taste of H

the **ULTIMATE** casserole
COOKBOOK

taste of home
the ULTIMATE
casserole
COOKBOOK

Senior Vice President, Editor in Chief	Catherine Cassidy
Vice President, Executive Editor/Books	Heidi Reuter Lloyd
Creative Director	Ardyth Cope
Food Director	Diane Werner RD
Senior Editor/Books	Mark Hagen
Editor	Krista Lanphier
Art Director	Gretchen Trautman
Content Production Supervisor	Julie Wagner
Layout Designer	Heather Meinen
Proofreaders	Linne Bruskewitz, Amy Glander
Editorial Intern	Danielle Calkins
Recipe Asset Management System	Coleen Martin
Premedia Supervisor	Scott Berger
Recipe Testing and Editing	Taste of Home Test Kitchen
Food Photography	Taste of Home Photo Studio
Administrative Assistant	Barb Czysz

U.S. Chief Marketing Officer	Lisa Karpinski
Vice President/Book Marketing	Dan Fink
Creative Director/Creative Marketing	Jim Palmen

The Reader's Digest Association, Inc.

President and Chief Executive Officer	Mary G. Berner
President, U.S. Affinities	Suzanne M. Grimes
SVP, Global Chief Marketing Officer	Amy J. Radin

Taste of Home and Reader's Digest are registered trademarks of
The Reader's Digest Association, Inc.

COVER PHOTOGRAPHY BY
Lori Foy and Grace Natoli Sheldon

FOOD STYLED BY
Diane Armstrong, Kaitlyn Besasie
and Sarah Thompson

SETS STYLED BY
Melissa Haberman
and Jennifer Bradley Vent

FRONT COVER PHOTOS
Italian Pasta Casserole (p. 69)
Zippy Macaroni and Cheese (p. 146)
Broccoli-Chicken Cups (p. 295)
Savory Spinach Pie (p. 175)
Makeover Manicotti Crepes (p. 33)

BACK COVER PHOTOS
Southwest Chicken and Rice (p. 241)
Chicken Salad Bake (p. 51)
Hamburger Noodle Casserole (p. 19)
Tuna-Chip Casserole (p. 128)
Fruited Holiday Vegetables (p. 209)

©2010 Reiman Media Group, Inc.
5400 S. 60th St., Greendale WI 53129
All rights reserved.

International Standard Book Number (10):
0-89821-867-5
International Standard Book Number (13):
978-0-89821-867-1
Library of Congress Control Number:
2009940176

Printed in China
3 5 7 9 10 8 6 4 2

For other *Taste of Home* books and products, visit
www.ShopTasteofHome.com

contents

welcome to our
BIGGEST COLLECTION OF CASSEROLES EVER!

We've outdone ourselves this time by creating a Taste of Home cookbook brimming with hearty hot dishes. With more than 450 heartwarming recipes to choose from, this truly is **THE ULTIMATE CASSEROLE COOKBOOK**.

No wonder casseroles are the most popular comfort food around! Not only are they delicious, their convenience in the kitchen is unmatched. Many of the meal-in-one dishes gracing these pages are freezer-friendly, can easily be assembled ahead of time and can be made using ingredients already on hand. Plus, cleanup is a snap because you don't use every pot and pan in the kitchen...and the leftovers taste great!

A VARIETY OF ONE-DISH WONDERS FOR EVERY OCCASION

All-American casseroles are as beloved as ever because they're so versatile and satisfying. Whether you need a robust dinner, breakfast meal or side dish, you won't have any trouble finding a recipe to suit your needs. You'll relish hundreds of user-friendly hot dish recipes perfect for brunch buffets, potlucks, family gatherings, church suppers, holiday events and easy-to-assemble weekday dinners.

This lovely, full-color cookbook is divided into 10 chapters. For the meat-lovers in your family, turn to the Beef, Poultry and Pork chapters. When you want to take a break from meat-and-potatoes fare, there are Seafood and Meatless chapters. You'll also find tantalizing dishes in the Breakfast & Brunch chapter, as well as Side Dishes, Quick & Easy and Serves Two. And finally, for scrumptious casseroles that serve 10 or more people, turn to Potluck Pleasers. There's something for everyone!

HEART-HEALTHY CHOICES AND HELPFUL KITCHEN TIPS

Casseroles are wonderfully easy, economical and deeply comforting...and now, you can add "healthy" as a description, too! We wanted to make sure that folks watching their calories, sodium and fat intake could also enjoy the delicious dishes in this cookbook. There are more than 55 recipes with Nutrition Facts and Diabetic Exchange information, so you can enjoy these tasty dishes and watch your diet. Just look for the recipe titles with the scale icon next to them.

You'll also find how-to tips for the busy cook placed throughout the book. From freezer hints to culinary tidbits, these handy ideas will help your culinary creations go a little smoother.

TRIED-AND-TRUE RECIPES FROM READERS LIKE YOU

With *Taste of Home The Ultimate Casserole Cookbook*, you'll find every type of classic casserole you and your family crave, plus delectable new twists on old favorites. Most every recipe is from a cook like you, and all are tested and approved by our experienced Test Kitchen...so you can trust that every dish is a winner. You'll warm the hearts of those you love for years to come with this family-pleasing keepsake!

beef

HARVEST HAMBURGER CASSEROLE • PAGE 28

BAKED ZITI WITH FRESH TOMATOES

PREP 70 minutes | **BAKE** 30 minutes

barbara johnson
DECKER, INDIANA

I prepare the sauce ahead of time, so it saves precious moments when we return to the house after working out in the farm fields.

1	pound ground beef
1	cup chopped onion
3	pounds plum tomatoes, peeled, seeded and chopped (about 15 tomatoes)
1-1/2	teaspoons salt
1	teaspoon dried basil
1/4	teaspoon pepper
8	ounces uncooked ziti
2	cups (8 ounces) shredded part-skim mozzarella cheese, *divided*
2	tablespoons grated Parmesan cheese

In a Dutch oven, cook the beef and onion over medium heat until meat is no longer pink; drain. Stir in the tomatoes, salt, basil and pepper. Reduce heat to low; cover and cook for 45 minutes, stirring occasionally.

Cook the ziti according to the package directions; drain. Stir in the sauce and 1 cup mozzarella cheese. Transfer to a greased 3-qt. baking dish; sprinkle with Parmesan and remaining mozzarella cheese.

Cover and bake at 350° for 15 minutes. Uncover; bake 15 minutes longer or until heated through.

YIELD: 6 SERVINGS.

MICROWAVE BEEF CASSEROLE

PREP/TOTAL TIME 30 minutes

- 1 pound ground beef
- 1 small onion, chopped
- 1/2 cup uncooked instant rice
- 1-1/2 cups water, *divided*
- 1 can (10-3/4 ounces) condensed cream of mushroom soup, undiluted
- 1 cup slivered almonds
- 5 large fresh mushrooms, chopped
- 1 package (6 ounces) seasoned stuffing mix
- 1/4 cup butter, melted

Crumble beef into a microwave-safe 3-qt. dish; add the onion. Loosely cover and microwave on high for 3-5 minutes or until meat is no longer pink, stirring twice; drain. Stir in rice and 1/2 cup water. Cover and cook for 2 minutes. Stir in the soup, almonds and mushrooms.

In a large bowl, combine the stuffing mix, butter and remaining water; spoon over beef mixture. Microwave, uncovered, for 1-3 minutes or until heated through.
YIELD: 4-6 SERVINGS.

joan hallford
NORTH RICHLAND HILLS, TEXAS

This microwave dish is great when time is short. I sometimes use cooked wild rice instead. Add a vegetable and crusty rolls for a delicious dinner.

freezing **GROUND BEEF**

When you have time, crumble, brown and drain several pounds of ground beef. Spread on a cookie sheet and freeze until solid. Transfer to freezer bags in 1/2- or 1-pound amounts (whatever your favorite recipes call for). When you are busy, pull out a bag and add to chili, tacos or any recipe that uses browned ground beef.

CHILI TOTS

PREP 15 minutes | **BAKE** 35 minutes

- 1 pound ground beef
- 2 cans (15 ounces *each*) chili without beans
- 1 can (8 ounces) tomato sauce
- 1 can (2-1/4 ounces) sliced ripe olives, drained
- 1 can (4 ounces) chopped green chilies
- 2 cups (8 ounces) shredded cheddar cheese
- 1 package (32 ounces) frozen Tater Tots

In a large skillet, cook beef over medium heat until no longer pink; drain. Stir in chili, tomato sauce, olives and chilies. Transfer to two greased 8-in. square baking dishes. Sprinkle with cheese and top with Tater Tots. Cover and freeze one casserole for up to 3 months.

Cover and bake the remaining casserole at 350° for 35-40 minutes or until heated through.
TO USE FROZEN CASSEROLE: Remove from the freezer 30 minutes before baking (do not thaw). Cover and bake at 350° for 1-1/4 to 1-1/2 hours or until heated through.
YIELD: 2 CASSEROLES (6 SERVINGS EACH).

linda baldwin
LONG BEACH, CALIFORNIA

Cook once and eat twice with these hearty Southwestern casseroles. With help from a few convenience products, they quickly go together before you freeze one and pop the other into the oven to bake.

GROUND BEEF NOODLE BAKE

PREP 35 minutes | **BAKE** 25 minutes

- 5 cups uncooked egg noodles
- 1-1/2 pounds ground beef
- 1 can (8 ounces) tomato sauce
- 1 teaspoon salt
- 1/4 teaspoon garlic salt
- 1/4 teaspoon pepper
- 2 teaspoons butter
- 1 cup (8 ounces) cream-style cottage cheese
- 1 cup (8 ounces) sour cream
- 4 green onions, chopped
- 1/2 cup minced fresh parsley
- 1 cup (4 ounces) shredded Swiss cheese

Cook the noodles according to the package directions. Meanwhile, in a large skillet, cook the beef over medium heat until no longer pink; drain. Stir in the tomato sauce, salt, garlic salt and pepper. Bring to a boil. Reduce heat; simmer, uncovered, for 5 minutes.

Drain noodles; toss with butter. Set aside. In a blender, process cottage cheese and sour cream until smooth. Transfer to a large bowl; stir in onions and parsley. Add noodles; toss to coat.

In a greased 11-in. x 7-in. baking dish, layer a third of the noodle mixture and half of the meat sauce. Repeat layers. Top with remaining noodle mixture; sprinkle with Swiss cheese.

Bake, uncovered, at 350° for 25-30 minutes or until bubbly and lightly browned.
YIELD: 6 SERVINGS.

judy taylor
KENNA, WEST VIRGINIA

This is a dressy recipe that will be a big hit. I think it's nice served with a side dish of hot vegetables and Texas toast. It's an oldie, but a goodie!

TATER-TOPPED CASSEROLE

PREP 15 minutes | **BAKE** 1 hour

- 1-1/2 pounds ground beef
- 1 package (16 ounces) frozen vegetables, thawed
- 1 can (2.8 ounces) french-fried onions
- 1/4 cup butter
- 1 can (10-3/4 ounces) condensed cream of celery soup, undiluted
- 1 can (10-3/4 ounces) condensed cream of chicken soup, undiluted
- 1/2 cup milk
- 1 package (16 ounces) frozen Tater Tots, thawed

In a large skillet, cook the beef over medium heat until no longer pink; drain. In a greased 13-in. x 9-in. baking dish, layer beef, vegetables and onions. Dot with butter.

In a bowl, combine soups and milk; spread over vegetables. Top with Tater Tots. Bake, uncovered, at 350° for 1 hour or until golden brown.
YIELD: 6-8 SERVINGS.

rosa dietzler
SANTA ROSA, CALIFORNIA

I often make this all-in-one dish ahead of time and reheat it for reunions and potlucks. No additional salt is needed...there's just enough in the canned soup.

BEEF AND POTATO NACHO CASSEROLE

PREP 20 minutes | **BAKE** 1-1/4 hours + standing

- 2 pounds lean ground beef
- 3/4 cup chopped onion, *divided*
- 1 envelope taco seasoning
- 1 can (8 ounces) tomato sauce
- 3/4 cup water
- 1 can (4 ounces) chopped green chilies, drained
- 1 can (16 ounces) kidney beans, rinsed and drained
- 1 package (24 ounces) frozen O'Brien potatoes, thawed
- 1 can (11 ounces) nacho cheese soup, undiluted
- 1/2 cup milk
- 1/4 cup chopped green pepper
- 1 teaspoon Worcestershire sauce
- 1/4 teaspoon sugar

Paprika

In a large skillet, cook beef and 1/2 cup onion over medium heat until the meat is no longer pink; drain. Stir in taco seasoning, tomato sauce and water. Bring to boil; reduce heat and simmer for 1 minute.

Spread into a greased 13-in. x 9-in. baking dish. Top with the green chilies, beans and potatoes. In large bowl, combine the soup, milk, green pepper, Worcestershire sauce, sugar and remaining onion; pour over potatoes. Sprinkle with paprika.

Cover and bake at 350° for 1 hour. Uncover and bake for 15 minutes or until lightly browned. Let stand for 10 minutes before cutting into squares.

YIELD: 8 SERVINGS.

gloria warczak
CEDARBURG, WISCONSIN

I created this recipe for my family a few years ago because we all love Mexican-style food. It was an instant success with them—and so easy to prepare for me!

MEXICAN CASSEROLE

PREP 20 minutes | **BAKE** 40 minutes

1-1/2 pounds ground beef
   1 envelope taco seasoning
 3/4 cup water
   1 can (16 ounces) refried beans
 1/2 cup salsa
   6 flour tortillas (6 inches)
   2 cups frozen corn, thawed
   2 cups (8 ounces) shredded cheddar
     cheese
Shredded lettuce, chopped tomatoes, sliced
   ripe olives and sour cream, optional

In a large skillet, cook beef over medium heat until no longer pink; drain. Stir in the taco seasoning and water. Bring to a boil. Reduce heat; simmer, uncovered, for 5 minutes.

Meanwhile, in a microwave-safe bowl, combine the beans and salsa. Cover and microwave for 1-2 minutes or until mixture is spreadable.

Place three tortillas in a greased round 2-1/2-qt. baking dish. Layer with half of the beef, bean mixture, corn and cheese; repeat the layers.

Bake, uncovered, at 350° for 40-45 minutes or until cheese is melted. Let stand for 5 minutes. Serve with lettuce, tomatoes, olives and sour cream if desired.
YIELD: 6 SERVINGS.

david mills
INDIANAPOLIS, INDIANA

Born out of a need to rid the fridge of extras, this recipe is flexible. Add more corn to make it sweeter, if you like. You can also spice it up as hot or mild as you want.

ZIPPY BEEF FIESTA

PREP 25 minutes | **BAKE** 35 minutes

1-1/2 pounds ground beef
1 large onion, chopped
2 tablespoons all-purpose flour
2 tablespoons chili powder
1 teaspoon salt
1/4 teaspoon ground cumin
2 cups water
2 cans (8 ounces *each*) tomato sauce
2 tablespoons vinegar
12 corn tortillas (6 inches)
2 cups (8 ounces) shredded process American cheese
1 can (2-1/4 ounces) sliced ripe olives, drained

In a skillet, cook beef and onion over medium heat until meat is no longer pink; drain. Stir in flour and seasonings until blended. Add the water, tomato sauce and vinegar; cook for 10 minutes or until heated through. Cut each tortilla into six wedges.

In a greased 13-in. x 9-in. baking dish, layer half of the tortillas, meat mixture, cheese and olives; repeat layers. Bake, uncovered, at 350° for 35 minutes or until heated through.

YIELD: 8 SERVINGS.

joyce ericksen
TURLOCK, CALIFORNIA

A cousin first introduced me to this rich casserole. The flavor is a cross between a taco and burrito. I like to serve it with a tossed salad and French bread.

slicing bell **PEPPERS**

Holding the pepper by the stem, using a chef's knife, slice from the top of the pepper down. Continue using this technique to slice around the seeds, then chop the strips into pieces. If the recipe calls for the pepper to be julienned, cut the pepper strips thinner.

BISCUIT-TOPPED BEEF AND BEANS

PREP 25 minutes | **BAKE** 20 minutes

1 pound ground beef
1/4 cup chopped green pepper
1 can (16 ounces) kidney beans, rinsed and drained
1 cup spaghetti sauce
1 can (4 ounces) mushroom stems and pieces, drained
1 tablespoon onion soup mix
1/4 teaspoon garlic powder
1 block (4 ounces) cheddar cheese, cut into 1/2-inch cubes
1 tube (12 ounces) refrigerated buttermilk biscuits
1 tablespoon butter, melted

In a skillet, cook beef and green pepper over medium heat until meat is no longer pink; drain. Stir in beans, spaghetti sauce, mushrooms, soup mix and garlic powder; mix well. Bring to a boil.

Meanwhile, place a cheese cube in the center of each biscuit. Fold dough over cheese to cover; pinch to seal.

Transfer hot meat mixture to a greased 2-qt. baking dish. Place biscuits seam side down over beef mixture. Brush with butter.

Bake, uncovered, at 400° for 18-20 minutes or until the biscuits are golden brown.

YIELD: 5 SERVINGS.

eleanor mcquiston
HARRISVILLE, PENNSYLVANIA

I entered this tasty recipe for the annual cookbook put out by our local newspaper and was thrilled to win a prize! I shared my winnings with the dear friend who gave the recipe to me.

BEEF POTATO SUPPER

PREP 25 minutes | **BAKE** 35 minutes

- 1-1/2 pounds ground beef
- 1 large onion, chopped
- 4 cups sliced peeled potatoes
- 1 can (14-1/2 ounces) cut green beans, drained
- 1 can (10-3/4 ounces) condensed cream of mushroom soup, undiluted
- 2/3 cup milk
- 2/3 cup water
- 1 can (2.8 ounces) french-fried onions
- 1 cup (4 ounces) shredded cheddar cheese

In a skillet, cook the beef and onion over medium heat until meat is no longer pink; drain. Meanwhile, place the potatoes in a saucepan and cover with water; bring to a boil. Cook for 7 minutes; drain.

In a greased 13-in. x 9-in. baking dish, layer beef mixture, beans and potatoes.

In a bowl, combine the soup, milk and water; pour over potatoes. Sprinkle with onions and cheese. Bake, uncovered, at 350° for 35 minutes or until browned.
YIELD: 6-8 SERVINGS.

lula mae mcelfresh
BYESVILLE, OHIO

This quick meal was often a featured item on the dinner table when our children were young. They're both married now and use this recipe in their own kitchens.

preparing **SPUDS**

Scrub with a vegetable brush under cold water. Remove eyes or sprouts. When working with lots of potatoes, peel and place in cold water to prevent discoloration. Before baking a whole potato, pierce with a fork.

GREEN CHILI FLAUTAS

PREP 25 minutes | **BAKE** 5 minutes

- 1-1/2 pounds ground beef
- 1 cup (4 ounces) shredded cheddar cheese
- 1 can (4 ounces) chopped green chilies, drained
- 1/2 teaspoon ground cumin
- 10 flour tortillas (6 inches)
- 1/3 cup butter, melted, *divided*

Shredded lettuce, guacamole, salsa and sour cream

In a large skillet, cook beef over medium heat until no longer pink; drain. Add the cheese, chilies and cumin; set aside.

Warm tortillas; brush both sides with some of the butter. Spoon about 1/3 cup beef mixture down center of each tortilla. Roll up tightly; place seam side down in a greased 13-in. x 9-in. baking pan.

Bake, uncovered, at 500° for 5-7 minutes or until golden brown, brushing once with remaining butter. Serve with toppings of your choice.
YIELD: 10 FLAUTAS.

lisa ann platt
BELLEVUE, NEBRASKA

This recipe has always been a great success at potlucks, especially when we lived in New Mexico. You can assemble this dish and freeze it to bake at a later date, too!

TWO-CHEESE SPAGHETTI BAKE

PREP 30 minutes | **BAKE** 25 minutes

janet knorr
GOLDEN, ILLINOIS

My kids and grandkids love this cheesy pasta dish. I prepare it at least once a month, but it's especially good during cooler seasons.

6 ounces uncooked spaghetti, broken into thirds

1 pound ground beef

1/4 cup chopped onion

1 jar (15 ounces) spaghetti sauce with mushrooms

2 tablespoons butter

4 teaspoons all-purpose flour

1/4 teaspoon salt

3/4 cup evaporated milk

1/3 cup water

4 ounces process cheese (Velveeta), cubed, *divided*

2 tablespoons grated Parmesan cheese

Cook the spaghetti according to package directions. Meanwhile, in a large skillet, cook the beef and onion over medium heat until meat is no longer pink; drain. Add spaghetti sauce; bring to a boil. Reduce heat; simmer, uncovered, for 10 minutes. Drain spaghetti; stir into beef mixture. Set aside.

In a small saucepan, melt the butter. Stir in the flour and salt; gradually stir in the milk and water. Bring to a boil; cook and stir until thickened and bubbly. Add 1/2 cup process cheese and Parmesan cheese; stir until melted.

Spread half of spaghetti mixture into a greased 11-in. x 7-in. baking dish. Cover with cheese sauce; top with remaining spaghetti mixture and process cheese.

Bake, uncovered, at 350° for 25-30 minutes or until heated through.

YIELD: 6 SERVINGS.

SICILIAN SUPPER

PREP 30 minutes | **BAKE** 20 minutes

gloria warczak

CEDARBURG, WISCONSIN

Ground beef, tomato and a tasty cream cheese sauce come together in this hot, hearty casserole. I recently took it to a banquet, and recipe requests came from every table.

2 cups uncooked egg noodles
1 pound ground beef
1/2 cup chopped onion
1/4 cup chopped green pepper
1 can (6 ounces) tomato paste
3/4 cup water
1-1/2 teaspoons sugar, *divided*
1/2 teaspoon salt
1/2 teaspoon dried basil
1/4 teaspoon garlic powder
1/4 teaspoon chili powder
1/4 teaspoon pepper, *divided*
1 tablespoon finely chopped green onion
1 tablespoon olive oil
1 package (8 ounces) cream cheese, cubed
3/4 cup milk
1/3 cup plus 2 tablespoons grated Parmesan cheese, *divided*

Cook the noodles according to the package directions. Meanwhile, in a large skillet, cook the beef, onion and green pepper over medium heat until the meat is no longer pink; drain. Stir in the tomato paste, water, 1 teaspoon sugar, salt, basil, garlic powder, chili powder and 1/8 teaspoon pepper.

In a large saucepan, saute the green onion in oil until tender. Add the cream cheese and milk; stir until blended. Stir in 1/3 cup Parmesan cheese, and remaining sugar and pepper. Drain noodles; stir into the cheese mixture.

In a greased 8-in. square baking dish, arrange alternate rows of beef and noodle mixtures. Sprinkle with the remaining Parmesan cheese. Cover and bake at 350° for 20-25 minutes or until bubbly.
YIELD: 4 SERVINGS.

TACO CASSEROLE

PREP 15 minutes | BAKE 30 minutes

- 3 cups uncooked bow tie pasta
- 1 pound ground beef
- 1/4 cup chopped onion
- 2 cups (8 ounces) shredded cheddar cheese
- 1 jar (16 ounces) salsa
- 1 can (14-1/2 ounces) diced tomatoes, undrained
- 1 envelope taco seasoning
- 2 cups nacho tortilla chips, crushed

Cook pasta according to package directions. Meanwhile, in a large skillet, cook beef and onion over medium heat until meat is no longer pink; drain. Add the cheese, salsa, tomatoes and taco seasoning. Drain pasta; stir into beef mixture.

Transfer to a greased 11-in. x 7-in. baking dish. Cover and bake at 350° for 20 minutes. Uncover; sprinkle with tortilla chips. Bake 10 minutes longer or until heated through.

YIELD: 7 SERVINGS.

kathy wilson
ROMEOVILLE, ILLINOIS

My child doesn't eat ground beef unless it's taco flavored, so I came up with this casserole we all like. To make assembly easy, I prepare the taco meat and freeze several bags at a time.

MEATY MACARONI

PREP/TOTAL TIME 20 minutes

- 1 pound ground beef
- 1 medium onion, chopped
- 1/2 cup chopped green pepper
- 1 jar (15 ounces) spaghetti sauce
- 1-1/2 cups uncooked elbow macaroni
- 1 cup water
- Salt and pepper to taste
- 1 cup (4 ounces) shredded part-skim mozzarella cheese

Crumble beef into a 2-qt. microwave-safe dish. Add onion and green pepper. Cover and microwave on high for 3-5 minutes or until meat is no longer pink, stirring once; drain. Stir in the spaghetti sauce, macaroni, water, salt and pepper.

Cover and microwave on high for 9 minutes, stirring once. Sprinkle with cheese. Let stand 5 minutes before serving.

YIELD: 6 SERVINGS.

carolyn rausch
ST. LUCAS, IOWA

This recipe is always fast to make, and the kids certainly enjoy it. I sometimes use my homemade canned spaghetti sauce.

STEAK POTPIE

PREP 20 minutes | BAKE 20 minutes

- 1-1/4 pounds boneless beef sirloin steak, cut into 1/2-inch cubes
- 2 tablespoons butter
- 1/4 teaspoon pepper
- 1 package (16 ounces) frozen vegetables for stew
- 2 tablespoons water
- 1/2 teaspoon dried thyme
- 1 jar (12 ounces) mushroom *or* beef gravy
- 1 tube (8 ounces) refrigerated crescent rolls

In a large ovenproof skillet, brown the beef in butter. Remove the beef; season with pepper and keep warm. In the same skillet, combine the vegetables, water and thyme. Stir in the gravy. Bring to a boil. Reduce heat; simmer, uncovered, until vegetables are thawed. Stir in beef; remove from heat.

Separate the crescent dough into eight triangles. Starting from the wide end of each triangle, roll up a third of the length and place over beef mixture with pointed ends toward the center. Bake, uncovered, at 375° for 16-18 minutes or until golden brown.

YIELD: 4-6 SERVINGS.

kristin shaw
CASTLETON, NEW YORK

This classic meat pie recipe really hits the spot on cold winter nights. With steak, vegetables and gravy, it's so satisfying.

LASAGNA TOSS

PREP 15 minutes | **BAKE** 20 minutes

1 pound ground beef
1/2 cup chopped onion
Dash minced garlic
1/2 teaspoon salt
1-3/4 cups spaghetti sauce
6 ounces spiral noodles, cooked and drained
1 cup (8 ounces) small curd 4% cottage cheese
2 cups shredded part-skim mozzarella cheese, *divided*
Grated Parmesan cheese

In a large skillet, brown the beef with onion, garlic and salt. Stir in spaghetti sauce; simmer until heated. Remove 1 cup meat sauce; set aside. Stir noodles into the remaining sauce. Place half of noodle-sauce mixture in greased 2-qt. casserole. Cover with cottage cheese and 1 cup mozzarella cheese.

Add remaining noodle-sauce mixture; top with 1 cup of reserved meat sauce and remaining mozzarella cheese. Sprinkle with Parmesan cheese. Cover; bake at 350° for 20-25 minutes. Let stand for 5 minutes before serving.

YIELD: 6-8 SERVINGS.

sharon martin
DENVER, PENNSYLVANIA

A combination of delicious cheeses is what makes this dish unforgettable. It's a comforting classic that will keep people coming back for more!

BURRITO BAKE

PREP 25 minutes | **BAKE** 30 minutes

1 pound ground beef
1 can (16 ounces) refried beans
1/4 cup chopped onion
1 envelope taco seasoning
1 tube (8 ounces) refrigerated crescent rolls
2 cups (8 ounces) shredded cheddar cheese
2 cups (8 ounces) shredded part-skim mozzarella cheese

TOPPINGS

Chopped green pepper, shredded lettuce, chopped tomatoes and sliced ripe olives

In a large skillet, cook beef over medium heart until no longer pink; drain. Add the beans, onion and taco seasoning.

Unroll crescent roll dough. Press onto the bottom and up the sides of a greased 13-in. x 9-in. baking dish; seal seams and perforations.

Spread the beef mixture over crust; sprinkle with cheeses. Bake, uncovered, at 350° for 30 minutes or until golden brown. Sprinkle with toppings of your choice.

YIELD: 6 SERVINGS.

cindee ness
HORACE, NORTH DAKOTA

Years ago when I was in college, my roommate would frequently make this economical casserole. It's so easy to put together, and one serving goes a long way.

HAMBURGER NOODLE CASSEROLE

PREP 30 minutes | **BAKE** 35 minutes

martha henson
WINNSBORO, TEXAS

People have a hard time believing this homey and hearty casserole uses lighter ingredients. The taste is so rich and creamy...a great weeknight family entree!

- 5 cups uncooked egg noodles
- 1-1/2 pounds lean ground beef
- 2 garlic cloves, minced
- 3 cans (8 ounces *each*) tomato sauce
- 1/2 teaspoon sugar
- 1/2 teaspoon salt
- 1/8 teaspoon pepper
- 1 package (8 ounces) reduced-fat cream cheese
- 1 cup reduced-fat ricotta cheese
- 1/4 cup reduced-fat sour cream
- 3 green onions, thinly sliced, *divided*
- 2/3 cup shredded reduced-fat cheddar cheese

Cook the noodles according to the package directions. Meanwhile, in a large nonstick skillet over medium heat, cook beef and garlic until meat is no longer pink; drain. Stir in the tomato sauce, sugar, salt and pepper; heat through. Drain noodles; stir into beef mixture.

In a small bowl, beat the cream cheese, ricotta cheese and sour cream until blended. Stir in half of the onions.

Spoon half of the noodle mixture into a 13-in. x 9-in. baking dish coated with cooking spray. Top with the cream cheese mixture and remaining noodle mixture.

Cover and bake at 350° for 30 minutes. Uncover; sprinkle with cheddar cheese. Bake 5-10 minutes longer or until heated through and cheese is melted. Sprinkle with remaining onions.

YIELD: 10 SERVINGS.

NUTRITION FACTS: 1 cup equals 319 calories, 14 g fat (8 g saturated fat), 92 mg cholesterol, 635 mg sodium, 23 g carbohydrate, 1 g fiber, 24 g protein. **DIABETIC EXCHANGES:** 3 lean meat, 1-1/2 starch, 1 fat.

minced **GARLIC**

Minced garlic in a jar that you can buy, garlic that's been finely chopped by hand and garlic that's been put through a press can all be used interchangeably in recipes. Choose whichever is easiest and the most convenient for you.

MEATY CORN BREAD CASSEROLE

PREP 20 minutes | **BAKE** 15 minutes

justina wilson
WEST SALEM, WISCONSIN

This casserole is as indulgent as it is delicious. This is stick-to-your-ribs, down-home comfort food at its finest.

- 1/2 pound ground beef
- 1/2 pound bulk pork sausage
- 1-3/4 cups frozen corn, thawed
- 1 cup water
- 1 envelope brown gravy mix
- 1 package (8-1/2 ounces) corn bread/muffin mix
- 1 tablespoon real bacon bits
- 1-1/2 teaspoons pepper
- 1/8 teaspoon garlic powder
- 1 envelope country gravy mix

In a large skillet, cook beef and sausage over medium heat until no longer pink; drain. Stir in the corn, water and brown gravy mix. Bring to a boil; cook and stir for 1 minute or until thickened. Spoon into a greased 8-in. square baking dish.

Prepare corn bread batter according to package directions; stir in the bacon bits, pepper and garlic powder. Spread over meat mixture.

Bake, uncovered, at 400° for 15-20 minutes or until a toothpick inserted into the corn bread layer comes out clean. Meanwhile, prepare the country gravy mix according to package directions; serve with casserole.

YIELD: 6 SERVINGS.

BEEF FLORENTINE

PREP 25 minutes | **BAKE** 30 minutes

- 2 pounds ground beef
- 1 medium onion, chopped
- 1 garlic clove, minced
- 1 jar (14 ounces) spaghetti sauce
- 1 cup water
- 1 can (8 ounces) tomato sauce
- 1 can (6 ounces) tomato paste
- 1 teaspoon salt
- 1 teaspoon pepper
- 2 eggs, lightly beaten
- 7 ounces elbow macaroni, cooked and drained
- 1-1/2 cups soft bread crumbs
- 1 package (10 ounces) frozen chopped spinach, thawed and squeezed dry
- 1 cup (4 ounces) shredded cheddar cheese

In a large skillet, cook the beef, onion and garlic over medium heat until no longer pink; drain.

In a small bowl, combine the spaghetti sauce, water, tomato sauce, tomato paste, salt and pepper. Add to skillet. Bring to a boil. Reduce heat; cover and simmer for 10 minutes.

In a large bowl, combine the eggs, macaroni, bread crumbs, spinach and cheese. Transfer to a greased 13-in. x 9-in. baking dish. Top with meat sauce.

Bake, uncovered, at 350° for 30 minutes or until a thermometer reads 160°. Let stand for 5 minutes before serving.

YIELD: 10-12 SERVINGS.

cindy waltner
COLUMBUS, MONTANA

Even my three small children, who won't touch spinach in any other way, enjoy this meal!

TEXAS STYLE LASAGNA

PREP 40 minutes | **BAKE** 30 minutes + standing

- 1-1/2 pounds ground beef
- 1 teaspoon seasoned salt
- 1 package (1-1/4 ounces) taco seasoning
- 1 can (14-1/2 ounces) diced tomatoes, undrained
- 1 can (15 ounces) tomato sauce
- 1 can (4 ounces) chopped green chilies
- 2 cups (16 ounces) 4% cottage cheese
- 2 eggs, lightly beaten
- 12 corn tortillas (6 inches), torn
- 3-1/2 to 4 cups shredded Monterey Jack cheese

In a large skillet, cook beef over medium heat until no longer pink; drain. Add the seasoned salt, taco seasoning mix, tomatoes, tomato sauce and chilies. Reduce heat and simmer, uncovered, for 15-20 minutes. In a small bowl, combine cottage cheese and eggs.

In a greased 13-in. x 9-in. baking dish, layer half of the meat sauce, half of the tortillas, half the cottage cheese mixture and half of the Monterey Jack cheese. Repeat layers.

Bake, uncovered, at 350° for 30 minutes or until bubbly. Let stand 10 minutes before serving.

YIELD: 10-12 SERVINGS.

effie gish
FORT WORTH, TEXAS

With its spicy flavor, this dish is a real crowd-pleaser. It goes great with side servings of picante sauce, guacamole, corn chips, olives and fresh fruit.

FIESTA MACARONI

PREP 15 minutes | **BAKE** 30 minutes

- 1 package (16 ounces) elbow macaroni
- 1 pound ground beef
- 1 jar (16 ounces) salsa
- 10 ounces process cheese (Velveeta), cubed
- 1 can (15 ounces) chili-style beans

Cook the macaroni according to package directions. Meanwhile, in a skillet, cook beef over medium heat until no longer pink; drain. Drain macaroni; set aside.

In a microwave-safe bowl, combine the salsa and cheese. Microwave, uncovered, on high for 2-3 minutes or until the cheese is melted. Stir into skillet; add the macaroni and beans. Transfer to a greased 13-in. x 9-in. baking dish.

Bake, uncovered, at 350° for 30-35 minutes or until heated through.
YIELD: 6-8 SERVINGS.

sandra castillo
JANESVILLE, WISCONSIN

When time is short, I rely on this family–pleasing main dish. It's so easy to fix, and everyone loves the zesty flavor that the salsa and chili beans provide.

BEEF AND NOODLE CASSEROLE

PREP 20 minutes | **BAKE** 45 minutes

- 1-1/2 pounds ground beef
- 1 tablespoon butter
- 1 large onion, chopped
- 1 cup chopped green pepper
- 1 tablespoon Worcestershire sauce
- 6-1/4 cups uncooked wide egg noodles, cooked and drained
- 2 cans (10-3/4 ounces *each*) condensed tomato soup, undiluted
- 1 can (10-3/4 ounces) condensed cream of mushroom soup, undiluted
- 1 cup (4 ounces) shredded cheddar cheese

In a large skillet, cook beef over medium heat until no longer pink; drain. In the same skillet, melt butter over medium-high heat. Saute the onion and pepper until tender. Stir in the beef, Worcestershire sauce, noodles and soups.

Transfer to a greased 3-qt. baking dish; top with cheese. Bake, uncovered, at 350° for 45-50 minutes or until heated through.
YIELD: 8 SERVINGS.

mary hinman
ESCONDIDO, CALIFORNIA

When I was working on the local election board in the '50s, one of my co–workers gave me this recipe, and it has been a family favorite ever since. It's quick to make for unexpected company or easily doubled for a potluck.

HOBO KNAPSACKS

PREP 15 minutes | **BAKE** 50 minutes

- 2 medium potatoes, peeled and thinly sliced
- 2 large tomatoes, chopped
- 1 large onion, chopped
- 1 package (10 ounces) frozen mixed vegetables, thawed
- 1 can (4 ounces) mushroom stems and pieces, drained
- 1 egg, beaten
- 1/2 cup tomato juice
- 1/2 cup old-fashioned oats
- 1 tablespoon finely chopped onion
- 1 teaspoon salt
- 1/4 teaspoon pepper
- 1 pound lean ground beef

Additional salt and pepper, optional

In a large bowl, combine the potatoes, tomatoes, onion, mixed vegetables and mushrooms; set aside.

In another large bowl, combine egg, tomato juice, oats, onion, salt and pepper; crumble beef over the mixture and mix well. Divide meat mixture into six portions; crumble each portion onto an 18-in. x 12-in. piece of foil.

Top with vegetable mixture; season with additional salt and pepper if desired. Bring edges of the foil together; crimp to seal, forming a packet. Place on baking sheets.

Bake at 350° for 50-60 minutes or until no pink remains and meat is thoroughly cooked.

YIELD: 6 SERVINGS.

ann millhouse
POLO, ILLINOIS

When our children were small, I invented this recipe to take along on trips to the park. We'd grill the packets, then eat the meal right out of the foil wrap.

PIZZA HOT DISH

PREP/TOTAL TIME 30 minutes

faythe anderson
RACINE, WISCONSIN

2 eggs

1/2 cup milk

1 package (7 ounces) elbow macaroni, cooked and drained

1 pound ground beef

1 medium onion, chopped

1 can (10-3/4 ounces) condensed tomato soup, undiluted

1 teaspoon salt

1/2 teaspoon dried basil

1/2 teaspoon dried oregano

1/4 teaspoon pepper

2 cups (8 ounces) shredded cheddar cheese

In a small bowl, beat eggs. Add milk and macaroni. Pour into a greased 13-in. x 9-in. baking dish; set aside.

In a large skillet, cook beef and onion over medium heat until meat is no longer pink; drain. Stir in the soup and seasonings.

Spoon over macaroni. Sprinkle with cheese. Bake, uncovered, at 350° for 20-25 minutes or until heated through.

YIELD: 12-16 SERVINGS.

Although we truly love pizza, the truth is, it can be expensive to order out and a task to put it together in the kitchen. This casserole offers the delicious flavor of pizza, without as much fuss. It's truly a family-tested recipe that will become a permanent part of your dinner repertoire.

BEEFY ENCHILADAS

PREP 30 minutes | **BAKE** 30 minutes

- 1-1/2 pounds ground beef
- 1/2 cup chopped onion
- 1 can (16 ounces) refried beans
- 1/2 teaspoon salt
- 1/4 teaspoon pepper
- 2 tomatoes, chopped
- 10 corn tortillas (6 inches), warmed

SAUCE

- 4 teaspoons butter
- 1/4 cup all-purpose flour
- 2 cups milk
- 1 can (10 ounces) enchilada sauce
- 1-1/2 cups (6 ounces) shredded cheddar cheese
- 3/4 cup sliced ripe olives, drained

In a skillet, brown beef and onion until beef is no longer pink and onion is tender. Drain fat. Stir in beans, salt and pepper. Place 1/3 cup of the mixture and a spoonful of the tomatoes on each tortilla. Roll up and place, seam side down, in a 13-in. x 9-in. baking pan.

For sauce, melt the butter in a saucepan. Stir in flour until smooth. Gradually add milk and enchilada sauce; stir until smooth. Add cheese and olives; cook over medium-high until mixture boils. Pour over the enchiladas. Bake at 350° for 30 minutes. Let stand a few minutes before serving.
YIELD: 5-6 SERVINGS.

connie shay
KENNEWICK, WASHINGTON

This family favorite is a meal-in-one when served with salad or fruit. Tortilla chips also make a tasty addition.

HAMBURGER 'N' FRIES DINNER

PREP 20 minutes | **BAKE** 30 minutes

- 1 pound ground beef
- 1 small onion, chopped
- 2 cups frozen french fries, thawed
- 1 can (15-1/4 ounces) whole kernel corn, drained
- 1 can (10-3/4 ounces) condensed cream of mushroom soup, undiluted
- 1/2 cup shredded process American cheese (Velveeta)

In a skillet, cook beef and onion over medium heat until the meat is no longer pink; drain. Line a greased 9-in. square baking dish with french fries. Top with the beef mixture, corn, soup and cheese.

Bake, uncovered, at 375° for 30 minutes or until hot and bubbly.
YIELD: 4-6 SERVINGS.

shelly ryun
MALVERN, IOWA

I got the idea for this recipe from our church cookbook. I played with the ingredients until it was just the way my brood likes it. Ground beef and fries are always a hit!

CHEESE-TOPPED BEEF BAKE

PREP 20 minutes | **BAKE** 25 minutes

- 1 package (16 ounces) medium pasta shells
- 1 pound ground beef
- 1 jar (26 ounces) spaghetti sauce
- 1 envelope taco seasoning
- 1 carton (8 ounces) spreadable chive and onion cream cheese
- 1 cup (8 ounces) sour cream
- 1 cup (4 ounces) shredded cheddar cheese

Cook the pasta according to the package directions. Meanwhile, in a large skillet, cook beef over medium heat until no longer pink; drain. Stir in the spaghetti sauce and taco seasoning.

In a small bowl, combine cream cheese and sour cream; set aside.

Drain the pasta; stir into beef mixture. Transfer to a greased 13-in. x 9-in. baking dish. Spread with cream cheese mixture; sprinkle with cheddar cheese.

Bake, uncovered, at 350° for 25-30 minutes or until cheese is melted.
YIELD: 8-10 SERVINGS.

debbie pirlot
GREEN BAY, WISCONSIN

One night when I was looking for something quick but different, I started browsing through a Taste of Home cookbook. I found two easy recipes with similar ingredients and decided to combine them. The result is this rich and delicious recipe that my gang really enjoys.

OVEN BEEF HASH

PREP/TOTAL TIME 30 minutes

dorothy pritchett
WILLS POINT, TEXAS

With just the two of us, we usually have leftovers of some sort, so hash is a regular menu item at our house. It's nice to have a hash that I can easily pop in the oven.

- 3 cups diced cooked potatoes
- 1-1/2 cups cubed cooked roast beef
- 1 can (5 ounces) evaporated milk
- 1/4 cup minced fresh parsley
- 1/4 cup finely chopped onion
- 2 teaspoons Worcestershire sauce
- 1/2 teaspoon salt
- 1/8 teaspoon pepper
- 1/3 cup crushed saltines
- 1 tablespoon butter, melted

In a large bowl, combine the first eight ingredients. Spoon into a greased 1-1/2-qt. baking dish. Combine saltines and butter; sprinkle over top. Bake, uncovered, at 350° for 30 minutes or until heated through.
YIELD: 4 SERVINGS.

a word about **MOLASSES**

Molasses is the byproduct of the process of refining sugarcane into table sugar. Made from the third boiling of sugar syrup, blackstrap molasses is stronger, darker and more bitter than light or dark molasses. While light and dark molasses can be used interchangeably, we suggest you use blackstrap molasses with caution in cooking or baking. The intense flavor can be overwhelming.

BARBECUED BEEF AND BEANS

PREP 15 minutes | **BAKE** 1 hour

mary lou ringhand
ALBANY, WISCONSIN

I like to make this dish for church potlucks. It's great for large groups. I always include at least six kinds of beans, but they're not the same every time.

- 1 pound ground beef
- 1 medium onion, finely diced
- 1 garlic clove, minced
- 1/2 cup barbecue sauce
- 1/2 cup ketchup
- 1/4 cup molasses
- 1/2 cup packed brown sugar
- 1 jar (32 ounces) northern beans, rinsed and drained
- 1 can (28 ounces) baked beans
- 1 can (16 ounces) red kidney beans
- 1 can (15-3/4 ounces) lima beans, rinsed and drained
- 1 can (15 ounces) garbanzo beans *or* chickpeas, rinsed and drained
- 1 can (14-1/2 ounces) cut green beans, drained

In a skillet, cook beef, onion and garlic over medium heat until beef is no longer pink. Drain; place in a large greased roaster or casserole. Stir in the barbecue sauce, ketchup, molasses and brown sugar. Add all beans and mix well.

Bake, uncovered, at 325° for 30 minutes. Cover and bake another 30 minutes.
YIELD: 8-10 SERVINGS.

CHEESE 'N' PASTA IN A POT

PREP 40 minutes | **BAKE** 30 minutes

2 pounds ground beef
1 large onion, chopped
1 garlic clove, minced
1 jar (14 ounces) spaghetti sauce
1 can (14-1/2 ounces) stewed tomatoes
1 can (4 ounces) mushroom stems and pieces, drained
8 ounces uncooked medium pasta shells
2 cups (16 ounces) sour cream, *divided*
6 ounces sliced provolone cheese
6 ounces sliced part-skim mozzarella cheese

In a large skillet, cook the beef, onion and garlic over medium heat until no longer pink; drain. Stir in the spaghetti sauce, tomatoes and mushrooms. Bring to a boil. Reduce heat; simmer, uncovered, for 20 minutes.

Meanwhile, cook macaroni according to package directions; drain and rinse with cold water. Spoon half of the shells into a 4-qt. baking dish. Layer with half of the meat mixture. Spread with 1 cup sour cream; top with provolone cheese. Layer with the remaining pasta, meat mixture and sour cream; top with mozzarella cheese.

Cover and bake at 350° for 30-40 minutes or until bubbly and heated through.
YIELD: 8-10 SERVINGS.

carmelita guinan
WOLLASTON, MASSACHUSETTS

I love to make this dish whenever friends are visiting. Since I can make it ahead, it gives me more time to spend with my guests. Warm rolls and a simple salad make this a complete meal.

HARVEST HAMBURGER CASSEROLE

PREP 20 minutes | **BAKE** 1-1/4 hours

1 pound lean ground beef
1 cup finely chopped onion
1 can (28 ounces) diced tomatoes, undrained
1 tablespoon Worcestershire sauce
1 teaspoon salt
2 cups sliced peeled potatoes
1/3 cup all-purpose flour
2 cups frozen corn, thawed
1-1/2 cups frozen lima beans, thawed
1 medium green pepper, julienned
1-1/2 cups (6 ounces) shredded cheddar cheese

In a large skillet, cook beef over medium heat until no longer pink; drain. Stir in the onion, tomatoes, Worcestershire sauce and salt. Transfer to a greased 3-qt. baking dish.

Layer with the potatoes, flour, corn, lima beans and green pepper. Cover and bake at 375° for 45 minutes. Sprinkle with cheese. Bake, uncovered, for 30 minutes or until bubbly.

YIELD: 8 SERVINGS.

grace hagen
RAGGEN, COLORADO

During harvesttime, I take this out to the field for my family's lunch. It sure makes things easy when you combine your meat and vegetables. And, as many times as I've carried a full casserole out to the field, I have never brought anything back to the house but the empty dish.

FIVE-VEGETABLE DELIGHT

PREP 20 minutes | BAKE 1-1/2 hours

  2 cups *each* diced carrots, celery and onion
  2 cups diced peeled potatoes and rutabagas
  1 pound lean ground beef
  1 can (10-3/4 ounces) condensed tomato soup, undiluted
1-1/3 cups water
  1 teaspoon salt
  1/4 teaspoon pepper

In a bowl, combine the vegetables; mix well. Crumble the beef over mixture and toss gently. Transfer mixture to a greased 13-in. x 9-in. baking dish.

In a bowl, combine soup, water, salt and pepper. Pour over vegetable mixture. Bake, uncovered, at 350° for 1-1/2 hours or until vegetables are tender.

YIELD: 8 SERVINGS.

rose mueller
INDEPENDENCE, WISCONSIN

I received this recipe from a friend many years ago; it's just about the only way my husband will eat onions. You can vary the vegetables depending on what you have in your garden.

CORN BREAD BEEF BAKE

PREP 20 minutes | BAKE 30 minutes

  1 pound ground beef
  2 cans (16 ounces *each*) pork and beans
  1/4 cup ketchup
  2 tablespoons brown sugar
  1/8 teaspoon pepper
  1 package (8-1/2 ounces) corn bread/muffin mix
  1/3 cup milk
  1 egg

In a skillet, cook beef over medium heat until no longer pink; drain. Add the beans, ketchup, brown sugar and pepper; mix well. Transfer to a greased 11-in. x 7-in. baking dish.

In a bowl, combine dry corn bread mix, milk and egg just until combined. Spoon over bean mixture.

Bake, uncovered, at 350° for 35 minutes or until a toothpick inserted in the corn bread comes out clean.

YIELD: 4-6 SERVINGS.

mary jane ogmundson
DANBURY, NEW HAMPSHIRE

My friend gave me this recipe one day when I was desperate for a quick yet wholesome meal. When my family knows this is in the oven, they come running!

MEAT 'N' PEPPER CORN BREAD

PREP 15 minutes | BAKE 25 minutes

  1 pound ground beef
  1 cup chopped green pepper
  1 cup chopped onion
  2 cans (8 ounces *each*) tomato sauce
1-1/2 teaspoons chili powder
  1/2 teaspoon salt
  1/4 teaspoon pepper
  1 cup all-purpose flour
  3/4 cup cornmeal
  1/4 cup sugar
  1 tablespoon baking powder
  1/2 teaspoon salt
  1 egg, beaten
  1 cup milk
  1/4 cup canola oil

In a 10-in. cast-iron skillet, lightly brown ground beef, green pepper and onion; drain. Add tomato sauce, chili powder, salt and pepper; simmer 10-15 minutes.

Meanwhile, combine dry ingredients. Combine the egg, milk and oil; stir into dry ingredients just until moistened. Pour over beef mixture.

Bake at 400° for 25-30 minutes or until golden. Run knife around edge of skillet and invert on serving plate. Cut into wedges.

YIELD: 4-6 SERVINGS.

rita carlson
IDAHO FALLS, IDAHO

It suits me to be able to brown and bake this corn bread in the same cast-iron skillet. It's such a convenience!

CORNMEAL

Cornmeal can be either white, yellow or blue depending on which strain of corn is used. White cornmeal is more popular in the South, and yellow is preferred in the North. Blue cornmeal can be found in specialty stores. All three types can be used interchangeably.

EGGPLANT CASSEROLE

PREP 20 minutes | **BAKE** 30 minutes

        4 cups water
        1 medium eggplant, peeled and cubed
    1-1/2 pounds ground beef
        1 medium onion, chopped
        1 medium green pepper, chopped
        3 medium tomatoes, chopped
Salt and pepper to taste
      1/2 cup milk
        1 egg, beaten
      1/2 cup dry bread crumbs
        2 tablespoons butter, melted

In a saucepan, bring the water to a boil; add the eggplant. Boil for 5-8 minutes or until tender; drain and set aside.

In a skillet, cook beef, onion and green pepper over medium heat until the meat is no longer pink; drain. Add the tomatoes, salt and pepper. Cook and stir for 5 minutes or until tomato is tender. Remove from the heat. Stir in the milk, egg and cooked eggplant; mix well.

Transfer to a greased 13-in. x 9-in. baking dish. Toss bread crumbs and butter; sprinkle over top. Bake, uncovered, at 375° for 30 minutes or until heated through.
YIELD: 8 SERVINGS.

marelyn baugher
HOLDREDGE, NEBRASKA

With lots of vegetables, this good-for-you dish is low in calories, but full of flavor. I make it often in summer when fresh produce is abundant.

BISCUITS AND BEANS

PREP 20 minutes | **BAKE** 20 minutes

        1 pound ground beef
        1 can (15-3/4 ounces) pork and beans
      3/4 cup barbecue sauce
        2 tablespoons brown sugar
        1 tablespoon dried minced onion
      1/2 teaspoon salt
        1 tube (12 ounces) refrigerated buttermilk biscuits
      1/2 to 1 cup shredded cheddar cheese

In a large skillet, cook beef over medium heat until no longer pink; drain. Add the beans, barbecue sauce, brown sugar, onion and salt; mix well. Bring to a boil.

Transfer to a greased 2-qt. baking dish. Separate biscuits and arrange over the hot beef mixture. Sprinkle with cheese.

Bake, uncovered, at 400° for 18-20 minutes or until biscuits are golden brown.
YIELD: 5 SERVINGS.

dolores grossenbacher
BELOIT, WISCONSIN

Biscuits and beans are common ingredients in traditional country cooking. This recipe earned an honorable mention when I entered it in a local cooking contest.

PARMESAN PENNE

PREP 30 minutes | **BAKE** 40 minutes

1 pound ground beef
1 medium onion, chopped
1 can (28 ounces) tomato sauce
1 cup grated Parmesan cheese, *divided*
1/2 teaspoon ground allspice
Salt and pepper to taste
1 package (16 ounces) penne pasta
1/2 cup butter, cubed, *divided*
1/4 cup all-purpose flour
2 cups milk
2 eggs, lightly beaten

In a large skillet, cook and stir the beef and onion over medium heat until the meat is no longer pink; drain. Stir in the tomato sauce, 1/3 cup cheese, allspice, salt and pepper. Bring to a boil. Reduce heat and simmer, uncovered, for 15 minutes.

Meanwhile, cook pasta according to package directions. In a large saucepan, melt 1/4 cup butter. Stir in flour until smooth. Gradually add milk. Bring to a boil; cook and stir for 2 minutes or until thickened. Remove from the heat; stir in 1/3 cup Parmesan cheese. Gradually whisk in eggs until blended.

Drain pasta. Add the remaining cheese and butter; toss to coat.

Spread a third of the meat mixture in a greased 13-in. x 9-in. baking dish. Layer with half of the pasta, a third of the meat mixture and half of the white sauce. Repeat layers.

Bake, uncovered, at 350° for 40-45 minutes or until bubbly.

YIELD: 12 SERVINGS.

vera soghomonian
MAPLE GROVE, MINNESOTA

My mother was not much of a cook, so I credit my husband for encouraging me to experiment in the kitchen. This is a fantastic all-in-one meal that features both a cream sauce and a meat sauce.

grated **PARMESAN**

If you decide to buy a chunk of Parmesan cheese and grate your own, be sure to use the finest section on your grating tool. You can also use a blender or food processor. Simply cut the cheese into 1-inch cubes and process 1 cup of cubes at a time on high until finely grated.

WESTERN BEEF AND CORN CASSEROLE

PREP 20 minutes | **BAKE** 25 minutes

FILLING

- 1 pound ground beef
- 1 can (11 ounces) Mexicorn, drained
- 1 can (8 ounces) tomato sauce
- 1 cup (4 ounces) shredded cheddar cheese
- 1/2 cup hickory-flavored sauce
- 1/2 teaspoon salt
- 1/2 teaspoon chili powder

CRUST

- 1 cup all-purpose flour
- 1/2 cup yellow cornmeal
- 2 tablespoons sugar
- 1 teaspoon salt
- 1 teaspoon baking powder
- 1 cup (4 ounces) shredded cheddar cheese, *divided*
- 1/4 cup cold butter
- 1/2 cup milk
- 1 egg, lightly beaten

In a large skillet, cook beef over medium heat until meat is no longer pink; drain. Stir in remaining filling ingredients; set aside.

For crust, in a large bowl, combine flour, cornmeal, sugar, salt and baking powder. Fold in the cheese. Cut in the butter until mixture resembles coarse crumbs. Stir in milk and egg.

Spread crust mixture over the bottom and up the sides of a greased 9-in. square baking dish. Pour filling into crust. Bake, uncovered, at 400° for 20-25 minutes or until bubbly. Sprinkle with remaining cheese; bake 5 minutes longer or until cheese is melted.

YIELD: 6-8 SERVINGS.

deb poitz
FORT MORGAN, COLORADO

I've been extra busy since our baby daughter was born a few months ago. That's why this easy-as-pie main dish is filed at the front of my recipe box! My husband really likes its Western flavors of beef, corn and wheat...especially since we raise the last two ingredients here on our family farm!

DOWN-HOME DINNER

PREP 20 minutes | **BAKE** 1 hour

- 1 pound ground beef
- 1 small onion, chopped
- 2 medium potatoes, peeled and thinly sliced
- 1 can (15 ounces) peas, drained
- 1 can (10-3/4 ounces) condensed cream of mushroom soup, undiluted
- 1 can (10-1/2 ounces) condensed vegetable beef soup, undiluted

Salt and pepper to taste

In a skillet, cook the beef and onion over medium heat until meat is no longer pink; drain. Add the potatoes, peas, soups, salt and pepper; mix well.

Transfer to a greased 11-in. x 7-in. baking dish. Cover and bake at 350° for 1 hour until potatoes are tender.

YIELD: 4-6 SERVINGS.

jeanette hiepler
BLOOMINGTON, MINNESOTA

This dish is a hit at every family gathering. It freezes well, so I always seem to have some on hand for last-minute meals.

MAKEOVER MANICOTTI CREPES

PREP 1-1/2 hours + simmering | **BAKE** 35 minutes

- 1 can (28 ounces) whole tomatoes, undrained
- 1-1/2 cups water
- 1 can (8 ounces) tomato sauce
- 3 teaspoons sugar
- 1 teaspoon dried oregano
- 1/4 teaspoon celery salt

CREPES
- 2 eggs
- 1 cup egg substitute
- 1-3/4 cups fat-free milk
- 1 teaspoon canola oil
- 1-1/2 cups all-purpose flour
- 1/4 teaspoon salt

FILLING
- 3 slices whole wheat bread, cubed
- 1/2 cup fat-free milk
- 1/4 cup egg substitute
- 1 cup finely chopped green pepper
- 3 tablespoons minced fresh parsley
- 2 garlic cloves, minced
- 1 teaspoon salt
- 1 teaspoon pepper
- 1 pound lean ground beef
- 1/2 pound Italian turkey sausage links, casings removed
- 1 cup (4 ounces) shredded part-skim mozzarella cheese
- 1/4 cup shredded Parmesan cheese

For sauce, place the tomatoes in a blender; cover and process until smooth. Transfer to a large saucepan; add the water, tomato sauce, sugar, oregano and celery salt. Bring to a boil. Reduce the heat; gently simmer, uncovered, for 2 hours or until reduced to 4-1/2 cups, stirring occasionally.

Meanwhile, for crepes, beat the eggs, egg substitute, milk and oil in a large bowl. Combine flour and salt; add egg mixture and stir until smooth. Cover and refrigerate for 1 hour.

For filling, in a large bowl, soak bread in milk for 5 minutes. Stir in the egg substitute, green pepper, parsley, garlic, salt and pepper. Crumble beef and sausage over mixture; mix well. Stir in mozzarella. Cover and refrigerate until assembling.

Coat an 8-in. nonstick skillet with cooking spray; heat. Stir crepe batter; pour 3 tablespoons into center of skillet. Lift and tilt pan to coat bottom evenly. Cook until top appears dry; turn and cook 15-20 seconds longer. Remove to a wire rack. Repeat with remaining batter, coating skillet with cooking spray as needed. When cool, stack crepes with waxed paper or paper towels in between.

Spread about 1/4 cup filling down the center of each crepe; roll up and place in a 13-in. x 9-in. baking dish and an 11-in. x 7-in. baking dish coated with cooking spray. Spoon sauce over top; sprinkle with Parmesan cheese. Cover and bake at 350° for 35-45 minutes or until a meat thermometer reads 165°.

YIELD: 10 SERVINGS.

christine rukavena
MILWAUKEE, WISCONSIN

This made-lighter dish will add a special touch to any event. Green pepper and garlic give it a fresh vegetable aroma.

freezing **CREPES**

Stack unfilled crepes between layers of waxed paper or white paper towels. Cool and place in an airtight container. Refrigerate for 2 to 3 days or freeze for 4 months. Thaw frozen crepes overnight in the refrigerator when ready to use.

MEATY PASTA CASSEROLES

PREP 45 minutes | **BAKE** 35 minutes

- 1 package (16 ounces) penne pasta
- 1 pound ground beef
- 1 pound bulk Italian pork sausage
- 1-3/4 cups sliced fresh mushrooms
- 1 medium onion, chopped
- 1 medium green pepper, chopped
- 2 cans (14-1/2 ounces *each*) Italian diced tomatoes
- 1 jar (25.6 ounces) Italian sausage and garlic spaghetti sauce
- 1 jar (16 ounces) chunky mild salsa
- 1 package (8 ounces) sliced pepperoni, chopped
- 1 cup (4 ounces) shredded Swiss cheese, *divided*
- 4 cups (16 ounces) shredded part-skim mozzarella cheese, *divided*
- 1-1/2 cups shredded Parmesan cheese, *divided*
- 1 jar (26 ounces) three-cheese spaghetti sauce

Cook the pasta according to the package directions. Meanwhile, in a Dutch oven, cook the beef, sausage, mushrooms, onion and green pepper over medium heat until meat is no longer pink; drain.

Drain pasta; add to the meat mixture. Stir in the tomatoes, sausage and garlic spaghetti sauce, salsa and pepperoni.

Divide half of pasta mixture between two greased 13-in. x 9-in. baking dishes. Sprinkle each with 1/4 cup Swiss cheese, 1 cup mozzarella cheese and 1/3 cup Parmesan cheese. Spread 3/4 cup of three-cheese spaghetti sauce over each. Top with remaining pasta mixture and three-cheese spaghetti sauce. Sprinkle with remaining cheeses.

Cover and freeze one casserole for up to 3 months. Cover and bake the remaining casserole at 350° for 25 minutes. Uncover and bake 10 minutes longer or until the cheese is melted.

TO USE FROZEN CASSEROLE: Thaw in the refrigerator overnight. Remove from the refrigerator 30 minutes before baking. Cover and bake at 350° for 45 minutes. Uncover; bake 10 minutes longer or until cheese is melted.

YIELD: 2 CASSEROLES (6 SERVINGS EACH).

debra butcher
DECATUR, INDIANA

I love this recipe because it makes a lot—two hearty casseroles. Every time I fix it, I add something different, such as extra garlic, to give it a little extra flavor.

storing CHEESE

Opened cheese should be wrapped with waxed paper, then wrapped again with a tight seal of plastic wrap or foil. Mozzarella cheese that is stored this way in the refrigerator will keep for several weeks. If mold develops, trim off the mold plus 1/2 inch extra of cheese and discard it. The rest of the cheese can be eaten.

BEEF BROCCOLI SUPPER

PREP 25 minutes | **BAKE** 35 minutes

- 3/4 cup uncooked long grain rice
- 1 pound ground beef
- 1-1/2 cups fresh broccoli florets
- 1 can (10-3/4 ounces) condensed broccoli cheese soup, undiluted
- 1/2 cup milk
- 1 teaspoon salt-free seasoning blend
- 1 teaspoon salt
- 1/2 teaspoon pepper
- 1/2 cup dry bread crumbs
- 2 tablespoons butter, melted

Cook the rice according to the package directions. Meanwhile, in a large skillet, cook beef over medium heat until no longer pink; drain. Add rice, broccoli, soup, milk, seasoning blend, salt and pepper; stir until combined. Transfer to a greased 2-qt. baking dish.

Toss bread crumbs and butter; sprinkle over the beef mixture. Cover and bake at 350° for 30 minutes. Uncover; bake 5-10 minutes longer or until heated through.

YIELD: 4-6 SERVINGS.

nita graffis
DOVE CREEK, COLORADO

When I put together a cookbook for our family reunion, my sister submitted this recipe. My husband and our boys usually don't care for broccoli, but they enjoy it in this dish.

ZUCCHINI PIZZA CASSEROLE

PREP 20 minutes | **BAKE** 40 minutes

- 4 cups shredded unpeeled zucchini
- 1/2 teaspoon salt
- 2 eggs
- 1/2 cup grated Parmesan cheese
- 2 cups (8 ounces) shredded part-skim mozzarella cheese, *divided*
- 1 cup (4 ounces) shredded cheddar cheese, *divided*
- 1 pound ground beef
- 1/2 cup chopped onion
- 1 can (15 ounces) Italian tomato sauce
- 1 medium green pepper, chopped

Place the zucchini in strainer; sprinkle with salt. Let stand for 10 minutes. Squeeze out moisture.

Combine the zucchini with the eggs, Parmesan and half of the mozzarella and cheddar cheeses. Press into a greased 13-in. x 9-in. baking dish.

Bake, uncovered, at 400° for 20 minutes. Meanwhile, cook beef and onion over medium heat until meat is no longer pink; drain. Add the tomato sauce; spoon over zucchini mixture.

Sprinkle with remaining cheeses; add green pepper. Bake 20 minutes longer or until heated through.

YIELD: 6-8 SERVINGS.

lynn bernstetter
WHITE BEAR LAKE, MINNESOTA

My spouse has a robust appetite...our two kids never tire of pizza...and I grow lots of zucchini. So this tasty, tomato-filled casserole is one of our favorites throughout the entire year. Once you've tried the recipe, you may even decide to grow more zucchini in your own garden.

REUBEN CRESCENT BAKE

PREP 20 minutes | **BAKE** 15 minutes

2 tubes (8 ounces *each*) refrigerated crescent rolls
1 pound sliced Swiss cheese, *divided*
1-1/4 pounds sliced deli corned beef
1 can (14 ounces) sauerkraut, rinsed and well drained
2/3 cup Thousand Island salad dressing
1 egg white, lightly beaten
3 teaspoons caraway seeds

Unroll one tube of crescent dough into one long rectangle; seal seams and perforations. Press onto bottom of a greased 13-in. x 9-in. baking dish. Bake at 375° for 8-10 minutes or until golden brown.

Layer with half of the cheese and all of the corned beef. Combine sauerkraut and salad dressing; spread over beef. Top with remaining cheese.

On a lightly floured surface, press or roll the second tube of crescent dough into a 13-in. x 9-in. rectangle, sealing seams and perforations. Place over cheese. Brush with egg white; sprinkle with caraway seeds.

Bake for 12-16 minutes or until heated through and crust is golden brown. Let stand for 5 minutes before cutting.
YIELD: 8 SERVINGS.

kathy kittell
LENEXA, KANSAS

This may not be a true Reuben, but the taste is still fantastic and it's easy to make. I like to serve this bake with homemade soup.

BAKED BLACK-EYED PEAS

PREP 25 minutes | **BAKE** 35 minutes

1-1/2 pounds ground beef
1 medium onion, chopped
2 garlic cloves, minced
1 can (15-1/2 ounces) black-eyed peas, rinsed and drained
1 can (10-3/4 ounces) condensed cream of mushroom soup, undiluted
1 can (10 ounces) enchilada sauce
1 cup tortilla chips, crushed
3 cups (12 ounces) shredded cheddar cheese

In a skillet, cook beef, onion and garlic over medium heat until the meat is no longer pink; drain. Add peas, soup and enchilada sauce; mix well.

Sprinkle tortilla chips in a greased 11-in. x 7-in. baking dish. Layer with half of the beef mixture and cheese. Repeat layers. Bake, uncovered, at 350° for 35 minutes or until heated through.

Baked Black-Eyed Peas can be served as an appetizer with tortilla chips for dipping.

YIELD: 6 SERVINGS.

janelle buschman
WAKA, TEXAS

Black-eyed peas are a nice change of pace in this extra-cheesy casserole. Use whatever type of enchilada sauce you prefer most...or try a yummy combination of cheddar and Monterey Jack cheeses.

HOMINY BEEF POLENTA

PREP/TOTAL TIME 30 minutes

2 tubes (1 pound *each*) polenta, cut into 1/2-inch slices
1 pound ground beef
1 cup chopped sweet red pepper
1 jar (16 ounces) picante sauce
1 can (15-1/2 ounces) hot chili beans, undrained
1 can (15-1/2 ounces) hominy, rinsed and drained
1/3 cup minced fresh cilantro
3 teaspoons ground cumin
2 teaspoons chili powder
2 cups (8 ounces) shredded Colby-Monterey Jack cheese

Line a greased 13-in. x 9-in. baking dish with a single layer of polenta slices. Bake, uncovered, at 350° for 15-20 minutes or until heated through.

Meanwhile, in a large skillet, cook beef and red pepper over medium heat until meat is no longer pink; drain. Stir in picante sauce, beans, hominy, cilantro, cumin and chili powder; heat through.

Sprinkle half of the cheese over polenta. Top with meat sauce and remaining cheese. Bake for 8 minutes or until cheese is melted.

YIELD: 6 SERVINGS.

taste of home
test kitchen
GREENDALE, WISCONSIN

Polenta can be found on the shelf in the Italian section of your local supermarket or in the refrigerated produce section. Store leftover polenta in the refrigerator. Cook leftover polenta slices in a skillet with olive oil for 1-2 minutes per side. Sprinkle with hot sauce and serve with scrambled eggs.

4-H CORN SPECIAL

PREP 15 minutes | **BAKE** 30 minutes

1   pound ground beef
1   small onion, finely chopped
1-1/2   cups cooked rice
2   cups seeded chopped fresh tomatoes
    or 1 can (16 ounces) tomatoes with
    liquid, cut up
2   cups fresh, frozen *or* canned sweet corn
Salt and pepper to taste
1   tablespoon Worcestershire sauce
1   teaspoon hot pepper sauce
1   cup crushed saltines
1/4   cup butter, melted

In a large skillet, brown beef and onion; drain. Stir in the cooked rice, tomatoes, corn, salt, pepper, Worcestershire sauce and hot pepper sauce.

Pour into a greased 13-in. x 9-in. baking dish. Combine the cracker crumbs and butter; sprinkle on top. Bake at 350° for 30 minutes.

YIELD: 6-8 SERVINGS.

donetta brunner
SAVANNA, ILLINOIS

I trace this hearty main dish back to a 4-H cooking project. I liked the recipe immediately, and it traveled through the years with me to become a favorite with my children and husband, too. The only change I've made to the original is to add extra seasonings.

SPIRAL PEPPERONI PIZZA BAKE

PREP 30 minutes | **BAKE** 40 minutes

1   package (16 ounces) spiral pasta
2   pounds ground beef
1   large onion, chopped
1   teaspoon salt
1/2   teaspoon pepper
2   cans (15 ounces *each*) pizza sauce
1/2   teaspoon garlic salt
1/2   teaspoon Italian seasoning
2   eggs
2   cups milk
1/2   cup shredded Parmesan cheese
4   cups (16 ounces) shredded part-skim
    mozzarella cheese
1   package (3-1/2 ounces) sliced
    pepperoni

Cook pasta according to package directions. Meanwhile, in a Dutch oven, cook beef, onion, salt and pepper over medium heat until meat is no longer pink; drain. Stir in pizza sauce, garlic salt and Italian seasoning; remove from the heat and set aside.

In a small bowl, combine the eggs, milk and Parmesan cheese. Drain pasta; toss with the egg mixture. Transfer to a greased 3-qt. baking dish. Top with beef mixture, mozzarella cheese and pepperoni.

Cover and bake at 350° for 20 minutes. Uncover; bake 20-25 minutes longer or until golden brown.

YIELD: 12 SERVINGS.

kimberly howland
FREMONT, MICHIGAN

My grandmother used to fix this yummy dish for my Girl Scout troop when I was growing up. Now, I make it for my stepdaughters' scout troop. It's easy to prepare, and the girls always beg me to make it.

make your OWN

Basic Italian Seasoning might contain marjoram, thyme, rosemary, savory, sage, oregano and basil. If you don't have all the ingredients, you can combine just a few of them with good results. Try substituting 1/4 teaspoon each of basil, thyme, rosemary and oregano for each teaspoon of Italian seasoning called for in a recipe.

LAYERED ITALIAN CASSEROLE

PREP 30 minutes | **BAKE** 50 minutes

joyce benninger
OWEN SOUND, ONTARIO

Yum! That's the response you'll get from your friends and family when they try this super supper. It tastes just like lasagna but with less preparation!

- 12 ounces uncooked spaghetti
- 1-1/2 pounds lean ground beef
- 1 large onion, chopped
- 2 garlic cloves, minced
- 2 cans (15 ounces *each*) Italian tomato sauce
- 3 tablespoons minced fresh parsley
- 1 tablespoon dried oregano
- 4 cups (32 ounces) 1% cottage cheese
- 2-1/2 cups (10 ounces) shredded part-skim mozzarella cheese, *divided*
- 1/2 cup grated Parmesan cheese, *divided*

Cook the spaghetti according to package directions. Meanwhile, in a large nonstick skillet over medium heat, cook the beef, onion and garlic until meat is no longer pink; drain. Add the tomato sauce, parsley and oregano; heat through.

In a large bowl, combine cottage cheese, 2 cups mozzarella cheese and 1/4 cup Parmesan cheese. Drain the spaghetti.

Spread 1 cup meat sauce into a 13-in. x 9-in. baking dish coated with cooking spray. Layer with half of the spaghetti, cheese mixture and remaining meat sauce. Repeat layers (dish will be full).

Cover and bake at 350° for 45 minutes. Uncover; sprinkle with the remaining mozzarella and Parmesan cheeses. Bake 5-10 minutes longer or until heated through and cheese is melted.
YIELD: 10 SERVINGS.

SHEPHERD'S PIE

PREP 20 minutes | **BAKE** 30 minutes

2-1/2 pounds potatoes, peeled and cooked
   1 to 1-1/2 cups (8 to 12 ounces) sour cream
Salt and pepper to taste
   2 pounds ground beef
 1/2 cup chopped onion
   1 medium sweet red pepper, chopped
   1 teaspoon garlic salt
   1 can (10-3/4 ounces) condensed cream
      of mushroom soup, undiluted
   1 can (16 ounces) whole kernel corn,
      drained
 1/2 cup milk
   2 tablespoons butter, melted
Chopped fresh parsley, optional

In a large bowl, mash potatoes with sour cream. Add salt and pepper; set aside. In a large skillet, cook beef with onion and red pepper until meat is no longer pink and vegetables are tender; drain. Stir garlic salt into meat mixture. Stir in the soup, corn and milk.

Spread meat mixture into a 13-in. x 9-in. baking dish. Top with mashed potatoes; drizzle with butter.

Bake, uncovered, at 350° for 30-35 minutes or until heated through. For additional browning, place under broiler for a few minutes. Sprinkle with parsley if desired.

YIELD: 8-10 SERVINGS.

valerie merrill
TOPEKA, KANSAS

This economical dish comes from a friend who was a whiz at pinching pennies without sacrificing hearty flavor. It's nice to have a satisfying meal on the table without breaking the bank.

HEARTY BEEF CASSEROLE

PREP 15 minutes | **BAKE** 30 minutes

- 1 package (8 ounces) medium noodles
- 1/3 cup sliced green onions
- 1/3 cup chopped green pepper
- 2 tablespoons butter
- 1 pound ground beef
- 1 can (6 ounces) tomato paste
- 1/2 cup sour cream
- 1 cup (8 ounces) 4% cottage cheese
- 1 can (8 ounces) tomato sauce

Cook the noodles according to the package directions; drain.

In a large skillet, saute the onions and green pepper in butter 3 minutes or until tender. Add beef and cook until no longer pink. Drain excess fat.

In a medium bowl, combine tomato paste and sour cream; stir in the noodles and cottage cheese. Layer half the noodle mixture in 2-qt. casserole; top with half the beef mixture. Repeat.

Pour tomato sauce evenly over the top of the casserole. Bake at 350° for 30-35 minutes or until heated through.
YIELD: 6 SERVINGS.

american dairy association
ROSEMONT, ILLINOIS

This casserole is delicious, because it's made with sour cream and cottage cheese. It's so yummy that even kids will adore it.

HERBED VEGETABLE MEDLEY

PREP 20 minutes | **BAKE** 30 minutes

- 2 pounds ground beef
- 1 medium eggplant, cubed
- 2 medium zucchini, cubed
- 1 medium onion, chopped
- 1 medium sweet yellow pepper
- 3 garlic cloves, minced
- 1 can (28 ounces) stewed tomatoes
- 1 cup cooked rice
- 1 cup (4 ounces) shredded cheddar cheese, *divided*
- 1/2 cup beef broth
- 1/2 teaspoon *each* oregano, savory and thyme
- 1/2 teaspoon salt
- 1/4 teaspoon pepper

betty blandford
JOHNS ISLAND, SOUTH CAROLINA

If your family is resistant to eating vegetables, offer them this dish! Eggplant, zucchini, onion and yellow pepper are disguised in a beefy tomato sauce.

In a Dutch oven, cook beef over medium heat until no longer pink; drain. Add the eggplant, zucchini, onion, yellow pepper and garlic; cook until tender. Add the tomatoes, rice, 1/2 cup of cheese, broth and seasonings; mix well.

Transfer to a greased 13-in. x 9-in. baking dish. Sprinkle with the remaining cheese. Bake, uncovered, at 350° for 30 minutes or until heated through.
YIELD: 10 SERVINGS.

MAKEOVER ZUCCHINI SUPPER

PREP 30 minutes | **BAKE** 50 minutes

mandy anderson
EAST MOLINE, ILLINOIS

This revised one-dish wonder boasts nearly 60% less saturated fat, 199 fewer calories and 46% less sodium per serving! But it's more colorful, nutritious and with all the cheesy, melt-in-your-mouth flavor my husband loves!

- 1-1/2 pounds lean ground beef
- 1/2 pound reduced-fat bulk pork sausage
- 1 large onion, chopped
- 1 medium carrot, chopped
- 1 celery rib, chopped
- 2 cups cubed day-old whole wheat bread
- 1/2 cup fat-free milk
- 1 tablespoon all-purpose flour
- 4 cups chopped zucchini
- 3/4 pound reduced-fat process cheese (Velveeta), cubed
- 1 can (10-3/4 ounces) reduced-fat reduced-sodium condensed cream of mushroom soup, undiluted
- 3/4 cup egg substitute
- 1 teaspoon garlic powder
- 1/2 teaspoon onion powder
- 1/2 teaspoon rubbed sage
- 1/2 teaspoon dried thyme
- 1/2 teaspoon pepper

In a Dutch oven, cook the beef, sausage, onion, carrot and celery over medium heat until the meat is no longer pink and vegetables are crisp-tender. Meanwhile, in a small bowl, combine bread cubes and milk; set aside.

Remove meat mixture from the heat; drain. Stir in flour until blended. Stir in the bread mixture and remaining ingredients. Transfer to a 13-in. x 9-in. baking dish coated with cooking spray.

Cover and bake at 350° for 40-45 minutes or until a meat thermometer reads 160°. Uncover and stir. Bake 8-12 minutes longer or until golden brown.

YIELD: 8 SERVINGS.

LAYERED BEEF CASSEROLE

PREP 25 minutes | **BAKE** 2 hours + standing

dorothy wiedeman
EATON, COLORADO

With my busy days, I treasure meal-in-one recipes like this. Toss together a salad, and you have a complete meal.

- 6 medium potatoes, peeled and thinly sliced
- 1 can (15-1/4 ounces) whole kernel corn, drained
- 1/2 cup chopped green pepper
- 1 cup chopped onion
- 2 cups sliced fresh carrots
- 1-1/2 pounds lean ground beef
- 1 can (8 ounces) tomato sauce
- Salt and pepper to taste
- 1 cup (4 ounces) shredded process American cheese

In a greased 13-in. x 9-in. baking dish, layer the potatoes, corn, green pepper, onion and carrots. Crumble beef over the vegetables. Pour tomato sauce over top. Sprinkle with salt and pepper.

Cover and bake at 350° for 2 hours. Sprinkle with cheese. Let stand for 10 minutes before serving.

YIELD: 8 SERVINGS.

HEARTY PENNE BEEF

PREP/TOTAL TIME 30 minutes

1-3/4 cups uncooked penne pasta
1 pound ground beef
1 teaspoon minced garlic
1 can (15 ounces) tomato puree
1 can (14-1/2 ounces) beef broth
1-1/2 teaspoons Italian seasoning
1 teaspoon Worcestershire sauce
1/4 teaspoon salt
1/4 teaspoon pepper
2 cups chopped fresh spinach
2 cups (8 ounces) shredded part-skim mozzarella cheese

Cook the pasta according to the package directions. Meanwhile, in a Dutch oven, cook beef and garlic over medium heat until meat is no longer pink; drain. Stir in the tomato puree, broth, Italian seasoning, Worcestershire sauce, salt and pepper.

Bring to a boil. Reduce heat; simmer, uncovered, for 10-15 minutes or until slightly thickened. Add spinach; cook for 1-2 minutes or until spinach is wilted.

Drain pasta; stir into beef mixture. Sprinkle with cheese; cover and cook for 3-4 minutes or until cheese is melted.
YIELD: 4 SERVINGS.

taste of home
test kitchen
GREENDALE, WISCONSIN

This is comfort food at its finest! The best of everything is found here—it's tasty, easy and a great way to sneak in some spinach for extra nutrition.

THREE-CHEESE LASAGNA

PREP 25 minutes | **BAKE** 15 minutes

2 pounds ground beef

1/2 cup chopped onion

1 package (6.4 ounces) lasagna dinner mix

2-1/4 cups hot water

2 cans (14-1/2 ounces *each*) diced tomatoes, undrained

1 package (10 ounces) frozen chopped spinach, thawed and squeezed dry

1 cup sliced fresh mushrooms

1/2 cup chopped green onions

1 cup (8 ounces) 4% cottage cheese

1/4 cup grated Parmesan cheese

1-1/2 cups (6 ounces) shredded part-skim mozzarella cheese

In a large skillet, cook beef and onion over medium heat for 10-12 minutes or until meat is no longer pink; drain.

Stir in the pasta from the dinner mix, contents of seasoning mix, water, tomatoes, spinach, mushrooms and onions. Bring to a boil. Reduce heat; cover and simmer for 10-13 minutes or until pasta is tender. Stir in cottage cheese and Parmesan cheese.

Transfer to two greased 8-in. square baking dishes. Sprinkle with mozzarella cheese.

Cover and freeze one casserole for up to 3 months. Cover and bake the remaining casserole at 350° for 15-20 minutes or until bubbly and cheese is melted.

TO USE FROZEN CASSEROLE: Remove from the freezer 30 minutes before baking (do not thaw). Cover and bake at 350° for 1 hour. Uncover; bake 15-20 minutes longer or until heated through.

YIELD: 2 CASSEROLES (4 SERVINGS EACH).

EDITOR'S NOTE: This recipe was tested with Hamburger Helper Lasagna Dinner Mix.

del mason
MARTENSVILLE, SASKATCHEWAN

With all the flavors of lasagna but none of the layering, this recipe is as easy as it is delicious. I like it especially because it makes two casseroles: one for now, and one for later. It's like getting two meals from the labor of one.

HEARTY HAMBURGER CASSEROLE

PREP 15 minutes | **BAKE** 30 minutes

- 1 pound ground beef
- 1 can (18.8 ounces) ready-to-serve chunky savory vegetable soup
- 1 package (6 ounces) stuffing mix
- 1/2 cup shredded cheddar cheese

In a skillet, cook beef until no longer pink; drain. Stir in soup and set aside. Prepare the stuffing mix according to package directions; spoon half into a greased 2-qt. baking dish. Top with beef mixture, cheese and remaining stuffing.

Bake, uncovered, at 350° for 30-35 minutes or until heated through.

YIELD: 4 SERVINGS.

regan delp
INDEPENDENCE, VIRGINIA

I love to invent my own recipes, so I used convenient stuffing mix and canned vegetable soup to come up with this satisfying supper.

JUMBLE LALA

PREP 15 minutes | **BAKE** 1 hour 20 minutes

- 1-1/2 pounds ground beef, browned and drained
- 1 medium onion, chopped
- 1 quart tomato juice
- 1 can (10-3/4 ounces) condensed tomato soup, undiluted
- 1 cup uncooked long grain rice
- 1 tablespoon brown sugar
- 1/4 teaspoon dried thyme
- 2 bay leaves
- 1/4 to 1/2 teaspoon curry powder
- 1 teaspoon salt
- 1/2 teaspoon pepper

Combine all ingredients in a large bowl. Pour into a greased 2-qt. baking dish. Cover and bake at 350° for 80-90 minutes or until hot and bubbly.

YIELD: 8-10 SERVINGS.

dora brahmer
SPRING VALLEY, WISCONSIN

Wondering about the silly name? It came about because this dish has all the spicy goodness of jambalaya—but requires a lot less time and work to prepare!

BAKED SPAGHETTI

PREP 25 minutes | **BAKE** 1 hour

- 1 package (16 ounces) spaghetti
- 1 pound ground beef
- 1 medium onion, chopped
- 1 jar (26 ounces) meatless spaghetti sauce
- 1/2 teaspoon seasoned salt
- 2 eggs
- 1/3 cup grated Parmesan cheese
- 5 tablespoons butter, melted
- 2 cups (16 ounces) 4% cottage cheese
- 4 cups (16 ounces) part-skim shredded mozzarella cheese

Cook the spaghetti according to package directions. Meanwhile, in a large skillet, cook the beef and onion over medium heat until meat is no longer pink; drain. Stir in spaghetti sauce and seasoned salt; set aside.

In a large bowl, whisk eggs, Parmesan cheese and butter. Drain the spaghetti; add to the egg mixture and toss to coat.

Place half of the spaghetti mixture in a greased 13-in. x 9-in. baking dish. Top with half of the cottage cheese, meat sauce and mozzarella cheese. Repeat layers.

Cover and bake at 350° for 40 minutes. Uncover; bake 20-25 minutes longer or until cheese is melted.

YIELD: 8-10 SERVINGS.

louise miller
WESTMINSTER, MARYLAND

This yummy spaghetti casserole will be requested again and again for potlucks and family gatherings. It's especially popular with my grandchildren, who just love all the cheese.

poultry

CRESCENT-TOPPED TURKEY AMANDINE • PAGE 62

CHICKEN AND HAM ROLL-UPS

PREP/TOTAL TIME 30 minutes

3 cups cooked rice
1-1/2 cups chopped cooked chicken
1 can (10-3/4 ounces) condensed cream of chicken soup, undiluted, *divided*
1/4 cup finely chopped celery
1 green onion, thinly sliced
1/4 teaspoon pepper, *divided*
6 slices fully cooked ham
1/4 cup sour cream *or* plain yogurt
1/4 cup milk
1/4 teaspoon dried thyme
1/2 cup shredded Swiss *or* part-skim mozzarella cheese
Paprika *or* additional chopped green onion

Spread the rice in a greased 11-in. x 7-in. microwave-safe baking dish; set aside. In a medium bowl, combine chicken, 1/3 cup soup, celery, onion and 1/8 teaspoon pepper. Place 1/4 cup on each ham slice and roll up. Secure with a toothpick if necessary. Place ham rolls, seam side down, on top of rice.

Combine the sour cream, milk, thyme and remaining soup and pepper; spoon over rolls. Cover and microwave on high, turning dish halfway through cooking time, for 6-10 minutes or until heated through. Sprinkle with cheese and paprika or onion; cover and let stand 5 minutes. Remove toothpicks before serving.
YIELD: 4-6 SERVINGS.

karen mawhinney
TEESEWATER, ONTARIO

I first started making these easy roll-ups as a way to use leftover chicken. My family raved about them so much that I now frequently serve them when entertaining.

TEMPTING TURKEY CASSEROLE

PREP 15 minutes | **BAKE** 25 minutes

3 ounces uncooked spaghetti, broken into 2-inch pieces
1/2 cup process cheese sauce, warmed
1/4 cup 2% milk
1-1/2 cups frozen chopped broccoli, thawed
3/4 cup cubed cooked turkey
1/3 cup canned mushroom stems and pieces, drained
1 tablespoon pimientos, chopped
1/8 to 1/4 teaspoon onion powder
1/8 teaspoon poultry seasoning

Cook the spaghetti according to package directions. Meanwhile, in a small bowl, whisk the cheese sauce and milk. Add the broccoli, turkey, mushrooms, pimientos, onion powder and poultry seasoning. Drain pasta; add to broccoli mixture.

Transfer to a 1-qt. baking dish coated with cooking spray. Cover and bake at 350° for 25-30 minutes or until heated through.
YIELD: 3 SERVINGS.

donna evans
MAYVILLE, WISCONSIN

Here's a great-tasting way to finish cooked turkey and eat your broccoli at the same time. We sure do like this casserole!

make your OWN

When a recipe calls for poultry seasoning, you can make your own at home with this simple idea. Combine 3/4 teaspoon rubbed sage and 1/4 teaspoon dried thyme or marjoram. This yields 1 teaspoon of poultry seasoning.

MEXICALI CASSEROLE

PREP 15 minutes | **BAKE** 55 minutes

1 pound ground turkey breast
1-1/2 cups chopped onions
1/2 cup chopped green pepper
1 garlic clove, minced
1 teaspoon chili powder
1/2 teaspoon salt
1 can (16 ounces) kidney beans, rinsed and drained
1 can (14-1/2 ounces) diced tomatoes, undrained
1 cup water
2/3 cup uncooked long grain rice
1/3 cup sliced ripe olives
1/2 cup shredded reduced-fat cheddar cheese

In a large skillet coated with cooking spray, cook turkey, onions, green pepper and garlic over medium heat until the meat is no longer pink and the vegetables are tender; drain. Sprinkle with chili powder and salt. Stir in beans, tomatoes, water, rice and olives.

Transfer to a 2-1/2-qt. baking dish coated with cooking spray. Cover and bake at 375° for 50-55 minutes or until the rice is tender. Uncover; sprinkle with cheese. Bake 5 minutes longer or until cheese is melted.
YIELD: 6 SERVINGS.

NUTRITION FACTS: 1 serving equals 348 calories, 10 g fat (3 g saturated fat), 66 mg cholesterol, 508 mg sodium, 41 g carbohydrate, 9 g fiber, 24 g protein. **DIABETIC EXCHANGES:** 2-1/2 lean meat, 2 starch, 2 vegetable.

gertrudis miller
EVANSVILLE, INDIANA

Kids will love this hearty yet mild tasting Mexican-style casserole. It's also popular at potluck dinners.

BROCCOLI CHICKEN SUPREME

PREP 30 minutes | **BAKE** 20 minutes

6 cups fresh broccoli florets
3 cups sliced fresh mushrooms
1 tablespoon butter
6 cups cubed cooked chicken
3 cans (8 ounces *each*) sliced water chestnuts, drained, *divided*

SAUCE

6 tablespoons butter, cubed
1/2 cup plus 1 tablespoon all-purpose flour
1-1/2 teaspoons seasoned salt
1/8 teaspoon pepper
3 cups chicken broth
1 cup heavy whipping cream
6 egg yolks, lightly beaten
3/4 teaspoon lemon juice
1/8 teaspoon ground nutmeg
3/4 cup slivered almonds, toasted

Place the broccoli in a steamer basket; place in a large saucepan over 1 in. of water. Bring to a boil; cover and steam for 5-7 minutes or until crisp-tender. Meanwhile, in a large skillet, saute the mushrooms in butter until tender.

In a greased 13-in. x 9-in. baking dish, layer 4 cups chicken, two-thirds of the mushrooms, two cans of water chestnuts and 4 cups broccoli. In a greased 8-in. square baking dish, layer the remaining chicken, mushrooms, water chestnuts and broccoli.

For sauce, in a large saucepan over medium heat, melt butter. Stir in the flour, seasoned salt and pepper until smooth. Gradually add broth and cream. Bring to a boil; cook and stir for 2 minutes or until thickened and bubbly. Remove from the heat.

Stir a small amount of hot mixture into egg yolks. Return all to the pan; cook and stir until mixture reaches 160° and coats the back of a metal spoon. Remove from the heat; stir in lemon juice and nutmeg.

Pour 3 cups sauce over the large casserole and the remaining sauce over the small casserole; sprinkle with almonds. Bake, uncovered, at 375° for 20-25 minutes or until bubbly and heated through.
YIELD: 12 SERVINGS.

vi neiding
SOUTH MILWAUKEE, WISCONSIN

This saucy, comforting casserole will draw compliments when it's served at your next potluck dinner. You can also try the rich sauce with leftover or cooked meats, fish or vegetables.

TURKEY RICE CASSEROLE

PREP 20 minutes | **COOK** 15 minutes

- 1 medium onion, chopped
- 1 celery rib, chopped
- 2 tablespoons butter
- 2 cups milk
- 1-1/4 cups uncooked instant rice
- 2 cups diced cooked turkey
- 1 can (10-3/4 ounces) condensed cream of mushroom soup, undiluted
- 1 cup seasoned stuffing cubes
- 1 can (4 ounces) chopped green chilies, drained
- 1 cup (4 ounces) shredded cheddar cheese, *divided*

In a 2-qt. microwave-safe dish, combine the onion, celery and butter. Cover and microwave on high for 1-1/2 to 3 minutes or until butter is melted. Stir in milk. Cover and cook on high for 3-5 minutes or until milk is steaming (do not boil). Stir in rice. Cover and let stand for 2 minutes.

Add turkey, soup, stuffing cubes, chilies and 1/2 cup cheese. Cover and microwave on high for 3-6 minutes or until heated through, stirring once. Sprinkle with the remaining cheese. Cover and let stand for 5 minutes.

YIELD: 6-8 SERVINGS.

tamy baker
KEARNEY, NEBRASKA

The recipe for this creamy and satisfying casserole came from my aunt as a way to use leftover turkey. I love it so much, however, that I don't wait for leftovers to make it. The green chilies provide the memorable flavor.

CHICKEN SALAD BAKE

PREP 20 minutes | **BAKE** 30 minutes

- 4 cups cubed cooked chicken breast
- 2 celery ribs, thinly sliced
- 1 small green *or* sweet red pepper, chopped
- 1/2 cup sliced water chestnuts, halved
- 1/2 cup sliced fresh mushrooms
- 1/4 cup finely chopped onion
- 1 cup reduced-fat salad dressing
- 1/2 teaspoon garlic powder
- 1/2 teaspoon pepper
- 1 cup soft bread crumbs
- 1 tablespoon butter, melted
- 1/4 cup shredded cheddar cheese

In a large bowl, combine the first six ingredients. Combine salad dressing, garlic powder and pepper; stir into chicken mixture.

Transfer to a 2-qt. baking dish coated with cooking spray. Bake, uncovered, at 350° for 20 minutes.

Toss bread crumbs with butter; sprinkle over chicken mixture. Top with cheese. Bake 7-10 minutes longer or until heated through and top is lightly browned.

YIELD: 6 SERVINGS.

darla germaux
SAXTON, PENNSYLVANIA

This amazing twist on the classic chicken salad is sure to impress guests. The main dish is one you can have seconds without feeling one bit of guilt.

reviving CELERY

Give limp, tired celery a second chance to season entrees, soups and stews. Cut the ends from any limp stalks. Place in a jar or glass of cold water. Then, store in the refrigerator for several hours or overnight.

FOUR-CHEESE CHICKEN FETTUCCINE

PREP 20 minutes | **BAKE** 30 minutes

- 8 ounces uncooked fettuccine
- 1 can (10-3/4 ounces) condensed cream of mushroom soup, undiluted
- 1 package (8 ounces) cream cheese, cubed
- 1 jar (4-1/2 ounces) sliced mushrooms, drained
- 1 cup heavy whipping cream
- 1/2 cup butter
- 1/4 teaspoon garlic powder
- 3/4 cup grated Parmesan cheese
- 1/2 cup shredded part-skim mozzarella cheese
- 1/2 cup shredded Swiss cheese
- 2-1/2 cups cubed cooked chicken

TOPPING

- 1/3 cup seasoned bread crumbs
- 2 tablespoons butter, melted
- 1 to 2 tablespoons grated Parmesan cheese

Cook the fettuccine according to package directions.

Meanwhile, in a large kettle, combine the soup, cream cheese, mushrooms, cream, butter and garlic powder. Stir in the cheeses; cook and stir until melted. Add chicken; heat through. Drain fettuccine; add to the sauce.

Transfer to a shallow greased 2-1/2-qt. baking dish. Combine topping ingredients; sprinkle over the chicken mixture. Cover and bake at 350° for 25 minutes. Uncover and bake 5-10 minutes longer or until the topping is golden brown.

YIELD: 6-8 SERVINGS.

rochelle brownlee
BIG TIMBER, MONTANA

As a cattle rancher, my husband is a big fan of beef. For him to comment on a poultry dish is rare. But he always tells me, "I love this casserole!" I first tasted it at a potluck; now, I fix it for my family once or twice a month, and I'm asked to take it to almost every get-together.

SOUTHWEST CREAMY PASTA BAKE

PREP 20 minutes | **BAKE** 30 minutes

- 12 ounces uncooked spiral pasta
- 3 cups cubed cooked chicken breast
- 2 cups (16 ounces) sour cream
- 2 cups (8 ounces) shredded Colby-Monterey Jack cheese
- 1 can (10-3/4 ounces) condensed cream of mushroom soup, undiluted
- 1 can (10-3/4 ounces) condensed cream of celery soup, undiluted
- 1 can (10 ounces) green chili salsa
- 1 cup chopped green onions
- 1 can (4-1/4 ounces) chopped ripe olives

Cook the pasta according to the package directions. Meanwhile, in a large bowl, combine the remaining ingredients. Drain pasta; stir into chicken mixture.

Transfer to a greased 13-in. x 9-in. baking dish. Bake, uncovered, at 350° for 30-35 minutes or until heated through.

YIELD: 8 SERVINGS.

patty putter
MARION, KANSAS

I like to cook a package of boneless chicken breasts in the microwave, then dice it up and store in freezer bags. On hectic nights, just pull one out and thaw in the microwave for a real time-saver with quick, tasty recipes like this.

HERBED TURKEY TETRAZZINI

PREP 30 minutes | **BAKE** 25 minutes

6 cups uncooked egg noodles
1/3 cup sliced green onions
1 garlic clove, minced
2 tablespoons olive oil
1 pound sliced fresh mushrooms
3 tablespoons minced fresh parsley
1 tablespoon minced fresh thyme *or*
   1 teaspoon dried thyme
2 bay leaves
2 teaspoons grated lemon peel
1/4 cup butter
1/4 cup all-purpose flour
2 cups chicken broth
1 egg yolk, beaten
1 cup milk
4 cups cubed cooked turkey
Salt and pepper to taste
1/3 cup dry bread crumbs
1/3 cup grated Parmesan cheese
1/2 cup sliced almonds, toasted

Cook the noodles according to the package directions. Meanwhile, in a Dutch oven, saute onions and garlic in oil for 3 minutes. Add the mushrooms, parsley, thyme and bay leaves. Cook until mushrooms are lightly browned. Discard bay leaves.

Transfer the mushroom mixture to a bowl; stir in lemon peel and set aside. Drain noodles; set aside.

In Dutch oven, melt the butter over medium heat. Stir in the flour until smooth. Whisk in the broth. Bring to a boil; cook and stir for 2 minutes or until thickened. Combine egg yolk and milk; stir into white sauce. Cook and stir 2 minutes longer.

Stir in mushroom mixture and turkey; heat through. Fold in noodles. Season with salt and pepper.

Spoon into a greased 13-in. x 9-in. baking dish. Toss the bread crumbs and cheese; sprinkle over the top. Bake, uncovered, at 350° for 25-30 minutes or until lightly browned. Sprinkle with almonds.
YIELD: 12 SERVINGS.

brigitte garringer
COPPER CANYON, TEXAS

There are many versions of this old-fashioned casserole. Mine offers a little more zip due to the thyme and lemon peel. It's a nice way to use up those turkey leftovers.

BUTTERNUT TURKEY BAKE

PREP 70 minutes | **BAKE** 25 minutes

1 medium butternut squash
(about 2-1/2 pounds)
3/4 cup finely chopped onion
2 tablespoons butter
2 cups seasoned salad croutons
1/2 teaspoon salt
1/2 teaspoon poultry seasoning
1/2 teaspoon pepper
2 cups cubed cooked turkey
1 cup chicken broth
1/2 cup shredded cheddar cheese

Cut squash in half; discard seeds. Place cut side down in a 15-in. x 10-in. x 1-in. baking pan; add 1/2 in. of hot water. Bake, uncovered, at 350° for 45 minutes.

Drain the water from pan; turn squash cut side up. Bake 10-15 minutes longer or until tender. Scoop out the pulp; mash and set aside.

In a large skillet, saute the onion in butter until tender. Stir in the croutons, salt, poultry seasoning and pepper. Cook 2-3 minutes longer or until croutons are toasted. Stir in the squash, turkey and broth; heat through.

Transfer to a greased 1-1/2-qt. baking dish. Bake, uncovered, at 350° for 20 minutes. Sprinkle with cheese. Bake 5-10 minutes longer or until the edges are bubbly and cheese is melted.

YIELD: 4 SERVINGS.

mary ann dell
PHOENIXVILLE, PENNSYLVANIA

Butternut squash adds a little sweetness to this comforting casserole. You can use leftover turkey and even replace the croutons with extra stuffing, if you wish. It's sure to satisfy your family.

CHICKEN MEAL-IN-ONE

PREP 10 minutes | **BAKE** 1-1/4 hours

4-1/2 cups frozen shredded hash brown
      potatoes
   2 cups frozen cut green beans, thawed
   1 cup frozen sliced carrots, thawed
   4 bone-in chicken breasts (6 ounces
      each)
   1 can (10-3/4 ounces) condensed
      cream of chicken *or* mushroom
      soup, undiluted
 3/4 cup water
   2 tablespoons onion soup mix
Salt and pepper to taste

In an ungreased 13-in. x 9-in. baking dish, combine the hash browns, beans and carrots. Top with the chicken. Combine the remaining ingredients; pour over chicken and vegetables.

Cover and bake at 375° for 50 minutes. Uncover; bake 25-30 minutes longer or until a meat thermometer reads 170°.
YIELD: 4 SERVINGS.

NUTRITION FACTS: 1 serving (prepared with skinless chicken breasts, reduced-fat reduced-sodium mushroom soup and reduced-sodium onion soup mix and without salt) equals 428 calories, 5 g fat (0 saturated fat), 73 mg cholesterol, 685 mg sodium, 62 g carbohydrate, 8 g fiber, 34 g protein. **DIABETIC EXCHANGES:** 3-1/2 starch, 3 very lean meat, 1 vegetable, 1/2 fat.

jina nickel
LAWTON, OKLAHOMA

As the parents of a young son, my husband and I don't have much time to prepare meals. While our boy is napping, I can assemble this dinner-in-a-dish in just 10 minutes and then pop it in the oven.

SPAGHETTI SQUASH SUPREME

PREP 45 minutes | **BAKE** 20 minutes

   1 medium spaghetti squash (4 pounds)
   1 can (14-1/2 ounces) diced tomatoes,
      undrained
   2 tablespoons prepared pesto
 1/2 teaspoon garlic powder
 1/2 teaspoon Italian seasoning
 1/4 cup dry bread crumbs
 1/4 cup shredded Parmesan cheese
   1 pound boneless skinless chicken
      breasts, cut into 1/2-inch cubes
   1 tablespoon plus 1 teaspoon olive oil,
      divided
 1/2 pound sliced fresh mushrooms
   1 medium onion, chopped
   1 garlic clove, minced
 1/2 cup chicken broth
 1/3 cup shredded cheddar cheese

Cut squash in half lengthwise; discard seeds. Place squash cut side down on a microwave-safe plate. Microwave, uncovered, on high for 14-16 minutes or until tender.

Meanwhile, in a blender, combine the tomatoes, pesto, garlic powder and Italian seasoning. Cover and process until blended; set aside. In a small bowl, combine bread crumbs and Parmesan cheese; set aside.

In a large skillet, cook chicken in 1 tablespoon oil until no longer pink; remove and keep warm. In the same skillet, saute mushrooms, onion and garlic in remaining oil until tender. Stir in the broth, chicken and reserved tomato mixture. Bring to a boil. Reduce heat; simmer, uncovered, for 5 minutes.

When squash is cool enough to handle, use a fork to separate strands. In a large ovenproof skillet, layer half of the squash, chicken mixture and the reserved crumb mixture. Repeat layers.

Bake, uncovered, at 350° for 15 minutes or until heated through. Sprinkle with cheddar cheese. Broil 3-4 in. from heat for 5-6 minutes or until cheese is melted and golden brown.
YIELD: 5 SERVINGS.

christina morris
CALABASAS, CALIFORNIA

While dreaming up a healthier pasta dish, I decided to experiment with spaghetti squash. After a few tries, I settled on this delicious casserole bursting with flavor, but with plenty of nutritious ingredients.

winter SQUASH

Here's a method to cut through the hard shells of winter squashes. Secure a food storage bag around a rubber mallet. Insert chef's knife lengthwise into the squash. Hold the knife handle with one hand and hit the knife blade (near the handle) with the mallet. Continue until the squash is cut in half.

CHICKEN AND DRESSING DISH

PREP 15 minutes + standing | **BAKE** 55 minutes

- 1 cup chopped onion
- 1 cup chopped celery
- 1/4 cup butter, cubed
- 2 cups chicken broth
- 1-1/2 teaspoons dried thyme
- 1 teaspoon poultry seasoning
- 1/2 teaspoon salt
- 1/2 teaspoon pepper
- 1/4 teaspoon ground nutmeg
- 2 eggs, lightly beaten *or* 1/2 cup egg substitute
- 1 package (12 ounces) unseasoned stuffing cubes
- 1/4 cup minced fresh parsley
- 3 cups cubed cooked chicken
- 1 can (10-3/4 ounces) condensed cream of chicken *or* mushroom soup, undiluted
- 1/3 cup water

In a large saucepan, saute the onion and celery in butter until tender; remove from heat. Stir in the broth, seasonings and eggs. Add bread cubes and parsley; toss to coat.

Transfer to a greased 13-in. x 9-in. baking dish. Top with chicken. Combine soup and water; spoon over chicken. Let stand for 10 minutes.

Cover and bake at 350° for 50 minutes. Uncover; bake 5-10 minutes longer or until a thermometer reads 160°.

YIELD: 8 SERVINGS.

NUTRITION FACTS: 1 serving (prepared with margarine, low-sodium broth, egg substitute and reduce-fat soup and without added salt) equals 390 calories, 13 g fat, 48 mg cholesterol, 572 mg sodium, 41 g carbohydrate, 26 g protein. **DIABETIC EXCHANGES:** 2-1/2 starch, 2 lean meat, 1-1/2 fat, 1 vegetable.

anne smith
TAYLORS, SOUTH CAROLINA

I've always enjoyed trying new recipes, and now that our children are grown, I have more time to do just that!

mincing **PARSLEY**

Here's a simple trimming tip. Don't mess up a cutting board! Simply place parsley leaves in a small glass container, then snip the sprigs with a pair of kitchen shears until they are minced.

CHICKEN ARTICHOKE BAKE

PREP 15 minutes | **BAKE** 55 minutes

- 2 cans (10-3/4 ounces *each*) condensed cream of celery soup, undiluted
- 1 cup mayonnaise
- 3 cups cubed cooked chicken
- 1 can (14 ounces) water-packed artichoke hearts, rinsed, drained and chopped
- 1 can (8 ounces) sliced water chestnuts, drained
- 1 package (6 ounces) long grain and wild rice mix
- 1 cup sliced fresh mushrooms
- 1 medium onion, finely chopped
- 1 jar (2 ounces) diced pimientos, drained
- 1/4 teaspoon pepper
- 1 cup seasoned stuffing cubes

In a large bowl, combine the soup and the mayonnaise. Stir in the chicken, artichokes, water chestnuts, rice mix with contents of seasoning packet, mushrooms, onion, pimientos and pepper.

Spoon into a greased 2-1/2-qt. baking dish. Sprinkle with stuffing cubes. Bake, uncovered, at 350° for 55-65 minutes or until edges are bubbly and rice is tender.

YIELD: 6 SERVINGS.

todd richards
WEST ALLIS, WISCONSIN

The first time I tasted this creamy casserole at a friend's get-together, I noted how much everyone loved it. All of the party guests went for seconds...and thirds. I can't believe how easy it is to prepare, and it is perfect on a buffet.

TURKEY ENCHILADA CASSEROLE

PREP 30 minutes | **BAKE** 25 minutes

debra martin
BELLEVILLE, MICHIGAN

Every time I make this for guests, I end up sharing my recipe! It's just got a lot of delicious things going on with it!

1 pound lean ground turkey
1 medium green pepper, chopped
1 medium onion, chopped
3 garlic cloves, minced
2 cans (15 ounces *each*) black beans, rinsed and drained
1 jar (16 ounces) salsa
1 can (15 ounces) tomato sauce
1 can (14-1/2 ounces) Mexican stewed tomatoes
1 teaspoon *each* onion powder, garlic powder and ground cumin
12 corn tortillas (6 inches)
2 cups (8 ounces) shredded reduced-fat cheddar cheese, *divided*

In a large nonstick saucepan coated with cooking spray, cook turkey, green pepper, onion and garlic over medium heat until meat is no longer pink. Stir in beans, salsa, tomato sauce, tomatoes, onion powder, garlic powder and cumin. Bring to a boil. Reduce heat; simmer, uncovered, for 10 minutes.

Spread 1 cup meat sauce into a 13-in. x 9-in. baking dish coated with cooking spray. Top with six tortillas. Spread with half of the remaining meat sauce; sprinkle with 1 cup cheese. Layer with remaining tortillas and meat sauce.

Cover and bake at 350° for 20 minutes. Uncover; sprinkle with remaining cheese. Bake 5-10 minutes longer or until bubbly and cheese is melted.
YIELD: 10 SERVINGS.

PEPPERONI ZITI CASSEROLE

PREP 20 minutes | **BAKE** 30 minutes

1 package (1 pound) uncooked ziti *or* small tube pasta
1/2 pound lean ground turkey
2 cans (one 29 ounces, one 8 ounces) tomato sauce, *divided*
1-1/2 cups (6 ounces) shredded part-skim mozzarella cheese, *divided*
1 can (8 ounces) mushroom stems and pieces, drained
5 ounces frozen chopped spinach, thawed and squeezed dry
1/2 cup reduced-fat ricotta cheese
4 teaspoons Italian seasoning
2 garlic cloves, minced
1/2 teaspoon garlic powder
1/2 teaspoon crushed red pepper flakes
1/4 teaspoon pepper
1/2 cup water
1 tablespoon grated Parmesan cheese
1-1/2 ounces sliced turkey pepperoni

Cook the pasta according to the package directions.

Meanwhile, in a large nonstick skillet, cook the turkey over medium heat until no longer pink; drain. Transfer to a large bowl. Add the 29-oz. can tomato sauce, 1 cup mozzarella cheese, mushrooms, spinach, ricotta cheese, Italian seasoning, garlic, garlic powder, pepper flakes and pepper. Drain pasta; fold into turkey mixture.

Transfer to a 13-in. x 9-in. baking dish coated with cooking spray. Combine the water and remaining tomato sauce; pour over pasta mixture. Sprinkle with the Parmesan cheese and remaining mozzarella cheese. Top with pepperoni.

Cover and bake at 350° for 24-30 minutes or until bubbly. Uncover; bake 5 minutes longer or until cheese is melted.
YIELD: 10 SERVINGS.

NUTRITION FACTS: 1 cup equals 306 calories, 7 g fat (3 g saturated fat), 37 mg cholesterol, 795 mg sodium, 42 g carbohydrate, 4 g fiber, 20 g protein. **DIABETIC EXCHANGES:** 2-1/2 starch, 2 lean meat, 1 vegetable.

andrea abrahamsen
BRENTWOOD, CALIFORNIA

I took a traditional family recipe and put my own nutritious spin on it. The chopped spinach and turkey pepperoni add color, pleasing both the eyes and the palate.

TURKEY SAUSAGE CASSEROLE

PREP 15 minutes | **BAKE** 20 minutes

- 1/2 cup finely chopped onion
- 2 teaspoons butter, *divided*
- 1 pound low-fat smoked turkey sausage, cut into 1/4-inch slices
- 1 package (10 ounces) spiral noodles, cooked and drained
- 1/2 pound fresh mushrooms, sliced
- 1 can (10-3/4 ounces) reduced-fat reduced-sodium condensed cream of chicken soup, undiluted
- 1 can (10-3/4 ounces) condensed cheddar cheese soup, undiluted
- 1 cup fat-free evaporated milk
- 1/2 cup crushed reduced-fat butter-flavored crackers

In a skillet, saute the onion in 1 teaspoon butter until tender. Add sausage, noodles, mushrooms, soups and milk; mix well. Transfer to a 13-in. x 9-in. baking dish coated with cooking spray. Sprinkle with cracker crumbs; dot with remaining butter.

Bake, uncovered, at 375° for 20-25 minutes or until heated through.
YIELD: 8 SERVINGS.

NUTRITION FACTS: 1 cup equals 344 calories, 11 g fat (0 saturated fat), 45 mg cholesterol, 1,128 mg sodium, 43 g carbohydrate, 0 fiber, 18 g protein. **DIABETIC EXCHANGES:** 2-1/2 starch, 2 meat, 1 vegetable.

nancy arnold
JOHNSON CITY, TENNESSEE

This is a much-requested dish with my gang. The blend of two kinds of meat with pasta and mushrooms is fantastic.

CRUNCHY CHICKEN CASSEROLE

PREP 15 minutes | **BAKE** 30 minutes

- 1 cup chopped celery
- 1 tablespoon butter
- 2 cups cubed cooked chicken
- 1-1/2 cups cooked rice
- 1 can (10-3/4 ounces) condensed cream of chicken soup, undiluted
- 3/4 cup mayonnaise
- 1 can (8 ounces) sliced water chestnuts, drained
- 1/2 cup sliced almonds
- 2 tablespoons chopped onion

Salt and pepper to taste

TOPPING
- 1 tablespoon butter, melted
- 1/2 cup crushed cornflakes

Sliced almonds, optional

In a skillet, saute celery in butter until tender. Remove from the heat; add the next nine ingredients. Spoon into an ungreased 2-1/2-qt. baking dish.

Combine melted butter and cornflakes: sprinkle on top of casserole. Sprinkle with almonds if desired. Bake, uncovered, at 350° for 30 minutes.
YIELD: 6-8 SERVINGS.

blanche hollingworth
RICHMOND, INDIANA

My 96-year-old mother wanted me to share her favorite recipe with readers. I hope you enjoy it as much as we do!

toasting **NUTS**

Toasting nuts before using them in a recipe intensifies their flavor. Spread the nuts on a baking sheet and bake at 350° for 5 to 10 minutes or until lightly toasted. Be sure to watch them carefully so they don't burn.

GROUND TURKEY NOODLE BAKE

PREP 35 minutes | **BAKE** 15 minutes

- 3 cups uncooked wide egg noodles
- 1/2 pound lean ground turkey
- 1 medium onion, chopped
- 1 can (15 ounces) tomato sauce
- 1 teaspoon Italian seasoning
- 2/3 cup nonfat dry milk powder
- 1/2 cup water
- 4 ounces reduced-fat cream cheese, cubed
- 1 tablespoon minced fresh parsley
- 1 garlic clove, minced
- 1-1/4 cups shredded part-skim mozzarella cheese

Cook the noodles according to the package directions. Meanwhile, in a large skillet, cook turkey and onion over medium heat until turkey is no longer pink; drain. Stir in tomato sauce and Italian seasoning. Bring to a boil. Reduce the heat; cover and simmer for 10 minutes.

In a small saucepan, combine the milk powder, water, cream cheese, parsley and garlic. Cook and stir over medium heat until cream cheese is melted.

Drain the noodles; add to the cream cheese mixture. Transfer to an 8-in. square baking dish coated with cooking spray. Top with the turkey mixture. Sprinkle with mozzarella cheese.

Bake, uncovered, at 375° for 15-20 minutes or until cheese is melted.
YIELD: 6 SERVINGS.

ruby williams
BOGALUSA, LOUISIANA

Back in the 1950s, when my husband was diagnosed as diabetic, we had five children at home to feed. I made this casserole often...and it satisfied us all. We agree it's still as delicious today as it was back then.

CHICKEN 'N' BISCUITS

PREP 25 minutes | **BAKE** 30 minutes

- 1 medium onion, chopped
- 2 teaspoons canola oil
- 1/4 cup all-purpose flour
- 1/2 teaspoon dried basil
- 1/2 teaspoon dried thyme
- 1/4 teaspoon pepper
- 2-1/2 cups fat-free milk
- 1 tablespoon Worcestershire sauce
- 1 package (16 ounces) frozen mixed vegetables
- 2 cups cubed cooked chicken
- 2 tablespoons grated Parmesan cheese

BISCUITS

- 1 cup all-purpose flour
- 1 tablespoon sugar
- 1-1/2 teaspoons baking powder
- 1/4 teaspoon salt
- 1/3 cup fat-free milk
- 3 tablespoons canola oil
- 1 tablespoon minced fresh parsley

In a large saucepan, saute the onion in oil until tender. Stir in the flour, basil, thyme and pepper until blended. Gradually stir in milk and Worcestershire sauce until smooth. Bring to a boil; cook and stir for 2 minutes or until thickened. Stir in the vegetables, chicken and Parmesan cheese; reduce heat to low.

Meanwhile, in a large bowl, combine the flour, sugar, baking powder and salt. In a small bowl, combine milk, oil and parsley; stir into dry ingredients just until combined.

Transfer hot chicken mixture to a greased 2-1/2-qt. baking dish. Drop biscuit batter by rounded tablespoonfuls onto chicken mixture.

Bake, uncovered, at 375° for 30-40 minutes or until biscuits are lightly browned.
YIELD: 8 SERVINGS.

NUTRITION FACTS: 1 serving equals 246 calories, 8 g fat (0 saturated fat), 24 mg cholesterol, 284 mg sodium, 31 g carbohydrate, 0 fiber, 13 g protein. **DIABETIC EXCHANGES:** 2 starch, 1 meat, 1/2 fat.

marilyn minnick
HILLSBORO, INDIANA

This comforting casserole has a colorful medley of vegetables and chunky chicken topped with golden homemade biscuits.

a bit of HISTORY

In 1835, English Lord Sandys commissioned two chemists from Worcestershire, John Lea and William Perrins, to duplicate a sauce he had acquired during his travels in India. The resulting batch proved disappointing and ended up in the cellar. When the pair stumbled upon the aged concoction 2 years later, they tasted it and were pleasantly surprised by its wonderfully unique taste.

HOT CHICKEN SALAD

PREP 15 minutes | **BAKE** 30 minutes

bernice knutson
DANBURY, IOWA

This recipe is a creamy mix of crunchy veggies and hot chicken topped with crispy potato chips. The whole family will love this scrumptious dish and the quick and easy prep!

1 package (9 ounces) frozen diced cooked chicken breast, thawed
2 cups thinly sliced celery
1 can (8 ounces) sliced water chestnuts, drained
1/2 cup chopped almonds
1/3 cup chopped green pepper
1 jar (2 ounces) diced pimientos, drained
2 tablespoons finely chopped onion
2/3 cup shredded Swiss cheese, *divided*
1 cup mayonnaise
2 tablespoons lemon juice
1/2 teaspoon salt
2 cups crushed potato chips

In a large bowl, combine chicken, celery, water chestnuts, almonds, green pepper, pimientos, onion and 1/3 cup cheese. In a small bowl, combine the mayonnaise, lemon juice and salt. Stir into the chicken mixture and toss to coat.

Transfer to a greased 8-in. square baking dish. Bake, uncovered, at 350° for 20 minutes.

Sprinkle with potato chips and remaining cheese. Bake 10-15 minutes longer or until heated through and cheese is melted.

YIELD: 4 SERVINGS.

CRESCENT-TOPPED TURKEY AMANDINE

PREP 20 minutes | BAKE 30 minutes

becky larson
MALLARD, IOWA

Quick to prepare, this tasty main dish is loaded with turkey flavor and a nice crunch from celery and water chestnuts. Topped with a golden crescent roll crust and a sprinkling of almonds and cheese, it's bound to become a favorite.

- 3 cups cubed cooked turkey
- 1 can (10-3/4 ounces) condensed cream of mushroom soup, undiluted
- 1 can (8 ounces) sliced water chestnuts, drained
- 2/3 cup mayonnaise
- 1/2 cup chopped celery
- 1/2 cup chopped onion
- 1 tube (4 ounces) refrigerated crescent rolls
- 2/3 cup shredded Swiss cheese
- 1/2 cup sliced almonds
- 1/4 cup butter, melted

In a large saucepan, combine the first six ingredients; heat through. Transfer to a greased 2-qt. baking dish. Unroll crescent dough and place over turkey mixture.

In a small bowl, combine the cheese, almonds and butter. Spoon over dough. Bake, uncovered, at 375° for 30-35 minutes or until crust is golden brown and filling is bubbly.

YIELD: 4 SERVINGS.

STUFFED CHICKEN BREASTS

PREP 20 minutes | **BAKE** 25 minutes

4 boneless skinless chicken breast halves (6 ounces *each*)

Salt and pepper to taste

1 package (6 ounces) chicken stuffing mix

1/2 cup chopped pecans

2 tablespoons butter

1 can (10-3/4 ounces) condensed cream of mushroom soup, undiluted

Flatten the chicken to 1/4-in. thickness; sprinkle with salt and pepper. Prepare the stuffing mix according to package directions. Meanwhile, in a small skillet, saute the pecans in butter until lightly browned; add to the stuffing.

Place 1/2 cup stuffing down the center of each chicken breast half; roll up and secure with a toothpick. Place seam side down in a greased shallow 1-qt. baking dish.

Spoon soup over chicken; sprinkle with remaining stuffing. Cover and bake at 400° for 25-30 minutes or until chicken juices run clear. Remove toothpicks before serving.
YIELD: 4 SERVINGS.

dolores kastello
WAUKESHA, WISCONSIN

Baked in a rich mushroom sauce, this easy entree is nice for a special family dinner. I serve this dish with rice, asparagus and a tossed salad.

HEARTY TURKEY CASSEROLE

PREP 20 minutes | **BAKE** 35 minutes

2 cups uncooked elbow macaroni

2 cups cubed cooked turkey breast

2 cups milk

1 can (10-3/4 ounces) condensed cream of mushroom soup, undiluted

1 can (10-3/4 ounces) condensed cream of celery soup, undiluted

1 can (8 ounces) sliced water chestnuts, drained

1/2 pound process cheese (Velveeta), cubed

3 hard-cooked eggs, chopped

1 jar (2 ounces) diced pimientos, drained

1 teaspoon grated onion

Cook the macaroni according to package directions; drain and place in a large bowl. Add the remaining ingredients; mix well.

Transfer to a greased 13-in. x 9-in. baking dish. Bake, uncovered, at 350° for 35-40 minutes or until bubbly.
YIELD: 9 SERVINGS.

eunice holmberg
WILLMAR, MINNESOTA

This recipe is a creamy, cheesy delight for guests of all ages. I think it's a real keeper!

HEARTY PASTA CASSEROLE

PREP 45 minutes | **BAKE** 35 minutes

- 2 cups cubed peeled butternut squash
- 1/2 pound fresh brussels sprouts, halved
- 1 medium onion, cut into wedges
- 2 teaspoons olive oil
- 1 package (13-1/4 ounces) whole wheat penne pasta
- 1 pound Italian turkey sausage links, casings removed
- 2 garlic cloves, minced
- 2 cans (14-1/2 ounces each) Italian stewed tomatoes
- 2 tablespoons tomato paste
- 1-1/2 cups (6 ounces) shredded part-skim mozzarella cheese, *divided*
- 1/3 cup shredded Asiago cheese, *divided*

In a large bowl, combine squash, brussels sprouts and onion; drizzle with oil and toss to coat. Spread the vegetables in a single layer in two 15-in. x 10-in. x 1-in. baking pans coated with cooking spray. Bake, uncovered, at 425° for 30-40 minutes or until tender.

Meanwhile, cook the pasta according to package directions. In a large nonstick skillet, cook the sausage and garlic over medium heat until meat is no longer pink; drain. Add tomatoes and tomato paste; cook and stir over medium heat until slightly thickened, about 5 minutes.

Drain pasta and return to the pan. Add sausage mixture, 1 cup mozzarella, 1/4 cup Asiago and roasted vegetables.

Transfer to a 13-in. x 9-in. baking dish coated with cooking spray. Cover and bake at 350° for 30-40 minutes or until heated through. Uncover; sprinkle with the remaining cheeses. Bake 5 minutes longer or until cheese is melted.

YIELD: 8 SERVINGS.

taste of home test kitchen
GREENDALE, WISCONSIN

Loaded with colorful, flavorful roasted veggies, this recipe became an instant hit with us when it was developed in the Test Kitchen. This rustic Italian–inspired casserole is also the perfect entree "to go," because it transports easily and retains heat well. A great make-ahead, too!

---

about **RUBBED SAGE**

In recipes calling for "rubbed" sage, take the whole dried leaf and crush or rub it to make a finely textured powder. Most dried sage that is sold in the spice section of grocery stores comes this way.

CORN BREAD CHICKEN BAKE

PREP 20 minutes | **BAKE** 45 minutes

- 1-1/4 pounds boneless skinless chicken breasts
- 6 cups cubed corn bread
- 8 bread slices, cubed
- 1 medium onion, chopped
- 2 cans (10-3/4 ounces each) condensed cream of chicken soup, undiluted
- 1 cup chicken broth
- 2 tablespoons butter, melted
- 1-1/2 to 2 teaspoons rubbed sage
- 1 teaspoon salt
- 1/2 to 1 teaspoon pepper

Place chicken in a large skillet and cover with water; bring to a boil. Reduce heat; cover and simmer for 12-14 minutes or until juices run clear. Drain and cut into cubes.

In a large bowl, combine the remaining ingredients. Add chicken. Transfer to a greased 13-in. x 9-in. baking dish. Bake, uncovered, at 350° for 45 minutes or until heated through.

YIELD: 8-10 SERVINGS.

madge britton
AFTON, TENNESSEE

To make the most of leftover corn bread, try this hearty casserole. It's moist, scrumptious and good on any occasion!

TASTES LIKE THANKSGIVING CASSEROLE

PREP 30 minutes | **BAKE** 30 minutes

mary lou timpson
COLORADO CITY, ARIZONA

This robust, rich-tasting main dish is sure to be a winner with your family. It's a delicious way to use up Thanksgiving turkey, and you can substitute 5-1/2 cups leftover mashed potatoes for the 6 potatoes.

- 6 medium potatoes, peeled and cut into chunks
- 1-1/4 cups chopped celery
- 3/4 cup chopped onion
- 1/2 cup butter, cubed
- 6 cups unseasoned stuffing cubes
- 1 teaspoon poultry seasoning
- 1/4 teaspoon rubbed sage
- 1 cup chicken broth
- 4 cups cubed cooked turkey
- 2 cans (10-3/4 ounces *each*) condensed cream of chicken soup, undiluted
- 1 teaspoon garlic powder
- 3/4 cup sour cream, *divided*
- 4 ounces cream cheese, softened
- 1/2 teaspoon pepper
- 1/4 teaspoon salt
- 1-1/2 cups (6 ounces) shredded cheddar cheese

Place the potatoes in a Dutch oven and cover with water. Bring to a boil. Reduce heat; cover and cook for 15-20 minutes or until tender.

Meanwhile, in a large skillet, saute the celery and onion in butter until tender. Remove from the heat. In a large bowl, combine the stuffing cubes, poultry seasoning and sage. Stir in the broth and celery mixture. Transfer to a greased 13-in. x 9-in. baking dish.

In another large bowl, combine the turkey, soup, garlic powder and 1/4 cup sour cream; spoon over stuffing mixture. Drain potatoes; mash in a large bowl. Beat in the cream cheese, pepper, salt and remaining sour cream; spread over turkey mixture. Sprinkle with cheese.

Bake, uncovered, at 350° for 30-35 minutes or until heated through.

YIELD: 8 SERVINGS.

MAKEOVER GREEK SPAGHETTI

PREP 30 minutes | **BAKE** 25 minutes

1 package (16 ounces) spaghetti, broken into 2-inch pieces
4 cups cubed cooked chicken breast
2 packages (10 ounces *each*) frozen chopped spinach, thawed and squeezed dry
1 can (10-3/4 ounces) reduced-fat reduced-sodium condensed cream of chicken soup, undiluted
3/4 cup reduced-fat mayonnaise
3/4 cup reduced-fat sour cream
3 celery ribs, chopped
1 small onion, chopped
1/2 cup chopped green pepper
1 jar (2 ounces) diced pimientos, drained
1/2 teaspoon salt-free lemon-pepper seasoning
3 tablespoons all-purpose flour
1-1/3 cups fat-free milk
1 teaspoon chicken bouillon granules
1 cup (4 ounces) shredded part-skim mozzarella cheese
1/2 cup soft bread crumbs
1/4 cup shredded Parmesan cheese

Cook the spaghetti according to package directions; drain. Return spaghetti to saucepan. Stir in the chicken, spinach, soup, mayonnaise, sour cream, celery, onion, green pepper, pimientos and lemon-pepper.

In a small saucepan, whisk flour and milk until smooth. Bring to a boil over medium heat; cook and stir for 2 minutes or until thickened. Stir in bouillon. Pour over spaghetti mixture and mix well.

Transfer to a 13-in. x 9-in. baking dish coated with cooking spray (dish will be full). Top with mozzarella cheese, bread crumbs and Parmesan cheese. Bake, uncovered, at 350° for 25-30 minutes or until heated through.

YIELD: 10 SERVINGS.

melanie dalbec
INVER GROVE HEIGHTS, MINNESOTA

My original hot-dish recipe is delicious but high in fat. This comforting version offers all of the goodness you'd expect from a casserole with nearly 60% less fat than the original.

CHOW MEIN CHICKEN

PREP 5 minutes | **BAKE** 45 minutes

- 1 can (10-3/4 ounces) condensed cream of chicken soup, undiluted
- 1 can (10-1/2 ounces) condensed chicken with rice soup, undiluted
- 1 can (5 ounces) evaporated milk
- 2 cups cubed cooked chicken
- 1 can (3 ounces) chow mein noodles

In a bowl, combine the soups and milk. Stir in chicken. Transfer to a greased 8-in. square baking dish. Bake, uncovered, at 350° for 40 minutes; stir. Sprinkle with the chow mein noodles. Bake 5-10 minutes longer or until bubbly and the noodles are crisp.
YIELD: 4 SERVINGS.

roberta fall
PAW PAW, MICHIGAN

This basic recipe can be expanded in many ways, but it's quite a success by itself. Sometimes I add sliced water chestnuts for extra crunch or a green vegetable for a burst of color.

TURKEY BISCUIT BAKE

PREP/TOTAL TIME 30 minutes

- 1 can (10-3/4 ounces) condensed cream of chicken soup, undiluted
- 1 cup diced cooked turkey *or* chicken
- 1 can (4 ounces) mushroom stems and pieces, drained
- 1/2 cup frozen peas
- 1/4 cup milk
- Dash *each* ground cumin, dried basil and thyme
- 1 tube (12 ounces) refrigerated biscuits

In a large bowl, combine the soup, turkey, mushrooms, peas, milk, cumin, basil and thyme. Pour into a greased 8-in. square baking dish. Arrange biscuits over the top.
Bake, uncovered, at 350° for 20-25 minutes or until biscuits are golden brown.
YIELD: 5 SERVINGS.

andy zinkle
MT. PLEASANT, IOWA

As a college student, I appreciate stick-to-your-ribs foods like this that are also easy on the budget. I often double the recipe to ensure there are leftovers.

🔲 WEEKNIGHT CHICKEN POTPIE

PREP 25 minutes | **BAKE** 25 minutes

- 1 small onion, chopped
- 1 teaspoon canola oil
- 1-1/2 cups fat-free milk, *divided*
- 1/2 cup reduced-sodium chicken broth
- 3/4 teaspoon rubbed sage
- 1/8 teaspoon pepper
- 1/4 cup all-purpose flour
- 4 cups cubed cooked chicken breast
- 3 cups frozen chopped broccoli, thawed and drained
- 1-1/2 cups (6 ounces) shredded reduced-fat cheddar cheese
- 1 tube (11.3 ounces) refrigerated dinner rolls

In a large nonstick saucepan, saute onion in oil until tender. Stir in 3/4 cup milk, broth, sage and pepper. In a small bowl, combine flour and remaining milk until smooth; gradually stir into onion mixture. Bring to a boil; cook and stir for 1-2 minutes or until thickened. Stir in the chicken, broccoli and cheese; heat through.

Transfer to a 2-qt. baking dish coated with cooking spray. Separate rolls; arrange over chicken mixture. Bake, uncovered, at 350° for 25-30 minutes or until filling is bubbly and rolls are golden brown.
YIELD: 8 SERVINGS.

NUTRITION FACTS: 3/4 cup chicken mixture with 1 roll equals 326 calories, 9 g fat (4 g saturated fat), 70 mg cholesterol, 511 mg sodium, 28 g carbohydrate, 2 g fiber, 33 g protein.
DIABETIC EXCHANGES: 4 very lean meat, 2 starch, 1 fat.

lisa sjursen-darling
SCOTTSVILLE, NEW YORK

I have long days at work, so I really appreciate quick recipes. My husband really enjoys this casserole, and often makes it while I'm working.

GREEN CHILI LUNCHEON BAKE

PREP 30 minutes | **BAKE** 55 minutes

- 1/2 pound lean ground turkey
- 1 large onion, chopped
- 1 can (16 ounces) fat-free refried beans
- 1-3/4 teaspoons ground cumin
- 1-1/2 teaspoons dried oregano
- 1/2 teaspoon garlic powder
- 1/2 teaspoon salt, *divided*
- 1/4 teaspoon pepper
- 2 cans (4 ounces *each*) chopped green chilies
- 1 cup (4 ounces) shredded reduced-fat Mexican cheese blend
- 1 cup frozen corn, thawed
- 1/3 cup all-purpose flour
- 2 eggs
- 2 egg whites
- 1-1/3 cups fat-free milk
- 1/8 teaspoon hot pepper sauce
- 1/4 cup thinly sliced red onion
- 3 tablespoons fresh cilantro leaves

In a large nonstick skillet coated with cooking spray, cook turkey and onion over medium heat until meat is no longer pink; drain. Stir in the beans, cumin, oregano, garlic powder, 1/4 teaspoon salt and pepper.

Sprinkle half of the chilies and cheese into a 2-qt. baking dish coated with cooking spray. Layer with bean mixture, corn and remaining chilies and cheese.

In a small bowl, combine the flour and remaining salt. In another small bowl, whisk eggs, egg whites, milk and pepper sauce; gradually whisk into flour mixture until smooth. Pour over the top.

Bake, uncovered, at 350° for 55-65 minutes or until set. Sprinkle with the red onion and cilantro.

YIELD: 6 SERVINGS.

NUTRITION FACTS: 1 piece equals 312 calories, 9 g fat (3 g saturated fat), 115 mg cholesterol, 884 mg sodium, 34 g carbohydrate, 7 g fiber, 25 g protein. **DIABETIC EXCHANGES:** 3 lean meat, 2 reduced-fat milk.

kathleen smith
PITTSBURGH, PENNSYLVANIA

Seasoned beans and ground turkey are layered with cheese, corn and an egg mixture, then baked until golden. This is a warm, comforting, low-fat meal that we always enjoy.

ITALIAN TURKEY AND NOODLES

PREP 35 minutes | **BAKE** 30 minutes

- 1-1/4 pounds lean ground turkey
- 1-1/2 cups sliced fresh mushrooms
- 1/2 cup chopped onion
- 1/2 cup chopped green pepper
- 1 jar (26 ounces) meatless spaghetti sauce
- 1/2 teaspoon onion salt
- 3 cups cooked yolk-free wide noodles
- 1 cup (4 ounces) shredded part-skim mozzarella cheese

In a large nonstick skillet, cook the turkey, mushrooms, onion and green pepper until turkey is no longer pink. Add spaghetti sauce and onion salt; bring to a boil. Reduce heat; simmer, uncovered, for 15 minutes.

Place cooked noodles in the bottom of a 2-1/2-qt. baking dish coated with cooking spray. Pour meat mixture over noodles. Sprinkle with cheese. Cover and bake at 350° for 20 minutes. Uncover; bake 10-15 minutes longer or until heated through.

YIELD: 6 SERVINGS.

NUTRITION FACTS: 1 serving equals 392 calories, 12 g fat (5 g saturated fat), 86 mg cholesterol, 798 mg sodium, 39 g carbohydrate, 5 g fiber, 28 g protein. **DIABETIC EXCHANGES:** 3 lean meat, 3 vegetable, 1-1/2 starch, 1/2 fat.

cindi roshia
RACINE, WISCONSIN

A jar of meatless spaghetti sauce makes this easy dish a perfect supper during the week...just add a green salad and dinner is set. Best of all, my whole family loves it!

ITALIC PASTA CASSEROLE

PREP 30 minutes | **BAKE** 20 minutes

denise rasmussen
SALINA, KANSAS

All the traditional flavors abound in this dish reminiscent of lasagna. This is a zippy and hearty recipe that our gang and guests really like.

- 2 cups uncooked spiral pasta
- 1/2 pound lean ground beef
- 1/2 pound Italian turkey sausage links, casings removed
- 1 small onion, finely chopped
- 1 garlic clove, minced
- 2 cans (14-1/2 ounces *each*) diced tomatoes, undrained
- 1/3 cup tomato paste
- 3/4 teaspoon Italian seasoning
- 1/2 teaspoon chili powder
- 1/4 teaspoon dried oregano
- 1/8 teaspoon salt
- 1/8 teaspoon garlic powder
- 1/8 teaspoon dried thyme
- 1/8 teaspoon pepper
- 2 ounces sliced turkey pepperoni
- 1 cup (4 ounces) shredded part-skim mozzarella cheese

Cook the pasta according to the package directions. Meanwhile, crumble the beef and sausage into a large skillet; add onion and garlic. Cook and stir over medium heat until meat is no longer pink; drain. Stir in the tomatoes, tomato paste and seasonings. Bring to a boil. Reduce the heat; simmer, uncovered, for 5 minutes.

Drain the pasta; stir in the meat mixture and pepperoni. Transfer half of pasta mixture to a 2-qt. baking dish coated with cooking spray. Sprinkle with half of cheese; repeat layers.

Cover and bake at 350° for 20-25 minutes or until bubbly.

YIELD: 6 SERVINGS.

NUTRITION FACTS: 1 cup equals 335 calories, 11 g fat (4 g saturated fat), 64 mg cholesterol, 752 mg sodium, 33 g carbohydrate, 4 g fiber, 26 g protein. **DIABETIC EXCHANGES:** 2 starch, 2 lean meat, 1-1/2 fat.

CHICKEN TORTILLA BAKE

PREP 25 minutes | **BAKE** 25 minutes

- 1 pound boneless skinless chicken breasts, cut into 1-inch cubes
- 1/2 teaspoon ground cumin
- 1/4 teaspoon salt
- 1 tablespoon plus 1 teaspoon olive oil, *divided*
- 1 can (16 ounces) refried beans
- 1 can (14-1/2 ounces) diced tomatoes with mild green chilies, drained
- 8 flour tortillas (8 inches), cut into 1-inch strips
- 1 can (11 ounces) Mexicorn, drained
- 2 cups (8 ounces) shredded cheddar cheese

In a large skillet, saute the chicken, cumin and salt in 1 tablespoon oil until chicken is no longer pink.

Combine refried beans and tomatoes; spread 1 cup into a greased 11-in. x 7-in. baking dish. Top with 24 tortilla strips and layer with half of the corn, bean mixture, chicken and cheese. Repeat layers.

Using the remaining tortilla strips, make a lattice crust over the filling; brush with the remaining oil. Bake, uncovered, at 350° for 25-30 minutes or until heated through and cheese is melted.

YIELD: 6 SERVINGS.

taste of home
test kitchen
GREENDALE, WISCONSIN

You get two for the price of one in this combo enchilada/lasagna hot dish. You get all the flavors of the Mexican staple, and all the ease of layering lasagna.

TASTY TURKEY CASSEROLE

PREP 20 minutes | **BAKE** 20 minutes

- 6 cups fresh broccoli florets
- 1 cup water
- 6 cups cubed cooked turkey breast
- 1 can (10-3/4 ounces) condensed cream of chicken soup, undiluted
- 1 cup (8 ounces) sour cream
- 3/4 cup shredded Swiss cheese

In a large saucepan, combine broccoli and water. Bring to a boil. Reduce heat. Cover and simmer for 6-8 minutes or until crisp-tender; drain. Transfer to a 13-in. x 9-in. baking dish coated with cooking spray. Sprinkle with turkey.

Combine soup and sour cream. Spoon over the turkey. Sprinkle with Swiss cheese. Bake, uncovered, at 375° for 20-25 minutes or until heated through.

YIELD: 10 SERVINGS.

maureen dongoski
PETERSBURG, WEST VIRGINIA

A can of cream soup makes it easy to assemble this crowd-pleasing casserole. Sour cream adds a rich taste to this saucy turkey-and-broccoli bake that's ideal for potlucks.

SECONDHAND TURKEY

PREP 30 minutes | **BAKE** 20 minutes

- 1/2 pound sliced fresh mushrooms
- 1/2 cup chopped celery
- 5 tablespoons butter, *divided*
- 2 tablespoons cornstarch
- 2 cups milk
- 2 cups cubed cooked turkey
- 2 cups cooked egg noodles
- 1/4 cup chicken broth
- 1 teaspoon salt
- 1/2 teaspoon dried thyme
- 1/8 teaspoon white pepper
- 1/2 cup dry bread crumbs

In a large skillet, saute the mushrooms and celery in 3 tablespoons butter until tender. Combine cornstarch and milk until smooth; stir into mushroom mixture. Bring to a boil over medium heat, stirring constantly. Cook for 1 minute or until thickened.

Stir in the turkey, noodles, broth, salt, thyme and pepper. Pour into a greased 2-qt. baking dish. Melt remaining butter; toss with bread crumbs. Sprinkle over casserole.

Bake, uncovered, at 375° for 20-25 minutes or until heated through.

YIELD: 4 SERVINGS.

dixie terry
GOREVILLE, ILLINOIS

Turkey leftovers taste fresh and flavorful in this satisfying casserole, which is the entree for my favorite post-Thanksgiving meal. Mushrooms, celery and thyme give it a familiar comforting appeal.

make your OWN

To make your own dry bread crumbs, simply break slices of dried bread into pieces and process in a blender or food processor until you have fine crumbs. If you like, add dried seasonings to the crumbs, such as basil, oregano, garlic or onion powder, grated Parmesan, salt or paprika. Start by adding small amounts, then add more as needed.

POPPY SEED CHICKEN

PREP 15 minutes | BAKE 30 minutes

- 1 cup (8 ounces) sour cream
- 1 can (10-3/4 ounces) condensed cream of chicken soup, undiluted
- 1 tablespoon poppy seeds
- 1 teaspoon dill weed
- 4 cups cubed cooked chicken
- 3 cups cooked rice
- 1-1/2 cups butter-flavored cracker crumbs
- 1/2 cup butter, melted

In a large bowl, combine the sour cream, soup, poppy seeds and dill. Stir in chicken and rice.

Spread into a greased 11-in. x 7-in. baking dish. Combine crumbs and butter; sprinkle over casserole. Bake, uncovered, at 350° for 30 minutes or until bubbly.
YIELD: 6-8 SERVINGS.

janet zoss
JACKSON, MICHIGAN

This flavorful chicken dish is hard to resist with its crunchy buttery topping.

CHEDDAR TURKEY BAKE

PREP 20 minutes | BAKE 35 minutes

- 2 cups chicken broth
- 2 cups water
- 4 teaspoons dried minced onion
- 2 cups uncooked long grain rice
- 2 cups frozen peas, thawed
- 4 cups cubed cooked turkey
- 2 cans (10-3/4 ounces *each*) condensed cheddar cheese soup, undiluted
- 2 cups milk
- 1 teaspoon salt
- 2 cups finely crushed butter-flavored crackers (about 60 crackers)
- 6 tablespoons butter, melted

In a large saucepan, bring the broth, water and onion to a boil. Reduce heat. Add rice; cover and simmer for 15 minutes. Remove from the heat; fluff with a fork.

Divide rice between two greased 9-in. square baking pans. Sprinkle each with peas and turkey. In a large bowl, combine the soup, milk and salt until smooth; pour over turkey. Toss the cracker crumbs and butter; sprinkle over the top.

Cover and freeze one casserole for up to 3 months. Bake second casserole, uncovered, at 350° for 35 minutes or until golden brown.
TO USE FROZEN CASSEROLE: Thaw in the refrigerator for 24 hours. Bake, uncovered, at 350° for 45-50 minutes or until heated through.
YIELD: 2 CASSEROLES (4-6 SERVINGS EACH).

carol dilcher
EMMAUS, PENNSYLVANIA

This recipe makes two creamy casseroles. Serve one for dinner and freeze the second for a night when you're racing against the clock. If you prefer, you can use chicken for the turkey and corn instead of peas.

⏲ BAKED MOSTACCIOLI

PREP 35 minutes | **BAKE** 30 minutes

donna ebert
RICHFIELD, WISCONSIN

I often prepare this for dinner parties and always get many compliments. It's as delicious as any entree that is served at a fancy Italian restaurant.

8	ounces uncooked mostaccioli
1/2	pound lean ground turkey
1	small onion, chopped
1	can (14-1/2 ounces) diced tomatoes, undrained
1	can (6 ounces) tomato paste
1/3	cup water
1	teaspoon dried oregano
1/2	teaspoon salt
1/8	teaspoon pepper
2	cups (16 ounces) fat-free cottage cheese
1	teaspoon dried marjoram
1-1/2	cups (6 ounces) shredded part-skim mozzarella cheese
1/4	cup grated Parmesan cheese

Cook the mostaccioli according to package directions. Meanwhile, in a large saucepan, cook the turkey and onion over medium heat until meat is no longer pink; drain if necessary.

Stir in tomatoes, tomato paste, water, oregano, salt and pepper. Bring to a boil. Reduce heat; cover and simmer for 15 minutes.

In a small bowl, combine cottage cheese and marjoram; set aside. Drain mostaccioli.

Spread 1/2 cup meat sauce into an 11-in. x 7-in. baking dish coated with cooking spray. Layer with half of the mostaccioli, meat sauce and mozzarella cheese. Top with cottage cheese mixture. Layer with the remaining mostaccioli, meat sauce and mozzarella cheese. Sprinkle with Parmesan cheese (dish will be full).

Bake, uncovered, at 350° for 30-40 minutes or until bubbly and heated through.
YIELD: 6 SERVINGS.

NUTRITION FACTS: 1 serving equals 278 calories, 7 g fat (3 g saturated fat), 39 mg cholesterol, 607 mg sodium, 32 g carbohydrate, 3 g fiber, 23 g protein. **DIABETIC EXCHANGES:** 2 lean meat, 2 vegetable, 1-1/2 starch.

MAKEOVER CHICKEN NOODLE DELIGHT

PREP 25 minutes | **BAKE** 40 minutes

4 cups uncooked yolk-free noodles

1 can (10-3/4 ounces) reduced-fat reduced-sodium condensed cream of chicken soup, undiluted

4 ounces reduced-fat cream cheese, cubed

1 cup (8 ounces) reduced-fat sour cream

1 cup (8 ounces) plain yogurt

1/4 cup fat-free milk

3 tablespoons minced fresh parsley *or* 1 tablespoon dried parsley flakes

1 teaspoon onion powder

1/4 teaspoon salt

2 cups cubed cooked chicken breast

1 cup crushed reduced-fat butter-flavored crackers (about 25 crackers)

3 tablespoons reduced-fat butter, melted

Cook the noodles according to the package directions. Meanwhile, in a large bowl, combine soup, cream cheese, sour cream, yogurt, milk, parsley, onion powder and salt. Stir in chicken.

Drain noodles; toss with the chicken mixture. Transfer to a 2-qt. baking dish coated with cooking spray.

Combine cracker crumbs and butter; sprinkle over the casserole. Bake, uncovered, at 350° for 40-45 minutes or until heated through.

YIELD: 6 SERVINGS.

EDITOR'S NOTE: This recipe was tested with Land O'Lakes light stick butter.

gail schumacher
BERTHOUD, COLORADO

A neighbor made this dish for us when we had our second child. It was so good! This lightened-up version is so delicious, my family never notices the difference!

STUFFED PASTA SHELLS

PREP 15 minutes | **BAKE** 30 minutes

1-1/2 cups cooked stuffing
2 cups diced cooked chicken *or* turkey
1/2 cup frozen peas, thawed
1/2 cup mayonnaise
18 jumbo pasta shells, cooked and drained
1 can (10-3/4 ounces) condensed cream of chicken soup, undiluted
2/3 cup water
Paprika
Minced fresh parsley

In a large bowl, combine stuffing, chicken, peas and mayonnaise; spoon into pasta shells. Place in a greased 13-in. x 9-in. baking dish. In a small bowl, combine soup and water; pour over shells. Sprinkle with paprika.

Cover and bake at 350° for 30 minutes or until heated through. Sprinkle with minced parsley.
YIELD: 6 SERVINGS.

judy memo
NEW CASTLE, PENNSYLVANIA

This is a delicious way to use up leftovers. A casserole of pasta shells filled with moist stuffing, tender chicken chunks and green peas is covered with an easy sauce.

CREAMY CHICKEN NOODLE BAKE

PREP 25 minutes | **BAKE** 40 minutes + standing

4 cups uncooked egg noodles
1/2 cup butter, *divided*
1/4 cup all-purpose flour
1/2 teaspoon salt
1/8 teaspoon white pepper
3-1/2 cups milk
4 cups cubed cooked chicken
2 jars (12 ounces *each*) chicken gravy
1 jar (2 ounces) diced pimientos, drained
1/2 cup cubed process cheese (Velveeta)
1/2 cup dry bread crumbs
4 teaspoons butter, melted

Cook the noodles according to package directions. Meanwhile, in a Dutch oven, melt 6 tablespoons butter. Stir in the flour, salt and pepper until smooth. Gradually add the milk. Bring to a boil; cook and stir for 1-2 minutes or until thickened. Remove from heat. Stir in chicken, gravy and pimientos.

Drain the noodles; toss with remaining butter. Stir into chicken mixture. Transfer to a greased 13-in. x 9-in. baking dish.

Cover and bake at 350° for 30-35 minutes or until bubbly. Combine the cheese, bread crumbs and melted butter. Sprinkle around edges of casserole. Bake, uncovered, for 10 minutes longer or until golden brown. Let stand for 10 minutes before serving.
YIELD: 12 SERVINGS (1 CUP EACH).

shirley unger
BLUFFTON, OHIO

Talk about a potluck pleaser! This comforting, creamy casserole is bursting with tender chunks of chicken. Even the pickiest eater will gobble up this tasty bake.

white PEPPER

When a recipe calls for white pepper, it's okay to substitute black pepper. White pepper actually comes from the same peppercorns as black pepper. However, with white pepper, the peppercorns are allowed to ripen longer before being dried and ground.

🕰 SUMMER SQUASH CHICKEN CASSEROLE

PREP 20 minutes | **BAKE** 30 minutes

1/2 cup uncooked instant rice
1 can (10-3/4 ounces) condensed cream of chicken soup, undiluted
1/3 cup reduced-fat mayonnaise
1/3 cup fat-free milk
4 cups cubed cooked chicken breast
2 cups pattypan squash, halved
1 small onion, finely chopped
1 jar (2 ounces) diced pimientos, drained
1 teaspoon dried thyme
1/4 teaspoon garlic powder
1/4 teaspoon pepper
1/3 cup shredded Parmesan cheese

Cook the rice according to the package directions. In a large bowl, combine the soup, mayonnaise and milk. Stir in the chicken, squash, onion, pimientos, thyme, garlic powder, pepper and cooked rice.

Spoon into a 2-qt. baking dish coated with cooking spray. Sprinkle with the Parmesan cheese. Bake, uncovered, at 350° for 30-40 minutes or until edges are bubbly and center is set.

YIELD: 6 SERVINGS.

NUTRITION FACTS: 1 cup equals 297 calories, 11 g fat (3 g saturated fat), 84 mg cholesterol, 633 mg sodium, 15 g carbohydrate, 2 g fiber, 32 g protein. **DIABETIC EXCHANGES:** 4 very lean meat, 2 fat, 1 starch.

taste of home
test kitchen
GREENDALE, WISCONSIN

This rich and saucy casserole features tender pattypans in a satisfying chicken and rice combination. Pair it with a salad for a family–friendly supper to feel good about.

TURKEY CABBAGE BAKE

PREP 30 minutes | **BAKE** 15 minutes

2 tubes (8 ounces *each*) refrigerated crescent rolls
1-1/2 pounds ground turkey
1/2 cup chopped onion
1/2 cup finely chopped carrot
1 teaspoon minced garlic
2 cups finely chopped cabbage
1 can (10-3/4 ounces) condensed cream of mushroom soup, undiluted
1/2 teaspoon dried thyme
1 cup (4 ounces) shredded part-skim mozzarella cheese

Unroll one tube of crescent dough into one long rectangle; seal seams and perforations. Press onto bottom of a greased 13-in. x 9-in. baking dish. Bake at 425° for 6-8 minutes or until golden brown.

Meanwhile, in a large skillet, cook the turkey, onion, carrot and garlic over medium heat until meat is no longer pink; drain. Add the cabbage, soup and thyme. Pour over crust; sprinkle with cheese.

On a lightly floured surface, press the second tube of crescent dough into a 13-in. x 9-in. rectangle, sealing seams and perforations. Place over casserole.

Bake, uncovered, at 375° for 14-16 minutes or until crust is golden brown.

YIELD: 6 SERVINGS.

irene gutz
FORT DODGE, IOWA

I revised this old recipe to make it healthier by using ground turkey instead of ground beef, by finely chopping the cabbage to improve texture and by adding thyme. Crescent rolls help it go together quickly, and it's requested often!

PESTO CHICKEN MOSTACCIOLI

PREP 25 minutes | **BAKE** 25 minutes

- 1 package (16 ounces) mostaccioli
- 1 package (16 ounces) frozen breaded chicken tenders
- 4 cups (16 ounces) shredded cheddar cheese
- 1 container (16 ounces) sour cream
- 1 carton (15 ounces) ricotta cheese
- 3/4 cup prepared pesto
- 2/3 cup heavy whipping cream
- 1/2 cup grated Parmesan cheese
- 1/2 cup dry bread crumbs
- 1/4 cup butter, melted

Cook mostaccioli and chicken according to package directions. Meanwhile, in a large bowl, combine cheddar cheese, sour cream, ricotta, pesto, cream and Parmesan cheese.

Chop the chicken tenders and drain mostaccioli; add to the cheese mixture. Toss to coat. Transfer to two greased 11-in. x 7-in. baking dishes (dishes will be full). Combine bread crumbs and butter; sprinkle over the top.

Bake, uncovered, at 350° for 25-30 or until heated through and golden brown.
YIELD: 2 CASSEROLES (5 SERVINGS EACH).

rebecca stablein
LAKE FOREST, CALIFORNIA

I was looking for something new to whip up and decided to invent my own recipe. We love pesto and mac and cheese...but who knew what a yummy combination it would be with chicken nuggets! Comfort food to the max, it's great for a crowd!

CHICKEN LASAGNA

PREP 25 minutes | **BAKE** 30 minutes + standing

- 2 cups (16 ounces) 2% cottage cheese
- 1 package (3 ounces) cream cheese, softened
- 4 cups cubed cooked chicken
- 1 can (10-3/4 ounces) condensed cream of chicken soup, undiluted
- 1 can (10-3/4 ounces) condensed cream of celery soup, undiluted
- 2/3 cup milk
- 1/2 cup chopped onion
- 1/2 teaspoon salt
- 6 lasagna noodles, cooked and drained
- 1 package (6 ounces) stuffing mix
- 1/2 cup butter, melted

In a small bowl, combine cottage cheese and cream cheese. In a large bowl, combine the chicken, soups, milk, onion and salt.

Spread half of chicken mixture into a greased 13-in. x 9-in. baking dish. Top with three noodles. Spread with half of the cheese mixture. Repeat layers. Toss stuffing mix with butter; sprinkle over casserole.

Bake, uncovered, at 350° for 30-40 minutes or until bubbly and golden brown. Let stand for 10 minutes before cutting.
YIELD: 8 SERVINGS.

janelle rutrough
ROCKY MOUNTAIN, VIRGINIA

A friend served this to us one night, and I just had to try it at home. It's quick, easy and so delicious! I love to serve it to guests with a Caesar salad and warm rolls. Also, it can be frozen and saved for a busy weeknight.

TURKEY GARDEN MEDLEY

PREP 25 minutes | **BAKE** 30 minutes

1 pound boneless skinless turkey breasts, cut into strips
1 garlic clove, minced
1/4 cup butter, *divided*
1 small yellow squash, julienned
1 small zucchini, julienned
1/2 cup *each* julienned green and sweet red pepper
1/4 cup thinly sliced onion
2 tablespoons all-purpose flour
1/2 teaspoon salt-free seasoning blend
1/4 teaspoon pepper
3/4 cup low-sodium chicken broth
1/2 cup evaporated skim milk
8 ounces angel hair pasta, cooked and drained
2 tablespoons shredded Parmesan cheese

In a large skillet over medium-high heat, saute turkey and garlic in 2 tablespoons butter for 10-12 minutes or until turkey juices run clear. Add the vegetables; cook until crisp-tender; set aside.

In a small saucepan, melt the remaining butter. Add flour, seasoning blend and pepper; stir to form a smooth paste. Gradually add broth, stirring constantly. Bring to a boil; cook for 2 minutes or until thickened. Stir in milk and heat through.

Pour over the turkey and vegetables; stir until well mixed. Place the pasta in a greased 2-qt. baking dish. Pour turkey mixture over top. Sprinkle with Parmesan cheese.

Cover and bake at 350° for 20 minutes; uncover and bake 10 minutes longer.
YIELD: 4-6 SERVINGS.

NUTRITION FACTS: 1/6 recipe equals 199 calories, 6 g fat (0 saturated fat), 47 mg cholesterol, 227 mg sodium, 14 g carbohydrate, 2 g fiber, 23 g protein. **DIABETIC EXCHANGES:** 2-1/2 lean meat, 1 vegetable, 1/2 starch, 1/2 fat.

dohreen winkler
HOWELL, MICHIGAN

After you sample this dish, it will quickly become a favorite. The vegetable variety is tasty and healthy!

evaporated MILK

To avoid wasting extra evaporated milk, pour it in ice cube trays that are specifically used for that purpose. Once frozen, the cubes store nicely in a resealable freezer bag. Simply pull out a few whenever a recipe uses evaporated milk.

MUSHROOM TURKEY TETRAZZINI

PREP 35 minutes | **BAKE** 25 minutes

12 ounces uncooked spaghetti, broken into 2-inch pieces
2 teaspoons chicken bouillon granules
1/2 pound sliced fresh mushrooms
2 tablespoons butter
2 tablespoons all-purpose flour
1/4 cup sherry *or* reduced-sodium chicken broth
3/4 teaspoon salt-free lemon-pepper seasoning
1/2 teaspoon salt
1/8 teaspoon ground nutmeg
1 cup fat-free evaporated milk
2/3 cup grated Parmesan cheese, *divided*
4 cups cubed cooked turkey breast
1/4 teaspoon paprika

In a large nonstick skillet, saute the mushrooms in butter until tender. Stir in flour until blended. Gradually stir in the sherry or broth and the reserved cooking liquid. Add the lemon-pepper, salt and nutmeg. Bring to a boil; cook and stir for 2 minutes or until thickened.

Reduce the heat to low; stir in milk and 1/3 cup Parmesan cheese until blended. Add turkey; cook and stir until heated through. Pour the turkey mixture over spaghetti and toss to combine. Sprinkle with paprika and remaining Parmesan cheese.

Cover and bake at 375° for 25-30 minutes or until bubbly.
YIELD: 8 SERVINGS.

NUTRITION FACTS: 1 cup equals 362 calories, 7 g fat (3 g saturated fat), 75 mg cholesterol, 592 mg sodium, 40 g carbohydrate, 2 g fiber, 33 g protein. **DIABETIC EXCHANGES:** 3 starch, 3 very lean meat, 1/2 fat.

Cook the spaghetti according to package directions. Drain, reserving 2-1/2 cups cooking liquid. Stir bouillon into cooking liquid and set aside. Place the spaghetti in a 13-in. x 9-in. baking dish coated with cooking spray; set aside.

linda howe
LISLE, ILLINOIS

This creamy, comforting casserole is a fantastic way to use up leftover Thanksgiving turkey. And it's a real family pleaser!

pork

SCALLOPED POTATOES 'N' HAM • PAGE 86

HAM AND NOODLE CASSEROLE

PREP 25 minutes | **BAKE** 30 minutes

- 2 cups uncooked egg noodles
- 1 cup cubed deli ham
- 1/2 cup shredded cheddar cheese
- 1/2 cup condensed cream of celery soup, undiluted
- 1/3 cup 2% milk
- 1 teaspoon finely chopped onion
- 2 teaspoons butter, melted, *divided*
- 1/4 teaspoon poppy seeds
- 1/4 teaspoon dried oregano
- 1/8 teaspoon salt
- 1/8 teaspoon dried basil
- 3 tablespoons dry bread crumbs

Cook the noodles according to the package directions. Meanwhile, in a small bowl, combine the ham, cheese, soup, milk, onion, 1 teaspoon butter, poppy seeds and seasonings. Drain noodles; add to the ham mixture.

Transfer to a 1-1/2-qt. baking dish coated with cooking spray. Combine bread crumbs and remaining butter; sprinkle over casserole. Bake, uncovered, at 325° for 30-35 minutes or until heated through.
YIELD: 3 SERVINGS.

laura burgess
MT. VERNON, SOUTH DAKOTA

I created this recipe when I had leftover ham to use up. You'll find it's the perfect little casserole for any night of the week!

SAUSAGE GREEN BEAN BAKE

PREP 5 minutes | **BAKE** 40 minutes

- 1 jar (28 ounces) spaghetti sauce
- 1-1/2 pounds Italian sausage links, cooked and cut into 1/2-inch pieces
- 1 package (16 ounces) frozen cut green beans
- 2 jars (4-1/2 ounces *each*) sliced mushrooms, drained
- 2 cups (8 ounces) shredded part-skim mozzarella cheese

In a large bowl, combine the spaghetti sauce, sausage, beans and mushrooms; mix well. Transfer to a greased 13-in. x 9-in. baking dish; sprinkle with mozzarella cheese.

Bake, uncovered, at 350° for 40-45 minutes or until cheese is melted.

YIELD: 6 SERVINGS.

mary detweiler
MIDDLEFIELD, OHIO

You can make and bake this saucy dish in less than an hour. The Italian sausage really makes it a treat. I sometimes serve it over noodles for a complete meal.

🕐 CHOPS 'N' KRAUT

PREP 25 minutes | **BAKE** 20 minutes

- 6 bone-in pork loin chops (3/4 inch thick and 7 ounces *each*)
- 1/4 teaspoon salt
- 1/4 teaspoon pepper
- 3 teaspoons canola oil, *divided*
- 1 medium onion, thinly sliced
- 2 garlic cloves, minced
- 1 can (14-1/2 ounces) petite diced tomatoes, undrained
- 1 can (14 ounces) sauerkraut, rinsed and well drained
- 1/3 cup packed brown sugar
- 1-1/2 teaspoons caraway seeds

Sprinkle both sides of pork chops with salt and pepper. In a large nonstick skillet coated with cooking spray, cook three chops in 1 teaspoon oil for 2-3 minutes on each side or until browned; drain. Repeat with remaining chops and 1 teaspoon oil.

Place the pork chops in a 13-in. x 9-in. baking dish coated with cooking spray; set aside. In the same skillet, cook onion and garlic in remaining oil until tender. Stir in the tomatoes, sauerkraut, brown sugar and caraway seeds. Cook and stir until mixture comes to a boil.

Carefully pour over chops. Cover and bake at 350° for 20-25 minutes or until a meat thermometer reads 160°.

YIELD: 6 SERVINGS.

NUTRITION FACTS: 1 pork chop with 2/3 cup sauerkraut mixture equals 311 calories, 11 g fat (3 g saturated fat), 86 mg cholesterol, 691 mg sodium, 21 g carbohydrate, 3 g fiber, 32 g protein. **DIABETIC EXCHANGES:** 4 lean meat, 1 vegetable, 1/2 starch, 1/2 fat.

ruth tamul
MOREHEAD CITY, NORTH CAROLINA

Diced tomatoes lend color to this hefty entree and brown sugar sweetens the sauerkraut.

brown **SUGAR**

To soften brown sugar, add a slice of bread or an apple wedge to the brown sugar in a covered container for a few days. If you are in a hurry, microwave on high for 20-30 seconds. Repeat if necessary, but be careful, because the sugar will begin to melt. Always store brown sugar in an airtight container.

HAM ROLLS CONTINENTAL

PREP 20 minutes | **BAKE** 25 minutes

- 6 thin slices fully cooked ham (about 5-inch square)
- 6 thin slices Swiss cheese (about 4-inch square)
- 6 thin slices cheddar cheese (about 4-inch square)
- 12 frozen broccoli spears, thawed
- 1 small onion, thinly sliced into rings
- 2 tablespoons butter
- 2 tablespoons all-purpose flour
- 1/2 teaspoon salt
- Dash white pepper
- 1-1/4 cups milk

Top each ham slice with a slice of Swiss cheese, a slice of cheddar and two broccoli spears (floret ends out); roll up jelly-roll style. Place, seam side down, in an ungreased 11-in. x 7-in. baking dish. Arrange onion rings on top.

In a small saucepan, melt the butter. Stir in flour, salt and pepper until smooth. Gradually stir in milk. Bring to a boil; boil and stir for 2 minutes. Pour over the center of ham rolls. Bake, uncovered, at 350° for 25-30 minutes or until the broccoli is tender. **YIELD:** 6 SERVINGS.

anita rogers
POPLAR GROVE, ILLINOIS

A neighbor shared many recipes with me when I was a newlywed. This is one I still use on a regular basis. With ham, broccoli and a creamy sauce, it's a pretty dish to serve to guests.

BROCCOLI SCALLOPED POTATOES

PREP 20 minutes | **BAKE** 1 hour

- 2 tablespoons chopped onion
- 4 garlic cloves, minced
- 1/4 cup butter, cubed
- 5 tablespoons all-purpose flour
- 1/4 teaspoon white pepper
- 1/8 teaspoon salt
- 2-1/2 cups milk
- 2 cups (8 ounces) shredded Swiss cheese, *divided*
- 2 pounds medium potatoes, peeled and thinly sliced
- 2 cups julienned fully cooked ham
- 2 cups frozen broccoli florets, thawed and patted dry

In a large skillet, saute the onion and garlic in butter for 3-4 minutes or until crisp-tender. Stir in the flour, pepper and salt until blended. Gradually stir in milk. Bring to a boil; cook and stir for 2 minutes or until thickened. Stir in 1 cup of cheese. Reduce heat; cook for 1-2 minutes or until cheese is melted (sauce will be thick).

Remove from the heat; gently stir in the potatoes, ham and broccoli. Transfer to a greased 13-in. x 9-in. baking dish.

Cover and bake at 350° for 40 minutes. Sprinkle with remaining cheese. Bake, uncovered, 20-25 minutes longer or until potatoes are tender and cheese is melted. **YIELD:** 8 SERVINGS.

denell syslo
FULLERTON, NEBRASKA

I love that I can cook this entire meal—vegetable and all—in one dish. I was looking for a twist on traditional scalloped potatoes and ham, and played in the kitchen until this dish was created.

freezing CHEESE

To stock up on shredded cheese, buy shredded cheese in bulk. Then divide it up, place it in heavy-duty resealable plastic bags and freeze. When it is time to use the cheese, there's no need to thaw a solid clump of cheese. The frozen pieces easily break apart.

CREAMY PEPPERONI ZITI

PREP 15 minutes | **BAKE** 25 minutes

1 package (16 ounces) ziti *or* small tube pasta

1 can (10-3/4 ounces) condensed cream of mushroom soup, undiluted

3/4 cup shredded part-skim mozzarella cheese

3/4 cup chopped pepperoni

1/2 cup *each* chopped onion, mushrooms, green pepper and tomato

1/2 cup half-and-half cream

1/4 cup chicken broth

1/4 teaspoon salt

1/4 teaspoon garlic powder

1/4 teaspoon pepper

1/2 cup grated Parmesan cheese

Cook the pasta according to the package directions; drain. In a large bowl, combine pasta, soup, mozzarella cheese, pepperoni, onion, mushrooms, green pepper, tomato, cream, broth and seasonings.

Transfer to a greased 13-in. x 9-in. baking dish. Sprinkle with Parmesan cheese. Cover and bake at 350° for 20 minutes. Uncover; bake 5-10 minutes longer or until bubbly.
YIELD: 9 SERVINGS.

charlane gathy
LEXINGTON, KENTUCKY

You can easily feed a crowd with this simple dish that's ready in about 40 minutes. The comforting sauce will become a fast favorite at your next potluck or weeknight dinner.

SCALLOPED POTATOES 'N' HAM

PREP 25 minutes | **BAKE** 1 hour

kathy johnson
LAKE CITY, SOUTH DAKOTA

3/4 cup powdered nondairy creamer
1-3/4 cups water
3 tablespoons butter
3 tablespoons all-purpose flour
2 tablespoons dried minced onion
1 teaspoon salt
3/4 teaspoon paprika
6 large potatoes, peeled and thinly sliced
2 cups diced fully cooked ham
1 cup (4 ounces) shredded cheddar cheese

In a small bowl, combine the creamer and water until smooth. In a small saucepan, melt butter. Stir in the flour, onion, salt and paprika until smooth; gradually add creamer mixture. Bring to a boil; cook and stir for 1-2 minutes or until thickened.

In a greased shallow 2-1/2-qt. baking dish, combine the potatoes and ham. Pour sauce over the top.

Cover and bake at 350° for 15 minutes. Uncover; bake 40-50 minutes longer or until potatoes are tender. Sprinkle with cheese; bake for 5-10 minutes or until edges are bubbly and cheese is melted.
YIELD: 6 SERVINGS.

I'm a home health nurse and got this recipe from one of my elderly clients, who had used it for years. Now, it's one of my family's favorites. It will never curdle, thanks to the secret ingredient of powdered nondairy creamer. You can serve this homey favorite for under a dollar per serving.

BAVARIAN CASSEROLE

PREP 40 minutes | **BAKE** 40 minutes

- 4 medium red potatoes
- 6 bacon strips, diced
- 6 bone-in pork loin chops (3/4 inch thick)
- 1 large onion, chopped
- 1 jar (32 ounces) sauerkraut, rinsed and well drained
- 1 can (28 ounces) stewed tomatoes, drained
- 1 teaspoon caraway seeds
- 1/2 teaspoon salt
- 1/4 teaspoon pepper

Place potatoes in a saucepan and cover with water. Bring to a boil. Reduce heat; cover and simmer for 25-30 minutes or until almost tender. Drain; when cool enough to handle, cut into 1/4-in. slices.

In a large skillet, cook the bacon over medium heat until crisp. Using a slotted spoon, remove to paper towels. In the drippings, brown the pork chops on both sides. Remove chops; drain, reserving 1 tablespoon drippings. Saute onion in drippings until tender. Stir in sauerkraut and bacon; cook for 3-4 minutes.

Spoon sauerkraut mixture into a greased 13-in. x 9-in. baking dish. Layer with the pork chops, potato slices and tomatoes. Sprinkle with caraway seeds, salt and pepper. Cover and bake at 350° for 40-45 minutes or until a meat thermometer reads 160°.
YIELD: 6 SERVINGS.

barbara laflair
HOUGHTON LAKE, MICHIGAN

This one-dish meal is a little different from the usual meat-and-potato casserole. The sauerkraut and tomatoes add a nice tangy flavor to the tender pork chops. I've also used boneless skinless chicken breasts and turkey bacon with good results.

LAZY DAY CASSEROLE

PREP 15 minutes | **BAKE** 30 minutes

- 8 ounces day-old Italian bread *or* French bread, sliced
- 1 pound bulk pork sausage, cooked and crumbled
- 8 eggs
- 2 cups milk
- 1/2 teaspoon pepper
- 8 ounces sliced Swiss cheese
- 1/4 cup minced fresh parsley

Line a greased 13-in. x 9-in. baking dish with bread. Sprinkle with sausage. Beat the eggs, milk and pepper; pour over sausage. Press bread down with a spatula to absorb egg mixture. Top with cheese and parsley.

Bake, uncovered, at 350° for 30-35 minutes or until a knife inserted near the center comes out clean. Let stand for 5 minutes before cutting.
YIELD: 8 SERVINGS.

trish parker
BLOWING ROCK, NORTH CAROLINA

When I first served this wonderful brunch casserole at a family reunion a few years ago, I think I wrote out at least a dozen copies of the recipe! My husband and I enjoy country living in the beautiful Blue Ridge Mountains.

refreshing fruit **SALAD**

An excellent accompaniment to the Lazy Day Casserole is fresh berries with a sweet, creamy topping. Beat 2 ounces softened cream cheese until smooth, Then stir in 1/2 cup sour cream, 1 tablespoon honey, 1-1/2 tablespoons orange juice and 1/8 teaspoon ground cinnamon. Serve over an assortment of fresh berries.

SAUSAGE SPINACH CASSEROLE

PREP 15 minutes | **BAKE** 30 minutes

- 2 packages (10 ounces *each*) frozen chopped spinach, thawed and drained
- 1 can (15 ounces) great northern beans, rinsed and drained
- 2 cooked Italian sausage links, sliced
- 1 can (12 ounces) evaporated milk
- 3/4 cup chopped onion
- 1/2 cup grated Parmesan cheese, *divided*
- 1 tablespoon lemon juice
- 1 teaspoon grated lemon peel
- 1/4 teaspoon ground nutmeg
- 1/8 teaspoon pepper
- 2 garlic cloves, minced
- 4 teaspoons butter
- 1/3 cup dry bread crumbs

In a bowl, combine first five ingredients. Stir in 1/4 cup cheese, lemon juice and peel, nutmeg and pepper. Transfer to a greased 2-qt. baking dish.

In a skillet, saute garlic in butter until tender. Remove from the heat; stir in bread crumbs and remaining cheese. Sprinkle over spinach mixture. Bake, uncovered, at 375° for 30 minutes or until heated through.

YIELD: 4 SERVINGS.

lynn salsbury
HERINGTON, KANSAS

This spinach casserole makes a light main dish or hearty side dish. It's really good with plenty of spinach, beans and nice garlic flavor. It's also a great way to use up leftover sausage.

CREAMY PORK CHOP CASSEROLE

PREP 15 minutes + marinating | **BAKE** 55 minutes

- 1/4 cup reduced-sodium teriyaki sauce
- 2 bone-in pork loin chops (8 ounces *each* and 1/2 inch thick)
- 1 can (10-3/4 ounces) condensed cream of mushroom soup, undiluted
- 1 cup frozen peas and carrots
- 3/4 cup water
- 1/2 small sweet red pepper, chopped
- 1/3 cup uncooked long grain rice
- 1 teaspoon dried minced onion
- 1/8 teaspoon pepper
- 1/4 cup shredded Mexican cheese blend

Place teriyaki sauce in a large resealable plastic bag; add pork chops. Seal bag and turn to coat; refrigerate for at least 1 hour.

In a large bowl, combine the soup, peas and carrots, water, red pepper, rice, onion and pepper. Transfer to an 11-in. x 7-in. baking dish coated with cooking spray.

Drain and discard marinade. Place pork chops over rice mixture. Cover and bake at 350° for 40 minutes. Uncover; sprinkle with cheese. Bake 15-20 minutes longer or until a meat thermometer reaches 160° and cheese is melted.

YIELD: 2 SERVINGS.

debbie hankins
IRONTON, OHIO

Tender pork chops are treated to a sweet-tangy marinade and topped with gooey melted cheese in this delightful meal. The rice and vegetable medley is a great complement.

cooking PORK

Fresh pork cooks quickly and needs only to be cooked to an internal temperature of 160° to 170°. At 160°, the internal color of boneless cuts of pork may be faint pink and bone-in cuts of pork may be slightly pink near the bone. But if the juices run clear, the meat is properly cooked.

BEANS AND FRANKS BAKE

PREP 20 minutes | **BAKE** 40 minutes

- 2 packages (8-1/2 ounces *each*) corn bread/muffin mix
- 1 can (28 ounces) baked beans
- 4 hot dogs, halved lengthwise and sliced
- 1/2 pound sliced bacon, cooked and crumbled
- 1 cup ketchup
- 1/2 cup packed brown sugar
- 1/2 cup chopped onion
- 2 cups (8 ounces) shredded part-skim mozzarella cheese

Prepare the corn bread batter according to the package directions; set aside. In a large bowl, combine beans, hot dogs, bacon, ketchup, brown sugar and onion. Transfer to two greased 8-in. square baking dishes. Sprinkle with cheese; top with the corn bread batter.

Cover and freeze one casserole for up to 3 months. Bake the second casserole, uncovered, at 350° for 40-45 minutes or until a toothpick inserted near the center comes out clean.

TO USE FROZEN CASSEROLE: Remove from the freezer 30 minutes before baking. Cover and bake at 350° for 40 minutes. Uncover; bake 15-20 minutes longer or until heated through.

YIELD: 2 CASSEROLES (4 SERVINGS EACH).

roxanne vangelder
ROCHESTER, NEW HAMPSHIRE

I have made this casserole several times, and it's always a hit. The kid-pleasing combo has a sweet flavor from the baked beans and the corn bread topping.

HAM AND BROCCOLI SUPPER

PREP 15 minutes | **BAKE** 35 minutes

angela liette
PIQUA, OHIO

I found this recipe in an old Amish cookbook a while back. It combines lots of my family's favorite foods, like ham, broccoli and rice, and it makes a very tasty meal.

1-1/2 cups chopped fresh broccoli
1/2 cup finely chopped onion
1-1/2 cups cooked rice
1-1/2 cups diced fully cooked ham
1 can (10-3/4 ounces) condensed cream of mushroom soup, undiluted
1-1/2 cups (6 ounces) shredded cheddar cheese
1/4 cup milk
2 slices bread, crusts removed
2 tablespoons butter

In a large saucepan, bring 1 in. water, broccoli and onion to a boil. Reduce heat; cover and simmer for 5-8 minutes or until vegetables are crisp-tender; drain.

In a greased 1-1/2-qt. baking dish, layer rice, ham and broccoli mixture. Combine the soup, cheese and milk; spoon over the broccoli. Bake, uncovered, at 350° for 20 minutes.

Meanwhile, coarsely crumble bread. In a small skillet, cook crumbs in butter over medium-high heat until lightly browned. Sprinkle over casserole. Bake 15 minutes longer or until heated through.

YIELD: 4 SERVINGS.

SAUCY SAUSAGE AND VEGGIES

PREP 15 minutes | **BAKE** 45 minutes

- 2 packages (1 pound *each*) frozen mixed broccoli, carrots and water chestnuts, thawed
- 1 pound fully cooked smoked sausage, cut into 1/2-inch pieces
- 1 can (10-3/4 ounces) condensed cream of celery soup, undiluted
- 3/4 cup milk
- 3/4 cup cubed process American cheese (Velveeta)
- 1/2 cup whole kernel corn, drained
- 1/2 teaspoon pepper
- 1/2 cup sour cream
- 1/2 cup seasoned dry bread crumbs
- 2 tablespoons butter, melted

Place vegetables in a greased 11-in. x 7-in. baking dish. In a skillet, brown sausage; drain. Layer over the vegetables.

In a saucepan, combine the soup, milk, cheese, corn and pepper. Cook over low heat until cheese is melted; remove from the heat. Stir in the sour cream; pour over the vegetables and sausage.

Combine the bread crumbs and butter; sprinkle over the casserole. Bake, uncovered, at 350° for 45 minutes or until browned and bubbly.

YIELD: 6-8 SERVINGS.

janice rose
ABILENE, KANSAS

This recipe calls for a broccoli-carrot-water chestnut frozen vegetable blend, but feel free to use whatever mixed vegetables you like.

RHUBARB AND PORK CHOP CASSEROLE

PREP 20 minutes | **BAKE** 40 minutes

- 4 boneless pork loin chops (3/4 inches thick and 4 ounces *each*)
- 1 tablespoon canola oil

Salt and pepper to taste

- 2-1/2 to 3 cups soft bread crumbs
- 3 cups sliced fresh *or* frozen rhubarb (1-inch pieces)
- 1/2 cup packed brown sugar
- 1/4 cup all-purpose flour
- 1 teaspoon ground cinnamon

In a large skillet, brown the pork chops in oil; sprinkle with salt and pepper. Remove and keep warm. Mix 1/4 cup pan drippings with the bread crumbs. Reserve 1/2 cup; sprinkle remaining crumbs into a 13-in. x 9-in. baking dish.

In a large bowl, combine the rhubarb, sugar, flour and cinnamon; spoon half over the bread crumbs.

Arrange the pork chops on top. Spoon the remaining rhubarb mixture over the pork chops. Cover with foil and bake at 350° for 30-45 minutes. Remove foil. Sprinkle with the reserved bread crumbs. Bake 10-15 minutes longer or until a meat thermometer reaches 160°.

YIELD: 4 SERVINGS.

jeanie castor
DECATUR, ILLINOIS

The usual reaction to this casserole is that it's a nice mix of sweet and tart—and a quite unusual use of rhubarb! I like rhubarb, but I'm not a dessert person. So I always thought there should be more to it than pies and cobblers.

about RHUBARB

Look for rhubarb stalks that are crisp and brightly colored. Tightly wrap in a plastic bag and store in the refrigerator for up to 3 days. Wash the stalks and remove the poisonous leaves before using. One pound of rhubarb yields about 3 cups chopped.

PIZZA CASSEROLE

PREP 25 minutes | **BAKE** 25 minutes + standing

3/4 cup chopped onion
1 medium sweet yellow pepper, diced
1 medium sweet red pepper, diced
1 tablespoon olive oil
1 medium zucchini, halved lengthwise and sliced
1 teaspoon minced garlic
2 cans (14-1/2 ounces *each*) diced tomatoes, drained
3/4 pound smoked sausage, sliced
1 can (6 ounces) tomato paste
1 teaspoon salt
1 teaspoon Italian seasoning
1/2 teaspoon pepper
1/4 cup grated Parmesan cheese, *divided*
2 cups (8 ounces) shredded part-skim mozzarella cheese
1 tube (11 ounces) refrigerated breadsticks

In a large skillet, saute onion and peppers in oil for 2-3 minutes or until crisp-tender. Add zucchini and garlic; saute 4-6 minutes longer or until vegetables are tender. Stir in tomatoes, sausage, tomato paste, salt, Italian seasoning, pepper and 2 tablespoons Parmesan cheese. Bring to a boil. Reduce heat; simmer, uncovered, for 8-10 minutes or until heated through.

Spoon half of the sausage mixture into a greased 13-in. x 9-in. baking dish. Sprinkle with mozzarella cheese; top with remaining sausage mixture. Separate breadsticks; arrange in a lattice pattern over the top. Sprinkle with remaining Parmesan cheese.

Bake, uncovered, at 375° for 25-30 minutes or until the topping is golden brown and filling is bubbly. Let stand for 10 minutes before serving.

YIELD: 6-8 SERVINGS.

EDITOR'S NOTE: This recipe was tested with Pillsbury refrigerated breadsticks.

nancy zimmerman
CAPE MAY COURT HOUSE, NEW JERSEY

Looking for a robust dish the whole family will love? I turn to this fast and flavorful pizza entree that fills my home with a simply wonderful aroma. Refrigerated breadsticks make the crust fuss–free, and any leftovers freeze well for another busy day. You can also substitute green peppers instead of yellow and red.

MEATBALLS SAUSAGE DINNER

PREP 25 minutes | **BAKE** 1 hour

3 cups frozen chopped broccoli, thawed
2 medium potatoes, peeled and cubed
3 medium carrots, sliced
1 medium onion, chopped
1 pound smoked kielbasa *or* Polish sausage, halved and cut into 1-inch pieces
1/2 pound lean ground beef
1 can (14-1/2 ounces) beef broth
Lemon-pepper seasoning to taste

In a large bowl, combine the first four ingredients. Transfer to a greased 13-in. x 9-in. baking pan. Sprinkle with sausage.

Shape the beef into 1-in. balls; arrange over top. Pour broth over the casserole. Sprinkle with lemon-pepper. Bake, uncovered, at 350° for 1 hour or until meatballs are no longer pink.

YIELD: 6-8 SERVINGS.

elizabeth martz
PLEASANT GAP, PENNSYLVANIA

One day I was having trouble deciding what to make for dinner. So I combined whatever was in the refrigerator and freezer. To my surprise, everyone loved it!

CHILI CHEESE DOG CASSEROLE

PREP 20 minutes | **BAKE** 30 minutes

- 1 package (8-1/2 ounces) corn bread/muffin mix
- 1 cup chopped green pepper
- 1/2 cup chopped onion
- 1/2 cup chopped celery
- 1 tablespoon olive oil
- 1 package (1 pound) hot dogs, halved lengthwise and cut into bite-size pieces
- 1 can (15 ounces) chili with beans
- 2 tablespoons brown sugar
- 1/2 teaspoon garlic powder
- 1/2 teaspoon chili powder
- 1 cup (4 ounces) shredded cheddar cheese, *divided*

Prepare the corn bread batter according to the package directions. Spread half the batter into a greased 8-in. square baking dish; set aside.

In a large skillet, saute the green pepper, onion and celery in oil until crisp-tender. Stir in hot dogs; saute 3-4 minutes longer or until lightly browned. Stir in chili, brown sugar, garlic powder and chili powder; heat through. Stir in 3/4 cup cheese. Spoon over prepared corn bread. Spread remaining batter onto hot dog mixture. Sprinkle with remaining cheese.

Bake, uncovered, at 350° for 28-32 minutes or until a toothpick inserted near the center comes out clean. Let stand for 5 minutes before serving.

YIELD: 6 SERVINGS.

taste of home
test kitchen
GREENDALE, WISCONSIN

Kids and dads alike will dive right into this hearty, comforting dish. With a crispy cheese topping on a warm corn bread crust, this recipe is a keeper.

POTATO SAUSAGE CASSEROLE

PREP 20 minutes | **BAKE** 65 minutes

- 1 pound bulk pork sausage
- 1 can (10-3/4 ounces) condensed cream of mushroom soup, undiluted
- 3/4 cup milk
- 1/2 cup chopped onion
- 1/2 teaspoon salt
- 1/4 teaspoon pepper
- 3 cups sliced peeled potatoes
- 2 cups (8 ounces) shredded cheddar cheese

Minced fresh parsley, optional

In a large skillet, cook the sausage over medium heat until no longer pink; drain and set aside. Combine the soup, milk, onion, salt and pepper.

In a greased 2-qt. baking dish, layer half of the potatoes, soup mixture and sausage. Repeat layers.

Cover and bake at 350° for 1 hour or until potatoes are tender. Sprinkle with cheese; bake, uncovered, for 2-3 minutes or until the cheese is melted. Garnish with parsley if desired.

YIELD: 6 SERVINGS.

mrs. fred osborn
THAYER, KANSAS

The subtle spices in the pork sausage give this dish a distinctive flavor that my family has loved for years. Not only is this hearty bake a great main dish on your dinner table, it reheats nicely.

ZUCCHINI PORK CHOP SUPPER

PREP 10 minutes | **BAKE** 1 hour

- 1 package (14 ounces) seasoned cubed stuffing mix, *divided*
- 1/4 cup butter, melted
- 2 pounds zucchini, cut into 1/2-inch pieces
- 1/2 cup grated carrots
- 1 can (10-3/4 ounces) condensed cream of celery soup, undiluted
- 1/2 cup milk
- 1 cup (8 ounces) sour cream
- 1 tablespoon chopped fresh parsley *or* 1 teaspoon dried parsley flakes
- 1/2 teaspoon pepper
- 6 pork loin chops (1 inch thick and 8 ounces *each*)

Water *or* additional milk

In a large bowl, combine two-thirds of stuffing mix with butter; place half in a greased 13-in. x 9-in. baking dish. In another large bowl, combine the zucchini, carrots, soup, milk, sour cream, parsley and pepper; spoon over stuffing. Sprinkle remaining buttered stuffing on top.

Crush remaining stuffing mix; place in a shallow bowl. In another shallow bowl, add the water or milk. Dip the pork chops in water or milk then roll in stuffing crumbs.

Place pork on top of stuffing mixture. Bake, uncovered, at 350° for 1 hour or until pork chops are tender.

YIELD: 6 SERVINGS.

linda martin
RHINEBECK, NEW YORK

My mom gave me a recipe for zucchini casserole, and I added the meat because I was trying to make a one-dish supper. I look forward to fresh zucchini now.

HAM AND CREAMY POTATO SCALLOPS

PREP 25 minutes | **BAKE** 50 minutes

- 5 pounds medium potatoes
- 3 tablespoons butter
- 1/4 cup all-purpose flour
- 1 can (14-1/2 ounces) chicken broth
- 1 pound diced fully cooked ham
- 1 cup process cheese sauce
- 1/2 cup sliced celery
- 1/4 cup chopped onion
- 1/4 cup mayonnaise

Salt and pepper to taste

Place potatoes in a Dutch oven and cover with water. Bring to a boil. Reduce heat; cover and cook for 20-25 minutes or until partially cooked. Drain and cool potatoes. Peel and cut into 1/4-in. slices. Spread in greased 3-qt. baking dish.

In large saucepan, melt butter. Stir in flour until smooth; add the broth. Bring to a boil. Cook and stir for 1-2 minutes or until thickened and bubbly. Remove from the heat. Stir in the remaining ingredients. Pour over the potatoes and toss gently to coat.

Bake, uncovered, at 350° for 50-60 minutes or until potatoes are tender.

YIELD: 12 SERVINGS.

EDITOR'S NOTE: Reduced-fat or fat-free mayonnaise is not recommended for this recipe.

mabel courtney
WAUSEON, OHIO

Everyone loves these scalloped potatoes. This dish is my own creation—it's a combination of three different recipes! Besides tasting good, this dish is foolproof to make, and the ingredients won't separate during baking.

CORN TORTILLA QUICHE

PREP 15 minutes | **BAKE** 45 minutes

- 3/4 pound bulk pork sausage
- 5 corn tortillas (6 inches)
- 1 cup (4 ounces) shredded Monterey Jack cheese
- 1 cup (4 ounces) shredded cheddar cheese
- 1/4 cup chopped canned green chilies
- 6 eggs, lightly beaten
- 1/2 cup heavy whipping cream
- 1/2 cup 4% cottage cheese
- 1/2 teaspoon chili powder
- 1/4 cup minced fresh cilantro

In a large skillet, cook the sausage until no longer pink; drain.

Place four tortillas in a greased 9-in. pie plate, overlapping and extending 1/2 in. beyond rim. Place remaining tortilla in the center. Layer with sausage, Monterey Jack and cheddar cheeses and chilies.

In a large bowl, combine the eggs, cream, cottage cheese and chili powder; slowly pour over chilies. Bake at 350° for 45 minutes or until center is set and puffed. Sprinkle with cilantro. Cut into wedges.
YIELD: 6 SERVINGS.

leicha welton
FAIRBANKS, ALASKA

A corn tortilla crust makes this tasty quiche a snap to assemble. Cheesy wedges are great for breakfast, lunch or dinner!

about **CILANTRO**

Cilantro gives a unique flavor to Mexican, Latin American and Asian dishes. (Coriander is the dried seed of the cilantro plant.) Like all fresh herbs, use cilantro as soon as possible.

SAUERKRAUT CASSEROLE

PREP 20 minutes | **BAKE** 70 minutes

- 1 pound mild Italian sausage links, cut into 1-inch slices
- 1 large onion, chopped
- 2 medium apples, peeled and quartered
- 1 can (27 ounces) sauerkraut, rinsed and well drained
- 1 cup water
- 1/2 cup packed brown sugar
- 2 teaspoons caraway seeds

In a large skillet, cook sausage and onion over medium heat until sausage is no longer pink and onion is tender; drain. Stir in the apples, sauerkraut, water, brown sugar and caraway seeds.

Transfer to a 2-1/2-qt. baking dish. Cover and bake at 350° for 1 hour.
YIELD: 6-8 SERVINGS.

rosemary pryor
PASADENA, MARYLAND

Mom brewed her own sauerkraut and, of course, the cabbage was from our big farm garden! Blending the kraut with spicy sausage and apples was Mom's favorite way to fix it, and I still love this country dish.

HAM CORN AU GRATIN

PREP/TOTAL TIME 30 minutes

- 2 teaspoons butter
- 5 teaspoons all-purpose flour
- 1/4 teaspoon ground mustard
- 1/8 teaspoon pepper
- 1 cup milk
- 1 cup diced fully cooked ham
- 1-1/4 cups frozen corn, thawed
- 2 tablespoons finely chopped green pepper
- 1 tablespoon finely chopped onion

TOPPING
- 1/4 cup shredded cheddar cheese
- 1/4 cup crushed butter-flavored crackers (about 7 crackers)
- 2 teaspoons butter, melted

Paprika

In a saucepan, melt butter. Stir in the flour, mustard and pepper until smooth; gradually add the milk. Bring to a boil; cook and stir for 2 minutes or until thickened.

In a greased 1-qt. baking dish, layer the ham, corn, green pepper and onion. Pour sauce over top. In a bowl, combine the cheese, crumbs and butter; sprinkle over top. Sprinkle with paprika.

Bake, uncovered, at 375° for 10-15 minutes or until heated through and top is golden brown.
YIELD: 2 SERVINGS.

carren chamberlin
NEW WATERFORD, OHIO

I found this recipe in one of my mother's cookbooks from during the Depression. It's still as satisfying today as it was back then.

MAC 'N' CHEESE WITH HAM

PREP 25 minutes | **BAKE** 25 minutes

- 1 package (7 ounces) elbow macaroni
- 2 tablespoons butter
- 3 tablespoons all-purpose flour
- 1 teaspoon dried parsley flakes
- 3/4 teaspoon ground mustard
- 1/4 teaspoon pepper
- 2 cups milk
- 1 package (16 ounces) process cheese (Velveeta), cubed
- 2 cups cubed fully cooked ham
- 1 package (10 ounces) frozen cut asparagus, thawed
- 1 jar (6 ounces) sliced mushrooms, drained
- 3 tablespoons dry bread crumbs

Cook the macaroni according to package directions. Meanwhile, in a large saucepan, melt butter. Stir in flour, parsley, mustard and pepper until blended. Gradually stir in the milk. Bring to a boil; cook and stir for 2 minutes or until thickened. Stir in cheese until melted.

Drain macaroni; add to cheese sauce. Stir in the ham, asparagus and mushrooms.

Transfer to a greased 2-1/2-qt. baking dish. Sprinkle with the bread crumbs. Bake, uncovered, at 350° for 25-30 minutes or until bubbly.

YIELD: 6 SERVINGS.

anita durst
MADISON, WISCONSIN

This hearty and comforting casserole features ingredients that everyone loves. It has a comforting homemade flavor.

CREAMY SPINACH SAUSAGE PASTA

PREP 15 minutes | **BAKE** 45 minutes

- 3 cups uncooked rigatoni *or* large tube pasta
- 1 pound bulk Italian sausage
- 1 cup finely chopped onion
- 1 can (14-1/2 ounces) Italian diced tomatoes, undrained
- 1 package (10 ounces) frozen creamed spinach, thawed
- 1 package (8 ounces) cream cheese, softened
- 2 cups (8 ounces) shredded part-skim mozzarella cheese, *divided*

Cook the pasta according to the package directions. Meanwhile, in a Dutch oven, cook sausage and onion over medium heat until sausage is no longer pink; drain. Stir in the tomatoes, spinach, cream cheese and 1 cup mozzarella cheese. Transfer to a greased 11-in. x 7-in. baking dish.

Cover and bake at 350° for 35 minutes. Uncover; sprinkle with the remaining cheese. Bake 10 minutes longer or until cheese is melted.

YIELD: 5 SERVINGS.

susie sizemore
COLLINSVILLE, VIRGINIA

So rich and creamy, this pasta dish is wonderfully cheesy and delicious! And for time-saving convenience, I like to assemble it the night before, then bake it the next day!

PLANTATION HAM PIE

PREP 20 minutes | **BAKE** 20 minutes

- 4 cups cubed fully cooked ham (2 pounds)
- 1 medium onion, chopped
- 2 tablespoons butter
- 2 cans (10-3/4 ounces *each*) condensed cream of chicken soup, undiluted
- 1 cup milk
- 2 cups fresh *or* frozen broccoli florets
- 2 cups biscuit/baking mix
- 1/2 cup water
- 1/2 cup minced fresh parsley

In a large skillet, saute the ham and onion in butter until onion is tender. Combine soup and milk; stir into ham mixture. Add the broccoli; heat through. Pour into an ungreased shallow 2-1/2-qt. baking dish.

Combine biscuit mix and water until a soft dough forms. On a lightly floured surface, knead the dough 10 times. Roll out into a 12-in. square; sprinkle with parsley.

Roll up the jelly-roll style. Cut into 12 pieces; place over the ham mixture. Bake, uncovered, at 425° for 20-25 minutes or until biscuits are golden and ham mixture is bubbly.

YIELD: 6 SERVINGS.

sharon white
MORDEN, MANITOBA

Pretty parsley pinwheels top this hearty casserole filled with a saucy mixture of broccoli, ham and onion. It can also be made with asparagus instead of broccoli. With a green salad, it's a satisfying supper.

ASPARAGUS AND HAM CASSEROLE

PREP 15 minutes | **BAKE** 35 minutes

- 1 pound fresh asparagus, trimmed, cut into 1-inch pieces
- 2 cups cubed fully cooked ham
- 3 cups cooked rice
- 1 cup finely chopped celery
- 1-1/2 teaspoons lemon-pepper seasoning
- 1 can (10-3/4 ounces) condensed cream of chicken soup, undiluted
- 1 cup chicken broth
- 1 cup (4 ounces) shredded cheddar cheese
- 1/2 cup dry bread crumbs
- 1 tablespoon butter, melted

In a large saucepan, bring 1/2 in. of water to a boil. Add asparagus; cover and boil for 3 minutes or until crisp-tender; drain well.

In a greased 2-1/2-qt. baking dish, combine the asparagus, ham, rice, celery and lemon-pepper; set aside. In a large saucepan, combine soup and broth; add cheese. Cook and stir over medium heat until the cheese is melted. Pour over the ham mixture.

Combine crumbs and butter; sprinkle over casserole. Bake, uncovered, at 350° for 35 minutes or until heated through.

YIELD: 6-8 SERVINGS.

helen ostronic
OMAHA, NEBRASKA

I created this casserole one day while trying to find a good recipe for leftover ham. Instead of resorting to scalloped potatoes and ham, or ham and noodles, I tried asparagus. Everyone liked it so much, I've made it ever since.

ASPARAGUS

The peak months for buying asparagus are April and May. When buying, look for firm, straight, uniform-size spears. The tips should be closed with crisp stalks. It's best to use asparagus within a few days of purchase. For longer storage, place bundled stalks upright in a bowl filled with 1 inch of water and refrigerate.

CHEESY MAC 'N' DOGS

PREP 25 minutes | **BAKE** 20 minutes

sue gonzalez
FORTSON, GEORGIA

I've made this casserole for 25 years, and my family never gets tired of it. I like to assemble it the night before, then pop it in the oven after work. A tossed salad completes the meal nicely.

- 1 package (8 ounces) elbow macaroni
- 1 small onion, finely chopped
- 1/4 cup butter, cubed
- 1/4 cup all-purpose flour
- 1 teaspoon salt
- 1/2 teaspoon ground mustard
- 2-1/2 cups milk
- 3/4 teaspoon Worcestershire sauce
- 12 ounces process cheese (Velveeta), cubed
- 7 cooked hot dogs, diced
- 1/4 cup dry bread crumbs

Cook the macaroni according to package directions. Meanwhile, in a large skillet, saute onion in butter until tender. Stir in the flour, salt and mustard. Gradually add the milk. Bring to a boil; cook and stir for 2 minutes or until thickened. Stir in the Worcestershire sauce and cheese until cheese is melted.

Drain macaroni; stir into the cheese sauce. Add the hot dogs. Transfer to a greased 2-1/2-qt. baking dish. Sprinkle with bread crumbs.

Bake, uncovered, at 350° for 20-25 minutes or until bubbly.

YIELD: 6-8 SERVINGS.

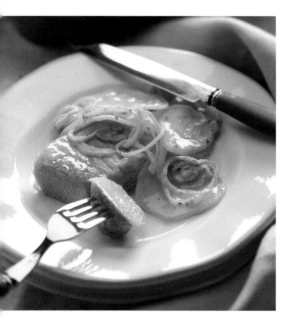

preheating the OVEN

It is important to preheat your oven before baking and roasting. Dishes depend on the correct oven temperature to help them cook properly. This takes about 15 to 20 minutes and can be done while preparing the recipe. Place the oven racks at the proper levels first, then set to the recommended temperature.

PERFECT PORK CHOP BAKE

PREP 15 minutes | **BAKE** 1-1/4 hours

jan lutz
STEVENS POINT, WISCONSIN

This recipe is especially useful on busy days during fall harvest or spring planting when we're short on time. It's packed with pork and produce for a filling meal.

- 6 pork chops (5 ounces *each*), trimmed
- 1/2 teaspoon salt, *divided*, optional
- 1 medium onion, thinly sliced and separated into rings
- 3 medium potatoes, peeled and thinly sliced
- 6 medium carrots, thinly sliced
- 1 teaspoon dried marjoram
- 3 tablespoons all-purpose flour
- 3/4 cup milk
- 1 can (10-3/4 ounces) condensed cream of mushroom soup, undiluted

Coat a large skillet with cooking spray; brown pork chops on both sides. Place in an ungreased 13-in. x 9-in. baking dish; sprinkle with 1/4 teaspoon salt if desired. Layer the onion, potatoes and carrots over chops. Sprinkle with marjoram and remaining salt if desired.

In a small bowl, whisk the flour and milk until smooth; add soup. Pour over the vegetables. Cover and bake at 350° for 1 hour. Uncover; bake 15 minutes longer or until pork is tender.

YIELD: 6 SERVINGS.

SPAGHETTI HAM BAKE

PREP 25 minutes | **BAKE** 30 minutes

mary killion
HERMISTON, OREGON

My sister passed along the recipe for this convenient casserole. I appreciate being able to freeze one pan for a hectic day. The generous portions are bound to feed a hungry family or an extra mouth or two that show up at your table.

- 2 packages (7 ounces *each*) thin spaghetti, broken into 2-inch pieces
- 4 cups cubed fully cooked ham
- 2 cans (10-3/4 ounces *each*) condensed cream of chicken soup, undiluted
- 2 cups (16 ounces) sour cream
- 1/2 pound sliced fresh mushrooms
- 1/2 cup chopped onion
- 1/2 cup sliced ripe olives, optional
- 1-1/2 teaspoons ground mustard
- 1 teaspoon seasoned salt
- 2 teaspoons Worcestershire sauce

TOPPING

- 2 cups soft bread crumbs
- 1/4 cup butter, melted
- 2 cups (8 ounces) shredded cheddar cheese

Cook the spaghetti according to package directions; drain and place in a large bowl. Stir in ham, soup, sour cream, mushrooms, onion, olives if desired, mustard, seasoned salt and Worcestershire sauce.

Transfer to two greased 11-in. x 7-in. baking dishes. In a small bowl, toss bread crumbs and butter; add cheese. Sprinkle over casseroles.

Cover and freeze one casserole for up to 2 months. Bake the remaining casserole, uncovered, at 325° for 30 minutes or until heated through.

TO USE FROZEN CASSEROLE: Thaw in the refrigerator overnight. Bake, uncovered, at 325° for 50-55 minutes or until heated through.

YIELD: 2 CASSEROLES (6 SERVINGS EACH).

HAM MAC AND CHEESE

PREP 30 minutes | **BAKE** 35 minutes

1 package (7-1/4 ounces) macaroni and cheese dinner mix
3/4 cup soft bread crumbs
2 tablespoons grated Parmesan cheese
1 tablespoon minced fresh parsley
1 tablespoon butter, melted
1 cup cubed fully cooked ham
1 cup (8 ounces) cream-style cottage cheese
1/2 cup sour cream
2 tablespoons sliced green onion
1 tablespoon diced pimientos, optional
1/4 teaspoon salt
1/4 teaspoon ground mustard

Prepare macaroni and cheese according to package directions. Meanwhile, in a small bowl, combine bread crumbs, Parmesan cheese, parsley and butter; set aside.

In a large bowl, combine the macaroni and cheese, ham, cottage cheese, sour cream, green onion, pimientos if desired, salt and mustard. Pour into a greased 1-1/2 qt. baking dish. Sprinkle with the bread crumb mixture.

Bake, uncovered, at 350° for 35-40 minutes or until heated through.
YIELD: 4 SERVINGS.

susan taul
BIRMINGHAM, ALABAMA

I've been using this recipe for years—everyone loves it and it's perfect with a side salad. It also makes a wonderful potluck dish.

MIX 'N' MATCH SQUASH CASSEROLE

PREP 20 minutes | **BAKE** 30 minutes

- 4 cups cubed summer squash (yellow, zucchini, pattypan *and/or* sunburst)
- 1 pound bulk pork sausage, cooked and drained
- 1 cup dry bread crumbs
- 1/4 cup chopped green pepper
- 1/4 cup chopped onion
- 1/2 cup grated Parmesan cheese
- 2 eggs, beaten
- 1/2 cup milk
- 1/2 teaspoon salt

Place the squash and a small amount of water in a large saucepan; cover and cook for 8-10 minutes or until tender. Drain. Add all the remaining ingredients; mix well. Transfer to a greased 11-in. x 7-in. baking dish. Bake, uncovered, at 325° for 30-35 minutes.

YIELD: 6-8 SERVINGS.

june mullins
LIVONIA, MISSOURI

Mix any kind of summer squash you have on hand for this flavorful casserole. Served with a salad and hot rolls or homemade bread, it makes a meal my family enjoys.

CAULIFLOWER HAM CASSEROLE

PREP 20 minutes | **BAKE** 40 minutes

- 4 cups chopped fresh cauliflower
- 1/4 cup butter, cubed
- 1/3 cup all-purpose flour
- 2 cups milk
- 1 cup (4 ounces) shredded cheddar cheese
- 1/2 cup sour cream
- 2 cups cubed fully cooked ham
- 1 jar (4-1/2 ounces) sliced mushrooms, drained

TOPPING

- 1 cup soft bread crumbs
- 1 tablespoon butter, melted

Place the cauliflower in a large saucepan; cover with water. Bring to a boil. Reduce heat; cover and simmer for 5-10 minutes or until tender.

Meanwhile, in another large saucepan, melt butter. Stir in flour until smooth; gradually add milk. Bring to a boil; cook and stir for 2 minutes or until thickened. Remove from the heat. Stir in the cheese and sour cream until melted.

Drain the cauliflower. In a large bowl, combine cauliflower, ham and mushrooms. Add the cheese sauce and toss to coat. Transfer to a greased 2-qt. baking dish.

Combine topping ingredients; sprinkle over casserole. Bake, uncovered, at 350° for 40-45 minutes or until heated through.

YIELD: 6 SERVINGS.

sue herlund
WHITE BEAR LAKE, MINNESOTA

Cauliflower replaces the potatoes in this comforting casserole, which I've been making for 30 years. Whenever we have leftover ham, my husband asks me to make this dish.

CAULIFLOWER

While purchasing fresh cauliflower heads, look for compact florets that are free from yellow or brown spots. The leaves should be crisp and green, not withered or discolored. Tightly wrap an unwashed head of cauliflower and refrigerate for up to 5 days. Before using, wash and remove the leaves at the base and trim the stem.

BUSY DAY HAM BAKE

PREP 15 minutes | **BAKE** 30 minutes

1 can (10-3/4 ounces) condensed cheddar cheese soup, undiluted
3 cups frozen chopped broccoli, thawed
1 cup cooked rice
1 cup cubed fully cooked ham
1/4 cup sour cream
1/4 cup mayonnaise
1/4 cup dry bread crumbs
1 tablespoon butter

In a large bowl, combine the first six ingredients. Transfer to a greased 1-1/2-qt. baking dish. Toss the bread crumbs with the butter; sprinkle over the top. Bake, uncovered, at 350° for 30 minutes or until heated through.
YIELD: 4 SERVINGS.

brenda daugherty
LAKE CITY, FLORIDA

I rely on a few everyday ingredients to make this eye-catching casserole. It's great with crusty rolls and fruit salad. Sometimes I replace the ham with cooked turkey for a change of pace.

about **RICOTTA**

When a cheese maker separates milk or cream into curds and whey, the curds are used to make cottage cheese and the whey is used to make ricotta. That's why both cheeses, although similarly soft and mild in flavor, have such different textures. Both are considered "fresh" or unripened cheeses.

HAM & SHELLS CASSEROLE

PREP 40 minutes | **BAKE** 25 minutes

1 package (16 ounces) medium pasta shells
3 large onions, halved and sliced
1 tablespoon olive oil
1 package (9 ounces) fresh spinach, torn
1 tablespoon minced fresh rosemary *or* 1 teaspoon dried rosemary, crushed
1/4 cup butter, cubed
1/3 cup all-purpose flour
1/4 teaspoon pepper
3-1/2 cups fat-free milk
1 cup part-skim ricotta cheese
1 cup crumbled goat cheese
2 cups cubed fully cooked ham
1/3 cup grated Parmesan cheese

Cook pasta according to package directions. Meanwhile, in a large skillet over medium heat, cook and stir the onions in oil for 15-20 minutes or until golden brown. Add spinach and rosemary; cook 1-2 minutes longer or until spinach is wilted.

In a large saucepan, melt butter. Stir in flour and pepper until smooth. Gradually add milk. Bring to a boil; cook and stir for 2 minutes or until thickened. Remove from the heat. Stir in the ricotta and goat cheeses until blended.

Drain pasta; place in a large bowl. Add the ham, onion mixture and sauce; toss to coat.

Transfer to a greased 13-in. x 9-in. baking dish; sprinkle with Parmesan cheese. Bake, uncovered, at 350° for 25-30 minutes or until bubbly.
YIELD: 12 SERVINGS (1 CUP EACH).

genise krause
STURGEON BAY, WISCONSIN

I altered this recipe to include ham and spinach, and I think it created a well-rounded meal guaranteed to win you rave reviews!

SAUSAGE AND WILD RICE CASSEROLE

PREP 35 minutes | **BAKE** 1 hour

elsie pritschau
RAVENNA, NEBRASKA

You can assemble this casserole and refrigerate until ready to bake. Remove from the refrigerator 30 minutes before baking.

1 package (6 ounces) long grain and wild rice mix
1 pound bulk pork sausage
1 can (10-3/4 ounces) condensed cream of mushroom soup, undiluted
1 cup chopped fresh mushrooms
1/2 cup chopped onion
1/2 cup chopped green pepper
1/2 cup shredded sharp cheddar cheese
1/2 cup chicken broth
1/4 cup finely chopped celery
1 teaspoon dried parsley flakes
1/2 teaspoon pepper

Cook the rice according to the package directions. Meanwhile, in a large skillet, cook the sausage over medium heat until no longer pink; drain. In a large bowl, combine the remaining ingredients; add the rice and sausage.

Transfer to a greased 2-qt. baking dish. Bake, uncovered, at 350° for 1 hour.

YIELD: 6-8 SERVINGS.

BAKED HAM TETRAZZINI

PREP 20 minutes | **BAKE** 20 minutes

4 ounces uncooked spaghetti, broken into 2-inch pieces

1 cup (4 ounces) shredded sharp cheddar cheese

2/3 cup condensed cream of mushroom soup, undiluted

1/2 cup 2% milk

1 tablespoon minced fresh parsley

2 teaspoons diced pimientos, drained

1 teaspoon finely chopped onion

1/2 teaspoon Worcestershire sauce

Dash pepper

3/4 cup cubed fully cooked ham

Cook the spaghetti according to package directions. Meanwhile, in a small bowl, combine the cheese, soup, milk, parsley, pimientos, onion, Worcestershire sauce and pepper.

Drain spaghetti; add to soup mixture. Spread half into a 1-1/2-qt. baking dish coated with cooking spray. Layer with ham and remaining spaghetti mixture.

Bake, uncovered, at 375° for 20-25 minutes or until bubbly.

YIELD: 2 SERVINGS.

elvi kaukinen
HORSEHEADS, NEW YORK

Rich, creamy pasta and cubed ham blend perfectly in this hearty meal for two. It's a great way to use up leftover holiday ham.

SAUSAGE HOT DISH

PREP 20 minutes | **COOK** 35 minutes

1 pound lean ground beef

3 medium potatoes, peeled and cut into 1/4-inch slices

2 medium carrots, thinly sliced

1 small onion, thinly sliced

1 teaspoon dried thyme

1 teaspoon salt

1/8 teaspoon pepper

1/4 cup water

1 pound bulk pork sausage

2 cups (8 ounces) shredded cheddar cheese

Crumble half of the beef into a 2-1/2-qt. microwave-safe dish. Layer with half of the potatoes, carrots and onion. Sprinkle with half of the thyme, salt and pepper. Repeat layers. Pour water over top. Cover and microwave at 70% power for 16 minutes.

Meanwhile, in a skillet, cook sausage over medium heat until no longer pink; drain. Spoon over the beef mixture.

Microwave, uncovered, on high for 5-7 minutes. Sprinkle with cheese. Heat 30 seconds longer. Let stand for 5 minutes before serving.

YIELD: 8 SERVINGS.

carol rydman
MIDLAND, MICHIGAN

I normally don't cook foods in the microwave, but this meal is the exception! The flavorful combination of ground beef and sausage makes it unique. We like it a lot.

PINEAPPLE HAM CASSEROLE

PREP 10 minutes | **BAKE** 40 minutes

1 can (20 ounces) pineapple tidbits

1/2 cup mayonnaise

1 teaspoon salt

1 teaspoon prepared mustard

1/4 teaspoon pepper

3 cups cooked rice

2 cups cubed fully cooked ham

1 cup chopped green pepper

1-1/2 cups (6 ounces) shredded Swiss cheese, *divided*

1/3 cup chopped onion

Drain the pineapple, reserving 1/2 cup juice; set pineapple aside. In a large bowl, combine the mayonnaise, salt, mustard, pepper and reserved pineapple juice; mix well. Fold in the rice, ham, green pepper, 1 cup of Swiss cheese, onion and pineapple.

Transfer to a greased 2-qt. baking dish. Cover and bake at 350° for 30 minutes. Sprinkle with remaining cheese. Bake, uncovered, for 10 minutes or until heated through and the cheese is melted.

YIELD: 6 SERVINGS.

EDITOR'S NOTE: Reduced-fat or fat-free mayonnaise is not recommended for this recipe.

gail earman
ALPHARETTA, GEORGIA

I turn to this recipe when I want to use leftover ham. The slightly sweet combination of ham, pineapple tidbits, rice and Swiss cheese is very popular at my house. We even featured this recipe in our family cookbook!

MOSTACCIOLI

PREP 15 minutes | **BAKE** 45 minutes

- 1 pound uncooked mostaccioli
- 1-1/2 pounds bulk Italian sausage
- 1 jar (28 ounces) meatless spaghetti sauce
- 1 egg, beaten
- 1 carton (15 ounces) ricotta cheese
- 2 cups (8 ounces) shredded part-skim mozzarella cheese
- 1/2 cup grated Romano cheese

Cook the pasta according to the package directions; drain. Crumble sausage into a Dutch oven. Cook over medium heat until no longer pink; drain. Stir in spaghetti sauce and pasta. In a bowl, combine the egg, ricotta cheese and mozzarella cheese.

Spoon half of the pasta mixture into a greased shallow 3-qt. baking dish; layer with cheese mixture and remaining pasta mixture. Cover and bake at 375° for 40 minutes. Uncover; top with Romano cheese. Bake 5 minutes longer or until heated through. **YIELD:** 10-12 SERVINGS.

nancy mundhenke
KINSLEY, KANSAS

Even though we're not Italian, this rich, cheesy pasta dish is a family tradition for holidays and special occasions. I was delighted the first time I tried this recipe—it has all the flavor of lasagna without the work of layering the ingredients. Try it...I'm sure it'll become one of your family's favorites, too!

BOW TIE HAM BAKE

PREP 20 minutes | **BAKE** 25 minutes

- 4 cups uncooked bowtie pasta
- 6 cups frozen broccoli florets
- 4 cups cubed fully cooked ham
- 2 cartons (10 ounces *each*) refrigerated Alfredo sauce
- 2 cups (8 ounces) shredded Swiss cheese
- 1 can (8 ounces) mushroom stems and pieces, drained

Cook the pasta according to the package directions, adding the broccoli during the last 5 minutes of cooking.

Meanwhile, in a large bowl, combine the ham, Alfredo sauce, cheese and mushrooms. Drain the pasta mixture; add to the ham mixture and toss to coat. Transfer to two greased 11-in. x 7-in. baking dishes. Cover and freeze one casserole for up to 3 months. Cover and bake remaining casserole at 375° for 20 minutes. Uncover; bake 5-10 minutes longer or until bubbly.

TO USE FROZEN CASSEROLE: Thaw in the refrigerator overnight. Remove from the refrigerator 30 minutes before heating. Cover; microwave on high for 8-10 minutes or until heated through, stirring once. **YIELD:** 2 CASSEROLES (6 SERVINGS EACH).

suzette jury
KEENE, CALIFORNIA

This recipe comes from our family cookbook that's filled with recipes from generations of women. We love casseroles—just pop one in the oven to warm your home and fill your stomach!

SAUSAGE-CORN BAKE

PREP 20 minutes | **BAKE** 30 minutes

1-1/2 pounds bulk pork sausage
1 medium green pepper, chopped
1 medium onion, chopped
4 tablespoons butter, *divided*
3 tablespoons all-purpose flour
1/2 teaspoon salt
1/2 teaspoon white pepper
1-1/2 cups milk
1 can (14-3/4 ounces) cream-style corn
3-1/2 cups (10 ounces) egg noodles, cooked and drained
1/4 cup shredded cheddar cheese
1/2 cup dry bread crumbs

In a large skillet, cook the sausage, green pepper and onion over medium heat until the sausage is no longer pink; drain and set aside.

In a large saucepan, melt 3 tablespoons butter over medium heat. Stir in the flour, salt and pepper. Gradually add milk. Bring to a boil; cook and stir for 2 minutes or until thickened. Stir in corn. Add noodles and corn mixture to the sausage mixture. Fold in the cheese.

Transfer to a greased 13-in. x 9-in. baking dish. Melt the remaining butter; stir in the bread crumbs. Sprinkle over casserole. Bake, uncovered, at 325° for 30-40 minutes or until heated through.

YIELD: 6-8 SERVINGS.

bernice morris
MARSHFIELD, MISSOURI

Corn gives this dish a mildly sweet flavor that folks find appealing. When cooking for two, I divide the ingredients into smaller dishes for fast meals in the future.

EASY HAM HASH

PREP 10 minutes | BAKE 35 minutes

esther johnson
danielson
GREENVILLE, TEXAS

- 1 pound finely ground fully cooked ham
- 1 large onion, finely chopped
- 3 medium potatoes, peeled and cooked
- 2 tablespoons butter, melted
- 2 tablespoons grated Parmesan cheese
- 1 tablespoon prepared mustard
- 2 teaspoons Worcestershire sauce
- 1 teaspoon prepared horseradish
- 1/4 teaspoon pepper
- 1 cup (4 ounces) shredded cheddar cheese
- 1/2 cup shredded Monterey Jack cheese

In a large bowl, combine the ham and onion. Shred the potatoes and add to ham mixture. Stir in the butter, Parmesan cheese, mustard, Worcestershire sauce, horseradish and pepper.

Spoon into a greased 11-in. x 7-in. baking dish, pressing down firmly. Combine cheeses; sprinkle over top. Bake, uncovered, at 350° for 35-40 minutes or until bubbly and cheese is melted.

YIELD: 6 SERVINGS.

As the oldest of six children, I learned to cook early in life. Now my files are bulging with a variety of recipes. This scrumptious casserole remains an old standby.

WILD RICE AND HAM CASSEROLE

PREP 15 minutes | **BAKE** 45 minutes

- 1 package (6-1/4 ounces) quick-cooking long grain and wild rice mix
- 1 package (10 ounces) frozen cut broccoli, thawed and drained
- 2 cups cubed fully cooked ham
- 1 can (10-3/4 ounces) condensed cream of mushroom soup, undiluted
- 1 cup mayonnaise
- 2 teaspoons prepared mustard
- 1 cup (4 ounces) shredded cheddar cheese

Prepare the rice according to the package directions. Spoon into an ungreased 2-1/2-qt. baking dish. Top with broccoli and ham. Combine the soup, mayonnaise and mustard. Spread over the rice mixture and mix gently.

Cover and bake at 350° for 45 minutes or until bubbly. Sprinkle with cheese. Let stand for 5 minutes before serving.

YIELD: 6 SERVINGS.

stacey diehl
LECANTO, FLORIDA

My grandmother gave me this recipe. The blend of flavors is fantastic. It's so simple to make and can easily be doubled for a large gathering.

OVEN-BAKED CHOP SUEY

PREP 15 minutes | **BAKE** 1 hour

- 2 pounds pork stew meat
- 1 package (7 ounces) shell macaroni, cooked and drained
- 2 cups diced celery
- 2 medium onions, diced
- 1 cup chopped green pepper
- 1 can (10-3/4 ounces) condensed cream of mushroom soup, undiluted
- 1 can (10-3/4 ounces) condensed cream of chicken soup, undiluted
- 1 can (4 ounces) mushroom stems and pieces, drained
- 1/4 cup soy sauce
- 1 jar (2 ounces) diced pimientos, drained
- 2 cups chow mein noodles

In a large skillet, cook pork over medium heat until meat is no longer pink; drain. Stir in the next nine ingredients.

Pour into a greased 13-in. x 9-in. baking dish. Top with the chow mein noodles. Bake, uncovered, at 350° for 1 to 1-1/4 hours or until pork is tender.

YIELD: 8 SERVINGS.

nadine dahling
ELKADER, IOWA

Whenever I take this casserole to a potluck, I always come home with an empty dish and with many recipe requests! The macaroni makes it a nice switch from other chop suey recipes.

UPSIDE-DOWN PIZZA BAKE

PREP 20 minutes | **BAKE** 25 minutes

- 1/2 pound Italian sausage links, cut into 1/4-inch slices
- 1 cup spaghetti sauce
- 1/2 cup sliced fresh mushrooms
- 1/2 cup julienned green pepper
- 1 cup (4 ounces) shredded part-skim mozzarella cheese, *divided*
- 1 cup biscuit/baking mix
- 1 egg
- 1/2 cup milk

In a large skillet, cook sausage over medium heat until meat is no longer pink; drain.

Pour spaghetti sauce into a greased 8-in. square baking dish. Top with the mushrooms, green pepper, sausage and 1/2 cup cheese.

In a small bowl, combine the biscuit mix, egg and milk until blended. Pour over top. Sprinkle with remaining cheese.

Bake, uncovered, at 400° for 25-30 minutes or until golden brown.

YIELD: 4 SERVINGS.

sandy bastian
TINLEY PARK, ILLINOIS

This super easy, but exceptionally delicious recipe is one I've been preparing and serving to my children and now to my grandchildren for over 30 years!

DELUXE POTATO HAM BAKE

PREP 10 minutes | **BAKE** 1 hour

- 2 cans (10-3/4 ounces *each*) condensed cream of chicken soup, undiluted
- 1/4 cup butter, melted
- 1 cup (8 ounces) sour cream
- 1-1/2 cups (6 ounces) shredded cheddar cheese
- 1 medium onion, chopped
- 2 cups cubed fully cooked ham
- 1 package (32 ounces) frozen Southern-style hash brown potatoes, thawed

TOPPING

- 1/4 cup butter, melted
- 3/4 cup crushed cornflakes

In a large bowl, combine the first five ingredients. Stir in ham and potatoes. Spread into a greased 13-in. x 9-in. baking dish.

For topping, combine the butter and cornflakes until crumbly. Sprinkle over top of ham mixture.

Bake, uncovered, at 350° for 1 hour or until potatoes are tender.

YIELD: 10-12 SERVINGS.

diane wilson wing
SALT LAKE CITY, UTAH

This tasty dish has the comforting combination of delicious flavors and a crisp, crunchy crust.

HAM AND CHICKEN CASSEROLE

PREP 25 minutes | **BAKE** 45 minutes

- 1 cup chopped onion
- 2 tablespoons butter
- 2 cups cubed fully cooked ham
- 2 cups diced cooked chicken
- 1 medium green pepper, chopped
- 1/2 cup chopped sweet red pepper
- 1 cup pimiento-stuffed olives
- 1 can (10-3/4 ounces) condensed cream of mushroom soup, undiluted
- 1 cup (8 ounces) sour cream
- 1-1/2 teaspoons salt
- 1/4 teaspoon pepper
- 8 ounces noodles, cooked and drained
- 3 tablespoons shredded Parmesan cheese

connie sanden
MENTOR, OHIO

This recipe has traveled to many parts of the country. That's because I've served it to guests from Washington to New Hampshire, and they always ask for the recipe before I leave! My grown children all have a copy, too—it never fails to get rave reviews.

In a skillet, saute onion in butter until tender. In a large bowl, combine the ham, chicken, peppers, olives, soup, sour cream, salt, pepper and onion. Fold in noodles.

Pour into a greased 2-1/2-qt. baking dish. Sprinkle with the Parmesan cheese. Bake, uncovered, at 325° for 45 minutes or until bubbly.

YIELD: 8 SERVINGS.

AUTUMN SAUSAGE CASSEROLE

PREP 20 minutes | **BAKE** 25 minutes

1 pound bulk pork sausage
1 medium apple, peeled and chopped
1 medium onion, chopped
1/2 cup chopped celery
3 cups cooked long grain rice
1/2 cup raisins
1/3 cup minced fresh parsley
1 tablespoon brown sugar
1/2 teaspoon salt
1/4 teaspoon ground allspice
1/4 teaspoon ground cinnamon
1/8 teaspoon pepper

In a large skillet, cook the sausage, apple, onion and celery over medium heat until the meat is no longer pink; drain. Stir in the remaining ingredients.

Transfer to a greased 2-qt. baking dish. Cover and bake at 350° for 25-30 minutes or until heated through.

YIELD: 4-6 SERVINGS.

diane brunell
WASHINGTON, MASSACHUSETTS

Apple, raisins and spices give this scrumptious sausage-rice casserole a taste of autumn. We enjoy it with a green salad on a cold fall day. It would be a nice potluck dish, too—just double the recipe if needed.

seafood

INDIVIDUAL SEAFOOD CASSEROLES • PAGE 124

TASTY TUNA CASSEROLE

PREP 20 minutes | **BAKE** 25 minutes

elsie epp
NEWTON, KANSAS

Reduced-fat cream cheese adds a delightful creaminess to this easy, tomato-flavored twist on classic tuna casserole.

  2 cups uncooked elbow macaroni
  1 can (12 ounces) solid white tuna, drained
  1 can (8 ounces) tomato sauce
  4 ounces reduced-fat cream cheese, cubed
  1 small onion, finely chopped
1/4 teaspoon salt
1/2 teaspoon dried oregano

Cook the macaroni according to package directions. Meanwhile, in a large bowl, combine the remaining ingredients. Drain macaroni; stir into tuna mixture.

Transfer to a 2-qt. baking dish coated with cooking spray. Cover and bake at 350° for 20-25 minutes or until heated through. **YIELD:** 4 SERVINGS.

NUTRITION FACTS: 1-1/2 cups equals 334 calories, 9 g fat (5 g saturated fat), 56 mg cholesterol, 851 mg sodium, 33 g carbohydrate, 2 g fiber, 29 g protein. **DIABETIC EXCHANGES:** 3 very lean meat, 2 starch, 1 fat.

BAYOU COUNTRY SEAFOOD CASSEROLE

PREP 35 minutes | **BAKE** 30 minutes

1 medium onion, chopped
1 medium green pepper, chopped
1 celery rib, chopped
1 garlic clove, minced
6 tablespoons butter
1 can (10-3/4 ounces) condensed cream of mushroom soup, undiluted
1 pound uncooked shrimp, peeled and deveined
1-1/2 cups cooked rice
2 cans (6 ounces *each*) crabmeat, drained, flaked and cartilage removed
4 slices day-old bread, cubed
3/4 cup half-and-half cream
1/4 cup chopped green onion tops
1/2 teaspoon salt
1/4 teaspoon pepper
Dash cayenne pepper

TOPPING

2 tablespoons butter, melted
1/3 cup dry bread crumbs
2 tablespoons snipped fresh parsley

In a large skillet, saute onion, green pepper, celery and garlic in butter until tender. Add the soup and shrimp; cook and stir over medium heat 10 minutes or until shrimp turn pink. Stir in rice, crab, bread cubes, cream, onion tops and seasonings.

Spoon into a greased 2-qt. baking dish. Combine topping ingredients; sprinkle over casserole. Bake uncovered at 375° for 25-30 minutes or until heated through.
YIELD: 8 SERVINGS.

ethel miller
EUNICE, LOUISIANA

Seafood is popular in our area. Since crabs and shrimp are so plentiful in our bayous and rivers, they're used in a variety of recipes. This casserole is nice enough for company, but it's always popular as a casual meal, too.

SPEEDY SALMON CASSEROLE

PREP/TOTAL TIME 30 minutes

1 tablespoon butter
1 tablespoon all-purpose flour
3 tablespoons ketchup
1/2 cup milk
1 can (14-3/4 ounces) salmon, drained, flaked and bones removed
2 cups mashed potato flakes
1 cup (4 ounces) shredded cheddar cheese

In a saucepan, melt butter over medium heat. Stir in flour and ketchup until smooth. Gradually stir in milk. Bring to a boil; cook and stir for 2 minutes. Add salmon. Prepare the mashed potato flakes according to the package directions.

Spoon half into a greased 11-in. x 7-in. baking dish. Top with the salmon mixture, remaining potatoes and cheese. Bake, uncovered, at 375° for 15-20 minutes or until heated through and cheese is melted.
YIELD: 6 SERVINGS.

evelyn gebhardt
KASILOF, ALASKA

Living here on the Kenai Peninsula, we have plenty of fresh salmon. This rich, comforting casserole tastes just as good with canned salmon. It's also a great way to use up leftover mashed potatoes or dress up instant ones.

SALMON BROCCOLI BAKE

PREP 15 minutes | **BAKE** 35 minutes

brigitte schaller
FLEMINGTON, MISSOURI

1 cup chopped onion

1 tablespoon butter

1-1/2 cups cooked wild rice

1 can (7-1/2 ounces) salmon, drained, bones and skin removed

1 egg

1/2 cup mayonnaise

1/2 cup grated Parmesan cheese

3 cups frozen chopped broccoli, thawed and drained

1-1/2 cups (6 ounces) shredded cheddar cheese, *divided*

In a skillet, saute onion in butter until tender. Remove from the heat; stir in rice and salmon. Combine egg and mayonnaise; add to the salmon mixture.

Spoon half into a greased 2-qt. baking dish; top with half of the Parmesan cheese and broccoli. Sprinkle with 1 cup cheddar cheese. Top with the remaining salmon mixture, Parmesan cheese and broccoli.

Bake, uncovered, at 350° for 30 minutes. Sprinkle with remaining cheddar. Bake 5 minutes longer or until cheese is melted. **YIELD:** 4 SERVINGS.

EDITOR'S NOTE: Reduced-fat or fat-free mayonnaise is not recommended for this recipe.

A good friend gave me this quick-and-easy recipe that uses canned salmon, wild rice and frozen broccoli. I often serve this hot dish with a wilted spinach salad for a complete meal.

WILD RICE SHRIMP BAKE

PREP 20 minutes | **BAKE** 20 minutes

lee stearns
MOBILE, ALABAMA

1 package (6 ounces) long grain and wild rice mix

1 pound uncooked medium shrimp, peeled and deveined

1 medium green pepper, chopped

1 medium onion, chopped

1 can (4 ounces) mushroom stems and pieces, drained

1/4 cup butter

1 can (10-3/4 ounces) condensed cream of chicken soup, undiluted

1/2 cup seasoned stuffing croutons

Fresh shrimp lends a special touch to this effortless entree that starts out with a boxed mix. I top off this creamy casserole with a handful of crunchy croutons.

deveining SHRIMP

Start on the underside by the head area to remove the shell from shrimp. Pull the legs and first section of shell to one side. Continue pulling shell up around the top and to the other side. Remove shell by tail if desired. Remove the black vein running down the back of shrimp by making a shallow slit with a paring knife along the back, from head to tail. Rinse under cold water to remove the vein.

Prepare the rice according to the package directions.

Meanwhile, in a large skillet, saute the shrimp, green pepper, onion and mushrooms in butter until shrimp turn pink. Add the soup to the rice; stir into the shrimp mixture.

Transfer mixture to a greased 2-qt. baking dish. Sprinkle with croutons. Bake, uncovered, at 350° for 20-25 minutes or until heated through. **YIELD:** 6 SERVINGS.

TUNA 'N' PEA CASSEROLE

PREP 20 minutes | **BAKE** 40 minutes

- 8 ounces uncooked egg noodles
- 2 cans (10-3/4 ounces *each*) condensed cream of mushroom soup, undiluted
- 1/2 cup mayonnaise
- 1/2 cup milk
- 2 to 3 teaspoons prepared horseradish
- 1/2 teaspoon dill weed
- 1/8 teaspoon pepper
- 1 cup frozen peas, thawed
- 1 can (4 ounces) mushroom stems and pieces, drained
- 1 small onion, chopped
- 1 jar (2 ounces) diced pimientos, drained
- 2 cans (6 ounces *each*) tuna, drained and flaked
- 1/4 cup dry bread crumbs
- 1 tablespoon butter, melted

Cook the noodles according to the package directions. Meanwhile, in a large bowl, combine soup, mayonnaise, milk, horseradish, dill and pepper. Stir in the peas, mushrooms, onion, pimientos and tuna.

Drain noodles; stir into soup mixture. Transfer to a greased 2-qt. baking dish. Toss bread crumbs and butter; sprinkle over the top. Bake, uncovered, at 375° for 40-45 minutes or until bubbly.

YIELD: 6 SERVINGS.

jackie smulski
LYONS, ILLINOIS

Turn to this recipe when you want a tuna casserole that's a little different—the horseradish adds extra flavor. This dish is a tried-and-true favorite in our family and never fails.

SEAFOOD AU GRATIN

PREP 30 minutes | **BAKE** 15 minutes

hazel mcmullin
AMHERST, NOVA SCOTIA

A seafood casserole is a "must" for a bountiful buffet. My father was a fisherman, so we ate fish almost every day. Over the years, I've tasted many seafood dishes, but none better than this one.

4 tablespoons butter, *divided*
2 tablespoons all-purpose flour
1/8 teaspoon pepper
1 cup chicken broth
1/2 cup milk
1/2 cup grated Parmesan cheese, *divided*
1/2 pound sea scallops
1 pound haddock *or* cod fillets, cut into six pieces
1-1/2 cups sliced fresh mushrooms
1/2 cup shredded part-skim mozzarella cheese
1/2 cup shredded cheddar cheese

In a large saucepan, melt 2 tablespoons of butter. Stir in the flour and pepper until smooth; gradually add the broth and milk. Bring to a boil; cook and stir for 2 minutes or until thickened. Stir in 1/4 cup Parmesan cheese; set aside.

Place the scallops in another saucepan; cover with water. Simmer, uncovered, for 4-5 minutes or until firm and opaque. Meanwhile, place fillets in a shallow 2-qt. microwave-safe dish. Cover and microwave on high for 2-4 minutes or until fish flakes easily with a fork. Drain scallops. Arrange fish and scallops in a greased 11-in. x 7-in. baking dish.

In a small skillet, saute the mushrooms in remaining butter until tender; stir into cheese sauce. Spoon over seafood. Sprinkle with mozzarella, cheddar and remaining Parmesan cheese.

Cover and bake at 350° for 15-20 minutes or until bubbly and cheese is melted.
YIELD: 6 SERVINGS.

CREAMY SEAFOOD CASSEROLE

PREP 15 minutes | **BAKE** 25 minutes

- 1 pound flounder fillets, cut into 1-1/2-inch pieces
- 1 pound uncooked medium shrimp, peeled and deveined
- 1 can (10-3/4 ounces) condensed cream of shrimp soup, undiluted
- 1/4 cup milk
- 1 cup crushed butter-flavored crackers (about 25 crackers)
- 1/4 cup grated Parmesan cheese
- 1 teaspoon paprika
- 2 tablespoons butter, melted

Arrange the fish and shrimp in a greased 11-in. x 7-in. baking dish. Combine the soup and milk; pour over the seafood. Combine the cracker crumbs, Parmesan cheese, paprika and butter; sprinkle over top.

Bake, uncovered, at 350° for 25-30 minutes or until fish flakes easily with a fork and shrimp turn pink.

YIELD: 6-8 SERVINGS.

mary brown
WHITMAN, MASSACHUSETTS

I love this recipe from my mother. It's easy, delicious and can be made the night before for added convenience, then popped in the oven the next day. Crushed potato chips or french-fried onions make other tasty topping options.

MAKEOVER SHRIMP RICE CASSEROLE

PREP 40 minutes | **BAKE** 30 minutes

- 1 pound uncooked medium shrimp, peeled and deveined
- 2 tablespoons butter, *divided*
- 12 ounces fresh mushrooms, sliced
- 1 large green pepper, chopped
- 1 medium onion, chopped
- 3 tablespoons all-purpose flour
- 3/4 teaspoon salt
- 1/8 teaspoon cayenne pepper
- 1-1/3 cups fat-free milk
- 3 cups cooked brown rice
- 1 cup (4 ounces) shredded reduced-fat cheddar cheese, *divided*

about **BROWN RICE**

Brown rice is rice that has had the husk removed but not the bran layer. The bran layer retains more vitamins, minerals and fiber content than white rice. When cooked, grains of brown rice are fluffy and have a chewy texture.

In a large nonstick skillet, saute shrimp in 1 tablespoon butter for 2-3 minutes or until shrimp turn pink. Remove and set aside. In the same skillet, saute mushrooms, green pepper and onion in the remaining butter until tender. Stir in the flour, salt and cayenne. Gradually add milk until blended. Bring to a boil; cook and stir for 2 minutes or until thickened. Add the rice, 1/2 cup cheese and shrimp; stir until combined.

Pour into a 1-1/2-qt. baking dish coated with cooking spray. Cover and bake at 325° for 30-35 minutes or until heated through. Sprinkle with the remaining cheese; cover and let stand for 5 minutes or until the cheese is melted.

YIELD: 6 SERVINGS.

NUTRITION FACTS: 1 cup equals 318 calories, 10 g fat (6 g saturated fat), 137 mg cholesterol, 621 mg sodium, 35 g carbohydrate, 4 g fiber, 24 g protein. **DIABETIC EXCHANGES:** 2 starch, 2 very lean meat, 1-1/2 fat, 1 vegetable.

marie roberts
LAKE CHARLES, LOUISIANA

Here's a lighter version of my shrimp casserole. It has half the calories and sodium and 76% less fat than my original recipe. I adore it!

MUSTARD SALMON PUFF

PREP 15 minutes | **BAKE** 35 minutes

2 eggs
2/3 cup milk
1/2 cup sour cream
3/4 cup dry bread crumbs
1 teaspoon seafood seasoning
1/2 teaspoon lemon-pepper seasoning
1/4 teaspoon dill weed
3 cups fully cooked flaked salmon
3 tablespoons chopped celery
2 tablespoons chopped onion
4-1/2 teaspoons lemon juice

TOPPING
1-1/3 cups mayonnaise
1 tablespoon prepared mustard
1 egg white
2 tablespoons minced parsley

In a large bowl, combine the eggs, milk and sour cream until smooth. Add the bread crumbs, seafood seasoning, lemon pepper and dill. Stir in the salmon, celery, onion and lemon juice.

Transfer to greased 11-in. x 7-in. baking dish. Bake at 350° for 25-30 minutes or until a knife inserted near center comes out clean.

Meanwhile, combine mayonnaise and mustard. In a small bowl, beat the egg white until stiff peaks form; fold into the mayonnaise mixture. Spread over the salmon mixture. Bake 10-15 minutes longer or until lightly browned. Sprinkle with parsley.
YIELD: 8 SERVINGS.

EDITOR'S NOTE: Reduced-fat or fat-free mayonnaise is not recommended for this recipe.

perlene hoekema
LYNDEN, WASHINGTON

This recipe is a delicious way to use leftover salmon.

lemon **JUICE**

When a recipe calls for lemon juice, you can use either fresh, frozen or bottled. When lemons are in season or you have excess lemons on hand, juice them and freeze the juice in ice cube trays. Measure 1-2 tablespoons of juice into each compartment in the tray. When frozen, remove the cubes and place in resealable freezer bags.

SALMON PUFF

PREP 15 minutes | **BAKE** 50 minutes

4 eggs, lightly beaten
1/2 cup milk
1 can (10-3/4 ounces) condensed cream of mushroom soup, undiluted
1 can (14-3/4 ounces) salmon, drained, bones and skin removed
2 cups soft bread cubes (about 2-1/2 slices)
1 tablespoon minced parsley
1 small onion, minced
2 tablespoons butter, melted
1/2 teaspoon lemon juice

In a large bowl, combine eggs, milk and soup; stir in remaining ingredients.

Pour into a greased 11-in. x 7-in. baking dish. Bake at 350° for 50 minutes or until set. Let stand for 5 minutes before serving.
YIELD: 6-8 SERVINGS.

marilyn kutzli
CLINTON, IOWA

This simple salmon dish is sure to be a hit at any occasion. It's a creative and yummy way to serve this tasty fish.

⚖ MAKEOVER SPINACH TUNA CASSEROLE

PREP 25 minutes | **BAKE** 40 minutes

karla hamrick
WAPAKONETA, OHIO

This thick, gooey casserole chock-full of tuna and spinach has been a family favorite for years.

- 5 cups uncooked egg noodles
- 1 cup (8 ounces) reduced-fat sour cream
- 1/2 cup fat-free mayonnaise
- 2 to 3 teaspoons lemon juice
- 2 tablespoons butter
- 1/4 cup all-purpose flour
- 2 cups fat-free milk
- 1/3 cup plus 2 tablespoons shredded Parmesan cheese, *divided*
- 1 package (10 ounces) frozen chopped spinach, thawed and squeezed dry
- 1 package (6 ounces) reduced-sodium chicken stuffing mix
- 1/3 cup seasoned bread crumbs
- 2 cans (6 ounces *each*) light water-packed tuna, drained and flaked

Cook the noodles according to the package directions. Meanwhile, in a small bowl, combine the sour cream, mayonnaise and lemon juice; set aside.

In a large saucepan or Dutch oven, melt the butter. Stir in the flour until blended. Gradually stir in the milk. Bring to a boil; cook and stir for 2 minutes or until thickened. Reduce heat; stir in 1/3 cup Parmesan cheese until melted. Remove from heat; stir in the sour cream mixture. Add the spinach, stuffing mix, bread crumbs and tuna; mix well.

Drain noodles and place in a 13-in. x 9-in. baking dish coated with cooking spray. Top with tuna mixture; sprinkle with remaining Parmesan cheese.

Cover and bake at 350° for 35 minutes. Uncover; bake 5-10 minutes longer or until lightly browned and heated through.
YIELD: 8 SERVINGS.

NUTRITION FACTS: 1 serving equals 346 calories, 9 g fat (5 g saturated fat), 50 mg cholesterol, 734 mg sodium, 41 g carbohydrate, 2 g fiber, 24 g protein. **DIABETIC EXCHANGES:** 2-1/2 starch, 2 very lean meat, 1-1/2 fat.

INDIVIDUAL SEAFOOD CASSEROLES

PREP 25 minutes | BAKE 20 minutes

jaelynne smigel
VANCOUVER, BRITISH COLUMBIA

My husband can't get enough of these mini casseroles and is disappointed when there aren't leftovers. This dish is a mainstay on my holiday menus.

- 1/3 cup chopped onion
- 1/3 cup butter, cubed
- 1/3 cup all-purpose flour
- 1/2 teaspoon salt
- 1/2 teaspoon white pepper
- 1 cup milk
- 1 cup heavy whipping cream
- 3 tablespoons *each* finely chopped sweet red and green pepper
- 2 teaspoons curry powder
- 1 teaspoon ground mustard
- 1/4 teaspoon dried thyme
- 1/4 teaspoon *each* ground ginger and turmeric
- 1/2 teaspoon lemon juice
- 3 to 5 drops hot pepper sauce
- 3 cans (6 ounces *each*) crabmeat, drained, flaked and cartilage removed
- 1 can (6 ounces) tuna, drained and flaked
- 1/4 pound cooked medium shrimp, peeled and deveined
- 2 hard-cooked eggs, chopped

TOPPING
- 1/2 cup shredded cheddar cheese
- 1/4 cup dry bread crumbs
- 1/4 teaspoon garlic powder
- 1 tablespoon *each* chopped sweet red and green pepper

In a large saucepan, saute onion in butter until tender. Stir in flour, salt and pepper until blended. Gradually whisk in milk and cream. Bring to a boil; cook and stir for 2 minutes or until thickened and bubbly. Stir in the peppers, seasonings, lemon juice and pepper sauce until blended.

Remove from heat; add the crab, tuna, shrimp and eggs. Transfer to six greased ovenproof 10-oz. dishes.

In a small bowl, combine the cheese, bread crumbs and garlic powder. Sprinkle over seafood mixture.

Bake, uncovered, at 350° for 15 minutes. Sprinkle with peppers. Bake 5-8 minutes longer or until heated through and the edges are bubbly.

YIELD: 6 SERVINGS.

DEVILED CRAB CASSEROLE

PREP/TOTAL TIME 30 minutes

- 1 can (6 ounces) crabmeat, drained, flaked and cartilage removed
- 1 cup dry bread crumbs, *divided*
- 3/4 cup milk
- 1/4 cup chopped green onions
- 2 hard-cooked eggs, chopped
- 1/2 teaspoon salt
- 1/4 teaspoon Worcestershire sauce
- 1/8 teaspoon ground mustard
- 1/8 teaspoon pepper
- 6 tablespoons butter, melted, *divided*

Paprika

In a bowl, combine the crab, 3/4 cup of bread crumbs, milk, onions, eggs, salt, Worcestershire sauce, mustard and pepper. Add 4 tablespoons of butter; mix well. Spoon into a greased 1-qt. baking dish.

Combine remaining bread crumbs and butter; sprinkle over casserole. Sprinkle with paprika. Bake, uncovered, at 425° for 16-18 minutes or until golden brown and edges are bubbly.

YIELD: 2 SERVINGS.

helen bachman
CHAMPAIGN, ILLINOIS

After creating this recipe, I later trimmed it down to serve two. I serve this dish often, since it's so easy to assemble. Along with a green salad, dessert and coffee, this mainstay makes a quick, delicious lunch or dinner.

SALMON SUPPER

PREP/TOTAL TIME 30 minutes

- 1/3 cup chopped green pepper
- 3 tablespoons chopped onion
- 2 tablespoons canola oil
- 1/4 cup all-purpose flour
- 1/2 teaspoon salt
- 1-1/2 cups milk
- 1 can (10-3/4 ounces) condensed cream of celery soup, undiluted
- 2 pouches (3 ounces *each*) boneless skinless pink salmon
- 1 cup frozen peas
- 2 teaspoons lemon juice
- 1 tube (8 ounces) refrigerated crescent rolls

In a large skillet, saute the green pepper and onion in the oil for 3-4 minutes or until crisp-tender.

In a small bowl, combine flour, salt, milk and soup until blended. Add to the skillet. Bring to a boil. Reduce heat; cook and stir for 2 minutes or until smooth. Stir in the salmon, peas and lemon juice.

Pour into an ungreased 11-in. x 7-in. baking dish. Do not unroll crescent dough; cut into eight equal slices. Arrange over salmon mixture. Bake, uncovered, at 375° for 10-12 minutes or until golden brown.

YIELD: 4 SERVINGS.

debra knippel
MEDFORD, WISCONSIN

With a husband and four children to cook for, I'm always on the lookout for quick recipes. This one was given to me many years ago by my mother-in-law. In addition to being very quick to fix, it has become a favorite family comfort food.

TUNA MUSHROOM CASSEROLE

PREP 20 minutes | **BAKE** 35 minutes

- 1 package (12 ounces) wide noodles, cooked and drained
- 2 cans (6 ounces *each*) tuna, drained
- 1 can (4 ounces) mushroom stems and pieces, drained
- 1 can (10-3/4 ounces) condensed cream of mushroom soup, undiluted
- 1-1/3 cups milk
- 1/2 teaspoon salt
- 1/4 teaspoon pepper
- 1/2 cup crushed saltines
- 3 tablespoons butter, melted

Paprika, tomato slices and fresh thyme, optional

In a large bowl, combine the noodles, tuna and mushrooms. Combine the soup, milk, salt and pepper; pour over the noodle mixture and mix well. Pour into a greased 2-1/2-qt. baking dish. Combine saltines and butter; sprinkle over noodles.

Bake, uncovered, at 350° for 35-45 minutes or until heated through. Sprinkle with paprika and garnish with tomato slices and thyme if desired.

YIELD: 6 SERVINGS.

connie moore
MEDWAY, OHIO

This robust dish is a rich-tasting entree. I usually serve this casserole when I'm short on time and we need something hearty and satisfying.

BAKED SOLE AND SPINACH

PREP 25 minutes | **BAKE** 30 minutes

1 package (8 ounces) egg noodles
3 tablespoons butter
3 tablespoons all-purpose flour
3 cups milk
1-1/2 cups (6 ounces) shredded cheddar cheese, *divided*
1 tablespoon lemon juice
1 teaspoon salt
1 teaspoon ground mustard
1 teaspoon Worcestershire sauce
1/8 teaspoon ground nutmeg
1/8 teaspoon pepper
2 packages (10 ounces *each*) frozen chopped spinach, thawed and squeezed dry
1-1/2 pounds sole fillets
1/4 cup slivered almonds, toasted

Cook the noodles according to the package directions. Meanwhile, in a large saucepan, melt butter. Stir in flour until smooth; gradually add milk. Bring to a boil; cook and stir for 2 minutes or until thickened.

Stir in 1 cup cheese, lemon juice, salt, mustard, Worcestershire sauce, nutmeg and pepper until cheese is melted. Set aside half of the cheese sauce. Drain noodles; add to the remaining sauce.

Transfer to a greased 13-in. x 9-in. baking dish. Top with the spinach, sole, reserved cheese sauce and remaining cheese; sprinkle with almonds.

Bake, uncovered, at 375° for 30-35 minutes or until fish flakes easily with a fork.
YIELD: 6 SERVINGS.

anna fuery
TAFTVILLE, CONNECTICUT

This crunched-for-time casserole can be fixed from start to finish in less than an hour. A cheesy pasta layer is topped with fish, spinach and almonds to make a meal-in-one that's a nice alternative to meat and potatoes.

SUNDAY SHRIMP PASTA BAKE

PREP 30 minutes | **BAKE** 25 minutes

12 ounces uncooked vermicelli
1 medium green pepper, chopped
5 green onions, chopped
6 garlic cloves, minced
6 tablespoons butter, cubed
2 tablespoons all-purpose flour
2 pounds deveined peeled cooked medium shrimp
1 teaspoon celery salt
1/8 teaspoon pepper
1 pound process cheese (Velveeta), cubed
1 can (10 ounces) diced tomatoes and green chilies, drained
1 can (4 ounces) mushroom stems and pieces, drained
1 tablespoon grated Parmesan cheese

Cook the vermicelli according to package directions. Meanwhile, in a large skillet, saute green pepper, onions and garlic in butter until tender. Gradually stir in flour until blended. Stir in the shrimp, celery salt and pepper; cook, uncovered, over medium heat for 5-6 minutes or until heated through.

In a microwave-safe bowl, combine the process cheese, tomatoes and mushrooms. Microwave, uncovered, on high for 3-4 minutes or until cheese is melted, stirring occasionally. Add to shrimp mixture. Drain vermicelli; stir into skillet.

Pour into a greased 13-in. x 9-in. baking dish. Sprinkle with Parmesan cheese. Bake, uncovered, at 350° for 25-30 minutes or until heated through.
YIELD: 8 SERVINGS.

sundra hauck
BOGALUSA, LOUISIANA

Pasta is popular in our home, so my favorite meals almost always include it in the main course. In this delicious casserole, vermicelli complements the shrimp our local fishermen bring in.

FLORIDA SEAFOOD CASSEROLE

PREP 15 minutes | **BAKE** 25 minutes

1/3 cup finely chopped onion
1/4 cup butter, cubed
1/4 cup all-purpose flour
1/2 teaspoon salt
1/2 teaspoon pepper
  1 cup milk
  1 cup half-and-half cream
  2 cups cooked long grain rice
  1 cup chopped cooked peeled shrimp
  1 cup crabmeat, drained, flaked and cartilage removed
  1 can (8 ounces) sliced water chestnuts, drained
  2 tablespoons lemon juice
  1 tablespoon chopped pimientos
  1 tablespoon minced fresh parsley
  1 cup (4 ounces) shredded cheddar cheese, *divided*

In a small saucepan, saute onion in butter. Stir in the flour, salt and pepper until blended. Gradually whisk in milk and cream. Bring to a boil. Cook and stir for 2 minutes or until thickened. Remove from the heat; stir in the rice, shrimp, crab, water chestnuts, lemon juice, pimientos, parsley and 1/2 cup cheese.

Transfer to a greased 2-1/2-qt. baking dish. Bake at 350° for 25-30 minutes or until heated through. Sprinkle with remaining cheddar cheese.

YIELD: 6 SERVINGS.

lucille pennington
ORMOND BEACH, FLORIDA

We have lots of friends from up North who come to Florida each winter to be out of the snow and in the sun. They always love to be served fresh seafood, a green salad and pie made with just–ripened strawberries. So I always try to accommodate them…and they usually compliment the chef!

TUNA-CHIP CASSEROLE

PREP 20 minutes | BAKE 20 minutes

1 package (7 ounces) plain potato chips, *divided*

1 can (7 ounces) water-packed tuna, drained

1 package (10-1/2 ounces) frozen asparagus tips, thawed and patted dry *or* 1 can (15 ounces) asparagus spears, drained and sliced

SAUCE

2/3 cup evaporated milk

1 tablespoon lemon juice

1/4 teaspoon ground mustard

1/8 teaspoon white pepper

TOPPING

1/4 cup shredded cheddar cheese

1/2 cup sliced almonds

Crush chips and place half in a greased 2-qt. baking dish. Arrange tuna over chips. Top with asparagus and the remaining chips. Combine sauce ingredients and pour over top. Sprinkle with cheese and almonds.

Bake, uncovered, at 325° for 20-25 minutes or until heated through. Let stand for 5 minutes before serving.

YIELD: 6 SERVINGS.

janis plourde
SMOOTH ROCK FALLS, ONTARIO

This crunchy spin on tuna casserole is a change from the ordinary that everyone will enjoy! With just a few steps, this tasty meal couldn't be easier to put together.

SHRIMP AND ASPARAGUS CASSEROLE

PREP 25 minutes | **BAKE** 30 minutes

- 2 packages (10 ounces *each*) frozen asparagus cuts
- 1/4 cup butter
- 1/4 cup all-purpose flour
- 1 cup milk
- 3/4 cup half-and-half cream
- 1/4 cup dry white wine *or* 1/4 cup more cream *or* 1/4 cup chicken broth
- 1/2 teaspoon salt
- 1/8 teaspoon pepper
- 1 egg yolk, lightly beaten
- 1/2 cup grated Parmesan cheese
- 1 pound cooked small shrimp
- 1/2 cup buttered soft bread crumbs

On stove top or in a microwave oven, blanch asparagus for 3 minutes. Drain well; set aside.

In a small saucepan, melt butter. Stir in the flour; cook, stirring constantly, for 1 minute. Gradually whisk in milk and cream; cook until thickened. Stir in wine (or substitute). Season with salt and pepper. Stir in beaten egg yolk, cheese and shrimp.

In a buttered 2-1/2-qt. casserole, arrange half the asparagus; pour on half the sauce. Repeat layers. Top with buttered crumbs. Bake at 350° for 30 minutes.

YIELD: 6 SERVINGS.

joan vallem
ARROYO GRANDE, CALIFORNIA

This scrumptious seafood dish "travels well." I make sure to pack the recipe in my handbag whenever my husband and I are preparing to visit out-of-state relatives. Now that we're retired, we travel often. And it's our custom to take over in the kitchen wherever we visit and whip up one of our own mainstay favorites—frequently this casserole. It never fails to win us many compliments...along with invitations to visit again!

OVERNIGHT TUNA CASSEROLE

PREP 25 minutes + chilling

- 1 can (10-3/4 ounces) condensed cream of celery soup, undiluted
- 1 cup milk
- 1 can (6 ounces) tuna, drained
- 1 cup uncooked elbow macaroni
- 1 cup frozen peas
- 1/2 cup chopped green onions
- 1 cup (4 ounces) shredded cheddar cheese, *divided*

In a bowl, combine soup and milk until smooth. Add the tuna, macaroni, peas, onions and 3/4 cup cheese; mix well.

Pour into a greased 2-qt. microwave-safe dish. Cover and refrigerate overnight. Microwave, covered, on high for 10-12 minutes or until bubbly. Uncover and sprinkle with remaining cheese; let stand for 5 minutes or until melted.

YIELD: 4 SERVINGS.

shirley glaab
HATTIESBURG, MISSISSIPPI

This may be the easiest tuna macaroni casserole ever! I prepare it the night before, and then just pop it in the microwave. There's no need to precook the macaroni, so there's really no fuss.

SPANISH CORN WITH FISH STICKS

PREP 20 minutes | **BAKE** 40 minutes

- 1/4 cup chopped onion
- 1/4 cup chopped green pepper
- 1/4 cup butter, cubed
- 1/4 cup all-purpose flour
- 1-1/2 teaspoons salt
- 1/4 teaspoon pepper
- 2 teaspoons sugar
- 2 cans (14-1/2 ounces *each*) stewed tomatoes
- 2 packages (10 ounces *each*) frozen corn, partially thawed
- 2 packages (12 ounces *each*) frozen fish sticks

In a large skillet, saute the onion and green pepper in butter until tender. Stir in the flour, salt, pepper and sugar until blended. Add tomatoes; bring to a boil. Cook and stir for 2 minutes or until thickened. Reduce heat; simmer, uncovered, for 3-5 minutes or until heated through, stirring occasionally. Stir in the corn.

Transfer to two greased 11-in. x 7-in. baking dishes. Cover and bake at 350° for 25 minutes. Uncover; arrange the fish sticks over top. Bake 15 minutes longer or until fish sticks are heated through.

YIELD: 8-10 SERVINGS.

roberta nelson
PORTLAND, OREGON

This yummy casserole is a family favorite and is my old standby for social functions. It's easy to assemble and economical, too.

FLOUNDER FLORENTINE

PREP 20 minutes | **BAKE** 20 minutes

debbie verbeck
FLORENCE, NEW JERSEY

I discovered this recipe several years ago when I was looking for a way to dress up fish fillets. Even though we're not big seafood fans, we enjoy this dish. It's tasty, healthful and inexpensive.

- 2 packages (10 ounces *each*) frozen chopped spinach, thawed and drained
- 1 pound flounder fillets
- 3 tablespoons chopped onion
- 2 tablespoons butter
- 3 tablespoons all-purpose flour
- 1/4 teaspoon salt
- 1/4 teaspoon pepper
- 1/8 teaspoon ground nutmeg
- 1-1/2 cups fat-free milk
- 1 tablespoon grated Parmesan cheese
- 1/4 teaspoon paprika

Sprinkle spinach in a 13-in. x 9-in. baking dish coated with cooking spray. Top with the fillets.

In a large saucepan, saute the onion in butter until tender. Stir in the flour, salt, pepper and ground nutmeg until blended. Gradually add milk. Bring to a boil; cook and stir for 2 minutes or until thickened.

Pour over fillets; sprinkle with Parmesan cheese and paprika. Bake, uncovered, at 350° for 20 minutes or until the fish flakes easily with a fork.

YIELD: 4 SERVINGS.

NUTRITION FACTS: 1 serving equals 253 calories, 8 g fat (4 g saturated fat), 73 mg cholesterol, 480 mg sodium, 16 g carbohydrate, 5 g fiber, 30 g protein. **DIABETIC EXCHANGES:** 3 lean meat, 2 vegetable, 1/2 fat-free milk.

CRAB 'N' PENNE CASSEROLE

PREP 20 minutes | **BAKE** 40 minutes

bernadette bennett
WACO, TEXAS

Purchased Alfredo sauce lends creaminess to my crab casserole while red pepper flakes kick up the taste. Summer squash and zucchini bring garden-fresh goodness to the comforting main dish.

- 1-1/2 cups uncooked penne pasta
- 1 jar (17 ounces) Alfredo sauce
- 1-1/2 cups imitation crabmeat, chopped
- 1 medium yellow summer squash, sliced
- 1 medium zucchini, sliced
- 1 tablespoon dried parsley flakes
- 1/8 to 1/4 teaspoon crushed red pepper flakes
- 1-1/2 cups (6 ounces) shredded part-skim mozzarella cheese
- 2 tablespoons dry bread crumbs
- 2 teaspoons butter, melted

Cook the pasta according to the package directions. Meanwhile, in a large bowl, combine Alfredo sauce, crab, yellow squash, zucchini, parsley and pepper flakes. Drain pasta; add to sauce mixture and toss to coat.

Transfer to a greased 13-in. x 9-in. baking dish. Sprinkle with cheese. Cover and bake at 325° for 35 minutes.

Toss bread crumbs and butter; sprinkle over casserole. Bake, uncovered, 5-6 minutes longer or until browned.

YIELD: 6 SERVINGS.

SEAFOOD CASSEROLE

PREP 20 minutes | **BAKE** 40 minutes

nancy billups
PRINCETON, IOWA

A family favorite, this rice casserole is stuffed with plenty of seafood and veggies. It's hearty, homey and so easy to make!

1 package (6 ounces) long grain and wild rice

1 pound frozen crabmeat, thawed *or* 2-1/2 cups canned lump crabmeat, drained

1 pound cooked medium shrimp, peeled, deveined and cut into 1/2-inch pieces

2 celery ribs, chopped

1 medium onion, finely chopped

1/2 cup finely chopped green pepper

1 can (4 ounces) mushroom stems and pieces, drained

1 jar (2 ounces) diced pimientos, drained

1 cup mayonnaise

1 cup milk

1/2 teaspoon pepper

Dash Worcestershire sauce

1/4 cup dry bread crumbs

Cook the rice according to the package directions. Meanwhile, in a large bowl, combine the crab, shrimp, celery, onion, green pepper, mushrooms and pimientos.

In a small bowl, whisk the mayonnaise, milk, pepper and Worcestershire sauce; stir into the seafood mixture. Stir in rice.

Transfer to a greased 13-in. x 9-in. baking dish. Sprinkle with bread crumbs. Bake, uncovered, at 375° for 40-50 minutes or until bubbly.

YIELD: 6 SERVINGS.

EDITOR'S NOTE: Reduced-fat or fat-free mayonnaise is not recommended for this recipe.

meatless

TORTELLINI SPINACH CASSEROLE • PAGE 138

SOUTHWEST VEGETARIAN BAKE

PREP 40 minutes | **BAKE** 35 minutes + standing

patricia gale
MONTICELLO, ILLINOIS

Creamy and comforting, this hearty Southwestern specialty is perfect for chilly nights.

3/4 cup uncooked brown rice
1-1/2 cups water
1 can (15 ounces) black beans, rinsed and drained
1 can (11 ounces) Mexicorn, drained
1 can (10 ounces) diced tomatoes and green chilies
1 cup salsa
1 cup (8 ounces) reduced-fat sour cream
1 cup (4 ounces) shredded reduced-fat cheddar cheese
1/4 teaspoon pepper
1/2 cup chopped red onion
1 can (2-1/4 ounces) sliced ripe olives, drained
1 cup (4 ounces) shredded reduced-fat Mexican cheese blend

In a large saucepan, bring rice and water to a boil. Reduce heat; cover and simmer for 35-40 minutes or until tender.

In a large bowl, combine the beans, Mexicorn, tomatoes, salsa, sour cream, cheddar cheese, pepper and rice. Transfer to a shallow 2-1/2-qt. baking dish coated with cooking spray. Sprinkle with onion and olives.

Bake, uncovered, at 350° for 30 minutes. Sprinkle with Mexican cheese. Bake 5-10 minutes longer or until heated through and cheese is melted. Let stand for 10 minutes before serving.

YIELD: 8 SERVINGS.

NUTRITION FACTS: 1 cup equals 284 calories, 10 g fat (6 g saturated fat), 30 mg cholesterol, 879 mg sodium, 35 g carbohydrate, 6 g fiber, 15 g protein. **DIABETIC EXCHANGES:** 2 starch, 2 vegetable, 1 very lean meat, 1 fat.

MEATLESS STUFFED CABBAGE

PREP 45 minutes | **BAKE** 40 minutes

1/2 cup uncooked brown rice
1 cup water
1 medium head cabbage
1 package (12 ounces) frozen vegetarian meat crumbles, thawed
1 large onion, chopped
1/2 teaspoon pepper
1 can (10-3/4 ounces) reduced-sodium condensed tomato soup, undiluted, *divided*
1 can (8 ounces) Italian tomato sauce, *divided*
1 can (14-1/2 ounces) Italian diced tomatoes, undrained

In a small saucepan, bring rice and water to a boil. Reduce heat; cover and simmer for 25-30 minutes or until tender. Meanwhile, cook cabbage in boiling water just until leaves fall off head. Set aside 12 large leaves for rolls (refrigerate the remaining cabbage for another use).

In a large bowl, combine the meat crumbles, onion, pepper, cooked rice and half of the soup. Cut out the thick vein from the bottom of each reserved leaf, making a V-shaped cut. Place 1/3 cup rice mixture on each cabbage leaf; overlap cut ends. Fold in sides, beginning from the cut end. Roll up completely to enclose filling.

Spread half of the tomato sauce into a 13-in. x 9-in. baking dish coated with cooking spray. Place rolls seam side down in dish.

Combine the tomatoes with the remaining soup and tomato sauce; pour over rolls. Cover and bake at 350° for 40-45 minutes or until bubbly and cabbage is tender.

YIELD: 6 SERVINGS.

NUTRITION FACTS: 2 cabbage rolls equals 232 calories, 3 g fat (trace saturated fat), trace cholesterol, 1,000 mg sodium, 37 g carbohydrate, 7 g fiber, 15 g protein. **DIABETIC EXCHANGES:** 2 starch, 1 lean meat, 1 vegetable.

linda evancoe-coble
LEOLA, PENNSYLVANIA

These stuffed cabbage bundles make a delicious alternative for the real thing, especially during meatless holidays. They're also a good source of fiber.

about BROCCOLI

The word "broccoli" comes from the Latin word "brachium," which means branch or arm. When purchasing broccoli, look for bunches that have a deep green color, tightly closed buds and crisp leaves. Store in a resealable plastic bag in the refrigerator for up to 4 days. Wash just before using. One pound of broccoli yields about 2 cups florets.

BROCCOLI CHEDDAR CASSEROLE

PREP 15 minutes | **BAKE** 45 minutes + standing

8 cups chopped fresh broccoli
1 cup finely chopped onion
3/4 cup butter, cubed
12 eggs
2 cups heavy whipping cream
2 cups (8 ounces) shredded cheddar cheese, *divided*
2 teaspoons salt
1 teaspoon pepper

In a skillet over medium heat, saute broccoli and onion in butter until crisp-tender; set aside. In a bowl, beat eggs. Add cream and 1-3/4 cups of cheese; mix well. Stir in the broccoli mixture, salt and pepper. Pour into a greased 3-qt. baking dish; set in a large pan filled with 1 in. of hot water.

Bake, uncovered, at 350° for 45-50 minutes or until a knife inserted near the center comes out clean. Sprinkle with the remaining cheddar cheese. Let stand for 10 minutes before serving.

YIELD: 12-16 SERVINGS.

carol strickland
YUMA, ARIZONA

We're lucky to have fresh fruits and vegetables year-round. I put bountiful Arizona broccoli to great use in this rich side dish. Even those who don't care for broccoli finish off big helpings.

⏲ ZESTY RICE 'N' BEAN CASSEROLE

PREP 35 minutes | **BAKE** 15 minutes

- 2 medium green peppers, chopped
- 1-1/2 cups sliced fresh mushrooms
- 1 medium onion, chopped
- 2 garlic cloves, minced
- 1/2 cup water
- 1 teaspoon canola oil
- 1 can (28 ounces) diced tomatoes, undrained
- 1 can (16 ounces) kidney beans, rinsed and drained
- 3/4 cup uncooked long grain rice
- 2 teaspoons ground cumin
- 1 teaspoon chili powder
- 1/4 teaspoon cayenne pepper
- 1 cup (4 ounces) shredded part-skim mozzarella cheese, *divided*

In a large nonstick skillet, saute the green peppers, mushrooms, onion and garlic in water and oil until onion is tender. Add the tomatoes, beans, rice and seasonings; bring to a boil. Reduce heat; cover and simmer for 25 minutes or until rice is tender and most of the liquid is absorbed. Remove from the heat; stir in 1/2 cup cheese.

Transfer to a 2-1/2-qt. baking dish coated with cooking spray. Sprinkle with the remaining cheese; bake, uncovered, at 350° for 15-20 minutes or until cheese is melted. **YIELD:** 8 SERVINGS.

NUTRITION FACTS: 1 cup equals 195 calories, 7 g fat (2 g saturated fat), 8 mg cholesterol, 392 mg sodium, 33 g carbohydrate, 7 g fiber, 10 g protein. **DIABETIC EXCHANGES:** 1-1/2 starch, 1 lean meat, 1 vegetable.

daphne blandford
GANDER, NEWFOUNDLAND AND LABRADOR

A savory mix of seasonings adds zip to this satisfying casserole that's loaded with beans, rice, vegetables and cheese. We enjoy it as a light entree with garlic bread and fresh spinach salad. It also makes a super side dish at potluck gatherings.

MARVELOUS SHELLS 'N' CHEESE

PREP 25 minutes | **BAKE** 30 minutes

- 1 package (16 ounces) medium pasta shells
- 1 package (8 ounces) process cheese (Velveeta), cubed
- 1/3 cup milk
- 2 cups (16 ounces) 2% cottage cheese
- 1 can (10-3/4 ounces) condensed cream of onion soup, undiluted
- 3 cups (12 ounces) shredded Mexican cheese blend
- 2/3 cup dry bread crumbs
- 1/4 cup butter, melted

Cook the pasta according to the package directions. Meanwhile, in a large saucepan, combine process cheese and milk; cook and stir over low heat until melted. Remove from the heat. Stir in the cottage cheese and soup.

Drain pasta and add to cheese sauce; stir until coated. Transfer to a greased 13-in. x 9-in. baking dish. Sprinkle with Mexican cheese blend. Toss bread crumbs with butter; sprinkle over the top.

Bake, uncovered, at 350° for 30-35 minutes or until heated through. **YIELD:** 6 SERVINGS.

lauren versweyveld
DELAVAN, WISCONSIN

This macaroni is so good! I adapted the recipe from one my mother makes, but she agrees that my version is rich and delicious. It's so easy to assemble and always receives rave reviews.

BAKED RIGATONI

PREP 35 minutes | **BAKE** 30 minutes

1 medium onion, chopped
1 small green pepper, diced
2 tablespoons canola oil
1 can (28 ounces) diced tomatoes, drained
1 can (8 ounces) tomato sauce
1 can (6 ounces) tomato paste
3/4 cup water
1 jar (4-1/2 ounces) sliced mushrooms, drained
1/4 cup minced fresh parsley
3 garlic cloves, minced
1 bay leaf
2 teaspoons sugar
1-1/2 teaspoons salt
1 teaspoon oregano
1/4 teaspoon pepper
1 package (16 ounces) rigatoni
2 tablespoons butter
2 eggs, lightly beaten

1 carton (15 ounces) ricotta cheese
1/2 cup grated Parmesan cheese
Additional Parmesan cheese

In a large skillet, saute onion and green pepper in oil until tender. Add tomatoes, sauce, paste, water, mushrooms, parsley, garlic and seasonings. Simmer, uncovered, for 30 minutes. Discard bay leaf.

Meanwhile, cook pasta according to package directions; drain and toss with the butter. In a small bowl, combine the eggs, ricotta and Parmesan cheese. Stir into rigatoni mixture. Transfer to a 3-qt. baking dish; top with tomato mixture.

Bake, uncovered, at 350° for 30-40 minutes or until heated through. Sprinkle with additional Parmesan cheese.

YIELD: 8-10 SERVINGS.

esther perea
VAN NUYS, CALIFORNIA

You can bet the pasta was homemade when my aunt made this dish. You don't have to make your own pasta, of course, especially if you want the preparation to go a lot quicker. The recipe calls for rigatoni, but you can substitute just about any pasta, especially mostaccioli. What I remember most from those afternoons at my aunt's house is the aroma of this sauce cooking. She'd have it simmering for 8 to 10 hours. It was worth the wait!

TORTELLINI SPINACH CASSEROLE

PREP 20 minutes | **BAKE** 20 minutes

- 2 packages (10 ounces *each*) frozen cheese tortellini
- 1 pound sliced fresh mushrooms
- 1 teaspoon garlic powder
- 1/4 teaspoon onion powder
- 1/4 teaspoon pepper
- 1/2 cup butter, *divided*
- 1 can (12 ounces) evaporated milk
- 1 block (8 ounces) brick cheese, cubed
- 3 packages (10 ounces *each*) frozen chopped spinach, thawed and squeezed dry
- 2 cups (8 ounces) shredded part-skim mozzarella cheese

Cook the tortellini according to package directions. Meanwhile, in a large skillet, saute the mushrooms, garlic powder, onion powder and pepper in 1/4 cup butter until the mushrooms are tender. Remove and keep warm.

In the same skillet, combine milk and remaining butter. Bring to a gentle boil; stir in brick cheese. Cook and stir until smooth. Drain tortellini; place in a large bowl. Stir in the mushroom mixture and spinach. Add cheese sauce and toss to coat.

Transfer to a greased 3-qt. baking dish; sprinkle with mozzarella cheese. Cover and bake at 350° for 15 minutes. Uncover; bake 5-10 minutes longer or until heated through and cheese is melted.
YIELD: 12 SERVINGS.

barbara kellen
ANTIOCH, ILLINOIS

Spinach gives this popular casserole a fresh taste that will delight even those who say they don't like spinach. In fact, people are often surprised at just how good it is! Whenever I bring it to a gathering, it doesn't sit around long.

BROCCOLI PASTA BAKE

PREP 30 minutes | **BAKE** 45 minutes

- 12 ounces uncooked spaghetti
- 8 cups chopped fresh broccoli
- 2 cans (10-3/4 ounces *each*) reduced-fat reduced-sodium condensed cream of mushroom soup, undiluted
- 1/4 cup fat-free milk
- 2 cups sliced fresh mushrooms
- 1 medium onion, finely chopped
- 1 can (8 ounces) whole water chestnuts, drained, halved and thinly sliced
- 1 can (3.8 ounces) sliced ripe olives, drained
- 1 teaspoon salt
- 1/2 teaspoon pepper
- 2 cups (8 ounces) shredded reduced-fat cheddar cheese, *divided*
- 1/4 cup sunflower kernels

Boil spaghetti according to the package directions for 7 minutes. Add the broccoli; return to a boil. Cook 2 minutes longer or until spaghetti is tender; drain.

In a large bowl, combine soup and milk. Stir in mushrooms, onion, water chestnuts, olives, salt, pepper and 1 cup cheese. Add spaghetti and broccoli; mix well.

Transfer to a 13-in. x 9-in. baking dish coated with cooking spray (dish will be full). Cover and bake at 350° for 40 minutes. Uncover; sprinkle with the sunflower kernels and remaining cheese. Bake 5-10 minutes longer or until heated through and cheese is melted.

YIELD: 8 SERVINGS.

evelyn peterson
CORVALLIS, MONTANA

I came up with this nutritious recipe in the middle of broccoli season, using ingredients I had on hand. My family loves this light and pleasing casserole.

half-and-half **SUBSTITUTE**

For dishes that are cooked or baked, you may substitute 4-1/2 teaspoons melted butter plus enough whole milk to equal 1 cup. One cup of evaporated milk may also be substituted for each cup of half-and-half cream.

OVER-THE-TOP MAC 'N' CHEESE

PREP 15 minutes | **BAKE** 40 minutes

- 1 package (16 ounces) elbow macaroni
- 2 ounces Muenster cheese, shredded
- 1/2 cup *each* shredded mild cheddar, sharp cheddar and Monterey Jack cheese
- 1/2 cup plus 1 tablespoon butter, *divided*
- 2 cups half-and-half cream
- 2 eggs, lightly beaten
- 1 cup cubed process cheese (Velveeta)
- 1/4 teaspoon seasoned salt
- 1/8 teaspoon pepper

Cook macaroni according to package directions. Meanwhile, in a small bowl, combine the Muenster, mild cheddar, sharp cheddar and Monterey Jack cheeses; set aside.

In a large saucepan, melt 1/2 cup butter over medium heat. Stir in the cream, eggs, process cheese, seasoned salt, pepper and 1-1/2 cups of the cheese mixture. Drain pasta; add to cheese sauce and stir to coat.

Transfer to a greased 2-1/2-qt. baking dish. Sprinkle with the remaining cheese mixture and dot with remaining butter. Bake, uncovered, at 350° for 40-45 minutes or until a thermometer reads 160°.

YIELD: 7 SERVINGS.

connie mcdowell
GREENWOOD, DELAWARE

This delicious dish is the ultimate comfort food. A blend of five cheeses, it makes a beautiful entree or a special side. I served it at our Thanksgiving dinner, and it received rave reviews.

CREAMY MACARONI AND CHEESE

PREP 20 minutes | **BAKE** 35 minutes

2 cups uncooked elbow macaroni
1/2 cup butter, cubed
1/2 cup all-purpose flour
1-1/2 cups milk
1 cup (8 ounces) sour cream
8 ounces process cheese (Velveeta), cubed
1/4 cup grated Parmesan cheese
1/2 teaspoon salt
1/2 teaspoon ground mustard
1/2 teaspoon pepper
2 cups (8 ounces) shredded cheddar cheese

Cook the macaroni according to package directions. Meanwhile, in a large saucepan, melt butter. Stir in flour until smooth. Gradually add milk. Bring to a boil; cook and stir for 2 minutes or until thickened.

Reduce heat; stir in the sour cream, process cheese, Parmesan cheese, salt, mustard and pepper until smooth and cheese is melted.

Drain macaroni; toss with cheddar cheese. Transfer to a greased 3-qt. baking dish. Stir in cream sauce.

Bake, uncovered, at 350° for 35-40 minutes or until golden brown and bubbly.
YIELD: 6 SERVINGS.

cindy hartley
CHESAPEAKE, VIRGINIA

This is the ultimate mac-and-cheese! It's creamy, thick and very rich, and it holds wonderful cheddar flavor. Once you taste it, you will be hooked.

BAKED EGGPLANT ITALIANO

PREP 30 minutes | **BAKE** 30 minutes

2 small eggplants, peeled and cut into 1/2-inch slices
3 tablespoons olive oil, *divided*
1 teaspoon garlic powder
1 teaspoon salt, *divided*
1/2 teaspoon pepper, *divided*
2 small tomatoes, finely chopped
1 small onion, finely chopped
1 tablespoon Italian seasoning
2 teaspoons minced garlic
1 package (6 ounces) fresh baby spinach
1 cup reduced-fat ricotta cheese
1 cup (4 ounces) shredded part-skim mozzarella cheese, *divided*
1 egg, lightly beaten
2 cups garden-style pasta sauce

Brush both sides of the eggplant slices with 2 tablespoons oil; sprinkle with garlic powder, 1/2 teaspoon salt and 1/4 teaspoon pepper. Grill, covered, over medium heat or broil 4-6 in. from the heat for 2-3 minutes on each side. Set aside.

In a large skillet, saute the tomatoes, onion, Italian seasoning, garlic, and the remaining salt and pepper in remaining oil. Add spinach; stir until wilted. Combine the ricotta, 1/2 cup mozzarella and egg; stir into tomato mixture.

Arrange the eggplant in a single layer in a 13-in. x 9-in. baking dish coated with cooking spray. Top with tomato mixture and pasta sauce. Sprinkle with remaining mozzarella. Bake, uncovered, at 350° for 30-35 minutes or until bubbly. Let stand for 5 minutes before serving.
YIELD: 6 SERVINGS.

NUTRITION FACTS: 1 serving equals 275 calories, 15 g fat (4 g saturated fat), 60 mg cholesterol, 885 mg sodium, 25 g carbohydrate, 7 g fiber, 13 g protein. **DAIBETIC EXCHANGES:** 2 vegetable, 2 fat, 1 starch, 1 lean meat.

traci chatterton
WINDSOR, NEW YORK

When my husband and I decided that we wanted to lose weight, I created this main dish as a downsized substitute to lasagna. It's fast, easy and cleans up in no time. And it makes a great dinner after a busy day at the office.

🏷 MOSTACCIOLI BAKE

PREP 15 minutes | **BAKE** 40 minutes

- 8 ounces uncooked mostaccioli
- 1 egg
- 1 egg white
- 2 cups (16 ounces) 1% cottage cheese
- 1 package (10 ounces) frozen chopped spinach, thawed and squeezed dry
- 1 cup (4 ounces) shredded part-skim mozzarella cheese, *divided*
- 2/3 cup shredded Parmesan cheese, *divided*
- 1/3 cup minced fresh parsley
- 1/4 teaspoon salt
- 1/4 teaspoon pepper
- 2-1/2 cups meatless spaghetti sauce, *divided*

Cook pasta according to package directions. Meanwhile, in a large bowl, combine the egg, egg white, cottage cheese, spinach, 2/3 cup mozzarella, 1/3 cup Parmesan, parsley, salt and pepper; set aside. Drain pasta; stir in 2 cups spaghetti sauce.

Layer half of the pasta mixture in a greased 11-in. x 7-in. baking dish coated with cooking spray. Top with spinach mixture, remaining pasta mixture and the remaining spaghetti sauce.

Cover and bake at 350° for 35-40 minutes or until bubbly. Uncover; sprinkle with remaining mozzarella and Parmesan cheeses. Bake 5 minutes longer or until cheese is melted.

YIELD: 8 SERVINGS.

NUTRITION FACTS: 1 serving equals 286 calories, 7 g fat (4 g saturated fat), 42 mg cholesterol, 837 mg sodium, 35 g carbohydrate, 4 g fiber, 21 g protein. **DIABETIC EXCHANGES:** 2 lean meat, 2 vegetable, 1-1/2 starch.

dorothy bateman
CARVER, MASSACHUSETTS

This homey lasagna–style casserole will appeal to the whole family. There's plenty of spaghetti sauce to keep the layers of tender pasta and spinach–cheese mixture moist.

extra **PASTA**

When you make more pasta than you can eat, freeze the leftovers. It's simple to put the frozen pasta in boiling water for just a few minutes to heat through.

VEGETARIAN ENCHILADA BAKE

PREP 20 minutes | **BAKE** 20 minutes

1 cup shredded zucchini
1 tablespoon finely chopped sweet red pepper
1 garlic clove, minced
1 teaspoon olive oil
3/4 cup frozen corn
3/4 cup black beans, rinsed and drained
1/8 teaspoon salt
1/8 teaspoon ground cumin
3/4 cup salsa
2 tablespoons minced fresh cilantro
3 corn tortillas (6 inches)
3/4 cup shredded cheddar cheese
Sour cream, optional

In a large skillet, saute the zucchini, pepper and garlic in oil until the pepper is crisp-tender. Add the corn, beans, salt and cumin; saute 2-3 minutes longer. Stir in salsa and cilantro.

Place a tortilla in the bottom of a 1-1/2-qt. round baking dish coated with cooking spray. Spread with 2/3 cup vegetable mixture; sprinkle with 1/4 cup cheese. Repeat layers twice.

Bake, uncovered, at 350° for 20-25 minutes or until heated through and cheese is melted. Let stand for 10 minutes before serving. Serve with sour cream if desired.
YIELD: 3 SERVINGS.

NUTRITION FACTS: 1 piece (calculated without sour cream) equals 286 calories, 11 g fat (6 g saturated fat), 30 mg cholesterol, 676 mg sodium, 37 g carbohydrate, 5 g fiber, 12 g protein. **DIABETIC EXCHANGES:** 2 starch, 2 fat, 1 lean meat.

barbara stelluto
DEVON, PENNSYLVANIA

I've had this economical vegetarian recipe for years. You'll enjoy the zippy Tex-Mex flavors, and you won't even miss the meat.

EGGPLANT PARMIGIANA

PREP 2 hours | **BAKE** 35 minutes

- 2 medium eggplant, peeled and cut into 1/2-inch slices
- 2 teaspoons salt
- 2 large onions, chopped
- 2 tablespoons minced fresh basil *or* 2 teaspoons dried basil
- 2 bay leaves
- 1 tablespoon minced fresh oregano *or* 1 teaspoon dried oregano
- 1 tablespoon minced fresh thyme *or* 1 teaspoon dried thyme
- 3 tablespoons olive oil
- 1 can (14-1/2 ounces) diced tomatoes, undrained
- 1 can (12 ounces) tomato paste
- 1 tablespoon honey
- 1-1/2 teaspoons lemon-pepper seasoning
- 4 garlic cloves, minced
- 2 eggs, lightly beaten
- 1/2 teaspoon pepper
- 1-1/2 cups dry bread crumbs
- 1/4 cup butter, *divided*
- 8 cups (32 ounces) shredded part-skim mozzarella cheese
- 1 cup grated Parmesan cheese

Place eggplant in a colander; sprinkle with salt. Let stand for 30 minutes. Meanwhile, in a large skillet, saute the onions, basil, bay leaves, oregano and thyme in oil until onions are tender.

Add the tomatoes, tomato paste, honey and lemon-pepper. Bring to a boil. Reduce heat; cover and simmer for 30 minutes. Add the garlic; simmer 10 minutes longer. Discard bay leaves.

Rinse eggplant slices; pat dry with paper towels. In a shallow bowl, combine eggs and pepper; place bread crumbs in another shallow bowl. Dip eggplant into eggs, then coat with crumbs. Let stand for 5 minutes.

In a large skillet, cook half of the eggplant in 2 tablespoons butter for 3 minutes on each side or until lightly browned. Repeat with remaining eggplant and butter.

In each of two greased 11-in. x 7-in. baking dishes, layer half of each of the eggplant, tomato sauce and mozzarella cheese. Repeat layers. Sprinkle with the Parmesan. Bake, uncovered, at 375° for 35 minutes or until bubbly.

YIELD: 10-12 SERVINGS.

valerie belley
ST. LOUIS, MISSOURI

This delicious eggplant casserole recipe from my mom makes a wonderful veggie meal. It's a resourceful way to use up the eggplant in your garden, and the homemade marinara sauce tastes so good.

SPAGHETTI CASSEROLE

PREP 20 minutes | **BAKE** 40 minutes

- 6 ounces uncooked spaghetti
- 1 tablespoon butter
- 1/3 cup shredded Parmesan cheese
- 1 jar (26 ounces) meatless spaghetti sauce
- 2 cups chopped green pepper
- 1 can (14-1/2 ounces) diced tomatoes, drained
- 1 carton (8 ounces) part-skim ricotta cheese
- 1 can (8 ounces) mushroom stems and pieces, drained
- 1 small onion, chopped
- 3 garlic cloves, minced
- 12 fresh basil leaves, thinly sliced
- 1/2 teaspoon dried oregano
- 3 cups (12 ounces) shredded part-skim mozzarella cheese, *divided*

Cook the spaghetti according to package directions; drain. Add butter and Parmesan cheese; toss to coat. In a large bowl, combine spaghetti sauce, green pepper and tomatoes.

In a blender, cover and process ricotta cheese until pureed. Add to spaghetti sauce mixture. Stir in mushrooms, onion, garlic, basil, oregano and 1-1/2 cups mozzarella cheese. Add the spaghetti; toss to coat.

Transfer to a 13-in. x 9-in. baking dish coated with cooking spray. Sprinkle with remaining mozzarella. Cover; bake at 350° for 40-45 minutes or until heated through.

YIELD: 9 SERVINGS.

NUTRITION FACTS: 1-1/2 cups equals 301 calories, 12 g fat (7 g saturated fat), 41 mg cholesterol, 774 mg sodium, 31 g carbohydrate, 4 g fiber, 18 g protein. **DIABETIC EXCHANGES:** 2 starch, 2 fat, 1 lean meat.

kathy bence
EDMONDS, WASHINGTON

I always get asked for a copy of this family-pleasing recipe. The hearty meatless main dish, which is a combination of spaghetti and lasagna ingredients, is cheesy and well seasoned with a creamy tomato sauce.

CHEESY ZUCCHINI BAKE

PREP 35 minutes | **BAKE** 25 minutes

4-1/2 cups sliced zucchini
    2 to 3 tablespoons olive oil
Salt and pepper to taste
    1 large onion, chopped
    2 tablespoons minced garlic
    1 can (10-3/4 ounces) tomato puree
    1 can (6 ounces) tomato paste
    3 tablespoons sugar
    1 teaspoon Italian seasoning
    1 teaspoon dried basil
    2 cans (2-1/4 ounces *each*) sliced ripe olives, drained
    3 cups (12 ounces) shredded part-skim mozzarella cheese
    6 eggs, lightly beaten
1-1/2 cups grated Parmesan cheese

In a large skillet, saute the zucchini in oil until tender. Sprinkle with salt and pepper; stir. Transfer to an ungreased 13-in. x 9-in. baking dish.

In the same skillet, saute onion until crisp-tender. Add garlic; saute 3 minutes longer. Stir in tomato puree, tomato paste, sugar, Italian seasoning and basil. Bring to a boil. Reduce heat; simmer, uncovered, for 10-15 minutes or until slightly thickened. Stir in olives. Pour over zucchini. Sprinkle with mozzarella.

Combine the eggs and Parmesan cheese; pour over zucchini. Bake, uncovered, at 375° for 25-30 minutes or until a knife inserted near the center comes out clean. Let stand for 15 minutes before serving.
YIELD: 12-16 SERVINGS.

sue stanton
LINVILLE, NORTH CAROLINA

Ever since a friend shared this classic hot dish with me, I actually look forward to our annual bounty of zucchini. This cheesy veggie bake makes a pretty entree or brunch item. I keep the recipe handy because I know I will get requests!

POLENTA CHILI CASSEROLE

PREP 20 minutes | **BAKE** 35 minutes + standing

1-1/4 cups yellow cornmeal
  1/2 teaspoon salt
    4 cups boiling water
    2 cups (8 ounces) shredded cheddar cheese, *divided*
    3 cans (15 ounces *each*) vegetarian chili with beans
    1 package (16 ounces) frozen mixed vegetables, thawed and well drained

In a large saucepan, combine cornmeal and salt. Gradually whisk in boiling water. Cook and stir over medium heat for 5 minutes or until thickened. Remove from the heat. Stir in 1/4 cup cheddar cheese until melted.

Spread into a 13-in. x 9-in. baking dish coated with cooking spray. Bake, uncovered, at 350° for 20 minutes. Meanwhile, heat chili according to package directions.

Spread vegetables over polenta; top with chili. Sprinkle with the remaining cheese. Bake 12-15 minutes longer or until the cheese is melted. Let stand for 10 minutes before serving.
YIELD: 8 SERVINGS.

dan kelmenson
WEST BLOOMFIELD, MICHIGAN

I created this delicious vegetarian bean and polenta bake that combines spicy chili, mixed veggies and homemade polenta. It's a warm and comfy casserole that is sure to please everyone, whether they're a vegetarian or not.

VEGETARIAN TORTILLA STACK

PREP 25 minutes | **BAKE** 35 minutes

1 medium green pepper, chopped
1 medium sweet red pepper, chopped
1 small onion, chopped
2 teaspoons olive oil
1 package (12 ounces) frozen vegetarian meat crumbles, thawed
2 tablespoons minced fresh cilantro
1 teaspoon ground cumin
1-1/2 cups salsa
5 flour tortillas (8 inches)
1-1/4 cups shredded reduced-fat Mexican cheese blend, *divided*
1/3 cup pickled jalapeno slices
5 tablespoons sliced ripe olives

In a large nonstick skillet coated with cooking spray, saute the peppers and onion in oil until tender. Stir in the meat crumbles, cilantro and cumin; heat through.

Spread 1/4 cup salsa into a 9-in. deep-dish pie plate coated with cooking spray. Layer with one tortilla, a fourth of the meat crumble mixture, 1/4 cup salsa, 1/4 cup cheese, 2-3 jalapeno slices and 1 tablespoon olives. Repeat layers three times. Top with remaining tortilla, salsa, jalapeno slices and olives.

Cover and bake at 350° for 30 minutes. Uncover; sprinkle with remaining cheese. Bake 5-10 minutes longer or until heated through and cheese is melted.

YIELD: 6 SERVINGS.

wendy fenstermacher
ALLENTOWN, PENNSYLVANIA

Nearly all the meals I make are meatless. This is one of my husband's favorites. If you like, you could vary the amount of jalapeno slices—or leave them out altogether. But I wouldn't!

ZIPPY MACARONI AND CHEESE

PREP: 20 minutes | **BAKE** 25 minutes

1-1/3 cups uncooked elbow macaroni
1 cup (8 ounces) 4% cottage cheese
1 cup (4 ounces) shredded part-skim mozzarella cheese
1/2 cup shredded cheddar cheese
1 teaspoon cornstarch
1 cup milk
1 small onion, grated
1/4 cup finely chopped green pepper
1 teaspoon Dijon mustard
1/2 teaspoon salt
1/4 to 1/2 teaspoon crushed red pepper flakes
1/2 cup crushed cornflakes
1 tablespoon butter, melted

Cook macaroni according to package directions; drain. Add the cottage, mozzarella and cheddar cheeses; set aside.

In a large saucepan, combine cornstarch and milk until smooth. Stir in the onion, green pepper, mustard, salt and pepper flakes. Bring to a boil; cook and stir for 2 minutes or until thickened. Pour over macaroni mixture; gently stir to coat.

Transfer to a greased 2-qt. baking dish. Combine cornflakes and butter; sprinkle over the top. Bake, uncovered, at 350° for 25-30 minutes or until bubbly and the top is golden brown.
YIELD: 4 SERVINGS.

glenda schwarz
MORDEN, MANITOBA

When I was asked to teach an advanced 4-H foods class, I included this recipe. The kids love it and have been making it for their families ever since.

CHICKPEA-STUFFED SHELLS

PREP 15 minutes | **BAKE** 30 minutes

- 18 uncooked jumbo pasta shells
- 1 can (15 ounces) garbanzo beans *or* chickpeas, rinsed and drained
- 2 egg whites
- 1 carton (15 ounces) reduced-fat ricotta cheese
- 1/2 cup minced fresh parsley
- 1/3 cup grated Parmesan cheese
- 1 small onion, quartered
- 1 garlic clove, minced
- 1 jar (28 ounces) meatless spaghetti sauce, *divided*
- 1-1/2 cups (6 ounces) shredded part-skim mozzarella cheese

Cook pasta shells according to package directions. Meanwhile, place garbanzo beans and egg whites in a food processor; cover and process until smooth. Add the ricotta, parsley, Parmesan cheese , onion and garlic; cover and process until well blended. Pour 1-1/4 cups of spaghetti sauce into an ungreased 13-in. x 9-in. baking dish; set aside.

Drain pasta shells; stuff with the bean mixture. Place over sauce. Drizzle with remaining sauce. Bake, uncovered, at 350° for 30 minutes. Sprinkle with mozzarella cheese. Bake 5-10 minutes longer or until cheese is melted and sauce is bubbly.
YIELD: 6 SERVINGS.

susan brown
SAUGERTIES, NEW YORK

I never thought my picky eaters would agree to try chickpeas, but they gobble them up when I disguise them this way. This pasta dish receives raves from my husband, kids and dinner guests, too. No one can guess my secret ingredient is the nutritious legumes!

GREEK SPINACH BAKE

PREP 10 minutes | **BAKE** 1 hour

- 2 cups (16 ounces) 4% cottage cheese
- 1 package (10 ounces) frozen chopped spinach, thawed and squeezed dry
- 8 ounces crumbled feta cheese
- 6 tablespoons all-purpose flour
- 1/2 teaspoon pepper
- 1/4 teaspoon salt
- 4 eggs, lightly beaten

In a large bowl, combine the cottage cheese, spinach and feta cheese. Stir in the flour, pepper and salt. Add the eggs and mix well.

Spoon into a greased 9-in. square baking dish. Bake, uncovered, at 350° for 1 hour or until a thermometer reads 160°.
YIELD: 6 SERVINGS.

sharon olney
GALT, CALIFORNIA

"Spanakopita" is the Greek name for this traditional dish featuring spinach and feta cheese. You can serve it as a side dish or a meatless main dish. My dad and I used to fight over the last piece!

THREE CHEESE BAKED PASTA

PREP 30 minutes | **BAKE** 30 minutes

- 2-1/2 cups uncooked elbow macaroni
- 6 tablespoons butter, *divided*
- 1/4 cup all-purpose flour
- 1 teaspoon salt
- 1 teaspoon sugar
- 2 cups milk
- 8 ounces process American cheese (Velveeta), cubed
- 1-1/3 cups 4% cottage cheese
- 2/3 cup sour cream
- 2 cups (8 ounces) shredded sharp cheddar cheese
- 1-1/2 cups soft bread crumbs

Cook the macaroni according to package directions; drain. Place in a greased 2-1/2-qt. baking dish. In a saucepan, melt 4 tablespoons butter. Stir in the flour, salt and sugar until smooth. Gradually stir in milk. Bring to a boil; cook and stir for 2 minutes or until thickened.

Reduce heat; stir in American cheese until melted. Stir in cottage cheese and sour cream. Pour over macaroni. Sprinkle with cheddar cheese. Melt remaining butter and toss with bread crumbs; sprinkle over top. Bake, uncovered, at 350° for 30 minutes or until golden brown.
YIELD: 6-8 SERVINGS.

gwen miller
ROLLING HILLS, ALBERTA

This delicious dish puts a new twist on traditional macaroni and cheese. The three different cheese flavors blend wonderfully. Plus, it's easy to prepare—I plan to make it often when my husband Ken and I start traveling.

SOUTHWESTERN RICE BAKE

PREP 25 minutes | **BAKE** 30 minutes

betty claycomb
ALVERTON, PENNSYLVANIA

We really enjoy this hearty dish. Just add a side salad for a nutritious, complete meal.

1-2/3 cups uncooked long grain rice
3-1/3 cups water
1 large onion, chopped
1 small green pepper, chopped
3 garlic cloves, minced
1 teaspoon olive oil
1 can (15 ounces) garbanzo beans *or* chickpeas, rinsed and drained
1 can (2-1/4 ounces) sliced ripe olives, drained
2 cups (8 ounces) shredded reduced-fat cheddar cheese, *divided*
1 cup reduced-fat ricotta cheese
1/4 cup reduced-fat sour cream
1-1/2 teaspoons chili powder
1 cup salsa

In a large saucepan, bring rice and water to a boil. Reduce heat; cover and simmer for 15-18 minutes or until water is absorbed and rice is tender.

In a large nonstick saucepan, saute the onion, green pepper and garlic in oil until tender. Remove from the heat; stir in the beans, olives and rice. Combine 1-1/2 cups cheddar cheese, ricotta cheese, sour cream and chili powder.

Spoon half of the rice mixture into a 13-in. x 9-in. baking dish coated with cooking spray; layer with half of cheese mixture and salsa. Repeat layers.

Bake, uncovered, at 350° for 25 minutes. Sprinkle with remaining cheddar cheese. Bake 3-5 minutes longer or until heated through and cheese is melted.
YIELD: 8 SERVINGS.

FOUR-CHEESE BAKED ZITI

PREP 20 minutes | **BAKE** 30 minutes

lisa varner
GREENVILLE, SOUTH CAROLINA

This pasta dish, made with Alfredo sauce, is deliciously different from typical tomato-based recipes. Extra cheesy, it goes together quickly and is always popular at potluck suppers.

1 package (16 ounces) ziti *or* small tube pasta
2 cartons (10 ounces *each*) refrigerated Alfredo sauce
1 cup (8 ounces) sour cream
2 eggs, lightly beaten
1 carton (15 ounces) ricotta cheese
1/2 cup grated Parmesan cheese, *divided*
1/4 cup grated Romano cheese
1/4 cup minced fresh parsley
1-3/4 cups shredded part-skim mozzarella cheese

Cook pasta according to package directions; drain and return to the pan. Stir in Alfredo sauce and sour cream. Spoon half into a lightly greased 3-qt. baking dish.

Combine the eggs, ricotta cheese, 1/4 cup Parmesan cheese, Romano cheese and parsley; spread over pasta. Top with the remaining pasta mixture; sprinkle with mozzarella and remaining Parmesan.

Cover and bake at 350° for 25 minutes. Uncover and bake 5-10 minutes longer or until bubbly.
YIELD: 12 SERVINGS.

BLACK BEAN TORTILLA CASSEROLE

PREP 20 minutes | **BAKE** 30 minutes

2 large onions, chopped
1-1/2 cups chopped green peppers
1 can (14-1/2 ounces) diced tomatoes, drained
3/4 cup picante sauce
2 garlic cloves, minced
2 teaspoons ground cumin
2 cans (15 ounces *each*) black beans, rinsed and drained
8 corn tortillas (6 inches)
2 cups (8 ounces) shredded reduced-fat Mexican cheese blend, *divided*

TOPPINGS
1-1/2 cups shredded lettuce
1 cup chopped fresh tomatoes
1/2 cup thinly sliced green onions
1/2 cup sliced ripe olives

In a large saucepan, combine the onions, peppers, tomatoes, picante sauce, garlic and cumin. Bring to a boil. Reduce the heat; simmer, uncovered, for 10 minutes. Stir in the beans.

Spread a third of the bean mixture in a 13-in. x 9-in. baking dish coated with cooking spray. Layer with four tortillas and 2/3 cup cheese. Repeat layers; top with the remaining beans.

Cover and bake at 350° for 30-35 minutes or until heated through. Sprinkle with remaining cheese. Let stand for 5 minutes or until cheese is melted. Serve with toppings.
YIELD: 9 SERVINGS.

NUTRITION FACTS: 1 serving equals 251 calories, 7 g fat (3 g saturated fat), 18 mg cholesterol, 609 mg sodium, 36 g carbohydrate, 8 g fiber, 14 g protein. **DIABETIC EXCHANGES:** 2 lean meat, 1-1/2 starch, 1 vegetable.

sue briski
APPLETON, WISCONSIN

A cousin gave me this recipe—she knows how much my family loves Southwestern fare.

BLACK BEAN CORNMEAL PIE

PREP 30 minutes | **BAKE** 20 minutes

tari ambler
SHOREWOOD, ILLINOIS

This hearty, meatless Southwestern main dish is delicious. If desired, you can vary the beans used. I like to serve it with salsa and reduced-fat sour cream.

- 1 large onion, chopped
- 1 large green pepper, chopped
- 1 teaspoon canola oil
- 1-1/2 teaspoons chili powder
- 1 garlic clove, minced
- 3/4 teaspoon ground cumin
- 1/4 teaspoon pepper
- 1 can (14-1/2 ounces) diced tomatoes, undrained
- 2 cans (15 ounces *each*) black beans, rinsed and drained
- 1 cup frozen corn

TOPPING
- 3/4 cup whole wheat pastry flour
- 3/4 cup yellow cornmeal
- 2 teaspoons sugar
- 2 teaspoons baking powder
- 2 teaspoons chopped seeded jalapeno pepper
- 1/4 teaspoon salt
- 1 egg
- 3/4 cup fat-free milk
- 1 tablespoon canola oil

Salsa and reduced-fat sour cream, optional

In a large skillet, saute onion and green pepper in oil until tender. Add the chili powder, garlic, cumin and pepper; saute 1 minute longer. Add tomatoes and bring to a boil. Reduce heat; cover and simmer for 5 minutes.

Stir in beans and corn; heat through. Transfer to an 11-in. x 7-in. baking dish coated with cooking spray.

For topping, in a small bowl, combine the flour, cornmeal, sugar, baking powder, jalapeno and salt. Whisk the egg, milk and oil; stir into dry ingredients just until moistened. Spoon over filling; gently spread to cover the top.

Bake at 375° for 20-25 minutes or until filling is bubbly and a toothpick inserted into topping comes out clean. Serve with salsa and sour cream if desired.
YIELD: 6 SERVINGS.

EDITOR'S NOTE: When cutting hot peppers, disposable gloves are recommended. Avoid touching your face.

BROCCOLI RICE HOT DISH

PREP 15 minutes | **BAKE** 25 minutes

- 2 cups hot cooked rice
- 3/4 cup shredded reduced-fat cheddar cheese
- 1/2 cup egg substitute
- 3/4 teaspoon garlic salt

FILLING

- 3 cups frozen chopped broccoli, thawed
- 4 ounces chopped fresh mushrooms
- 1/2 cup chopped sweet red pepper
- 1/2 medium onion, chopped
- 1 cup egg substitute
- 1/2 cup fat-free milk
- 1/2 teaspoon onion salt
- 1/2 teaspoon pepper
- 1 cup (4 ounces) shredded reduced-fat cheddar cheese

In a large bowl, combine rice, cheese, egg substitute and garlic salt. Press firmly into a 2-qt. baking dish coated with cooking spray. Bake at 375° for 10 minutes.

Meanwhile, for filling, place the broccoli, mushrooms, red pepper and onion in a steamer basket over 1 in. boiling water in a saucepan. Bring to a boil; cover and steam for 5 minutes or until crisp-tender.

In a large bowl, combine the egg substitute, milk, onion salt and pepper; stir in vegetables. Pour over crust. Sprinkle with cheese. Bake, uncovered, at 375° for 25-30 minutes or until a knife inserted near the center comes out clean.

YIELD: 6 SERVINGS.

NUTRITION FACTS: 1 cup equals 226 calories, 7 g fat (5 g saturated fat), 24 mg cholesterol, 527 mg sodium, 23 g carbohydrate, 2 g fiber, 19 g protein. **DIABETIC EXCANGES:** 2 lean meat, 1 starch, 1 vegetable.

gretchen widner
SUN CITY WEST, ARIZONA

With green broccoli, golden cheese and sweet red peppers, this bountiful bake has plenty of eye appeal...and it makes a tasty and satisfying meatless entree or side dish.

UPSIDE-DOWN MEATLESS PIZZA

PREP 25 minutes | **BAKE** 20 minutes

- 1 small onion, chopped
- 1/4 cup chopped green pepper
- 3 tablespoons canola oil, *divided*
- 2 tablespoons plus 1 cup all-purpose flour, *divided*
- 1/2 teaspoon dried basil
- 1/2 teaspoon fennel seed
- 1 package (10 ounces) frozen chopped spinach, thawed and squeezed dry
- 1 cup sliced fresh mushrooms
- 1 can (15 ounces) tomato sauce
- 2 cups (8 ounces) shredded cheddar cheese
- 2 eggs
- 3/4 cup milk
- 1/2 teaspoon salt
- 2 tablespoons grated Parmesan cheese

In a large skillet, saute the chopped onion and green pepper in 2 tablespoons oil until tender. Stir in 2 tablespoons flour, basil and fennel until blended. Add the spinach, mushrooms and tomato sauce. Bring to a boil; cook and stir sauce for 2 minutes or until thickened.

Pour into a greased 11-in. x 7-in. baking dish. Sprinkle with cheddar cheese.

Place the remaining flour in a large bowl. Beat the eggs, milk, salt and remaining oil until smooth. Stir in Parmesan cheese. Pour over vegetable mixture.

Bake, uncovered, at 425° for 20-25 minutes or until a thermometer reads 160°.

YIELD: 8 SERVINGS.

marie figueroa
WAUWATOSA, WISCONSIN

I experimented with a recipe for upside-down pizza so I could turn it into a veggie dish. It turned out very tasty!

dried **HERBS**

Dried herbs don't spoil, but they do lose flavor and potency over time. For maximum flavor in your cooking, you may want to replace herbs that are over a year old. Store dried herbs in an airtight container and keep away from heat and light. Don't store them above the stove.

breakfast & brunch

CAJUN-STYLE BRUNCH BAKE • PAGE 184

BREAKFAST ENCHILADA BAKE

PREP 15 minutes | **BAKE** 55 minutes

- 2 cups chopped shaved deli ham
- 1/2 cup chopped green onions
- 1/2 cup chopped green pepper
- 1 package (10 ounces) frozen chopped spinach, thawed and squeezed dry
- 1 can (4 ounces) chopped green chilies
- 1-1/4 cups shredded cheddar cheese
- 1-1/4 cups shredded Monterey Jack cheese
- 8 flour tortillas (6 inches)
- 6 eggs
- 2-1/2 cups half-and-half cream
- 2 tablespoons all-purpose flour
- 1/4 teaspoon garlic powder
- 1/4 teaspoon salt
- 2 to 3 drops hot pepper sauce

In a large bowl, combine the first five ingredients. In another bowl, combine the cheeses. Spoon about 1/4 cup of the ham mixture off-center on each tortilla; sprinkle with 2 tablespoons cheese mixture. Fold sides and ends over filling and roll up. Place seam side down in a greased 13-in. x 9-in. baking dish.

In a bowl, whisk the eggs, cream, flour, garlic powder, salt and hot pepper sauce. Pour over tortillas. Sprinkle with remaining ham mixture.

Cover and bake at 350° for 50 minutes. Uncover; sprinkle with remaining cheese mixture. Bake 5-10 minutes longer or until the cheese is melted.
YIELD: 8 SERVINGS.

loree ellis
COLORADO SPRINGS, COLORADO

My sister gave me this fuss–free recipe for a hot, hearty breakfast dish, and I can't tell you how many times I've used it for holiday brunch. I love it because it's full of flavor, fast and filling enough to hold us through Christmas Day.

HAM 'N' EGG CASSEROLE

PREP 15 minutes + chilling | **BAKE** 1 hour

- 1/2 cup chopped green pepper
- 1/2 cup butter, cubed
- 10 slices white bread, cubed
- 2 cups cubed fully cooked ham
- 1/2 pound process American cheese, cubed
- 6 eggs
- 2 cups milk
- 1 teaspoon ground mustard

In a skillet, saute green pepper in butter until tender. Remove green pepper, reserving drippings. Combine green pepper, bread and ham; place in an ungreased 13-in. x 9-in. baking dish. Add cheese to drippings; cook and stir over low heat until the cheese melts. Pour over bread mixture. Beat the eggs, milk and mustard; pour over the cheese.

Cover and refrigerate overnight. Remove from the refrigerator 30 minutes before baking. Bake, uncovered, at 300° for 1 hour.
YIELD: 10-12 SERVINGS.

elizabeth hesse
SPRINGVILLE, NEW YORK

I like to prepare this when I have leftovers of ham and day–old bread on hand. It's a delicious dish for brunch. Besides being so tasty, it's prepared the night before, which allows me more time to complete other dishes for the meal. This dish still tastes good hours after being baked, so it's also a favorite to take along for various potluck gatherings.

SAUSAGE-POTATO BAKE

PREP 20 minutes | **BAKE** 55 minutes + standing

ruth rigoni
HURLEY, WISCONSIN

1/2 pound bulk pork sausage
  3 large potatoes, peeled and thinly sliced
1/2 teaspoon salt
1/4 teaspoon pepper
  1 jar (2 ounces) diced pimientos, drained
  3 eggs
  1 cup milk
  2 tablespoons minced chives
3/4 teaspoon dried thyme *or* oregano
Additional minced chives, optional

I not only make this dish for breakfast, but sometimes for a main meal. It's very good. You can substitute finely diced lean ham or crumbled turkey bacon for the sausage for a change of pace.

In a large skillet, cook the sausage over medium heat until no longer pink; drain.

Arrange half of the potatoes in a greased 8-in. square baking dish; sprinkle with salt, pepper and half of the sausage. Top with the remaining potatoes and sausage; sprinkle with pimientos. In a bowl, whisk the eggs, milk, chives and thyme; pour over the top.

Cover and bake at 375° for 45-50 minutes or until potatoes are tender. Uncover; bake 10 minutes longer or until lightly browned. Let stand for 10 minutes before cutting. Sprinkle with additional chives if desired.
YIELD: 6 SERVINGS.

OVERNIGHT STUFFED FRENCH TOAST

PREP 20 minutes + chilling | **BAKE** 45 minutes

bren childress
BROKEN ARROW, OKLAHOMA

This brunch dish is so rich that no one will suspect each generous serving is low in fat. I don't like to cook a lot in the morning, so this make-ahead dish is perfect for us.

20	slices French bread (1 inch thick)
1	package (8 ounces) fat-free cream cheese
3	cups egg substitute
2	cups fat-free milk
1/3	cup plus 1-3/4 cups sugar-free maple-flavored syrup, *divided*
1	teaspoon vanilla extract
1/4	teaspoon ground cinnamon
2-1/2	cups sliced fresh strawberries

Arrange 10 slices of bread in a 13-in. x 9-in. baking dish coated with cooking spray. Spread each slice with cream cheese. Top with remaining bread. In a large bowl, whisk the egg substitute, milk, 1/3 cup syrup, vanilla and cinnamon; pour over bread. Cover and refrigerate overnight.

Remove from the refrigerator 30 minutes before baking. Bake, uncovered, at 350° for 45-50 minutes or until top is lightly browned and a thermometer reads at least 160°. Serve with strawberries and remaining syrup.

YIELD: 10 SERVINGS.

ASPARAGUS STRATA

PREP 20 minutes + chilling | **BAKE** 55 minutes + standing

12 slices white bread
12 ounces sharp process cheese, diced
1-1/2 pounds fresh asparagus, trimmed
2 cups diced cooked ham
6 eggs
3 cups milk
2 tablespoons finely chopped onion
1/2 teaspoon salt
1/4 teaspoon ground mustard

Using a doughnut cutter, cut 12 circles and holes from bread; set aside. Tear the remaining bread in pieces and place in a greased 13-in. x 9-in. baking dish.

Layer with cheese, asparagus and ham; arrange bread circles and holes on top. Lightly beat eggs with milk. Add onion, salt and mustard; mix well. Pour egg mixture over bread circles and holes. Cover and refrigerate at least 6 hours or overnight.

Bake, uncovered, at 325° for 55 minutes or until top is light golden brown. Let stand for 10 minutes before serving.

YIELD: 6-8 SERVINGS.

ethel pressel
NEW OXFORD, PENNSYLVANIA

You can easily prepare this the night before for a luncheon or during the morning for a dinner. I serve it year-round for large groups, like my card club, garden club, picnics and at other occasions. When I do, someone always requests the recipe!

BLUEBERRY BLINTZ SOUFFLE

PREP 10 minutes | **BAKE** 65 minutes

3 tablespoons butter, melted
2 packages (13 ounces *each*) frozen blueberry blintzes
4 eggs, lightly beaten
1-1/2 cups (12 ounces) sour cream
1/4 cup sugar
1 tablespoon orange juice
1 teaspoon vanilla extract
Confectioners' sugar, optional

Place butter in a 13-in. x 9-in. baking dish. Top with blintzes. In a bowl, combine the eggs, sour cream, sugar, orange juice and vanilla. Pour over blintzes.

Cover and bake at 350° for 55 minutes. Uncover; bake 10-15 minutes longer or until lightly browned and a knife inserted in the egg mixture comes out clean. Sprinkle with confectioners' sugar if desired.

YIELD: 6 SERVINGS.

iris katz
POMPANO BEACH, FLORIDA

Store-bought blintzes speed up the preparation of this rich blueberry souffle. This wonderful brunch entree tastes great with just about any breakfast meat served alongside.

CHILI RELLENO MINI CASSEROLES

PREP 15 minutes | **BAKE** 25 minutes

4 flour tortillas (8 inches)
4-1/2 teaspoons butter, melted
2 cups (8 ounces) shredded Monterey Jack cheese
1 tablespoon all-purpose flour
1/4 teaspoon salt
1/4 teaspoon pepper
6 eggs, lightly beaten
1 can (4 ounces) chopped green chilies
1 garlic clove, minced
1 tablespoon finely chopped onion
Salsa

Brush both sides of tortillas with butter. Place each tortilla in an individual oven-proof 10-oz. custard cup or casserole, pressing down in center to form a shell.

In a bowl, combine the cheese, flour, salt and pepper; set half aside. To the other half, add the eggs, chilies, garlic and onion; pour into tortilla shells. Top with the reserved cheese mixture.

Bake, uncovered, at 325° for 25 minutes or until eggs are set. Let stand for 5 minutes before serving. Serve with salsa.

YIELD: 4 SERVINGS.

mary jo amos
NOEL, MISSOURI

This recipe came about by accident 20 years ago. My sons had begged me to hurry up with breakfast so that we could play a game of catch. I whipped this up, spent time with my sons and then we all enjoyed our own spicy, fun casserole.

TEX-MEX EGGS

PREP 15 minutes + chilling | **BAKE** 50 minutes

- 10 slices English muffin toasting bread, cut into 1-inch cubes
- 3/4 pound bulk pork sausage
- 1 medium onion, chopped
- 1 can (4 ounces) chopped green chilies
- 2 cups (8 ounces) shredded Monterey Jack cheese
- 4 ounces process American cheese, cubed
- 5 eggs
- 2 cups milk
- 1 cup salsa

Place half of the bread cubes in a greased 13-in. x 9-in. baking dish; set remaining bread aside. In a skillet over medium heat, cook sausage and onion until meat is no longer pink and onion is tender; drain. Stir in chilies.

Spoon half of the sausage mixture over bread; top with half of each cheese. Repeat layers of bread sausage mixture and cheeses.

In a bowl, lightly beat eggs. Stir in milk and salsa. Pour over the cheeses; cover and refrigerate 8 hours or overnight. Remove from refrigerator 1 hour before baking.

Bake, uncovered, at 325° for 50-55 minutes or until a knife inserted in the center comes out clean. Let stand for 5 minutes before cutting.
YIELD: 6-8 SERVINGS.

mary ellen abel
WELCOME, MINNESOTA

Every biteful of this egg dish is loaded with crusty bread, hearty sausage, rich cheeses and outstanding flavor! Whenever I make this, the men ask for seconds and the women ask for the recipe.

CINNAMON RAISIN STRATA

PREP 20 minutes + chilling | **BAKE** 40 minutes

- 1/4 cup butter, softened
- 3 tablespoons ground cinnamon
- 8 slices day-old raisin bread
- 4 tablespoons brown sugar, *divided*
- 6 eggs
- 1-1/2 cups milk
- 3 tablespoons maple syrup
- 1 teaspoon vanilla extract

Additional maple syrup

In a small bowl, combine the butter and cinnamon; spread over one side of each slice of bread. Place four slices, buttered side up, in a greased 8-in. square baking dish (trim to fit if necessary). Sprinkle with 2 tablespoons brown sugar. Repeat with the remaining bread and brown sugar.

In a large bowl, whisk the eggs, milk, syrup and vanilla; pour over bread. Cover and refrigerate overnight.

Remove from the refrigerator 30 minutes before baking. Bake, uncovered, at 350° for 40-50 minutes or until golden and puffed. Serve with additional syrup.
YIELD: 4 SERVINGS.

barbara tritch
HOPE, IDAHO

This delightful dish, made with day-old raisin bread, is full of cinnamon flavor. I like to serve it for brunch with sliced bacon and a fruit compote.

BROCCOLI-TURKEY BRUNCH CASSEROLE

PREP 20 minutes | **BAKE** 45 minutes

1-1/2 cups fat-free milk

1 can (10-3/4 ounces) reduced-fat reduced-sodium condensed cream of chicken soup, undiluted

1 carton (8 ounces) egg substitute

1/4 cup reduced-fat sour cream

1/2 teaspoon pepper

1/4 teaspoon poultry seasoning

1/8 teaspoon salt

2-1/2 cups cubed cooked turkey breast

1 package (16 ounces) frozen chopped broccoli, thawed and drained

2 cups seasoned stuffing cubes

1 cup (4 ounces) shredded reduced-fat cheddar cheese, *divided*

In a large bowl, combine the milk, soup, egg substitute, sour cream, pepper, poultry seasoning and salt. Stir in the turkey, broccoli, stuffing cubes and 3/4 cup cheese. Transfer to a 13-in. x 9-in. baking dish coated with cooking spray.

Bake, uncovered, at 350° for 40 minutes. Sprinkle with remaining cheese. Bake 5-10 minutes longer or until a knife inserted near the center comes out clean. Let stand for 5 minutes before serving.

YIELD: 6 SERVINGS.

NUTRITION FACTS: 1 serving equals 303 calories, 7 g fat (4 g saturated fat), 72 mg cholesterol, 762 mg sodium, 26 g carbohydrate, 3 g fiber, 33 g protein. **DIABETIC EXCHANGES:** 3 very lean meat, 1-1/2 starch, 1 vegetable, 1 fat.

kellie mulleavy
LAMBERTVILLE, MICHIGAN

I have a lot of company at Thanksgiving, and I enjoy making new things for them. I came up with this recipe as a way to use up leftover turkey. Don't have any turkey leftovers? That's okay, cooked chicken works well, too!

DELUXE BREAKFAST BAKE

PREP 15 minutes + chilling | BAKE 65 minutes + standing

lavonne hegland
ST. MICHAEL, MINNESOTA

My husband and three sons love this rich and creamy egg bake because it is so filling. I like it because it's so versatile, (you can alter the ingredients) and you can prepare it ahead of time.

1	package (6 ounces) onion and garlic salad croutons
2	cups (8 ounces) shredded cheddar cheese
1-1/2	cups cubed fully cooked ham
4	eggs
2-3/4	cups milk, *divided*
3/4	teaspoon ground mustard
1	can (10-3/4 ounces) condensed cream of mushroom soup, undiluted
1	package (26 ounces) frozen shredded hash brown potatoes, thawed
1/2	teaspoon paprika
1/4	teaspoon pepper

Place croutons in a greased 3-qt. baking dish. Sprinkle with cheese and ham. In a large bowl, whisk the eggs, 2-1/4 cups milk and mustard; pour over ham and cheese. Cover and refrigerate overnight.

Remove from the refrigerator 30 minutes before baking. Combine soup and remaining milk until blended; spread over casserole. Top with hash browns; sprinkle with paprika and pepper.

Cover and bake at 350° for 30 minutes. Uncover; bake 35-40 minutes longer or until edges are browned. Let stand for 10 minutes before serving.
YIELD: 12 SERVINGS.

SAN JOSE TORTILLA PIE

PREP 25 minutes | **BAKE** 25 minutes

anne boesiger
BILLINGS, MONTANA

Because my husband is in the Navy, we've lived in many parts of the country and have had the great opportunity of trying different foods in each region. This is a family favorite served with fried potatoes and fruit.

6 corn tortillas (6 inches)
Oil for deep-fat frying
Salt
1 pound ground beef
1 large onion, chopped
1 medium green pepper, chopped
1 garlic clove, minced
1 tablespoon chili powder
1 tablespoon dried oregano
1 teaspoon ground cumin
2 cups (8 ounces) shredded cheddar cheese
1 to 2 cans (4 ounces *each*) chopped green chilies
6 eggs
1-1/2 cups milk
1/2 teaspoon salt
Sliced ripe olives, optional

Cut each tortilla into eight wedges. Saute a few at a time in hot oil until crisp. Drain on paper towels; sprinkle with salt.

In a large skillet, cook ground beef, onion, green pepper and garlic until beef is no longer pink and vegetables are tender; drain. Stir in chili powder, oregano and cumin.

In a greased 13-in. x 9-in. baking dish, layer half of the tortilla wedges, half the meat mixture and half the cheese. Sprinkle with green chilies, and top with remaining meat mixture and cheese. Tuck remaining tortilla wedges, point side up, around the edge of dish.

In a small bowl, beat eggs, milk and salt. Pour evenly over top. Bake, uncovered at 375° for 25-30 minutes. Garnish with olives if desired.

YIELD: 10-12 SERVINGS.

TOMATO AND CHEESE STRATA

PREP 15 minutes + chilling | **BAKE** 45 minutes

molly seidel
EDGEWOOD, NEW MEXICO

This is a great make-ahead dish for supper or brunch. It's delicious! People who try it always ask for the recipe.

10 slices white bread
4 medium tomatoes, sliced 1/2 inch thick
1 cup (4 ounces) shredded cheddar cheese
4 green onions, thinly sliced
4 eggs
2 cups milk
1/2 teaspoon salt

Line a greased 8-in. square baking dish with four bread slices. Layer with half of the tomatoes, cheese and onions. Top with the remaining bread (slices will overlap). Layer with the remaining tomatoes, cheese and onions.

In a small bowl, whisk eggs, milk and salt. Pour over the top. Cover and refrigerate overnight.

Remove from the refrigerator 30 minutes before baking. Bake, uncovered, at 350° for 45-50 minutes or until a knife inserted near the center comes out clean. Let stand for 5 minutes before cutting.

YIELD: 4-6 SERVINGS.

green ONIONS

If you washed, dried and chopped more green onions than you need in your recipe, store the leftovers in a covered clean glass jar in the refrigerator. They'll last a couple of weeks this way. Just shake them out as needed.

CHERRY STRATA

PREP 35 minutes | **BAKE** 35 minutes

- 12 cups day-old Italian bread cubes (1/2-inch cubes)
- 1 package (8 ounces) cream cheese, softened
- 1/2 cup sugar, *divided*
- 1/2 teaspoon almond extract
- 1/2 cup dried cherries *or* cranberries
- 1/2 cup chopped pecans
- 4 eggs
- 1-1/2 cups half-and-half cream
- 1 teaspoon ground cinnamon

CHERRY SYRUP

- 1 can (14-1/2 ounces) sour cherries, chopped
- 1 cup sugar
- 1 cup corn syrup
- 1/2 teaspoon almond extract

Place 8 cups of the bread cubes in a greased 13-in. x 9-in. baking pan. In a bowl, beat the cream cheese, 1/4 cup sugar and extract until smooth. Stir in cherries and pecans; spoon over bread. Top with remaining bread cubes.

In a bowl, whisk eggs, cream, cinnamon and remaining sugar; pour over the bread. Bake, uncovered, at 350° for 35-40 minutes or until browned. Let stand 5 minutes before serving.

For syrup, combine cherries, sugar and corn syrup in a saucepan; bring to a boil. Reduce the heat; simmer for 15 minutes. Remove from the heat; stir in extract. Serve warm over strata.

YIELD: 6-8 SERVINGS.

carrie sherrill
FORESTVILLE, WISCONSIN

This dressed-up French toast always gets rave reviews! The cherry syrup, made with sour cherries, really brings it over the top.

sour cream SUBSTITUTE

Plain yogurt can be substituted in equal amounts for sour cream in baking recipes, as well as in casseroles, dips and sauces. You may notice dips and sauces might be thinner in consistency when using yogurt—and nonfat yogurt doesn't work well in baked recipes.

HAM 'N' POTATO CASSEROLE

PREP 25 minutes | **BAKE** 30 minutes

- 1/4 cup butter, cubed
- 1/4 cup all-purpose flour
- 1 teaspoon salt
- 1/4 teaspoon pepper
- 1-1/2 cups (12 ounces) sour cream
- 4 ounces process cheese (Velveeta), cubed
- 1 cup (4 ounces) shredded Colby cheese
- 8 hard-cooked eggs
- 3 cups cubed cooked potatoes
- 2 cups cubed fully cooked ham
- 2 tablespoons dried minced onion
- 2 tablespoons minced fresh parsley

In a large saucepan over medium heat, melt butter. Stir in the flour, salt and pepper until smooth. Cook and stir for 1-2 minutes. Remove from the heat; stir in sour cream and cheeses. Cook and stir over low heat just until cheese is melted (mixture will be thick). Remove from the heat. Stir in the eggs, potatoes, ham, onion and parsley.

Transfer to a greased 2-qt. baking dish. Bake, uncovered, at 350° for 30-35 minutes or until bubbly and edges are golden brown.

YIELD: 6 SERVINGS.

rosetta miller
MIDDLEBURY, INDIANA

Sour cream and cheese give this hearty casserole an irresistible richness. Paired with fresh fruit, it is a filling breakfast, lunch or dinner.

⏱ START-RIGHT STRATA

PREP 15 minutes + chilling | **BAKE** 35 minutes + standing

- 4 slices white bread, torn into pieces
- 4 breakfast turkey sausage links, casings removed, crumbled
- 1/3 cup chopped onion
- 1 cup fat-free milk
- 3/4 cup egg substitute
- 1/2 cup reduced-fat sour cream
- 1/4 cup shredded reduced-fat cheddar cheese
- 1/4 cup salsa

Place bread in an 8-in. square baking dish coated with cooking spray; set aside.

In a small nonstick skillet, cook sausage and onion over medium heat until meat is no longer pink; drain. Spoon over bread. In a small bowl, combine milk, egg substitute and sour cream. Stir in cheese. Pour over meat mixture. Cover and refrigerate overnight.

Remove from the refrigerator 30 minutes before baking. Bake, uncovered, at 325° for 35-40 minutes or until a knife inserted near the center comes out clean. Let stand for 10 minutes before cutting. Serve with salsa.
YIELD: 4 SERVINGS.

NUTRITION FACTS: 1 piece with 1 tablespoon salsa equals 247 calories, 10 g fat (4 g saturated fat), 39 mg cholesterol, 580 mg sodium, 21 g carbohydrate, 1 g fiber, 17 g protein.
DIABETIC EXCHANGES: 2 lean meat, 1-1/2 starch, 1 fat.

cecile brown
CHILLICOTHE, TEXAS

I substituted reduced-fat ingredients and reworked this recipe to fit my diet...and my tastes! Served with melon or grapes on the side, it's ideal for overnight guests.

BRUNCH PIZZA

PREP 20 minutes | **BAKE** 25 minutes

jessica salman
DUBLIN, OHIO

2/3   cup reduced-fat biscuit/baking mix

2   tablespoons plus 1 teaspoon water

2   cups fresh baby spinach, chopped

1/2   cup egg substitute

1/3   cup sour cream

1/3   cup shredded reduced-fat cheddar cheese

2   green onions, chopped

1/2   teaspoon garlic powder

2   bacon strips, cooked and crumbled

In a small bowl, combine biscuit mix and water to form a soft dough. Press onto the bottom and up the sides of a 7-in. pie plate coated with cooking spray.

Bake at 450° for 5 minutes or until golden brown. Remove from the oven. Reduce heat to 375°.

In a small bowl, combine the spinach, egg substitute, sour cream, cheese, onions and garlic powder. Pour into crust. Sprinkle with bacon. Bake for 25-30 minutes or until golden brown.

YIELD: 2 SERVINGS.

Whether you serve it for your morning meal or for supper, this flavorful "pie" will fill you up without all the cholesterol. You can make it even healthier by substituting turkey bacon for the bacon.

BISCUIT EGG BAKE

PREP 20 minutes | **BAKE** 40 minutes

- 1 tube (16.3 ounces) large refrigerated buttermilk biscuits
- 12 eggs
- 1 cup milk
- 1 cup chopped fresh tomatoes
- 1/2 cup chopped green onions
- 1 can (4 ounces) chopped green chilies
- 1 teaspoon salt
- 1/2 teaspoon pepper
- 1/2 teaspoon salt-free garlic seasoning blend
- 1 package (2.1 ounces) ready-to-serve fully cooked bacon, diced
- 2 cups (8 ounces) shredded cheddar cheese

Separate biscuits. Cut each biscuit into fourths; arrange in a greased 13-in. x 9-in. baking dish.

In a large bowl, whisk the eggs, milk, tomatoes, onions, chilies, salt, pepper and seasoning blend. Pour over the biscuits. Sprinkle with bacon and cheese.

Bake, uncovered, at 350° for 40-45 minutes or until a thermometer reads 160°.
YIELD: 10-12 SERVINGS.

jenny flake
GILBERT, ARIZONA

Determined to come up with a brunch dish that didn't keep me in the kitchen all morning, I created this casserole made with everyone's favorite ingredients. Preparation is minimal, and then it goes right into the oven, so you can spend more time with the ones you love. Simply serve with a fruit salad for a hearty weekend breakfast guests will love.

OMELET CASSEROLES

PREP 35 minutes | **BAKE** 40 minutes

- 1 cup butter, melted
- 100 eggs
- 2-1/2 quarts milk
- 1-1/4 teaspoons white pepper
- 7-1/2 cups (30 ounces) shredded Swiss cheese
- 7-1/2 cups cubed fully cooked ham

Divide the butter among five 13-in. x 9-in. baking dishes; set aside. In a large bowl, beat 20 eggs, 2 cups milk and 1/4 teaspoon pepper until blended. Stir in 1-1/2 cups cheese and 1-1/2 cups ham; pour into one prepared dish. Repeat four times.

Bake, uncovered, at 350° for 40-45 minutes or until a knife inserted near the center comes out clean (cover with foil if the top browns too quickly). Let stand for 5 minutes before cutting.
YIELD: 60 SERVINGS.

renee schwebach
DUMONT, MINNESOTA

This dish is perfect for a church breakfast or an afternoon brunch. The Swiss cheese and diced ham add nice flavor.

storing **EGGS**

The American Egg Board states that fresh eggs can be refrigerated in their carton up to 5 weeks beyond the pack date. Some cartons are stamped with a date that is 30 days beyond the pack date.

SAUSAGE EGG CASSEROLE

PREP 20 minutes + chilling | **BAKE** 30 minutes + standing

- 10 eggs
- 2-1/4 cups milk
- 1-1/2 teaspoons ground mustard
- 1/2 teaspoon salt
- 1 pound bulk pork sausage, cooked and drained
- 2 cups cubed white bread
- 1-1/2 cups (6 ounces) shredded cheddar cheese

In a large bowl, whisk the eggs, milk, mustard and salt. Stir in the sausage, bread cubes and cheese. Pour into a greased 13-in. x 9-in. baking dish. Cover and refrigerate overnight.

Remove from the refrigerator 30 minutes before baking. Bake, uncovered, at 350° for 30-40 minutes or until a knife inserted near the center comes out clean. Let stand for 10 minutes before serving.
YIELD: 12 SERVINGS.

janice hose
HAGERSTOWN, MARYLAND

Subtle bursts of mustard and savory pork sausage add flavor to this mainstay. I like to refrigerate it overnight, then pop it in the oven shortly before guests arrive.

SPICY BREAKFAST LASAGNA

PREP 20 minutes + chilling | **BAKE** 35 minutes

- 3 cups (24 ounces) 4% cottage cheese
- 1/2 cup minced chives
- 1/4 cup sliced green onions
- 18 eggs
- 1/3 cup milk
- 1/2 teaspoon salt
- 1/4 teaspoon pepper
- 1 tablespoon butter
- 8 lasagna noodles, cooked and drained
- 4 cups frozen shredded hash browns
- 1 pound bulk pork sausage, cooked and crumbled
- 8 ounces sliced Monterey Jack cheese with jalapeno peppers
- 8 ounces sliced Muenster cheese

In a large bowl, combine the cottage cheese, chives and onions; set aside. In a large bowl, whisk the eggs, milk, salt and pepper. In a large skillet, heat butter until hot. Add egg mixture; cook and stir over medium heat until eggs are completely set. Remove from heat; set aside.

In a greased 13-in. x 9-in. baking dish, place four lasagna noodles. Top with 2 cups hash browns, scrambled eggs, sausage and half of cottage cheese mixture. Cover with Monterey Jack cheese. Repeat layers with the remaining lasagna noodles, hash browns and cottage cheese mixture. Top with Muenster cheese.

Cover and refrigerate for 8 hours or overnight. Remove from the refrigerator 30 minutes before baking. Bake, uncovered, at 350° for 35-40 minutes or until a knife inserted near the center comes out clean. Let stand for 5 minutes before cutting.
YIELD: 12-16 SERVINGS.

guthrie torp jr.
HIGHLAND RANCH, COLORADO

It's fun to cook up something new for family and friends—especially when it gets rave reviews. When I brought this dish to our breakfast club at work, people said it really woke up their taste buds!

COUNTRY OVEN OMELET

PREP 20 minutes | **BAKE** 50 minutes

- 1 large onion, chopped, *divided*
- 3 tablespoons canola oil
- 3-1/2 cups frozen shredded hash brown potatoes
- 1-1/2 teaspoons salt, *divided*
- 1/2 teaspoon pepper, *divided*
- 1 pound ground beef
- 1/4 cup chopped green pepper
- 1/4 cup chopped sweet red pepper
- 1 tablespoon dried parsley flakes
- 1 cup (4 ounces) shredded Swiss cheese *or* shredded part-skim mozzarella cheese
- 4 eggs
- 1-1/4 cups milk
- 1/4 teaspoon paprika

In a skillet, saute 1/2 cup onion in oil. Add the hash browns, 3/4 teaspoon salt and 1/4 teaspoon pepper. Cook over medium heat for 5 minutes or until hash browns are thawed. Press mixture into an ungreased 10-in. pie plate, forming a shell.

Bake at 400° for 20 minutes. Meanwhile, in a skillet, cook beef, peppers and remaining onion over medium heat until meat is no longer pink; drain. Stir in parsley. Spoon into the potato shell. Sprinkle with cheese.

In a bowl, beat the eggs, milk, paprika and remaining salt and pepper; pour over meat mixture. Bake at 400° for 30 minutes or until a knife inserted near the center comes out clean. Let stand 5 minutes before cutting.
YIELD: 4-6 SERVINGS.

kim pettipas
OROMOCTO, NEW BRUNSWICK

I love to make this pie on weekends when my husband and I have time to enjoy every savory bite. Green and red peppers add color and flavor.

HASH BROWN SAUSAGE BAKE

PREP 30 minutes | **BAKE** 40 minutes

1 package (20 ounces) refrigerated shredded hash brown potatoes
1/3 cup butter, melted
1 teaspoon beef bouillon granules
1 pound bulk pork sausage
1/3 cup chopped onion
1 cup (8 ounces) 4% cottage cheese
3 eggs, lightly beaten
4 slices process American cheese, chopped

In a large bowl, combine the hash browns, butter and bouillon. Press onto the bottom and up the sides of a greased 10-in. pie plate. Bake at 350° for 25-30 minutes or until edges are lightly browned.

Meanwhile, in a large skillet, cook the sausage and onion over medium heat until meat is no longer pink; drain. In a large bowl, combine the sausage mixture, cottage cheese, eggs and American cheese.

Pour into the crust. Bake at 350° for 40-45 minutes or until a knife inserted near the center comes out clean. Let stand for 5 minutes before cutting.
YIELD: 6-8 SERVINGS.

vicky dempsey
LOUISVILLE, MISSISSIPPI

This is one of my son's favorites. Buttered hash browns form a mouth-watering crust for the yummy filling of sausage and cheese. It's sure to please at breakfast, brunch or even lunch.

BAKED SPINACH SUPREME

PREP 15 minutes | **BAKE** 30 minutes

- 1 cup reduced-fat biscuit/baking mix
- 2 egg whites
- 1 egg
- 1/4 cup fat-free milk
- 1/4 cup finely chopped onion

FILLING

- 1 package (10 ounces) frozen chopped spinach, thawed and squeezed dry
- 1-1/2 cups fat-free cottage cheese
- 3/4 cup shredded Monterey Jack cheese
- 1/2 cup grated Parmesan cheese
- 2 egg whites
- 1 egg
- 1 teaspoon dried minced onion

In a small bowl, combine biscuit mix, egg whites, egg, milk and onion. Spread into a greased 11-in. x 7-in. baking dish.

In another bowl, combine the filling ingredients. Gently spoon over the biscuit mixture.

Bake, uncovered, at 350° for 28-32 minutes or until golden brown and a knife inserted near the center comes out clean.

YIELD: 6 SERVINGS.

NUTRITION FACTS: 1 piece equals 251 calories, 9 g fat (5 g saturated fat), 92 mg cholesterol, 725 mg sodium, 21 g carbohydrate, 2 g fiber, 20 g protein. **DIABETIC EXCHANGES:** 1-1/2 fat, 1 starch, 1 lean meat, 1/2 fat-free milk.

betty claycomb
ALVERTON, PENNSYLVANIA

This healthful recipe makes a lovely brunch bake or main dish for lunch. The cheese mixture will convince anyone to eat his or her spinach. Plus, it adds extra protein.

CHEDDAR HAM STRATA

PREP 20 minutes + chilling | **BAKE** 1 hour + standing

- 10 slices day-old bread, crusts removed and cubed
- 1 medium onion, finely chopped
- 4 medium fresh mushrooms, finely chopped
- 1/4 cup butter, cubed
- 4 cups (16 ounces) shredded cheddar cheese
- 2 cups cubed fully cooked ham
- 2 tablespoons all-purpose flour
- 8 eggs
- 3 cups milk
- 2 tablespoons prepared mustard
- 1 teaspoon garlic powder
- 1/2 teaspoon salt

Place bread cubes in a greased 13-in. x 9-in. baking dish. In a small skillet, saute onion and mushrooms in butter; spoon over bread. Sprinkle with the cheese, ham and flour. In a large bowl, whisk eggs, milk, mustard, garlic powder and salt. Pour over ham and cheese. Cover and refrigerate overnight.

Remove from the refrigerator 30 minutes before baking. Bake, uncovered, at 350° for 60-70 minutes or until a knife inserted near the center comes out clean. Let stand for 10 minutes before serving.
YIELD: 12 SERVINGS.

ann pool
JEROME, IDAHO

I put together this ham and egg dish on Christmas Eve and refrigerate it. Then, while we open presents on Christmas morning, I pop it in the oven for breakfast. It's a family tradition.

testing for **DONENESS**

To test egg dishes containing beaten eggs, such as quiche, strata or custard, for doneness, insert a knife near the center of the dish. If the knife comes out clean, the eggs are cooked.

EGG BISCUIT BAKE

PREP/TOTAL TIME 30 minutes

- 1 can (5 ounces) evaporated milk
- 8 ounces process cheese (Velveeta), cubed
- 1 teaspoon prepared mustard
- 3/4 cup cubed fully cooked ham
- 1/2 cup frozen peas
- 2 tablespoons butter
- 10 eggs, lightly beaten
- 1 tube (12 ounces) refrigerated buttermilk biscuits

In a large saucepan, combine milk, cheese and mustard; cook over low heat until smooth, stirring constantly. Stir in ham and peas.

Melt the butter in a large skillet, heat butter until hot. Add eggs; cook and stir over medium heat until eggs are completely set. Add cheese sauce and stir gently.

Spoon into an ungreased shallow 2-qt. baking dish. Separate the biscuits and cut in half. Place with cut side down around outer edge of dish.

Bake, uncovered, at 375° for 15-20 minutes or until a knife inserted near the center comes out clean and biscuits are golden brown.
YIELD: 4-6 SERVINGS.

alice le duc
CEDARBURG, WISCONSIN

Convenient refrigerated biscuits create a golden border around this all-in-one brunch dish. It's a variation of a simple egg–cheese combination my mother used to make. It's become our favorite comfort food.

BROCCOLI-CHICKEN STRATA

PREP 15 minutes + chilling | **BAKE** 1 hour

margery moore
RICHFIELD SPRINGS, NEW YORK

On our dairy farm, chores often delay dinner. That's when this strata comes in handy. I'll prepare it beforehand and pop it in the oven for a quick and easy meal.

- 12 slices buttered bread
- 2-1/4 cups (10 ounces) shredded cheddar cheese, *divided*
- 3 cups frozen chopped broccoli, thawed and drained
- 2 cups diced cooked chicken
- 6 eggs
- 3 cups milk
- 2 tablespoons finely chopped onion
- 3/4 teaspoon salt
- 1/2 teaspoon ground mustard
- 1/4 teaspoon pepper

Using a doughnut cutter, cut 12 rings and holes from bread; set aside. Tear bread scraps and place in a greased 13-in. x 9-in. baking dish. Sprinkle with 2 cups cheese, broccoli and chicken. Arrange rings and holes, with buttered sides up, on top.

Beat the eggs, milk, onion, salt, mustard and pepper; pour over the top. Cover and refrigerate 8 hours or overnight.

Remove from the refrigerator 30 minutes before baking. Bake, uncovered, at 325° for 55-60 minutes. Sprinkle with remaining cheese; bake 5 minutes longer or until a knife inserted near the center comes out clean. Let stand for 5-10 minutes before cutting.
YIELD: 6-8 SERVINGS.

WEEKEND BREAKFAST BAKE

PREP 15 minutes | **BAKE** 30 minutes

melissa ball
PEARISBURG, VIRGINIA

My family really enjoys this breakfast casserole on weekends or holidays. It's so quick to prepare and very filling. Great for those on a low-carb diet, too!

- 1 pound bulk pork sausage
- 1/3 cup chopped onion
- 4 cups (16 ounces) shredded Monterey Jack *or* cheddar cheese
- 8 eggs, lightly beaten
- 1 can (10-3/4 ounces) condensed cream of mushroom soup, undiluted

In a large skillet, cook the sausage and onion over medium heat until meat is no longer pink; drain. Transfer to a greased 13-in. x 9-in. baking dish. Sprinkle with cheese. Combine eggs and soup; pour over cheese.

Bake, uncovered, at 400° for 30-35 minutes or until a knife inserted near the center comes out clean. Let stand for 5 minutes before cutting.
YIELD: 8 SERVINGS.

SOUTHWEST BRUNCH CASSEROLE

PREP 15 minutes + chilling | **BAKE** 20 minutes

- 4 teaspoons butter, softened
- 2 English muffins, split
- 1/2 pound bulk pork sausage
- 4 eggs
- 1/4 cup sour cream
- 1/2 cup shredded sharp cheddar cheese
- 1/4 cup canned chopped green chilies

Spread the butter over cut sides of each muffin half. Place the buttered side up in an 8-in. square baking dish coated with cooking spray; set aside.

In a small skillet, cook the sausage over medium heat until no longer pink; drain. Spoon sausage over muffin halves. In a small bowl, whisk eggs and sour cream; pour over sausage. Sprinkle with cheese and chilies. Cover and refrigerate for 3 hours or overnight.

Remove from the refrigerator 30 minutes before baking. Bake at 350° for 20-25 minutes or until a knife inserted near the center comes out clean. Let stand for 5 minutes before cutting.

YIELD: 4 SERVINGS.

linda hinkley
FLORENCE, OREGON

My husband used to take this casserole, doubled, to office potlucks, and it was a favorite. I serve it at home as a special-occasion breakfast or even dinner for the two of us. Any leftovers taste just as good reheated in the microwave.

BACON SPINACH STRATA

PREP 30 minutes + chilling | **BAKE** 45 minutes + standing

- 1 package (8 ounces) sliced mushrooms
- 1 bunch green onions, sliced
- 2 teaspoons canola oil
- 1 loaf (1 pound) day-old bread, cut into 3/4-inch cubes
- 1 cup (4 ounces) shredded Swiss cheese
- 1 package (1 pound) sliced bacon, cooked and crumbled
- 2 cups (8 ounces) shredded cheddar cheese
- 1 package (10 ounces) frozen chopped spinach, thawed and squeezed dry
- 9 eggs
- 3 cups milk
- 1/2 teaspoon *each* onion powder, garlic powder and ground mustard
- 1/4 teaspoon salt
- 1/4 teaspoon pepper

In a large skillet, saute mushrooms and onions in oil until tender. Place half of the bread cubes and 1/2 cup Swiss cheese in a greased 13-in. x 9-in. baking dish. Layer with bacon, cheddar cheese, mushroom mixture, spinach and remaining Swiss cheese and bread cubes.

In a large bowl, combine the eggs, milk and seasonings. Pour over casserole. Cover and refrigerate overnight.

Remove from the refrigerator 30 minutes before baking. Bake, uncovered, at 375° for 45-55 minutes or until a knife inserted near the center comes out clean (cover loosely with foil if top browns too quickly). Let stand for 10 minutes before cutting.

YIELD: 12 SERVINGS.

kris kebisek
BROOKFIELD, WISCONSIN

Full of flavor, fast and filling, this make–ahead breakfast dish is pretty enough for any holiday brunch buffet. It disappears in minutes, and being able to prepare it the night before makes handling hectic mornings a snap!

MEXICAN BREAKFAST CASSEROLE

PREP 15 minutes + chilling | **BAKE** 40 minutes

- 4 cups cubed day-old French bread
- 1 cup cubed fully cooked lean ham
- 1 can (4 ounces) chopped green chilies
- 1/4 cup chopped sweet red pepper
- 1-1/4 cups egg substitute
- 1 cup fat-free milk
- 1/4 teaspoon onion powder
- 1/4 teaspoon ground cumin
- 1/4 teaspoon ground mustard
- 1/8 to 1/4 teaspoon cayenne pepper
- 1/4 teaspoon paprika
- 1-1/4 cups shredded reduced-fat cheddar cheese

Salsa, optional

In an 8-in. square baking dish coated with cooking spray, combine the bread cubes, ham, chilies and red pepper.

Whisk the egg substitute, milk, onion powder, cumin, mustard and cayenne. Pour over bread mixture; sprinkle with paprika. Cover and refrigerate overnight.

Remove from the refrigerator 30 minutes before baking. Bake at 350° for 30 minutes. Uncover; sprinkle with cheese. Bake for 10-15 minutes longer or until a knife inserted near the center comes out clean. Let stand for 5 minutes before cutting. Serve with salsa if desired.

YIELD: 4 SERVINGS.

leona hansen
KENNEDY MEADOWS, CALIFORNIA

I make this recipe whenever I'm having overnight guests. Fresh fruit and tortillas or sweet rolls go very well to complete breakfast.

SAUSAGE-MUSHROOM BREAKFAST BAKE

PREP 25 minutes | **BAKE** 50 minutes + standing

- 1 pound bulk pork sausage
- 2 cups sliced fresh mushrooms
- 6 cups cubed bread
- 2 cups (8 ounces) shredded sharp cheddar cheese
- 1 cup chopped fresh tomatoes
- 10 eggs, lightly beaten
- 3 cups milk
- 2 teaspoons ground mustard
- 1/2 teaspoon salt
- 1/4 teaspoon pepper

In a large skillet, cook the sausage and mushrooms over medium heat until meat is no longer pink; drain. Place half of the bread cubes in a greased 13-in. x 9-in. baking dish; top with 2 cups sausage mixture and half of the cheese and tomatoes. Repeat layers. In a large bowl, combine eggs, milk, mustard, salt and pepper; pour over bread mixture.

Bake, uncovered, at 350° for 50-55 minutes or until a knife inserted near the center comes out clean. Let stand for 10 minutes before serving.

YIELD: 12 SERVINGS.

diane babbitt
LUDLOW, MASSACHUSETTS

My mom shared this delicious recipe when I needed to bring a dish to a breakfast potluck. Everyone loved it!

dry MUSTARD

Dry mustard (referred to as ground mustard in many recipes) is made from mustard seeds that have been finely ground. When a recipe calls for prepared mustard, use yellow or brown mustard commonly served as a condiment.

ITALIAN SAUSAGE CASSEROLE

PREP 15 minutes + chilling | **BAKE** 1 hour 20 minutes

nancy robinson
KANSAS CITY, KANSAS

- 1 pound bulk pork sausage
- 1 pound bulk Italian sausage
- 1 medium green pepper, chopped
- 1 cup sliced fresh mushrooms
- 1/2 cup chopped onion
- 2-1/2 cups onion and garlic croutons
- 8 eggs
- 1-1/2 cups milk
- 1 cup (4 ounces) shredded part-skim mozzarella cheese
- 1 cup (4 ounces) shredded cheddar cheese
- 3 to 4 Roma tomatoes, thinly sliced
- 1/2 cup Parmesan cheese, shredded

In a large skillet, cook sausage, green pepper, mushrooms and onion until meat is browned and vegetables are tender; drain. Place croutons in a greased 13-in. x 9-in. baking dish; top with sausage mixture. Beat eggs and milk; pour over sausage.

Cover and chill for 8 hours or overnight. Remove from the refrigerator 30 minutes before baking. Bake, uncovered, at 300° for 1 hour.

Sprinkle with the mozzarella and cheddar cheeses. Place tomato slices over top; sprinkle with Parmesan cheese. Bake 20 minutes longer or until a knife inserted near the center comes out clean. Let stand 5 minutes before cutting.

YIELD: 12 SERVINGS.

At the start of each week, my family is already looking forward to our traditional weekend breakfasts, when I serve warm and wonderful dishes such as this. The make-ahead convenience lets me relax with the family as the savory aroma fills the house.

HASH BROWN EGG DISH

PREP 25 minutes | **COOK** 15 minutes

diann sivley
SIGNAL MOUNTAIN, IOWA

- 3/4 to 1 pound sliced bacon
- 6 cups frozen shredded hash brown potatoes
- 1 small onion, chopped
- 1 medium green pepper, chopped
- 1 jar (4-1/2 ounces) sliced mushrooms, drained
- 3 tablespoons butter
- 6 eggs
- 1/4 cup milk
- 3/4 teaspoon salt
- 1/4 teaspoon dried basil
- 1/8 teaspoon pepper
- 2 cups (8 ounces) shredded cheddar cheese

Place bacon on a microwave-safe plate lined with paper towels. Cover with another paper towel; microwave on high for 5-7 minutes or until crisp. Cool; crumble and set aside.

In a 2-1/2-qt. microwave-safe dish, combine the potatoes, onion, green pepper, mushrooms and butter. Cover and microwave on high for 5-7 minutes or until the vegetables are tender, stirring once.

Whisk eggs, milk, salt, basil and pepper; stir into vegetable mixture. Cover and cook at 70% power for 4-6 seconds or until eggs are almost set, stirring every 2 minutes.

Sprinkle with cheese and bacon. Cook, uncovered, on high for 30-60 seconds or until cheese is melted. Let stand for 5 minutes before serving.

YIELD: 6-8 SERVINGS.

I cook the bacon and chop up the vegetables for this hearty casserole the night before, so it only takes a few minutes to finish in the morning. When we have overnight guests, I serve it for breakfast along with blueberry muffins. My family also thinks it's good for dinner.

SAVORY SPINACH PIE

PREP 15 minutes | **BAKE** 45 minutes

1/4 cup chopped onion

2 tablespoons butter

1 package (10 ounces) frozen chopped spinach, thawed and well drained

1/4 to 1/2 teaspoon salt

1/4 teaspoon ground nutmeg

1 cup (8 ounces) 4% cottage cheese

1/2 cup half-and-half cream

1/4 cup grated Parmesan cheese

3 eggs, lightly beaten

1 unbaked pastry shell (9 inches)

In a skillet, saute onion in butter. Remove from heat; stir in spinach, salt and nutmeg.

In a bowl, combine cottage cheese, cream, Parmesan cheese and eggs; mix well. Stir in spinach mixture. Pour into pie shell.

Bake at 350° for 45-50 minutes, or until a knife inserted near the center comes out clean. Let stand for 5 minutes before cutting.

YIELD: 6 SERVINGS.

pam krenzke
HILLIARD, OHIO

Even those who aren't morning people will break into smiles when they taste this super spinach pie. Served with cinnamon rolls and fresh fruit, it will surely get your day off to a sunny start!

SPRING BRUNCH BAKE

PREP 15 minutes | **BAKE** 35 minutes + standing

8 cups cubed French bread

2 cups cut fresh asparagus (1-inch pieces)

1 cup cubed fully cooked lean ham

3/4 cup shredded part-skim mozzarella cheese

6 egg whites

3 eggs

1-1/2 cups fat-free milk

2 tablespoons lemon juice

1/4 teaspoon garlic powder

In a large bowl, combine bread, asparagus, ham and cheese. Whisk the egg whites, eggs, milk, lemon juice and garlic powder; pour over the bread mixture and stir until blended. Transfer to a 13-in. x 9-in. baking dish coated with cooking spray.

Cover and bake at 350° for 25 minutes. Uncover and bake 8-10 minutes longer or until a knife inserted near the center comes out clean. Let stand for 10 minutes before serving.

YIELD: 6 SERVINGS.

nancy zimmerman
CAPE MAY COURT HOUSE, NEW JERSEY

What a delicious way to use up leftover ham and fresh asparagus! Fluffy and moist, this dish will be a welcomed sight at any meal.

BREAKFAST IN A CUP

PREP/TOTAL TIME 25 minutes

3 cups cooked long grain rice
1 cup (4 ounces) shredded cheddar cheese, *divided*
1 can (4 ounces) chopped green chilies, drained
1 jar (2 ounces) diced pimientos, drained
1/3 cup milk
2 eggs
1/2 teaspoon ground cumin
1/2 teaspoon salt
1/4 teaspoon pepper

In a large bowl, combine the rice, 1/2 cup cheese, chilies, pimientos, milk, eggs, cumin, salt and pepper.

Spoon into 12 greased muffin cups. Sprinkle with remaining cheese. Bake at 400° for 15 minutes or until eggs are set.
YIELD: 12 SERVINGS.

donna chapman
ANCHOR POINT, ALASKA

These single-serving breakfast surprises are perfect when you're looking to serve something different. Your guests will want seconds!

leftover **TORTILLAS**

Have an opened package of tortillas in the refrigerator? Brush the tortillas with butter and sprinkle with herbs or cinnamon-sugar. Then, bake on a cookie sheet until crisp. Or, let the tortillas dry on racks until brittle, then crumble into small pieces to use on soups or salads in place of croutons.

EGG AND CORN QUESADILLA

PREP 25 minutes | BAKE 10 minutes

1 medium onion, chopped
1 medium green pepper, chopped
1 garlic clove, minced
2 tablespoons olive oil
3 cups fresh *or* frozen corn
1 teaspoon minced chives
1/2 teaspoon dried cilantro flakes
1/2 teaspoon salt
1/4 teaspoon pepper
4 eggs, beaten
4 flour tortillas (10 inches)
1/2 cup salsa
1 cup (8 ounces) sour cream
1 cup (4 ounces) shredded cheddar cheese
1 cup (4 ounces) shredded part-skim mozzarella cheese
Additional salsa and sour cream, optional

In a skillet, saute the onion, green pepper and garlic in oil until tender. Add the corn, chives, cilantro, salt and pepper. Cook until heated through, about 3 minutes. Stir in eggs; cook until completely set, stirring occasionally. Remove from the heat.

Place one tortilla on a lightly greased baking sheet or pizza pan; top with a third of the corn mixture, salsa and sour cream. Sprinkle with a fourth of the cheeses. Repeat layers twice. Top with the remaining tortilla and cheeses.

Bake at 350° for 10 minutes or until the cheese is melted. Cut into wedges. Serve with salsa and sour cream if desired.
YIELD: 6-8 SERVINGS.

stacy joura
STONEBORO, PENNSYLVANIA

For a deliciously different breakfast or brunch, try this excellent quesadilla. It's also great for a light lunch or supper. Corn is a natural in Southwestern cooking and a tasty addition to this zippy egg dish.

FETA BREAKFAST BAKE

PREP 15 minutes | **BAKE** 1 hour + standing

- 4 cups seasoned salad croutons
- 1-1/2 cups (6 ounces) crumbled feta cheese
- 8 eggs
- 4 cups milk
- 1 tablespoon minced fresh basil
  or 1 teaspoon dried basil
- 1 tablespoon minced fresh oregano
  or 1 teaspoon dried oregano
- 1/4 teaspoon pepper
- 1-1/2 cups cubed fully cooked ham

In a large bowl, combine the croutons and feta cheese; transfer to a greased 13-in. x 9-in. baking dish. In a large bowl, whisk the eggs, milk, basil, oregano and pepper. Slowly pour over crouton mixture. Sprinkle with ham.

Bake, uncovered, at 325° for 60-65 minutes or until a knife inserted near center comes out clean. Let stand for 10 minutes before cutting.

YIELD: 12-14 SERVINGS.

cheryl rude
WINFIELD, KANSAS

Guests at our family's bed-and-breakfast love this easy-prep brunch item. You can try several variations of the egg dish with your favorite types of cheese. Add a sprig of oregano as a pretty garnish.

about GROUND HAM

Many meat departments will grind a ham for you if you're buying the ham from them. Others, however, will not grind ham because of safety concerns. The same grinders may be used to grind red meats, and even though they've been cleaned, the grinders can pose a risk of cross-contamination.

BRUNCH ENCHILADAS

PREP 20 minutes | **BAKE** 45 minutes

- 2 cups ground fully cooked ham
- 1/2 cup sliced green onions
- 1/2 cup finely chopped green pepper
- 2 tablespoons canola oil
- 8 flour tortillas (8 inches)
- 2-1/2 cups (10 ounces) shredded cheddar cheese, *divided*
- 4 eggs
- 2 cups half-and-half cream
- 1 tablespoon all-purpose flour
- 1/4 teaspoon garlic powder
- 2 to 3 drops hot pepper sauce

Salsa

Sour cream

In a skillet, saute the ham, onions and green pepper in oil until vegetables are tender. Place 1/3 cup down the center of each tortilla; top with 3 tablespoons cheese. Roll up and place seam side down in a greased 11-in. x 7-in. baking dish.

In a bowl, beat the eggs. Add cream, flour, garlic powder and hot pepper sauce; mix well. Pour over tortillas. Cover and chill 8 hours or overnight. Remove from refrigerator 30 minutes before baking.

Bake, uncovered, at 350° for 45-50 minutes or until a knife inserted near the center comes out clean. Let stand 5 minutes. Serve with salsa and sour cream.

YIELD: 4 SERVINGS.

pat o'brien
SOQUEL, CALIFORNIA

This recipe takes me back to when my grandmother would visit. While she prepared one of her delicious meals, she'd give me dough to make my own tortillas. With such tasty memories, it's no surprise this is my most asked for recipe!

HEARTY BREAKFAST EGG BAKE

PREP 10 minutes + chilling | **BAKE** 45 minutes + standing

1-1/2 pounds bulk pork sausage

3 cups frozen shredded hash brown potatoes, thawed

2 cups (8 ounces) shredded cheddar cheese

8 eggs

1 can (10-3/4 ounces) condensed cream of mushroom soup, undiluted

3/4 cup evaporated milk

Crumble the sausage into a large skillet. Cook over medium heat until no longer pink; drain. Transfer to a greased 13-in. x 9-in. baking dish. Sprinkle with the hash browns and cheese.

In a large bowl, whisk the remaining ingredients; pour over the top. Cover and refrigerate overnight.

Remove from the refrigerator 30 minutes before baking. Bake, uncovered, at 350° for 45-50 minutes or until a knife inserted near the center comes out clean. Let stand for 10 minutes before cutting.

YIELD: 8 SERVINGS.

pamela norris

FENTON, MISSOURI

I always fix this casserole ahead when overnight guests are visiting, so I have more time to spend with them. Then, I simply add some toast or biscuits and fresh fruit for a complete meal that everyone loves. It also reheats well.

CREAMY HAM 'N' EGG CASSEROLE

PREP 15 minutes | **BAKE** 20 minutes

dixie terry
GOREVILLE, ILLINOIS

Have leftover cooked potatoes or eggs on hand? Here's a terrific way to use them up! This breakfast main dish is a great way to fill up family members before they leave for work, school or wherever they need to be.

2	medium cooked potatoes, peeled and sliced
4	hard-cooked eggs, chopped
1	cup diced fully cooked ham
1/2	teaspoon salt
1/4	teaspoon pepper
1	egg
1-1/2	cups (12 ounces) sour cream
1/4	cup dry bread crumbs
1	tablespoon butter, melted

In a large bowl, combine the potatoes, eggs, ham, salt and pepper. Combine the egg and sour cream; add to potato mixture and gently toss to coat. Transfer to a greased 11-in. x 7-in. baking dish.

Toss the bread crumbs with the melted butter; sprinkle over the casserole. Bake, uncovered, at 350° for 20 minutes or until a thermometer reaches 160°.

YIELD: 6 SERVINGS.

WINE 'N' CHEESE STRATA

PREP 15 minutes + chilling | **BAKE** 70 minutes

- 1 pound day-old Italian bread, cubed
- 3 tablespoons butter, melted
- 1-1/3 cups shredded Swiss cheese
- 1 cup (4 ounces) shredded Monterey Jack cheese
- 2 ounces salami, coarsely chopped
- 8 eggs
- 1-1/2 cups milk
- 1/4 cup dry white wine *or* water
- 2 green onions, chopped
- 1-1/2 teaspoons spicy brown mustard
- 1/4 teaspoon pepper
- Dash crushed red pepper flakes
- 3/4 cup sour cream
- 1/2 cup shredded Parmesan cheese

Place bread cubes in a greased 13-in. x 9-in. baking dish; drizzle with butter. Sprinkle with cheeses and salami. In a bowl, beat eggs, milk, wine, onions, mustard, pepper and pepper flakes. Pour evenly over top. Cover and refrigerate overnight.

Remove from refrigerator 30 minutes before baking. Cover and bake at 325° for 1 hour. Uncover; spread sour cream evenly over the top. Sprinkle with Parmesan cheese. Bake 10 minutes longer or until cheese is melted.

YIELD: 10-12 SERVINGS.

tiffany mitchell
SUSANVILLE, CALIFORNIA

When hosting a shower or brunch, I double this recipe's ingredients and use two 13-in. x 9-in. dishes. You don't need many other foods to complete the meal.

SAUSAGE SPINACH BAKE

PREP 20 minutes | **BAKE** 35 minutes

- 1 package (6 ounces) savory herb-flavored stuffing mix
- 1/2 pound bulk pork sausage
- 1/4 cup chopped green onions
- 1/2 teaspoon minced garlic
- 1 package (10 ounces) frozen chopped spinach, thawed and squeezed dry
- 1-1/2 cups (6 ounces) shredded Monterey Jack cheese
- 1-1/2 cups half-and-half cream
- 3 eggs
- 2 tablespoons grated Parmesan cheese

Prepare the stuffing according to package directions. Meanwhile, crumble the sausage into a large skillet; add onions and garlic. Cook over medium heat until meat is no longer pink; drain.

In a large bowl, combine the stuffing, sausage mixture and spinach. Transfer to a greased 13-in. x 9-in. baking dish; sprinkle with Monterey Jack cheese. In a small bowl, combine the cream and eggs; pour over sausage mixture.

Bake at 400° for 30 minutes or until a thermometer reads 160°. Sprinkle with Parmesan cheese; bake 5 minutes longer or until bubbly.

YIELD: 12 SERVINGS.

kathleen grant
SWAN LAKE, MONTANA

This delicious recipe, which uses a packaged stuffing mix, was given to me some years ago by a friend. A salad and bread of your choice is all you'll need for a filling lunch or dinner. It's so versatile, you can even serve it at brunch.

CHILI CHEESE STRATA

PREP 15 minutes + chilling | **BAKE** 30 minutes + standing

- 1 loaf (12 ounces) French bread, cut into 1-inch cubes
- 2 cups shredded cheddar *or* Monterey Jack cheese, *divided*
- 1 jar (8 ounces) mild green chili salsa *or* 4 ounces chopped green chilies and 4 ounces salsa, combined
- 4 eggs
- 1 can (10-3/4 ounces) condensed cheddar cheese soup, undiluted
- 2 cups milk *or* half-and-half cream
- 2 tablespoons finely chopped onion
- 1 teaspoon Worcestershire sauce

Place bread cubes evenly in a greased 2-qt. shallow baking dish. Sprinkle with 1 cup cheese. Pour salsa over cheese; set aside. In blender, combine eggs, soup, milk, onion and Worcestershire sauce; pour over bread mixture. Sprinkle with remaining cheese. Cover and refrigerate 6 hours or overnight.

Remove from the refrigerator 30 minutes before baking. Bake, uncovered, at 350° for 30 minutes or until a knife inserted near the center comes out clean. Let stand for 10 minutes before serving.

YIELD: 8 SERVINGS.

shirley smith
ANAHEIM, CALIFORNIA

This do-ahead casserole has a south-of-the-border flavor. Adjust the chilies and salsa to suit your tastes.

MEATLESS SAUSAGE EGG BAKE

PREP 25 minutes | **BAKE** 35 minutes + standing

- 1 small onion, chopped
- 1 small green pepper, chopped
- 1 small sweet red pepper, chopped
- 2 teaspoons canola oil
- 12 egg whites
- 6 eggs
- 1 cup fat-free milk
- 1 package (16 ounces) frozen shredded hash brown potatoes, thawed
- 1 package (8 ounces) frozen vegetarian breakfast sausage patties, thawed and crumbled
- 1 cup (4 ounces) shredded reduced-fat cheddar cheese
- 1 teaspoon salt
- 1/2 teaspoon pepper

taste of home
test kitchen
GREENDALE, WISCONSIN

This eye-opener is sure to please every palate at your breakfast table. Crumbled vegetarian patties make the potato casserole a hearty option that doesn't pack on the pounds.

In a small nonstick skillet, saute onion and peppers in oil until tender. In a large bowl, beat the egg whites, eggs and milk. Stir in hash browns, crumbled sausage, cheese, salt, pepper and onion mixture.

Transfer to a 13-in. x 9-in. baking dish coated with cooking spray. Bake, uncovered, at 350° for 35-45 minutes or until a knife inserted near the center comes out clean. Let stand for 10 minutes before cutting.

YIELD: 8 SERVINGS.

NUTRITION FACTS: 1 piece equals 256 calories, 11 g fat (3 g saturated fat), 170 mg cholesterol, 733 mg sodium, 19 g carbohydrate, 4 g fiber, 22 g protein. **DIABETIC EXCHANGES:** 3 lean meat, 1 starch, 1/2 fat.

ZIPPY EGG CASSEROLE

PREP 20 minutes + chilling | **BAKE** 40 minutes + standing

1 pound bulk pork sausage

1 package (5-1/2 ounces) seasoned salad croutons

1-1/2 cups (6 ounces) shredded cheddar cheese

1 cup (4 ounces) shredded Swiss cheese

1 cup (4 ounces) shredded pepper Jack cheese

8 eggs

2 cups half-and-half cream

1-1/2 cups milk

1 tablespoon finely chopped onion

1-1/2 teaspoons ground mustard

1/4 teaspoon salt

1/4 teaspoon pepper

In a large skillet, cook sausage over medium heat until no longer pink; drain. Place the croutons in a greased 13-in. x 9-in. baking dish. Sprinkle with cheeses and sausage.

In a large bowl, whisk the remaining ingredients; pour over the casserole. Cover and refrigerate overnight.

Remove from the refrigerator 30 minutes before baking. Bake, uncovered, at 350° for 40-45 minutes or until a knife inserted near the center comes out clean. Let stand for 10 minutes before serving.

YIELD: 8-10 SERVINGS.

anita jones
RAYTOWN, MISSOURI

This casserole has a bit of a zip to it because of the pepper Jack cheese. Instead of plain white bread, it uses seasoned croutons, which give it more flavor.

CAJUN-STYLE BRUNCH BAKE

kathie deusser
CHURCH POINT, LOUISIANA

PREP 10 minutes + chilling | BAKE 45 minutes + standing

6 eggs, lightly beaten

2 cups milk

1 pound sliced bacon, cooked and crumbled

6 slices bread, cubed

1 medium potato, peeled and diced

1 cup (4 ounces) shredded cheddar cheese

1/2 cup finely chopped onion

1 to 1-1/2 teaspoons Cajun seasoning

1 teaspoon salt

In a large bowl, combine all ingredients. Transfer to a greased 11-in. x 7-in. baking dish. Cover and refrigerate overnight.

Remove from the refrigerator 30 minutes before baking. Bake, uncovered, at 350° for 45-50 minutes or until a knife inserted near the center comes out clean. Let stand for 10 minutes before cutting.

YIELD: 6 SERVINGS.

It's so handy to fix this robust breakfast casserole the night before and refrigerate it until morning. It was given to me by a co-worker and has turned out to be a family hit! I adapted it to our tastes, adding onion, potato and Cajun seasoning. Serve it with your favorite fruits, coffee and juice.

ALL-IN-ONE EGG CASSEROLE

PREP 25 minutes | **BAKE** 20 minutes

- 10 bacon strips, diced
- 1 cup sliced fresh mushrooms
- 1/2 cup sliced green onions
- 1/4 cup butter
- 1/4 cup all-purpose flour
- 1/4 teaspoon salt
- 1/4 teaspoon pepper
- 2 cups milk
- 1-1/2 cups (6 ounces) shredded cheddar cheese

SCRAMBLED EGGS

- 8 eggs
- 1/2 cup milk
- 1/2 teaspoon pepper
- 1/4 teaspoon salt
- 4 English muffins, split, toasted and lightly buttered
- 2 tablespoons minced fresh parsley

In a large skillet, cook the bacon until crisp. Remove bacon and set aside; discard all but 2 tablespoons of drippings. Saute mushrooms and onions in drippings until tender; set aside.

In a saucepan, melt butter. Stir in the flour, salt and pepper until smooth; cook until bubbly. Gradually stir in milk and cheese; cook and stir until thickened. Stir in bacon, mushrooms and onions; remove from the heat and set aside.

For scrambled eggs, beat the eggs, milk, pepper and salt; pour into a greased skillet. Cook and stir gently until the eggs are set. Remove from the heat and set aside.

Cut English muffin halves in half again. Place in the bottom of a greased 11-in. x 7-in. baking dish. Cover with half of the cheese sauce. Spoon eggs over all; top with remaining sauce. Sprinkle with parsley.

Bake, uncovered, at 325° for 20-25 minutes or until bubbly.

YIELD: 4-6 SERVINGS.

carol trotter
INMAN, SOUTH CAROLINA

I've had this unique recipe for years. It's always a hit at our house because it combines eggs, bacon, cheese, vegetables and bread all in one pan. I enjoy cooking for my husband of 31 years, two sons, one daughter and two grandsons.

diced **BACON**

To dice bacon with ease, cut the uncooked bacon with kitchen shears and brown as usual. Freeze leftover cooked bacon by placing in a resealable plastic bag, then storing in the freezer.

HAM AND BROCCOLI BAKE

PREP 15 minutes + chilling | **BAKE** 35 minutes

- 1 loaf (8 ounces) day-old French bread, cubed
- 1/2 cup butter, melted
- 2 cups (8 ounces) shredded cheddar cheese
- 2 cups frozen chopped broccoli, thawed
- 2 cups cubed fully cooked ham
- 4 eggs
- 2 cups milk
- 1/4 teaspoon pepper

Toss the bread cubes with butter. Place half in a greased 13-in. x 9-in. baking dish. Top with half of the cheese and broccoli; sprinkle with ham. Top with remaining broccoli, cheese and bread cubes.

In a large bowl, whisk the eggs, milk and pepper. Pour over casserole. Cover and refrigerate overnight.

Remove from the refrigerator 30 minutes before baking. Bake, uncovered, at 350° for 35-40 minutes or until a knife inserted near the center comes out clean. Let stand for 5 minutes before cutting.

YIELD: 8 SERVINGS.

harmony tardugno
VERNON CENTER, NEW YORK

Plan ahead and start this satisfying and comforting casserole the night before you plan to enjoy it. This hearty hot dish is a bargain at only 75 cents per serving.

side dishes

GO FOR THE GRAINS CASSEROLE • PAGE 207

CREAMY SPINACH CASSEROLE

PREP 10 minutes | **BAKE** 35 minutes

annette marie young
WEST LAFAYETTE, INDIANA

Rich and comforting, this savory spinach casserole will be a welcome addition to the table. You'll love the short preparation time and decadent taste.

- 2 cans (10-3/4 ounces *each*) reduced-fat reduced-sodium condensed cream of chicken soup, undiluted
- 1 package (8 ounces) reduced-fat cream cheese, cubed
- 1/2 cup fat-free milk
- 1/2 cup grated Parmesan cheese
- 4 cups herb seasoned stuffing cubes
- 2 packages (10 ounces *each*) frozen chopped spinach, thawed and squeezed dry

In a large bowl, beat the soup, cream cheese, milk and Parmesan cheese until blended. Stir in stuffing cubes and spinach.

Spoon mixture into a 2-qt. baking dish coated with cooking spray. Bake, uncovered, at 350° for 35-40 minutes or until heated through.

YIELD: 10 SERVINGS.

ASPARAGUS TOMATO BAKE

PREP 15 minutes | BAKE 35 minutes

- 1/4 cup butter, melted
- 1 pound fresh asparagus, cut into 2-inch pieces
- 3 tablespoons finely chopped onion
- 1 garlic clove, minced
- 3 tablespoons minced celery
- 2 tablespoons grated Parmesan cheese
- 2 tablespoons seasoned bread crumbs
- 1 can (14-1/2 ounces) stewed tomatoes, drained and diced
- 1/2 teaspoon dried oregano
- 1/2 teaspoon salt
- 1/4 teaspoon pepper
- 1/4 teaspoon dried thyme

Pour butter into an 8-in. square baking dish. Lay asparagus over butter. Sprinkle with onion, garlic, celery, cheese and bread crumbs. Top with tomatoes. Sprinkle with oregano, salt, pepper and thyme.

Cover and bake at 375° for 35-40 minutes or until the asparagus is tender.

YIELD: 6 SERVINGS.

jan vanchena
KENOSHA, WISCONSIN

Country roads and railroad tracks near my home are favorite places to hunt for wild asparagus—one of the true treats of spring. Both of my sons can eye wild asparagus from afar!

TURNIP PUFF

PREP 30 minutes | BAKE 25 minutes

- 3 medium turnips, peeled and cubed
- 4 tablespoons butter, *divided*
- 2 eggs
- 3 tablespoons all-purpose flour
- 1 tablespoon brown sugar
- 3 teaspoons baking powder
- 3/4 teaspoon salt
- 1/4 teaspoon pepper
- Dash ground nutmeg
- 1/2 cup dry bread crumbs

Place turnips in a small saucepan and cover with water. Bring to a boil. Reduce the heat; cover and simmer for 10-12 minutes or until tender. Drain.

In a small bowl, combine the turnips, 2 tablespoons butter and eggs. Combine the flour, brown sugar, baking powder, salt, pepper and nutmeg; add to the turnip mixture and mix well. Transfer to a greased 8-in. square baking dish.

Melt remaining butter; toss with the bread crumbs. Sprinkle over the top. Bake, uncovered, at 375° for 25-30 minutes or until a knife inserted near the center comes out clean. Serve immediately.

YIELD: 8 SERVINGS.

EDITOR'S NOTE: Carrots, parsnips or rutabagas may be substituted for the turnips.

helen hackwood
MEAFORD, ONTARIO

This recipe has been in our family for years. We like turnips with turkey, so my mother used to serve this side dish with our turkey dinner at Christmas. Then I served this dish, and now my daughter, who has taken over preparing Christmas dinner, is carrying on the tradition.

about TURNIPS

When you are shopping for turnips, select those with smooth, unblemished skin, and that are heavy, firm and not spongy. Look for turnips no larger than 2 inches in diameter. Keep unwashed turnips in a plastic bag in the refrigerator crisper drawer for up to 1 week. Just before using, wash, trim ends and peel.

⏱ CORN BREAD VEGETABLE COBBLER

PREP 25 minutes | **BAKE** 1-1/4 hours

1 butternut squash (2 pounds), peeled and cut into 1/2-inch pieces
1 pound red potatoes, cut into 1/2-inch wedges
3 medium parsnips, peeled and cut into 1/2-inch pieces
1 medium red onion, cut into 1/2-inch wedges
3 tablespoons olive oil
1 teaspoon salt
1 teaspoon dried tarragon
1 can (14-1/2 ounces) vegetable *or* chicken broth
2 cups fresh broccoli florets
1/2 teaspoon grated lemon peel
4 teaspoons cornstarch
1-1/2 cups milk, *divided*
1-3/4 cups biscuit/baking mix
1/2 cup yellow cornmeal
Dash cayenne pepper

Place squash, potatoes, parsnips and onion in a shallow 3-qt. baking dish. Combine oil, salt and tarragon; drizzle over vegetables and toss to coat. Bake, uncovered, at 375° for 1 hour or until tender, stirring once.

Meanwhile, in a large saucepan, bring broth to a boil. Add broccoli and lemon peel. Reduce the heat; cover and cook for 2 minutes or until broccoli is crisp-tender.

In a small bowl, combine the cornstarch and 1/2 cup milk until smooth. Add to broccoli. Bring to a boil; cook and stir for 2 minutes or until thickened. Add to the roasted vegetables; stir to combine.

Combine the baking mix, cornmeal, cayenne and remaining milk until smooth. Drop the batter in 12 mounds over the hot vegetables. Bake, uncovered, for 15-20 minutes or until topping is browned.
YIELD: 12 SERVINGS.

NUTRITION FACTS: 1 cup (prepared with reduced-sodium chicken broth and reduced-fat baking mix) equals 205 calories, 6 g fat (1 g saturated fat), 4 mg cholesterol, 514 mg sodium, 34 g carbohydrate, 4 g fiber, 5 g protein. **DIABETIC EXCHANGES:** 2 starch, 1 fat.

edna hoffman
HEBRON, INDIANA

Here's a new flavor spin on the traditional cobbler. A medley of delicious veggies, this warm and savory treat is topped with a delicious cornbread mixture.

about **PARSNIPS**

Parsnips are a root vegetable similar to carrots. Look for parsnips that are small to medium, and that are firm and have smooth skin. Avoid ones that are shriveled, limp, cracked or spotted. Store in a plastic bag for up to 2 weeks. Peel and trim ends just before using. Four medium parsnips equal about one pound or two cups chopped.

SWISS POTATO GRATIN

PREP 15 minutes | **BAKE** 20 minutes

1-1/2 cups grated peeled potatoes
1/2 cup 2% milk
1/4 cup heavy whipping cream
1/2 teaspoon salt
1/4 to 1/2 teaspoon minced garlic
Dash ground nutmeg
Pepper to taste
1/4 cup shredded Swiss *or* Gruyere cheese

In a saucepan, combine the potatoes, milk, whipping cream, salt, garlic, nutmeg and pepper. Bring to a boil over medium heat, stirring occasionally.

Pour into a 3-cup baking dish coated with cooking spray. Sprinkle with cheese. Bake, uncovered, at 425° for 20-25 minutes or until heated through and golden brown.
YIELD: 2 SERVINGS.

connie bryan
LINWOOD, KANSAS

Grated potatoes and creamy Swiss or Gruyere cheese make this side dish a satisfying alternative to mashed or baked potatoes.

VEGGIE BEAN CASSEROLE

PREP 30 minutes | **BAKE** 45 minutes

- 2 medium carrots, diced
- 2 celery ribs, chopped
- 1 large onion, chopped
- 1 medium green pepper, chopped
- 3 garlic cloves, minced
- 2 tablespoons canola oil
- 2 tablespoons chili powder
- 1/2 teaspoon ground cumin
- 1 can (28 ounces) diced tomatoes, undrained
- 2 cups frozen corn
- 1 can (16 ounces) kidney beans, rinsed and drained
- 1 can (15 ounces) garbanzo beans *or* chickpeas, rinsed and drained
- 1 can (15 ounces) tomato sauce
- 2 tablespoons picante sauce

In a large Dutch oven, saute the carrots, celery, onion, green pepper and garlic in oil for 5 minutes. Add chili powder and cumin; saute 2 minutes longer. Stir in remaining ingredients; bring to a boil.

Cover and bake at 350° for 45-50 minutes or until thickened and vegetables are tender. **YIELD:** 8 SERVINGS.

larue ritchie
BELLEVUE, ALBERTA

I serve this as a meatless main dish, but it also makes a nice side dish. It freezes and reheats well, so I'll sometimes double the recipe. It has a colorful combination of carrots, corn, beans and tomatoes.

CHILI-CHEESE RICE BAKE

PREP/TOTAL TIME 30 minutes

cathlene willis
RIGBY, IDAHO

Rich and satisfying, this easy side is sheer comfort. On occasion, I top it with canned onions or crumbled potato chips before baking.

1/2 cup uncooked instant rice
1/2 cup chopped onion
  1 tablespoon butter
1/2 cup sour cream
1/4 cup canned chopped green chilies
  2 tablespoons cream-style cottage cheese
  2 tablespoons ricotta cheese
1/8 teaspoon salt
Dash pepper
1/2 cup shredded sharp cheddar cheese
  1 teaspoon minced fresh parsley

Cook the rice according to the package directions. Meanwhile, in a large skillet, saute onion in butter until tender. Remove from the heat; stir in the sour cream, chilies, cottage cheese, ricotta cheese, salt, pepper and cooked rice.

Transfer rice mixture to a 2-cup baking dish coated with cooking spray. Sprinkle with cheddar cheese. Bake at 375° for 15-20 minutes or until the cheese is melted. Sprinkle with parsley.
YIELD: 2 SERVINGS.

HEARTY VEGETABLE CASSEROLE

PREP 15 minutes | **BAKE** 1-1/2 hours

1 cup sliced turnips
1 cup diced carrots
1 cup diced potatoes
1 cup frozen peas
1 cup diced parsnips
1 cup shredded cabbage
Salt and pepper to taste
1 can (8 ounces) cut green beans
2 tablespoons chopped onion
1 package (12 ounces) fresh pork sausage links
1 can (10-3/4 ounces) condensed cream of mushroom soup, undiluted

In a greased 13-in. x 9-in. glass baking dish, layer the first six vegetables in order given, seasoning with salt and pepper between layers. Drain beans, reserving liquid; set the liquid aside.

Place beans over cabbage; sprinkle with salt and pepper. Top with onion. Brown the sausage; drain. Place over onion. Combine soup and bean liquid; pour over sausage.

Cover and bake at 350° for 1 hour. Turn sausage over; bake, uncovered, 30 minutes longer or until vegetables are tender.

YIELD: 6 SERVINGS.

bill cowan
HANOVER, ONTARIO

This layered dish has lots of fall vegetables and a package of pork sausage for flavor. It is great for potluck meals at our church. As a side dish this casserole serves twelve; as a one-dish entree it serves six people.

about DRIED BEANS

It can take a long time to cook dried beans. To save time, prepare an entire bag of beans at once. Soak them overnight, cook in a large pot the next day, then drain and cool them. Place cupfuls in freezer bags and keep them in the freezer for up to 1 year to use whenever you need them for a recipe.

OLD-FASHIONED BAKED BEANS

PREP 1-1/2 hours + soaking | **BAKE** 45 minutes

1 pound dried great northern beans
1 quart water
1/2 teaspoon salt
1 medium onion, chopped
2 tablespoons prepared mustard
2 tablespoons brown sugar
2 tablespoons dark molasses
1/2 pound sliced bacon, cooked and crumbled

Place beans in a Dutch oven or kettle; add enough water to cover by 2 in. Bring to a boil; boil for 2 minutes. Remove from the heat; cover and let stand for 1 hour.

Drain and rinse the beans, discarding liquid. Return the beans to pan. Add the water and salt; bring to a boil. Reduce the heat; cover and simmer for 1 to 1-1/4 hours or until beans are tender. Drain, reserving 2 cups of cooking liquid.

In a greased 13-in. x 9-in. baking dish, combine the beans, onion, mustard, brown sugar, molasses, bacon and 1 cup reserved cooking liquid. Cover and bake at 400° for 45 minutes or until the beans have reached desired thickness, stirring occasionally (add additional reserved cooking liquid if needed).

YIELD: 8 SERVINGS.

marjorie thompson
WEST SACRAMENTO, CALIFORNIA

These savory beans were a specialty my dear grandma frequently prepared. When I even think of this dish, I can smell the enticing aroma that met us at the door when we went over to Grandma's for Sunday dinner. Every dish she made was a labor of love.

KOHLRABI 'N' CARROT BAKE

PREP 35 minutes | **BAKE** 20 minutes

- 3 medium kohlrabies, peeled and sliced
- 4 medium carrots, sliced
- 1/4 cup chopped onion
- 3 tablespoons butter, *divided*
- 2 tablespoons all-purpose flour
- 1/2 teaspoon salt
- Dash pepper
- 1-1/2 cups milk
- 1/4 cup minced fresh parsley
- 1 tablespoon lemon juice
- 3/4 cup soft bread crumbs

Place kohlrabies and carrots in a large saucepan and cover with water. Bring to a boil. Reduce heat; cover and cook for 15-20 minutes or until tender. Drain well; set aside.

In a large skillet, saute onion in 2 tablespoons butter until tender. Stir in the flour, salt and pepper until blended. Gradually whisk in milk. Bring to a boil; cook and stir for 2 minutes or until thickened.

Remove from heat. Stir in the vegetable mixture, parsley and lemon juice. Transfer to a shallow 2-qt. baking dish coated with cooking spray.

In a small skillet, melt remaining butter over medium heat. Add bread crumbs; cook and stir for 2-3 minutes or until lightly browned. Sprinkle over vegetable mixture.

Bake, uncovered, at 350° for 20-25 minutes or until heated through.

YIELD: 6 SERVINGS.

NUTRITION FACTS: 3/4 cup (prepared with reduced-fat butter and fat-free milk) equals 108 calories, 4 g fat (2 g saturated fat), 11 mg cholesterol, 321 mg sodium, 16 g carbohydrate, 4 g fiber, 5 g protein. **DIABETIC EXCHANGES:** 2 vegetable, 1/2 starch, 1/2 fat.

dianne bettin
TRUMAN, MINNESOTA

We love kohlrabies from our garden, but there don't seem to be many recipes that use this flavorful vegetable. This one is wonderful!

about KOHLRABI

The word kohlrabi is of German origin (kohl meaning cabbage and rabi meaning turnip). The taste is a blend of cabbage, turnip, water chestnut and artichoke. To prepare kohlrabi, peel the outer fibrous layer and boil or steam either whole or halved for 15-30 minutes or until tender. Kohlrabi is also tasty served raw. Peeled and cut into sticks or slices, it can be served with dips or spreadable cheese. Look for kohlrabi at bargain prices during the summer months.

GREEN BEAN CASSEROLE

PREP/TOTAL TIME 20 minutes

- 1/2 cup condensed cream of mushroom soup, undiluted
- 3 tablespoons milk
- 1/2 teaspoon soy sauce
- Dash pepper
- 1-1/3 cups frozen cut green beans *or* cut fresh green beans
- 1/2 cup french-fried onions, *divided*

In a large bowl, combine the soup, milk, soy sauce and pepper. Stir in beans and 1/4 cup onions. Transfer to a 2 or 3 cup baking dish coated with cooking spray. Sprinkle with remaining onions.

Bake, uncovered, at 400° for 12-15 minutes or until bubbly.

YIELD: 2 SERVINGS.

christy hinrichs
PARKVILLE, MISSOURI

Who doesn't love green beans when they're dressed up in a creamy sauce and topped with golden french-fried onions? This traditional side dish is sized right for two people.

SNAPPY HERBED SPINACH

PREP/TOTAL TIME 20 minutes

1 teaspoon butter
2 tablespoons finely chopped onion
2 eggs
1/3 cup fat-free milk
1/2 teaspoon Worcestershire sauce
1/2 teaspoon salt
1/4 teaspoon dried rosemary, crushed
1 package (10 ounces) frozen chopped spinach, thawed and squeezed dry
1 cup cooked long grain rice
1/2 cup shredded cheddar cheese, *divided*

In a small microwave-safe bowl, melt the butter. Add onion; cover and microwave at 50% power for 1 minute, stirring after 30 seconds. Set aside.

In a large bowl, whisk the eggs, milk, Worcestershire sauce, salt and rosemary. Stir in spinach, rice, onion mixture and 1/4 cup cheese. Transfer to an 8-in. x 4-in. microwave-safe dish coated with cooking spray.

Microwave, uncovered, on high for 6-8 minutes. Sprinkle with remaining cheese; microwave 1-2 minutes longer or until firm and a thermometer reads 160°. Cover and let stand for 5 minutes before cutting.

YIELD: 4 SERVINGS.

NUTRITION FACTS: 1 piece equals 174 calories, 8 g fat (4 g saturated fat), 124 mg cholesterol, 492 mg sodium, 16 g carbohydrate, 2 g fiber, 10 g protein. DIABETIC EXCHANGES: 1 starch, 1 lean meat, 1 vegetable, 1 fat.

eva brookman
DAVIS, ILLINOIS

We have a small group that meets once a week to exercise and share ideas for light and tasty foods that are good for us but also quick. This is one of our favorite recipes.

CRANBERRY CORNMEAL DRESSING

PREP 30 minutes | **BAKE** 40 minutes

corinne portteus
ALBUQUERQUE, NEW MEXICO

This moist dressing is perfect when paired with poultry or pork. The sweet-tart flavor of the dried cranberries really complements the dish's turkey sausage.

- 3 cups reduced-sodium chicken broth, *divided*
- 1/2 cup yellow cornmeal
- 1/2 teaspoon salt
- 1/2 teaspoon white pepper
- 1/2 pound Italian turkey sausage links, casings removed
- 1 large onion, diced
- 1 large fennel bulb, diced (about 1 cup)
- 1 garlic clove, minced
- 1 egg yolk
- 4 cups soft French *or* Italian bread crumbs
- 3/4 cup dried cranberries
- 2 tablespoons minced fresh parsley
- 1 tablespoon balsamic vinegar
- 1 teaspoon minced fresh sage
- 1 teaspoon minced fresh savory
- 1/4 teaspoon ground nutmeg

In a small bowl, whisk 1 cup broth, cornmeal, salt and pepper until smooth. In a large saucepan, bring remaining broth to a boil. Add cornmeal mixture, stirring constantly. Return to a boil; cook and stir for 3 minutes or until thickened. Remove from the heat; set aside.

Crumble the sausage into a large nonstick skillet, add onion, fennel and garlic. Cook over medium heat until sausage is no longer pink; drain. Stir in egg yolk and cornmeal mixture. Add the bread crumbs, cranberries, parsley, vinegar, sage, savory and nutmeg.

Transfer to a 1-1/2-qt. baking dish coated with cooking spray. Cover and bake at 350° for 40-45 minutes or until heated through. **YIELD:** 8 SERVINGS.

NUTRITION FACTS: 2/3 cup equals 205 calories, 4 g fat (1 g saturated fat), 42 mg cholesterol, 695 mg sodium, 33 g carbohydrate, 3 g fiber, 9 g protein. **DIABETIC EXCHANGES:** 2 starch, 1 lean meat.

VEGETABLE RICE CASSEROLE

PREP 40 minutes | **BAKE** 45 minutes

6 cups water
2 tablespoons butter
3 cups uncooked long grain rice
2 tablespoons dried parsley flakes
3 teaspoons dill weed, *divided*
2 teaspoons celery salt, *divided*
1 cup diced carrots
1 cup diced fresh tomato
1 cup diced green pepper
1 cup diced onion
1 cup diced celery
1/4 to 1/2 cup diced hot banana peppers *or* hot peppers of your choice
2 tablespoons olive oil
2 cans (10-3/4 ounces *each*) condensed cream of chicken soup, undiluted
1/2 cup milk
2 teaspoons dried basil
1 teaspoon dried thyme
1/2 teaspoon pepper

In a large saucepan, bring the water and butter to a boil; add the rice. Cover and simmer for 20 minutes or until liquid is absorbed. Stir in the parsley, 2 teaspoons dill and 1 teaspoon celery salt; set aside.

In a skillet, saute the carrots, tomato, green pepper, onion, celery and hot peppers in oil until vegetables are crisp-tender. Stir in the soup, milk, basil, thyme, pepper and remaining dill and celery salt.

Divide half of rice mixture between two greased 11-in. x 7-in. baking dishes. Top with vegetable mixture and remaining rice mixture.

Cover and bake at 350° for 45 minutes or until heated through.
YIELD: 2 CASSEROLES (12 SERVINGS EACH).

blaine baker
KELSEYVILLE, CALIFORNIA

As an avid gardener and occasional cook, I use fresh vegetables and herbs when trying out new recipes on my wife and children. This zesty rice dish always pleases.

HEARTY CALICO BEAN BAKE

PREP 10 minutes | **BAKE** 1 hour

1 can (16 ounces) pork and beans, undrained
1 can (16 ounces) kidney beans, rinsed and drained
1 can (15-1/2 ounces) great northern beans, rinsed and drained
1 can (15-1/2 ounces) chili beans, undrained
1 can (14-1/2 ounces) cut wax beans, drained
1-1/2 cups packed brown sugar
1-1/2 cups cubed fully cooked ham
1-1/2 cups cubed cheddar cheese
1/2 cup ketchup
1 small onion, chopped
2 tablespoons Worcestershire sauce

In a large bowl, combine all the ingredients. Transfer to a greased shallow 3-qt. baking dish. Bake, uncovered, at 350° for 1 hour or until bubbly and heated through.
YIELD: 10 SERVINGS.

heather biedler
LAURA, ILLINOIS

For years, my mother made this savory-sweet bean dish. I was always thrilled when it was on the menu, and now I serve it often to my own family. You can vary the types of beans used if you wish.

GREEN RICE

PREP 15 minutes | **BAKE** 55 minutes

    2 cups uncooked long grain rice
1-1/2 cups milk
    1 pound shredded process American cheese
    1 cup chopped green pepper
    1 cup minced fresh parsley
 1/4 cup canola oil
    1 to 2 garlic cloves, minced
Salt and pepper to taste

Cook the rice according to the package directions. Add remaining ingredients. Transfer to a greased 2-1/2-qt. baking dish. Bake, uncovered, at 350° for 55-60 minutes or until the green pepper is tender.
YIELD: 10-12 SERVINGS.

ruth glabe
ORONOCO, MINNESOTA

This colorful twist on rice is a flavorful side dish that will impress your guests, with hardly any effort!

TWO-CHEESE ZITI

PREP 25 minutes | **BAKE** 25 minutes

    3 cups uncooked ziti *or* small tube pasta
    1 tablespoon butter
    2 tablespoons all-purpose flour
 1/2 teaspoon salt
 1/4 teaspoon pepper
1-3/4 cups fat-free milk
 3/4 cup shredded reduced-fat cheddar cheese
    2 tablespoons grated Parmesan cheese

TOPPING
    3 tablespoons dry bread crumbs
1-1/2 teaspoons butter, melted
 1/4 cup shredded reduced-fat cheddar cheese
    3 tablespoons grated Parmesan cheese

Cook ziti according to package directions. Meanwhile, in a large nonstick skillet, melt butter. Stir in flour, salt and pepper until smooth; gradually add milk. Bring to a boil; cook and stir for 2 minutes or until thickened. Remove from the heat; stir in cheeses until melted.

    Drain ziti; add to sauce and stir to coat. Transfer to a shallow 1-1/2-qt. baking dish coated with cooking spray. Cover and bake at 350° for 20 minutes.

    In a small bowl, combine the bread crumbs and butter; stir in the cheeses. Sprinkle over the ziti. Bake, uncovered, for 5-10 minutes or until heated through and the topping is lightly browned.
YIELD: 5 SERVINGS.

NUTRITION FACTS: 3/4 cup equals 340 calories, 11 g fat (7 g saturated fat), 31 mg cholesterol, 590 mg sodium, 44 g carbohydrate, 2 g fiber, 18 g protein. **DIABETIC EXCHANGES:** 3 starch, 1 lean meat, 1 fat.

flo burtnett
GAGE, OKLAHOMA

My grandkids really like this rich, buttery macaroni and cheese. And adults go for the home-style bread crumb topping and creamy, comforting flavor. It doesn't taste light at all! It's easy to make twice as much for a larger crowd. It's a great dish to take to potlucks.

VEGGIE MAC 'N' CHEESE

PREP 30 minutes | **BAKE** 15 minutes

1-1/2 cups uncooked elbow macaroni
3 cups fresh broccoli florets
2 cups fresh cauliflowerets
3 large carrots, halved and thinly sliced
2 celery ribs, sliced
1 medium onion, chopped
1 tablespoon butter
1/4 cup all-purpose flour
1 cup milk
1 cup chicken broth
3 cups (12 ounces) shredded sharp cheddar cheese
1 tablespoon Dijon mustard
1/4 teaspoon salt
1/8 teaspoon pepper
1/4 teaspoon paprika

Cook the macaroni according to package directions, adding broccoli, cauliflowerets, carrots and celery during the last 6 minutes. Drain; transfer to a greased 13-in. x 9-in. baking dish.

Meanwhile, in a Dutch oven, saute onion in butter until tender. Sprinkle with flour; stir until blended. Gradually stir in milk and broth. Bring to a boil; cook and stir for 2 minutes or until thickened. Stir in the cheese, mustard, salt and pepper. Pour over the macaroni mixture; stir to coat. Sprinkle with paprika.

Bake, uncovered, at 350° for 15-20 minutes or until heated through.
YIELD: 12 SERVINGS.

marsha morrill
BROWNSVILLE, OREGON

This creamy, filling mac 'n' cheese definitely doesn't come from a box! Fresh veggies add crunch and color and will leave everyone saying, "More, please!"

BUTTERY SWEET POTATO CASSEROLE

PREP 15 minutes | **BAKE** 20 minutes

sue miller
MARS, PENNSYLVANIA

2 cans (15-3/4 ounces *each*) sweet potatoes, drained and mashed

1/2 cup sugar

1 egg

1/4 cup butter, melted

1/2 teaspoon ground cinnamon

Dash salt

TOPPING

1 cup coarsely crushed butter-flavored crackers (about 25 crackers)

1/2 cup packed brown sugar

1/4 cup butter, melted

In a large bowl, combine first six ingredients. Transfer to a greased 8-in. square baking dish. Combine the topping ingredients; sprinkle over sweet potato mixture.

Bake, uncovered, at 350° for 20-25 minutes or until a thermometer reads 160°.

YIELD: 6-8 SERVINGS.

Whenever we get together as a family for major holidays, my kids, nieces and nephews literally beg me to make this dish. It goes together in minutes with canned sweet potatoes, which is ideal for the busy holiday season.

POTATO CHIP POTATOES

PREP 10 minutes | **BAKE** 40 minutes

- 6 medium potatoes, peeled and cut into 1/2-inch cubes
- 3/4 cup crushed potato chips, *divided*
- 1/2 cup chopped onion
- 2 tablespoons butter, melted
- 3/4 teaspoon salt
- 1/4 teaspoon pepper

In a large bowl, combine the potatoes, 1/2 cup of potato chips, onion, butter, salt and pepper; toss to combine.

Transfer to a greased shallow 2-qt. baking dish. Sprinkle with remaining potato chips. Bake, uncovered, at 350° for 40-50 minutes or until potatoes are tender.
YIELD: 6-8 SERVINGS.

debra hartze
ZEELAND, NORTH DAKOTA

If you are looking to bring a new side dish to the table, try this recipe. I hate to throw out the crushed chips at the bottom of potato chip bags, so they make a savory and crunchy topping for this hearty favorite.

LIGHT SCALLOPED POTATOES

PREP 15 minutes | **BAKE** 1-1/4 hours + standing

- 6 medium potatoes, peeled and thinly sliced
- 3 cups water
- 4 reduced-sodium chicken bouillon cubes
- 1 garlic clove, minced
- 1/2 cup grated Parmesan cheese

Minced fresh parsley, optional

Place potatoes in a greased 2-qt. baking dish that has been coated with cooking spray. In a small saucepan, heat the water, bouillon and garlic until bouillon is dissolved; pour over potatoes. Sprinkle with Parmesan.

Bake, uncovered, at 350° for 1-1/4 to 1-1/2 hours or until tender. Let stand 10 minutes before serving. Sprinkle with parsley if desired. Serve with a slotted spoon.
YIELD: 6 SERVINGS.

tamie foley
THOUSAND OAKS, CALIFORNIA

Even with lighter ingredients like chicken bouillon and Parmesan cheese, this is a comforting potato dish.

CREAMY ASPARAGUS CASSEROLE

PREP 20 minutes | **BAKE** 30 minutes

- 2 pounds fresh asparagus, trimmed, cut into 1-inch pieces
- 1/4 cup butter, cubed
- 1/4 cup all-purpose flour
- 2 cups milk *or* half-and-half cream
- 1/2 teaspoon salt
- 1/4 teaspoon pepper
- 6 hard-cooked eggs, sliced
- 1 cup (4 ounces) shredded cheddar cheese
- 1 cup crushed potato chips

In a large saucepan, bring 1/2 in. of water to a boil. Add asparagus; cover and boil for 3 minutes or until crisp-tender. Drain well; set aside.

In a large saucepan over medium heat, melt butter. Stir in flour until smooth. Gradually add milk. Bring to a boil over medium heat; cook and stir for 2 minutes or until thickened. Add salt and pepper.

In a ungreased 11-in. x 7-in. baking dish, layer half of the asparagus. Cover with half of the eggs, cheese and sauce. Repeat layers. Sprinkle with potato chips.

Bake, uncovered, at 350° for 30 minutes or until heated through.
YIELD: 6-8 SERVINGS.

joyce allison
MILLSAP, TEXAS

My sister created this recipe and shared it with me. I always serve it on special occasions, particularly Easter. My husband says he hates asparagus, but he loves this casserole. He doesn't know he's eating his "enemy vegetable!"

BROWN RICE VEGETABLE CASSEROLE

PREP 20 minutes | **BAKE** 1 hour 20 minutes

- 3 cups chicken broth
- 1-1/2 cups uncooked brown rice
- 2 cups chopped onions, *divided*
- 3 tablespoons soy sauce
- 2 tablespoons butter, melted
- 1/2 teaspoon dried thyme
- 4 cups fresh cauliflowerets
- 4 cups fresh broccoli florets
- 2 medium sweet red peppers, julienned
- 2 garlic cloves, minced
- 3 tablespoons olive oil
- 1 cup salted cashew halves
- 2 cups (8 ounces) shredded cheddar cheese, optional

In a greased 3-qt. baking dish, combine the broth, rice, 1 cup onion, soy sauce, butter and thyme. Cover and bake at 350° for 65-70 minutes or until rice is tender.

Meanwhile, in a large skillet, saute the cauliflower, broccoli, peppers, garlic and remaining onion in oil until crisp-tender; spoon over rice mixture.

Cover and bake for 10 minutes. Uncover and sprinkle with the cashews and cheese if desired. Bake 5-7 minutes longer or until cheese is melted.

YIELD: 8-10 SERVINGS.

gloria de beradinis
GREENTOWN, PENNSYLVANIA

One taste of this crowd-pleasing casserole brings compliments and requests for my recipe. It's been in my file for as long as I can remember. The blend of tender vegetables and rice is perfect for special meals and dish-to-pass affairs.

GREEN BEAN 'N' CORN BAKE

PREP 15 minutes | **BAKE** 30 minutes

- 1 can (14-1/2 ounces) French-style green beans, drained
- 1 can (11 ounces) shoepeg corn, drained
- 1 can (10-3/4 ounces) condensed cream of celery soup, undiluted
- 1/2 cup sliced celery
- 1/2 cup chopped onion
- 1/2 cup sour cream
- 1/2 cup shredded cheddar cheese
- 1 jar (2 ounces) diced pimientos, drained
- 1/2 teaspoon salt
- 1/2 teaspoon pepper
- 1/2 cup crushed butter-flavored crackers (about 13 crackers)
- 2 tablespoons butter, melted

In a large bowl, combine first 10 ingredients. Transfer to a greased 1-1/2-qt. baking dish. Combine the cracker crumbs and butter; sprinkle over vegetable mixture.

Bake, uncovered, at 350° for 30-35 minutes or until topping is golden brown.

YIELD: 6 SERVINGS.

christy hughes
SUNSET BEACH, NORTH CAROLINA

I serve this side dish for many occasions and holidays—it's a must for Thanksgiving—because it goes well with many entrees. The creamy casserole includes green beans, corn, pimientos and cheddar cheese with a buttery cracker topping. If your family is like mine, there won't be any left!

CREAMED POTATO CASSEROLES

PREP 1-1/4 hours | **BAKE** 40 minutes

- 10 pounds medium potatoes (about 30)
- 2/3 cup plus 3 tablespoons butter, *divided*
- 2/3 cup all-purpose flour
- 5 cups chicken broth
- 5 cups half-and-half cream
- 8 egg yolks, lightly beaten
- 1-1/2 cups minced fresh parsley
- 3 teaspoons salt
- 3/4 teaspoon pepper
- 1/4 teaspoon cayenne pepper
- 1 cup seasoned bread crumbs

Place potatoes in a large stockpot or soup kettle; cover with water. Bring to a boil. Reduce heat; cover and simmer for 20 minutes or until just tender. Drain and rinse in cold water. When cool enough to handle, peel potatoes and cut into 1/4-in. slices; set aside.

In a large saucepan, melt 2/3 cup butter. Stir in flour until smooth; gradually add broth and cream. Bring to a boil; cook and stir for 2 minutes or until thickened. Remove from the heat. Stir 1 cup hot cream mixture into egg yolks; return all to the pan, stirring constantly. Add the parsley, salt, pepper and cayenne. Bring to a gentle boil; cook and stir 2 minutes longer. Remove from the heat.

Spread 1 cup sauce into each of two 3-qt. baking dishes. Top with a third of the potato slices. Repeat layers twice. Spread with remaining sauce. Melt the remaining butter; toss with bread crumbs. Sprinkle over the casseroles. Bake, uncovered, at 375° for 40-45 minutes or until bubbly.

YIELD: 2 CASSEROLES (12 SERVINGS EACH).

norma harder
SASKATOON, SASKATCHEWAN

This classic potato dish makes enough for 24 hungry people. It's great with ham and other meats. Guests always remark on its rich sauce and seasoned crumb topping.

MAKEOVER FAVORITE CORN BAKE

PREP 20 minutes | **BAKE** 30 minutes + standing

- 1 cup all-purpose flour
- 1 cup cornmeal
- 3 tablespoons sugar
- 1/2 teaspoon salt
- 1/2 teaspoon baking soda
- 1 egg
- 1 cup (8 ounces) reduced-fat sour cream
- 1/4 cup unsweetened applesauce
- 1/4 cup butter, melted
- 1 can (15-1/4 ounces) whole kernel corn, undrained
- 1 can (14-3/4 ounces) cream-style corn

In a large bowl, combine the first five ingredients. In a small bowl, whisk egg, sour cream, applesauce and butter. Stir in the corn. Stir into the dry ingredients just until moistened. Transfer to a 13-in. x 9-in. baking dish coated with cooking spray.

Bake at 350° for 30-35 minutes or until a toothpick inserted near the center comes out clean. Serve warm. Refrigerate leftovers.

YIELD: 12 SERVINGS.

NUTRITION FACTS: 1 serving equals 211 calories, 7 g fat (4 g saturated fat), 34 mg cholesterol, 395 mg sodium, 32 g carbohydrate, 2 g fiber, 5 g protein. **DIABETIC EXCHANGES:** 2 starch, 1 fat.

ruthann clore
WEST PEORIA, ILLINOIS

My family loves this dish—even my picky youngster. The Test Kitchen helped slash the fat in my recipe for a sweet corn bake with fewer calories but all the flavor of the original.

CREAMY BRUSSELS SPROUTS BAKE

PREP 15 minutes | BAKE 30 minutes

- 1 package (8 ounces) cream cheese, softened
- 1 cup (8 ounces) sour cream
- 1/2 pound sliced fresh mushrooms
- 1 medium onion, chopped
- 2 tablespoons butter
- 2 packages (10 ounces *each*) frozen brussels sprouts, thawed and drained
- 3/4 cup shredded cheddar cheese

In a small bowl, beat cream cheese and sour cream until smooth; set aside. In a large skillet, saute the mushrooms and onion in butter until tender. Stir in the brussels sprouts. Remove from the heat; stir in cream cheese mixture.

Spoon into a greased shallow 2-qt. baking dish. Cover and bake at 350° for 25-30 minutes or until bubbly. Uncover and sprinkle with cheddar cheese. Bake for 5 minutes longer or until cheese is melted. **YIELD:** 6-8 SERVINGS.

elizabeth metz
ALBUQUERQUE, NEW MEXICO

Eating brussels sprouts was a ho-hum experience at our house until I put together this cheesy bake. After one taste, my husband declared it a "keeper." It's nice alongside ham, pork or beef roasts.

BARLEY AND CORN CASSEROLE

PREP 15 minutes | BAKE 70 minutes

- 3 garlic cloves, minced
- 1 cup chopped onion
- 2/3 cup chopped carrots
- 1 tablespoon canola oil
- 3 cups chicken broth
- 1 cup medium pearl barley
- 1/4 teaspoon salt
- 1/8 teaspoon pepper
- 2 cups frozen corn, thawed
- 1/2 cup chopped fresh parsley

In a large skillet, saute the garlic, onion and carrots in oil over medium heat, until tender.

Transfer to a greased 2-qt. baking dish; add chicken broth, barley, salt and pepper. Mix well. Cover and bake at 350° for 1 hour.

Stir in corn and parsley. Cover and bake 10-15 minutes longer or until barley is tender and corn is heated through. **YIELD:** 12 SERVINGS.

NUTRITION FACTS: 1/2 cup (prepared with low-sodium chicken broth; calculated w/o added salt) equals 108 calories, 2 g fat (0 saturated fat), 1 mg cholesterol, 36 mg sodium, 21 g carbohydrate, 0 fiber, 4 g protein. **DIABETIC EXCHANGES:** 1 starch, 1 vegetable.

diane molberg
EMERALD PARK, SASKATCHEWAN

This hearty and colorful casserole goes well with everything from pork and chicken to beef and fish. For convenience, this dish can be prepared ahead and refrigerated until mealtime. After it's been in the oven for awhile, I simply stir in the last two ingredients and finish baking it.

SAUCY GREEN BEAN BAKE

PREP/TOTAL TIME 30 minutes

- 1 can (8 ounces) tomato sauce
- 2 tablespoons diced pimientos
- 1 tablespoon prepared mustard
- 1/4 teaspoon salt
- 1/8 teaspoon pepper
- 1 pound fresh *or* frozen cut green beans, cooked
- 1/2 cup chopped onion
- 1/3 cup chopped green pepper
- 1 garlic clove, minced
- 2 tablespoons butter
- 3/4 cup shredded process cheese (Velveeta)

In a large bowl, combine the first five ingredients. Add green beans; toss to coat. Transfer to an ungreased 1-qt. baking dish. Cover; bake at 350° for 20 minutes.

Meanwhile, in a large skillet, saute the onion, green pepper and garlic in butter until tender. Sprinkle over beans. Top with cheese. Bake, uncovered, for 3-5 minutes or until cheese is melted. **YIELD:** 4-6 SERVINGS.

june formanek
BELLE PLAINE, IOWA

Here's a different way to serve green beans. It's a nice change of pace from plain vegetables.

MONTEREY CORN BAKE

PREP 15 minutes | **BAKE** 25 minutes

- 1 medium onion, chopped
- 1 garlic clove, minced
- 5 tablespoons butter, *divided*
- 2 cups sliced fresh mushrooms
- 1 medium sweet red pepper, chopped
- 1/2 teaspoon salt
- 1/4 teaspoon pepper
- 1 package (16 ounces) frozen corn, thawed
- 2 cups (8 ounces) shredded Colby-Monterey Jack cheese
- 2 teaspoons brown sugar
- 1/2 cup dry bread crumbs
- 2 tablespoons minced fresh parsley

In a large skillet, saute onion and garlic in 2 tablespoons butter until tender. Add the mushrooms, red pepper, salt and pepper; cook and stir for 5 minutes or until the vegetables are tender. Drain.

In a greased 2-qt. baking dish, layer half of the corn, mushroom mixture, cheese and brown sugar; repeat layers.

Melt the remaining butter; toss with the bread crumbs and parsley. Sprinkle over the casserole. Bake, uncovered, at 375° for 25-30 minutes or until golden brown.
YIELD: 4-6 SERVINGS.

irene redick
TRENTON, ONTARIO

I am happy to share this 50-year-old recipe. It came from my mother-in-law, who taught me how to cook. It is one of my family's favorite dishes, yielding enough for a group or the perfect serving for a few if you cut the recipe in half.

SWEET POTATO CASSEROLE

PREP 45 minutes | **BAKE** 40 minutes

- 6 medium sweet potatoes
- 1/2 cup butter, cubed
- 3/4 cup sugar
- 1 can (20 ounces) crushed pineapple, drained
- 2 eggs, beaten
- 1 teaspoon vanilla extract
- 1/2 teaspoon ground nutmeg
- 1/2 teaspoon salt
- 15 large marshmallows

Place sweet potatoes in a large kettle and cover with water; bring to a boil. Boil gently until potatoes can easily be pierced with the tip of a sharp knife, about 30-45 minutes. Drain; cool slightly.

Peel potatoes and place in a large bowl; mash. Stir in butter and sugar until butter is melted. Add the pineapple, eggs, vanilla, nutmeg and salt.

Spoon into a greased 2-qt. baking dish. Top with marshmallows. Bake, uncovered, at 350° for 40-45 minutes or until a knife inserted near the center comes out clean.
YIELD: 8 SERVINGS.

ruth leach
SHREVEPORT, LOUISIANA

Pineapple, sugar and marshmallows lend a superb sweetness to these potatoes. I've been making this casserole for years, both for special occasions and casual dinners.

sweet POTATOES

The sweet potato is a member of the morning glory family and native to Central America. Two varieties are readily available. One has a pale skin with light yellow flesh and dry mealy texture, the other has dark skin with orange flesh that cooks to a moist texture. This variety is often commonly known as a yam. True yams, though, are not readily available in the United States and are seldom grown here.

GO FOR THE GRAINS CASSEROLE

PREP 25 minutes | **BAKE** 55 minutes

    5 medium carrots, thinly sliced
    2 cups frozen corn, thawed
    1 medium onion, diced
    1 cup quick-cooking barley
  1/2 cup bulgur
  1/3 cup minced fresh parsley
    1 teaspoon salt
  1/2 teaspoon pepper
    3 cups vegetable broth
    1 can (15 ounces) black beans, rinsed and
      drained
1-1/2 cups (6 ounces) shredded reduced-fat
      cheddar cheese

In a large bowl, combine carrots, corn, onion, barley, bulgur, parsley, salt and pepper. Stir in broth and beans. Transfer to a 13-in. x 9-in. baking dish coated with cooking spray.

Cover and bake at 350° for 50-55 minutes or until the grains are tender, stirring once. Sprinkle with the cheese. Bake, uncovered, 3-5 minutes longer or until cheese is melted. **YIELD:** 10 SERVINGS.

NUTRITION FACTS: 3/4 cup equals 226 calories, 5 g fat (3 g saturated fat), 12 mg cholesterol, 741 mg sodium, 38 g carbohydrate, 8 g fiber, 12 g protein. **DIABETIC EXCHANGES:** 2 starch, 1 lean meat, 1 vegetable.

melanie blair
WARSAW, INDIANA

This casserole is hearty and delicious. A friend of mine gave me the recipe when I was compiling healthier recipes. This colorful medley has "good-for-you" written all over it.

DIJON SCALLOPED POTATOES

PREP 25 minutes | **BAKE** 50 minutes + standing

2/3 cup chopped onion

2 teaspoons canola oil

1 can (14-1/2 ounces) chicken broth

2 packages (3 ounces *each*) cream cheese, cubed

1 tablespoon Dijon mustard

3 medium russet potatoes, peeled and thinly sliced

2 medium sweet potatoes, peeled and thinly sliced

1-1/2 to 2 cups crushed butter-flavored crackers

3 tablespoons grated Parmesan cheese

2 tablespoons butter, melted

2 teaspoons minced fresh parsley

In a Dutch oven, saute onion in oil until tender. Reduce heat to medium; stir in the broth, cream cheese and mustard until blended. Remove from heat. Stir in potatoes.

Transfer to a 13-in. x 9-in. baking dish coated with cooking spray. Combine the crushed crackers, Parmesan cheese and butter; sprinkle over the top.

Bake, uncovered, at 350° for 50-60 minutes or until potatoes are tender. Sprinkle with parsley. Let stand for 10 minutes before serving.

YIELD: 8 SERVINGS.

carolyn putnam
NORWALK, OHIO

My family loves this creamy and colorful recipe for cheesy potatoes. What's not to love? It has both sweet and white potatoes, lots of rich, buttery flavor and a pretty, golden-crumb topping.

FRUITED HOLIDAY VEGETABLES

PREP 1 hour | **BAKE** 30 minutes

- 1 large rutabaga, peeled and cubed
- 3 small red potatoes, cubed
- 3 medium sweet potatoes, peeled and cubed
- 4 teaspoons cornstarch
- 1/2 cup cold water
- 1/2 cup orange juice
- 1 cup prepared mincemeat
- 1/4 cup butter, melted
- 1/4 cup packed dark brown sugar
- 1/4 cup dark corn syrup
- 1/4 teaspoon ground ginger
- 1/4 teaspoon ground cinnamon
- 1-3/4 cups frozen unsweetened sliced peaches, thawed and chopped
- 1 medium tart apple, chopped
- 1 tablespoon lemon juice
- 1/2 cup chopped pecans

Place rutabaga in a Dutch oven; cover with water. Bring to a boil. Reduce heat; cover and simmer for 15 minutes. Add the red potatoes and enough additional water to cover. Return to a boil. Reduce heat; cover and simmer for 5 minutes.

Add the sweet potatoes and enough additional water to cover. Bring to a boil. Reduce heat; cover and simmer 15 minutes longer or until vegetables are tender.

Meanwhile, in a small saucepan, combine the cornstarch and cold water until smooth. Gradually stir in the orange juice. Bring to a boil; cook and stir for 1-2 minutes or until thickened. Stir in mincemeat, butter, brown sugar, corn syrup, ginger and the cinnamon; heat through.

In a large bowl, combine the peaches, apple and lemon juice. Drain vegetables; stir in fruit mixture. Transfer to a greased 4-qt. baking dish. Add mincemeat; stir gently. Sprinkle with pecans. Bake, uncovered, at 325° for 30-35 minutes or until fruit is tender.
YIELD: 12 SERVINGS.

paula marchesi
LENHARTSVILLE, PENNSYLVANIA

Mom and I made a great team in the kitchen, cooking and baking for hours at a time. I treasure this holiday favorite from her the most.

make your OWN

If you are out of corn syrup, here's how to make your own. For each cup of light corn syrup in a recipe, substitute with 1 cup of sugar mixed with 1/4 cup water. For each cup of dark corn syrup, substitute with 1 cup of packed brown sugar mixed with 1/4 cup water.

SWEET ONION RICE CASSEROLE

PREP 15 minutes | **BAKE** 45 minutes

- 1/3 cup uncooked instant rice
- 2-1/2 cups chopped sweet onions
- 1 tablespoon butter
- 1/4 cup shredded Swiss cheese
- 1/4 cup half-and-half cream

Cook the rice according to the package directions. Meanwhile, in a large skillet, saute onions in butter until tender. Stir in the cheese, cream and rice.

Transfer to a 2-cup baking dish coated with cooking spray. Bake, uncovered, at 325° for 45-55 minutes or until golden brown.
YIELD: 2 SERVINGS.

NUTRITION FACTS: 1 cup equals 277 calories, 13 g fat (8 g saturated fat), 43 mg cholesterol, 115 mg sodium, 32 g carbohydrate, 4 g fiber, 8 g protein. **DIABETIC EXCHANGES:** 2 starch, 1-1/2 fat, 1 lean meat.

julie rea
BATTLE GROUND, WASHINGTON

This rich onion casserole is warm, comforting and perfect for a cool evening. Everyone who tries it, loves it!

CHEESY BROCCOLI CAULIFLOWER CASSEROLE

PREP 35 minutes | **BAKE** 25 minutes

1 tablespoon butter
4-1/2 teaspoons all-purpose flour
1-1/4 cups 1% milk
3/4 cup shredded reduced-fat cheddar cheese
1/3 cup grated Parmesan cheese
5 cups frozen broccoli florets, thawed
2-1/4 cups frozen cauliflowerets, thawed
1 cup cubed fully cooked lean ham
1 cup soft bread crumbs
Butter-flavored cooking spray

In a saucepan, melt butter. Stir in flour until smooth; gradually add the milk. Bring to a boil; cook and stir for 1-2 minutes or until thickened. Remove from the heat. Add cheeses; stir until melted.

Place vegetables in a 2-qt. baking dish coated with cooking spray; sprinkle with ham. Pour sauce over ham. Place bread crumbs in a bowl; spray with butter-flavored spray. Sprinkle around the edge of the casserole. Bake, uncovered, at 350° for 25-30 minutes or until heated through and bubbly.

YIELD: 5 SERVINGS.

NUTRITION FACTS: 1 serving equals 227 calories, 10 g fat (6 g saturated fat), 34 mg cholesterol, 707 mg sodium, 16 g carbohydrate, 3 g fiber, 18 g protein. **DIABETIC EXCHANGES:** 2 lean meat, 1 vegetable, 1 fat, 1/2 starch.

nancy whitford
EDWARDS, NEW YORK

After I found this recipe in an old church cookbook, I adjusted it to make it lower in calories and fat. The creamy cheese sauce makes it a tasty way to get children to eat their vegetables.

POTATO CHEESE CASSEROLE

PREP 20 minutes | **BAKE** 50 minutes

4 pounds potatoes, peeled and cubed
1 package (8 ounces) cream cheese, softened
1/2 cup butter, softened
1/4 cup milk
1 to 1-1/4 teaspoons salt
1/4 teaspoon pepper
1 cup chopped green pepper
1/2 cup shredded cheddar cheese
1/2 cup grated Parmesan cheese
1/2 cup minced chives
1 jar (2 ounces) diced pimientos, drained

Cook the potatoes in boiling water until tender; drain and mash. Add the cream cheese, butter, milk, salt and pepper; mix well. Stir in the green pepper, cheeses, chives and pimientos.

Transfer the mixture to a greased 13-in. x 9-in. baking dish. Bake, uncovered, at 350° for 50-60 minutes or until browned and heated through.

YIELD: 12-15 SERVINGS.

jane luzem
GREEN BAY, WISCONSIN

This rich, flavorful side dish is a Christmas tradition at our house. Plain potatoes are the start, but they get dressed up with a creamy sauce and colorful ingredients like peppers and chives.

VEGETABLE BARLEY BAKE

PREP 25 minutes | BAKE 55 minutes

3 medium sweet red or green peppers, chopped
4 cups sliced fresh mushrooms
2 medium onions, chopped
2 tablespoons butter
2 cups reduced-sodium chicken broth or vegetable broth
1-1/2 cups medium pearl barley
1/8 teaspoon pepper

In a large nonstick skillet, saute peppers, mushrooms and onions in butter for 8-10 minutes or until tender. Transfer to a 13-in. x 9-in. baking dish coated with cooking spray. Stir in the broth, barley and pepper.

Cover and bake at 350° for 50 minutes. Uncover; bake 5-10 minutes longer or until barley is tender and liquid is absorbed.
YIELD: 10 SERVINGS.

shirley doyle
MT. PROSPECT, ILLINOIS

Forget the potatoes and rice, and consider this change-of-pace dinner accompaniment. I rely on wholesome barley for this heart-smart dish that complements most any main course.

HASH BROWN BROCCOLI BAKE

PREP 25 minutes | **BAKE** 50 minutes

  4 tablespoons butter, *divided*
  2 tablespoons all-purpose flour
  1 teaspoon salt
1/8 teaspoon ground nutmeg
1/8 teaspoon pepper
  2 cups milk
  1 package (8 ounces) cream cheese, cubed
  2 cups (8 ounces) shredded Swiss cheese
  6 cups frozen shredded hash brown potatoes, thawed
  1 package (16 ounces) frozen chopped broccoli, thawed
1/2 cup dry bread crumbs

In a large saucepan, melt 2 tablespoons butter. Stir in the flour, salt, nutmeg and pepper until smooth; gradually add milk. Bring to a boil; cook and stir for 2 minutes or until thickened. Remove from the heat. Add cheeses; stir until melted. Stir in potatoes.

Spoon half of the potato mixture into a greased 2-qt. baking dish. Top with the broccoli and remaining potato mixture. Cover and bake at 350° for 35 minutes.

Melt remaining butter; toss with bread crumbs. Sprinkle over the casserole. Bake, uncovered, for 15-20 minutes or until heated through and topping is golden.
YIELD: 12-14 SERVINGS.

jeanette volker
WALTON, NEBRASKA

Here's a perfect dish for a potluck or holiday buffet. It goes well with fish, poultry, pork or beef. Cheddar cheese can be substituted for Swiss. Often, I double the recipe to serve a crowd.

SCALLOPED CORN

PREP 20 minutes | **BAKE** 25 minutes

- 1/2 cup chopped green pepper
- 1/4 cup chopped onion
- 5 tablespoons butter, *divided*
- 2 cups soft bread crumbs
- 2 cans (8-1/2 ounces *each*) cream-style corn
- 1 can (11 ounces) whole kernel corn, drained
- 2 eggs
- 1/4 cup dry bread crumbs

In a large skillet, saute the green pepper and onion in 4 tablespoons butter until tender. Stir in soft bread crumbs, corn and eggs. Transfer to a greased 8-in. square baking dish.

Melt the remaining butter; toss with dry bread crumbs. Sprinkle over casserole. Bake, uncovered, at 350° for 25-30 minutes or until bubbly.

YIELD: 5 SERVINGS.

doris thomas
SCOTTSVILLE, NEW YORK

This is one of my favorite recipes, and my family loves it! It's been handed down from generation to generation. I love that it can be made the day before.

MAKEOVER SOUTHERN FAVORITE SWEET POTATOES

PREP 15 minutes | **BAKE** 40 minutes

- 2 eggs, beaten
- 1/2 cup fat-free milk
- 1/3 cup sugar
- 1/3 cup unsweetened pineapple juice
- 1/4 cup reduced-fat butter, melted
- 1 teaspoon vanilla extract
- 2 cans (40 ounces *each*) sweet potatoes, drained and coarsely chopped

TOPPING
- 1 cup chopped pecans
- 2/3 cup packed brown sugar
- 1/4 cup reduced-fat butter, melted

In a large bowl, combine eggs, milk, sugar, pineapple juice, butter and vanilla. Gently stir in sweet potatoes. Transfer to a 3-qt. baking dish coated with cooking spray.

Combine the topping ingredients; spoon over sweet potato mixture. Bake, uncovered, at 350° for 40-50 minutes or until bubbly and golden brown.

YIELD: 12 SERVINGS.

EDITOR'S NOTE: This recipe was tested with Land O'Lakes light stick butter.

sonia chimenti
CONCORD, CALIFORNIA

Thanksgiving wouldn't be the same for my family without the buttery, pecan-topped sweet potato bake they've come to love with their turkey. This recipe is one any holiday cook can be thankful for!

ZUCCHINI TOMATO BAKE

PREP 30 minutes | **BAKE** 25 minutes

- 1 medium onion, chopped
- 1 tablespoon butter
- 3 medium zucchini (about 1 pound), shredded and patted dry
- 3 medium tomatoes, seeded and chopped
- 1 cup (4 ounces) shredded reduced-fat Swiss cheese, *divided*
- 1/3 cup reduced-fat sour cream
- 1 teaspoon paprika
- 1/2 teaspoon salt
- 1/2 teaspoon garlic powder
- 1/4 teaspoon pepper
- 2 tablespoons shredded Parmesan cheese

In a large nonstick skillet, saute onion in butter until tender. Transfer to a large bowl. Add zucchini, tomatoes, 1/2 cup Swiss, sour cream and seasonings; mix well.

Transfer to an 11-in. x 7-in. baking dish coated with cooking spray. Sprinkle with Parmesan cheese and remaining Swiss cheese. Bake, uncovered, at 350° for 25-30 minutes or until vegetables are tender.

YIELD: 6 SERVINGS.

NUTRITION FACTS: 1 serving equals 113 calories, 5 g fat (3 g saturated fat), 18 mg cholesterol, 321 mg sodium, 9 g carbohydrate, 2 g fiber, 9 g protein. **DIABETIC EXCHANGES:** 2 vegetable, 1 lean meat, 1/2 fat.

tina repak
JOHNSTOWN, PENNSYLVANIA

This flavorful side makes the most of those bountiful tomatoes and zucchinis. Melted Swiss cheese and sour cream lend a touch of decadence to this healthy and appealing dish.

ITALIAN BROCCOLI BAKE

PREP 20 minutes | **BAKE** 30 minutes

1-1/2 cups (16 ounces) fat-free cottage cheese
2 egg whites
1/4 cup grated Parmesan cheese
3 tablespoons all-purpose flour
1/2 teaspoon Italian seasoning
1 large bunch broccoli, sliced lengthwise into spears
1 cup reduced-sodium meatless spaghetti sauce
1 cup (4 ounces) shredded part-skim mozzarella cheese

In a blender or food processor, place the cottage cheese, egg whites, Parmesan cheese, flour and Italian seasoning; cover and process until smooth. Set aside.

Place the broccoli and a small amount of water in a skillet; cover and cook for 5-8 minutes or until crisp-tender. Drain. Place half of the broccoli in a single layer in a 13-in. x 9-in. baking dish coated with cooking spray. Top with cottage cheese mixture and remaining broccoli. Pour spaghetti sauce over broccoli. Sprinkle with mozzarella cheese.

Bake, uncovered, at 375° for 30-35 minutes or until cheese is melted and bubbly. Let stand 5 minutes before serving.

YIELD: 9 SERVINGS.

NUTRITION FACTS: 1 serving equals 147 calories, 5 g fat (0 saturated fat), 13 mg cholesterol, 341 mg sodium, 13 g carbohydrate, 0 fiber, 15 g protein. **DIABETIC EXCHANGES:** 1-1/2 meat, 1 vegetable, 1/2 starch.

carol wilson
CHELSEA, OKLAHOMA

There are several diabetics in my family, and I've enjoyed adapting dishes to meet their needs. This flavorful Italian recipe is such a dish. This tasty side is also easy on the waistline!

UNSTUFFING SIDE DISH

PREP 15 minutes | **BAKE** 40 minutes

1/2 pound bulk Italian sausage
1/4 cup butter
1/2 pound fresh mushrooms, sliced
3/4 cup chopped celery
1 medium onion, chopped
1 teaspoon poultry seasoning
1/2 teaspoon salt
1/4 teaspoon pepper
6 cups unseasoned stuffing croutons *or* dry bread cubes
2-1/2 to 3 cups chicken broth

In a large skillet, brown sausage; drain. Add butter, mushrooms, celery and onion; saute 2-3 minutes or until onion is tender. Stir in the poultry seasoning, salt and pepper. Transfer to a large bowl; add croutons and enough broth to moisten.

Place in a greased 2-qt. baking dish. Cover and bake at 350° for 30 minutes. Uncover and bake 10 minutes more.

YIELD: 8 SERVINGS.

ken churches
SAN ANDREAS, CALIFORNIA

With sausage, mushrooms, celery and the perfect blend of seasonings, this moist dressing is irresistible. I like to call it "Unstuffing" since it bakes separately from the turkey, which I do on the grill.

PECAN SWEET POTATO CASSEROLE

PREP 10 minutes | **BAKE** 1 hour

2 cans (40 ounces *each*) sweet potatoes, drained

8 eggs

1/2 cup sugar

1/4 cup all-purpose flour

2 teaspoons vanilla extract

1 teaspoon salt

TOPPING

1 cup packed brown sugar

1/3 cup all-purpose flour

1 cup chopped pecans

1/4 cup cold butter

In a large bowl, mash the sweet potatoes. Add the eggs, sugar, flour, vanilla and salt; beat until smooth. Transfer to a greased 13-in. x 9-in. baking dish.

In a small bowl, combine brown sugar, flour and pecans; cut in butter until crumbly. Sprinkle over sweet potato mixture.

Bake, uncovered, at 325° for 60-70 minutes or until a thermometer reads 160°. Refrigerate leftovers.

YIELD: 12 SERVINGS.

anita briner
ETTERS, PENNSYLVANIA

This convenient casserole calls for canned sweet potatoes, so preparation time is minimal. The nutty brown sugar topping adds a bit of crunch.

BROCCOLI RICE CASSEROLE

PREP 15 minutes | **BAKE** 30 minutes

1-1/2 cups water
1/2 cup butter, cubed
1 tablespoon dried minced onion
2 cups uncooked instant rice
1 package (16 ounces) frozen chopped broccoli, thawed
1 can (10-3/4 ounces) condensed cream of mushroom soup, undiluted
1 jar (8 ounces) process cheese sauce

In a large saucepan, bring water, butter and onion to a boil. Stir in rice. Remove from the heat; cover and let stand for 5 minutes or until water is absorbed.

Stir in broccoli, soup and cheese sauce. Transfer to a greased 2-qt. baking dish. Bake, uncovered, at 350° for 30-35 minutes or until bubbly.

YIELD: 8 SERVINGS.

jennifer fuller
BALLSTON SPA, NEW YORK

When I was little, serving this dish was the only way my mother could get me to eat broccoli. It's an excellent recipe to serve anytime and is especially good with poultry.

OLD-FASHIONED CHEESE POTATOES

PREP 15 minutes | **BAKE** 1 hour

1/4 cup butter, cubed
1/4 cup all-purpose flour
2 teaspoons salt
1/2 teaspoon pepper
2-1/2 cups milk
1-1/2 cups (6 ounces) shredded process cheese (Velveeta)
6 medium potatoes, peeled and thinly sliced

In a large saucepan, melt butter. Whisk in the flour, salt and pepper until smooth. Gradually add milk. Bring to a boil. Cook and stir for 2 minutes or until thickened. Reduce heat. Add the cheese; cook and stir until melted.

Place potatoes in a greased 13-in. x 9-in. baking dish. Pour sauce over potatoes. Bake, uncovered, at 350° for 1 hour or until potatoes are tender.

YIELD: 8-10 SERVINGS.

martha sue stroud
CLARKSVILLE, TEXAS

When my husband and I got married in 1951, one of the first appliances we bought was an apartment-size electric range. The range came with a cookbook that included this recipe. I've used the same recipe ever since!

FESTIVE PEAS AND ONIONS

PREP 35 minutes | **BAKE** 40 minutes

1 package (16 ounces) frozen pearl onions
2 cups water
1 package (10 ounces) frozen peas, thawed
1 can (10-3/4 ounces) condensed cream of celery soup, undiluted
1 jar (2 ounces) diced pimientos, *divided*
1/3 cup shredded sharp cheddar cheese

In a covered saucepan, cook the onions in water for 25 minutes or until tender. Drain, reserving 1/4 cup liquid. Combine onions, peas, soup, 2 tablespoons pimientos and reserved cooking liquid; stir to coat. Transfer to a greased 1-1/2-qt. baking dish.

Bake, uncovered, at 350° for 35 minutes. Sprinkle with cheese and remaining pimientos. Bake 5 minutes longer or until the cheese is melted.

YIELD: 4-6 SERVINGS.

caramella robichaud
RICHIBUCTO, NEW BRUNSWICK

The first time I tried this recipe, my friend finished half of it while my back was turned! That was over 30 years ago, but the dish is just as popular today.

CREAMY CORN CASSEROLE

PREP 15 minutes | **BAKE** 25 minutes

1 cup finely chopped celery
1/4 cup finely chopped onion
1/4 cup finely chopped sweet red pepper
3 tablespoons butter, *divided*
1 can (10-3/4 ounces) condensed cream of chicken soup, undiluted
3 cups fresh, frozen *or* drained canned corn
1 can (8 ounces) sliced water chestnuts, drained
1/3 cup slivered almonds, optional
1/2 cup soft bread crumbs

In a medium skillet, saute celery, onion and red pepper in 2 tablespoons of butter for 2-3 minutes or until vegetables are tender. Remove from the heat; stir in soup, corn, water chestnuts and almonds if desired.

Transfer to a 2-qt. baking dish. Melt the remaining butter; toss with bread crumbs. Sprinkle on top of the casserole. Bake, uncovered, at 350° for 25-30 minutes or until bubbly.

YIELD: 8 SERVINGS.

brenda wood
EGBERT, ONTARIO

If you're looking for a different way to serve vegetables, give this recipe a try. This dish is one of my family's favorites. It just might become a favorite at your house, too.

quick & easy

SWEET POTATO HAM BAKE

PREP 10 minutes | **BAKE** 30 minutes

- 1 can (15 ounces) cut sweet potatoes, drained and quartered lengthwise
- 2 cups cubed fully cooked ham
- 1 cup (4 ounces) shredded cheddar cheese

In a greased 1-qt. baking dish, layer half of the sweet potatoes, ham and cheddar cheese. Repeat layers. Cover and bake at 350° for 20 minutes. Uncover; bake 8-10 minutes longer or until cheese is melted.

YIELD: 2-3 SERVINGS.

jennette fourne
DETROIT, MICHIGAN

Three ingredients are all you need for this colorful hot dish, sized perfectly for two. It's a good way to use up ham from the holidays.

HOT PORK SALAD SUPREME

PREP 10 minutes | **BAKE** 30 minutes

- 2 cups diced cooked pork
- 2 cups cooked rice
- 1 can (10-3/4 ounces) condensed cream of chicken soup, undiluted
- 1 cup diced celery
- 1/2 cup mayonnaise
- 1 can (4 ounces) mushroom stems and pieces, drained
- 1 tablespoon lemon juice
- 1 tablespoon finely chopped onion
- 1/4 teaspoon salt
- 1 cup cornflake crumbs
- 1/2 cup sliced almonds
- 2 tablespoons butter, melted

Combine the first nine ingredients; mix well. Spoon into an ungreased 11-in. x 7-in. baking dish. Combine crumbs, almonds and butter; sprinkle on top.

Bake, uncovered, at 350° for 30-40 minutes or until lightly browned.

YIELD: 4-6 SERVINGS.

dawn eason
CARMICHAEL, CALIFORNIA

The original recipe for this dish called for chicken, but I decided to use "the other white meat." It's a nice dish to pass at a luncheon or shower.

BRUNCH EGG CASSEROLE

PREP 10 minutes | **BAKE** 1 hour

- 2 cups unseasoned croutons
- 1 cup (4 ounces) shredded cheddar cheese
- 4 eggs, lightly beaten
- 2 cups milk
- 1/2 teaspoon salt
- 1/2 teaspoon ground mustard
- 1/8 teaspoon onion powder
- Dash pepper
- 4 bacon strips, cooked and crumbled

Place the croutons and cheese in a greased 11-in. x 7-in. baking dish. Combine the eggs, milk and seasonings; pour into baking dish. Sprinkle with bacon.

Bake at 325° for 1 hour or until a knife inserted near the center comes out clean.

YIELD: 6 SERVINGS.

lelia brown
ANNANDALE, VIRGINIA

There aren't many foods that do a better job of combining breakfast and lunch than cheese and eggs. This savory dish satisfies a mouthful of taste buds for both hearty and light eaters.

make your **OWN**

To make croutons, use heels from loaves of bread or leftover buns. Cube the bread, coat with cooking spray and season with dried garlic powder, parsley, basil or oregano. Then bake on a cookie sheet at 250° until crisp and brown.

THREE-BEAN CASSOULET

PREP 5 minutes | **BAKE** 1 hour

- 2 cans (14-1/2 ounces *each*) stewed tomatoes
- 1 can (15 ounces) garbanzo beans *or* chickpeas, rinsed and drained
- 1 can (15-1/2 ounces) great northern beans, rinsed and drained
- 1 can (15 ounces) butter beans, rinsed and drained
- 1 cup finely chopped carrots
- 1 cup finely chopped onion
- 2 garlic cloves, minced
- 1 bay leaf
- 2 teaspoons dried parsley flakes
- 1 teaspoon dried basil
- 1/2 teaspoon salt
- 1/2 teaspoon dried thyme
- 1/8 teaspoon pepper

In an ungreased 3-qt. baking dish, combine all ingredients. Cover and bake at 350° for 60-70 minutes or until the vegetables are tender, stirring occasionally. Discard the bay leaf.

YIELD: 9 SERVINGS.

NUTRITION FACTS: 3/4 cup equals 197 calories, 1 g fat (0.55 g saturated fat), 0 cholesterol, 687 mg sodium, 41 g carbohydrate, 9 g fiber, 10 g protein. **DIABETIC EXCHANGES:** 2 starch, 2 vegetable.

carol berigan
GOLDEN, COLORADO

Brimming with a trio of bean varieties, this recipe is as easy as one, two, three. You can serve it on the side or as a satisfying meatless main dish. The veggies add an interesting mix of tastes, colors and textures.

SWEET POTATO BANANA BAKE

PREP 10 minutes | **BAKE** 30 minutes

2 cups mashed sweet potatoes
1 cup mashed ripe bananas (2 to 3 medium)
1/2 cup reduced-fat sour cream
1 egg, lightly beaten
3/4 teaspoon curry powder
1/2 teaspoon salt

In a large bowl, combine all ingredients until smooth. Transfer to a 1-qt. baking dish coated with cooking spray.

Cover and bake at 350° for 30-35 minutes or until a thermometer inserted near the center reads 160°.

YIELD: 6 SERVINGS.

susan mccartney
ONALASKA, WISCONSIN

This yummy casserole makes what's good for you taste good, too. Pairing bananas with sweet potatoes unites two power foods into a change-of-pace side dish. Try it with roasted poultry.

ZESTY CHICKEN AND RICE

PREP 5 minutes | **BAKE** 1 hour 20 minutes

6 chicken breast halves (bone in)
1/3 cup Italian salad dressing
1 can (14-1/2 ounces) chicken broth
1 package (16 ounces) frozen broccoli, carrots and water chestnuts
2/3 cup uncooked long grain rice
1-1/4 teaspoons Italian seasoning

Place chicken in a greased 13-in. x 9-in. baking dish. Pour dressing over chicken. Bake, uncovered, at 400° for 20 minutes. Combine the broth, vegetables, rice and Italian seasoning; pour over chicken.

Cover and bake at 350° for 30 minutes. Uncover; bake 30 minutes more or until chicken juices run clear and rice is tender.
YIELD: 6 SERVINGS.

NUTRITION FACTS: 1 serving (prepared with fat-free salad dressing and low-sodium chicken broth) equals 363 calories, 14 g fat (0 saturated fat), 94 mg cholesterol, 344 mg sodium, 22 g carbohydrate, 3 g fiber, 34 g protein. **DIABETIC EXCHANGES:** 4-1/2 lean meat, 1 starch, 1/2 vegetable, 1/2 fat.

ella west
LAKE CHARLES, LOUISIANA

A dear friend gave me this recipe years ago. Italian dressing and seasoning add just the right amount of "zip" to ordinary chicken and white rice.

BACON TATER BAKE

PREP 10 minutes | **BAKE** 1 hour

2 cans (10-3/4 ounces *each*) condensed cream of mushroom soup, undiluted
1-1/3 cups sour cream
1 large onion, chopped
1 pound sliced bacon, cooked and crumbled
1 package (32 ounces) frozen Tater Tots

In a large bowl, combine the soup, sour cream and onion. Add the bacon and Tater Tots; stir until combined.

Transfer to a greased 13-in. x 9-in. baking dish. Cover and bake at 350° for 50 minutes. Uncover and bake 8-10 minutes longer or until golden brown.
YIELD: 10 SERVINGS.

nita cinquina
SURPRISE, ARIZONA

I make the most of convenient Tater Tots in this down-home dish. A ham dinner would not be complete without this creamy casserole. It always gets compliments.

PORK CHOP CASSEROLE

PREP 10 minutes | **BAKE** 65 minutes

4 boneless pork loin chops (3/4 inch thick)
1/4 teaspoon Italian seasoning
1/4 teaspoon pepper
2 large potatoes, peeled and sliced 1/4 inch thick
1 medium onion, chopped
1 tablespoon all-purpose flour
3 tablespoons reduced-fat margarine
1 tablespoon chopped green pepper

Sprinkle pork chops with Italian seasoning and pepper. Arrange in the center of a 13-in. x 9-in. baking dish that has been coated with cooking spray. Combine the potatoes, onion and flour; place around chops. Dot with margarine; sprinkle with green pepper.

Cover and bake at 325° for 55 minutes. Uncover and bake 10-15 minutes longer or until potatoes are tender and meat juices run clear.
YIELD: 4 SERVINGS.

NUTRITION FACTS: 1 serving equals 278 calories, 13 g fat (0 saturated fat), 63 mg cholesterol, 137 mg sodium, 14 g carbohydrate, 0 fiber, 27 g protein. **DIABETIC EXCHANGES:** 3 lean meat, 1 starch.

linda wynn
IOWA PARK, TEXAS

My family raves about this casserole with its tender chops and nicely seasoned potatoes. I can just pop it in the oven and let it bake.

RICH AND CREAMY POTATO BAKE

PREP 10 minutes | **BAKE** 45 minutes

> 3 cups half-and-half cream
> 1/2 cup butter, cubed
> 1-1/2 teaspoons salt
> 1 package (32 ounces) frozen Southern-style hash brown potatoes, thawed
> 1/2 cup grated Parmesan cheese

Minced fresh parsley, optional

In a large saucepan, combine cream, butter and salt. Cook and stir over medium heat until butter is melted. Place potatoes in a greased 13-in. x 9-in. baking dish; pour cream mixture over potatoes. Sprinkle with Parmesan cheese.

Bake, uncovered, at 350° for 45-55 minutes or until the potatoes are tender and top is golden brown. Sprinkle with parsley if desired.

YIELD: 12 SERVINGS.

joy simpkins
CAMBRIDGE CITY, INDIANA

Here's a delicious side dish that goes well with any meat entree. It's a wonderful recipe to make for potluck dinners.

LIMA BEAN CASSEROLE

PREP/TOTAL TIME 30 minutes

> 8 bacon strips, diced
> 1 medium onion, chopped
> 1 can (10-3/4 ounces) condensed tomato soup, undiluted
> 5 slices process American cheese, cut into 1/2-inch pieces
> 1 package (16 ounces) frozen baby lima beans, cooked and drained

Additional cheese slices, optional

In a large skillet, cook the bacon until crisp. Remove to paper towels; drain, reserving 1 tablespoon of the drippings. Saute the onion in drippings until tender. Stir in the soup, cheese, beans and bacon. Cover and simmer over low heat for 5 minutes or until the cheese melts. Spoon into an ungreased 1-1/2-qt. casserole dish.

Cover and bake at 350° for 20-30 minutes or until casserole is bubbly and beans are tender. Garnish with additional cheese if desired.

YIELD: 8-10 SERVINGS.

about **LIMA BEANS**

Also called "butter beans" because of their buttery texture, lima beans are known as a component, along with corn, in succotash. They are thought to originate from Peru in South America, but some historians believe they may have actually come from Guatemala. Lima beans are an excellent source of fiber, manganese and folate.

margaret taylor
WEST HAVEN, CONNECTICUT

This versatile casserole makes a delicious side dish for any meal. I've made it often for buffets and potlucks, and it's always a crowd-pleaser. It can be prepared the day before, so it fits into any cook's busy schedule.

CHEESY EGG CASSEROLE

PREP 10 minutes + chilling | **BAKE** 40 minutes

- 4 cups (16 ounces) shredded Monterey Jack cheese
- 1 tablespoon all-purpose flour
- 2 cups (8 ounces) shredded sharp cheddar cheese
- 1 pound sliced bacon, cooked and crumbled
- 12 eggs
- 1 cup milk

Toss Monterey Jack cheese with flour; place in a greased 13-in. x 9-in. baking dish. Top with cheddar cheese; sprinkle with bacon. Beat the eggs and milk; pour over all. Cover and chill for 8 hours or overnight. Remove from the refrigerator 30 minutes before baking.

Bake, uncovered, at 325° for 40-45 minutes or until a knife inserted near the center comes out clean. Let stand 5 minutes before cutting.
YIELD: 12-16 SERVINGS.

dawn reeve
SALT LAKE CITY, UTAH

This dish is perfect for potlucks because it looks so pretty on the table and, best of all, it can be made ahead of time. Although we live in the city, my family and I love the country flavor of this hearty egg casserole.

QUICK TATER TOT BAKE

PREP 10 minutes | **BAKE** 30 minutes

jean ferguson
ELVERTA, CALIFORNIA

I like to make this dish when time before supper is limited. It serves two to three people, but if we have unexpected company I double the ingredients and use a 9-in. x 13-in. pan. I call it my "Please Stay Casserole!"

3/4 to 1 pound ground beef *or* turkey
1 small onion, chopped
Salt and pepper to taste
1 package (16 ounces) frozen Tator Tot potatoes
1 can (10-3/4 ounces) condensed cream of mushroom soup, undiluted
2/3 cup milk *or* water
1 cup (4 ounces) shredded cheddar cheese

In a large skillet, cook beef and onion over medium heat until no longer pink; drain. Season with salt and pepper.

Transfer to a greased 2-qt. baking dish. Top with potatoes. Combine the soup and milk; pour over the potatoes. Sprinkle with cheese. Bake, uncovered, at 350° for 30-40 minutes or until heated through.
YIELD: 2-3 SERVINGS.

BREAKFAST BREAD PUDDING

PREP 10 minutes + chilling | BAKE 40 minutes

- 12 slices white bread
- 1 package (8 ounces) cream cheese, cubed
- 12 eggs
- 2 cups milk
- 1/3 cup maple syrup
- 1/4 teaspoon salt

Remove and discard the crusts from bread; cut the bread into cubes. Toss lightly with the cream cheese cubes; place in a greased 13-in. x 9-in. baking pan. In a large bowl, beat eggs. Add milk, syrup and salt; mix well. Pour over bread mixture. Cover and refrigerate 8 hours or overnight.

Remove from refrigerator 30 minutes before baking. Bake, uncovered, at 375° for 40-45 minutes or until a knife inserted near the center comes out clean. Let stand 5 minutes before cutting.

YIELD: 6-8 SERVINGS.

alma andrews
LIVE OAK, FLORIDA

I assemble this dish the day before our grandchildren visit, giving me more time to spend with them and have fun!

CHEESY POTATOES AND HAM

PREP 10 minutes | BAKE 30 minutes

- 1 can (10-3/4 ounces) condensed cream of mushroom soup, undiluted
- 1 cup cubed process cheese (Velveeta)
- 2 tablespoons butter, cubed
- 2 cups cubed fully cooked ham
- 1/4 cup chopped onion
- 1-1/2 teaspoons Worcestershire sauce
- 6 cups mashed potatoes (with added milk and butter)

In a large saucepan, combine soup, cheese and butter. Cook and stir over medium heat until cheese is melted. Stir in the ham, onion and Worcestershire sauce.

Pour into a greased 2-qt. baking dish. Top with the mashed potatoes. Bake, uncovered, at 350° for 30-35 minutes or until heated through.

YIELD: 4-6 SERVINGS.

esther yoder
MILLERSBURG, OHIO

I combine leftover ham with canned soup, cheese and a few other ingredients to make this mashed potato-topped casserole. My family loves it!

PEPPERONI CHEESE BAKE

PREP 10 minutes | BAKE 20 minutes + standing

- 2 cups (8 ounces) shredded part-skim mozzarella cheese
- 1/2 cup diced pepperoni
- 5 eggs
- 3/4 cup milk
- 1/4 teaspoon dried basil

In a greased 9-in. pie plate, layer mozzarella cheese and pepperoni. In a bowl, whisk the eggs, milk and basil; pour over the cheese. Bake at 400° for 20-25 minutes or until a knife inserted near the center comes out clean. Let stand for 10 minutes before cutting.

YIELD: 6-8 SERVINGS.

sharon deur
FREMONT, MICHIGAN

We have this cheesy, pepperoni-filled casserole monthly because it's a welcome dish for me after coming home from work. It requires minimal prep time so it's easy to make in a jiffy, but it's also chock-full of protein and flavor.

FAST CHICKEN DIVAN

PREP 5 minutes | **BAKE** 30 minutes

- 8 cups frozen broccoli florets *or* chopped broccoli
- 3 cups cubed cooked chicken
- 2 cans (10-3/4 ounces *each*) condensed cream of chicken soup, undiluted
- 1 cup mayonnaise
- 1 teaspoon lemon juice
- 1 cup (4 ounces) shredded sharp cheddar cheese
- 3/4 cup dry bread crumbs
- 3 tablespoons butter, melted
- 1 tablespoon sliced pimientos, optional

In a large saucepan, cook the broccoli in boiling water for 1 minute; drain. Transfer to a greased 11-in. x 7-in. baking dish; top with chicken. Combine soup, mayonnaise and lemon juice; spread over chicken. Sprinkle with cheese. Combine bread crumbs and butter; sprinkle over top.

Bake, uncovered, at 325° for 30 minutes or until bubbly and golden brown. Let stand for 10 minutes before serving. Garnish with pimientos if desired.

YIELD: 4-6 SERVINGS.

EDITOR'S NOTE: Reduced-fat or fat-free mayonnaise is not recommended for this recipe.

bertille cooper
CALIFORNIA, MARYLAND

Frozen broccoli and leftover chicken get an easy, but elegant, treatment in this dish. I dress them up with a saucy blend of cream soup and mayonnaise, then cover it all with a golden, cheesy crumb topping.

GREEN BEANS DELUXE

PREP/TOTAL TIME 30 minutes

- 1 package (16 ounces) frozen French-style green beans
- 1 small onion, chopped
- 2 tablespoons butter
- 1 tablespoon all-purpose flour
- 3/4 cup sour cream
- 1/2 teaspoon salt
- 1/4 teaspoon pepper
- Pinch ground nutmeg
- 1/4 cup shredded cheddar cheese

Prepare green beans according to package directions. Meanwhile, in a large skillet, saute onion in butter until tender. Reduce heat; stir in flour until blended. Add the sour cream, salt, pepper and nutmeg; heat through (do not boil).

Drain the beans; stir into the sour cream mixture. Transfer to a greased 1-qt. baking dish. Bake, uncovered, at 350° for 15-20 minutes or until heated through. Sprinkle with cheese; bake 5 minutes longer or until cheese is melted.

YIELD: 4-6 SERVINGS.

lucy martin
DALLAS, TEXAS

We have belonged to a dinner/bridge group for many years, and this green bean dish has been a favorite. The pinch of nutmeg enhances the flavor, which is creamy and rich. It goes well with a holiday meal, both by color and taste.

using fresh **GREEN BEANS**

To use fresh green beans for Green Beans Deluxe, wash and trim one pound of green beans or French green beans, blanch until crisp-tender, then rinse with cold water. Heat and drain the beans (a microwave works great), then use according to the recipe.

SAUSAGE RICE CASSEROLE

PREP 10 minutes | **BAKE** 30 minutes

1/2 pound bulk Italian sausage
1/4 cup chopped onion
1/4 cup chopped sweet red pepper
1/2 cup uncooked instant rice
1/4 teaspoon dried basil
1 can (10-3/4 ounces) condensed tomato soup, undiluted
1/4 cup water
1/4 cup plus 2 tablespoons shredded part-skim mozzarella cheese, *divided*

In a small skillet, cook the sausage, onion and red pepper over medium heat until sausage is no longer pink; drain. Remove from the heat. Stir in the rice, basil, soup, water and 1/4 cup cheese.

Transfer to an ungreased 3-cup baking dish. Cover and bake at 350° for 25-30 minutes or until the rice is tender. Uncover; sprinkle with the remaining cheese. Bake 5 minutes longer or until cheese is melted.
YIELD: 2 SERVINGS.

eleanor deaver
FRESNO, CALIFORNIA

The key to the distinctive flavor in this casserole is the use of Italian sausage. The nice balance of ingredients gives it an old-fashioned taste, and it's just the right amount for two.

VEGGIE TURKEY CASSEROLE

PREP 10 minutes | **BAKE** 30 minutes

- 3 cups cubed cooked turkey
- 2 cups frozen mixed vegetables
- 2 cups frozen broccoli florets
- 1 can (10-3/4 ounces) condensed cream of chicken soup, undiluted
- 1 can (10-3/4 ounces) condensed cream of mushroom soup, undiluted
- 1/2 cup chopped onion
- 1/4 teaspoon garlic powder
- 1/4 teaspoon celery seed

In a large bowl, combine all the ingredients. Transfer to a greased 11-in. x 7-in. baking dish. Bake, uncovered, at 350° for 30-35 minutes or until heated through. Stir before serving.

YIELD: 4 SERVINGS.

michelle summers
CHATTANOOGA, TENNESSEE

I rely on canned goods and frozen vegetables to hurry along this creamy main dish. I like this quick casserole so much that I've requested it for my birthday dinner. Serve it with biscuits for a meal your family will love...mine sure does!

FRENCH TOAST STRATA

PREP 10 minutes + chilling | **BAKE** 35 minutes

1 loaf (1 pound) cinnamon bread, cubed
1 package (8 ounces) cream cheese, cubed
8 eggs
2-1/2 cups milk
6 tablespoons butter, melted
1/4 cup maple syrup

CIDER SYRUP

1/2 cup sugar
4 teaspoons cornstarch
1/2 teaspoon ground cinnamon
1 cup apple cider
1 tablespoon lemon juice
2 tablespoons butter

Arrange half of the bread cubes in a greased 13-in. x 9-in. baking dish. Top with cream cheese and remaining bread. In a blender, combine the eggs, milk, butter and maple syrup; cover and process until smooth. Pour over the bread. Cover and refrigerate overnight.

Remove from the refrigerator 30 minutes before baking. Bake, uncovered, at 350° for 35-40 minutes or until a knife inserted near the center comes out clean. Let stand for 10 minutes before serving.

For syrup, in a small saucepan, combine sugar, cornstarch and cinnamon. Gradually whisk in cider and lemon juice. Bring to a boil; cook and stir for 2 minutes or until thickened. Stir in butter until melted. Serve warm with strata.
YIELD: 8 SERVINGS (1 CUP SYRUP).

jill middleton
BALDWINSVILLE, NEW YORK

I'm always on the lookout for different breakfast and brunch ideas. I like to serve this easy make-ahead casserole when we have out-of-town guests.

CAJUN RICE DISH

PREP 5 minutes | **BAKE** 1 hour

5 cups beef broth
2 cups uncooked long grain rice
1 pound ground beef
1 medium onion, chopped
1 cup sliced carrots
1/2 cup sliced celery
1/2 cup frozen corn
1/2 cup frozen peas
1/2 cup chopped sweet red pepper
1 teaspoon salt
1 teaspoon Cajun seasoning

In a roasting pan, combine the broth and rice; mix well. Cover and bake at 350° for 30 minutes.

Meanwhile, in a large skillet, cook beef and onion over medium heat until meat is no longer pink; drain. Add to rice. Stir in the vegetables, salt and Cajun seasoning.

Cover and bake 30 minutes longer or until rice is tender.
YIELD: 6-8 SERVINGS.

rose kostynuik
CALGARY, ALBERTA

A variety of vegetables make this delicious casserole a hit with everyone. I team up generous servings with garlic bread and a tossed salad.

make your OWN

Look for Cajun seasoning in the spice section of your grocery store. You can also make your own. There are many different blends, but a typical mix might include salt, onion powder, garlic powder, cayenne pepper, ground mustard, celery seed and black pepper.

BAKED CREAMY SPINACH

PREP 10 minutes | **BAKE** 30 minutes

sue dodd
FRIENDSVILLE, TENNESSEE

Even folks not fond of spinach find this creamy casserole irresistible. It's a holiday favorite for my family!

- 1 large onion, chopped
- 1 tablespoon butter
- 1 package (8 ounces) cream cheese, cubed
- 1/4 cup milk
- 1-1/2 cups (6 ounces) shredded Parmesan cheese, *divided*
- 1/2 teaspoon cayenne pepper
- 1/4 teaspoon salt
- 1/8 teaspoon pepper
- 2 packages (10 ounces *each*) frozen chopped spinach, thawed and squeezed dry

In a large saucepan, saute the onion in butter until tender. Add the cream cheese and milk; stir until melted. Stir in 1 cup Parmesan cheese, cayenne, salt and pepper. Stir in spinach.

Transfer to a greased 1-1/2-qt. baking dish. Sprinkle with remaining Parmesan. Bake, uncovered, at 350° for 30-35 minutes or until hot and bubbly.

YIELD: 6-8 SERVINGS.

PINTO BEAN CASSEROLE

PREP/TOTAL TIME 30 minutes

sherry lee
SHELBY, ALABAMA

This trouble-free casserole is perfect for munching at a celebration. Bring it to your next party and people will ask for seconds!

- 1 package (9 ounces) tortilla chips
- 2 cans (15 ounces *each*) pinto beans, rinsed and drained
- 1 can (15 ounces) whole kernel corn, drained
- 1 can (14-1/2 ounces) diced tomatoes
- 1 can (8 ounces) tomato sauce
- 1 envelope taco seasoning
- 2 cups (8 ounces) shredded cheddar cheese
  Shredded lettuce, sour cream and salsa, optional

cheddar **CHEESE**

Select sharp cheddar cheese when using packaged shredded cheese for recipes that you'd prefer to have a bolder flavor. If you will be shredding the cheese at home from bulk cheddar, you can choose from either mild, medium, sharp or extra sharp.

Crush tortilla chips and sprinkle into a greased 13-in. x 9-in. baking dish. In a large bowl, combine the beans, corn, tomatoes, tomato sauce and taco seasoning. Pour over chips. Sprinkle with cheese.

Bake, uncovered, at 350° for 18-25 minutes or until heated through. Serve with lettuce, sour cream and salsa if desired.

YIELD: 6-8 SERVINGS.

SPICY SPANISH RICE

PREP 10 minutes | **BAKE** 55 minutes

1 cup uncooked long grain rice

1 small onion, chopped

1 can (2-1/4 ounces) sliced ripe olives, drained

1 teaspoon ground cumin

2 cans (10 ounces *each*) diced tomatoes and green chilies, undrained

1 cup water

2 tablespoons canola oil

1 cup (4 ounces) shredded Monterey Jack cheese

2 tablespoons minced fresh cilantro, optional

In a greased 2-qt. baking dish, combine rice, onion, olives, cumin, tomatoes, water and oil. Cover and bake at 350° for 45 minutes.

Stir in cheese. Bake, uncovered, 10-15 minutes longer or until rice is tender and liquid is absorbed. Stir in cilantro if desired.

YIELD: 6-8 SERVINGS.

marilyn warner
SHIRLEY, ARKANSAS

This is a tasty dish to serve with a Mexican meal or to perk up any dinner. We especially like it with chicken enchiladas. I also prepare it for potlucks and family get-togethers. It's a little different to bake rice, but it's handy to not have to watch it on the stove. To make the rice less spicy, choose a milder variety of the canned tomatoes with green chilies.

COLORFUL VEGETABLE BAKE

PREP 10 minutes | **BAKE** 55 minutes + standing

betty brown
BUCKLEY, WASHINGTON

My sister gave me the recipe for this side dish years ago, and it's become a favorite in our household. Chock-full of colorful veggies, it's delicious and feeds a crowd.

3 cups frozen cut green beans, thawed and drained

2 medium green peppers, chopped

6 plum tomatoes, chopped and seeded

2 to 3 cups (8 to 12 ounces) shredded cheddar cheese

3 cups chopped zucchini

1 cup biscuit/baking mix

1/2 teaspoon salt

1/2 teaspoon cayenne pepper

6 eggs

1 cup milk

Place beans and peppers in a greased 13-in. x 9-in. baking dish. Top with tomatoes, cheese and zucchini. In a bowl, combine biscuit mix, salt, cayenne, eggs and milk just until moistened. Pour over the vegetables.

Bake, uncovered, at 350° for 55-60 minutes or until puffed and a knife inserted near the center comes out clean. Let stand for 10 minutes before serving.

YIELD: 12 SERVINGS.

NUTRITION FACTS: 1 serving (prepared with 2 cups reduced-fat cheese, reduced-fat biscuit/baking mix, 1-1/2 cups egg substitute and fat-free milk) equals 146 calories, 5 g fat (2 g saturated fat), 11 mg cholesterol, 400 mg sodium, 15 g carbohydrate, 2 g fiber, 12 g protein. **DIABETIC EXCHANGES:** 2 vegetable, 1 lean meat, 1 fat.

CHICKEN ASPARAGUS STROGANOFF

PREP 10 minutes | **BAKE** 30 minutes

- 1 can (10-3/4 ounces) condensed cream of chicken soup, undiluted
- 1/4 cup milk
- 1/4 cup sour cream
- 2 cups cooked sliced asparagus
- 1 cup diced cooked chicken
- 1/4 teaspoon dried rosemary, crushed
- 1/4 cup shredded cheddar cheese

Hot cooked noodles *or* rice

Combine the soup, milk and sour cream. Pour half into a greased 1-qt. baking dish; top with asparagus, chicken and rosemary. Pour remaining soup over top. Sprinkle with cheese.

Bake, uncovered, at 350° for 30 minutes or until heated through. Serve with cooked noodles or rice.

YIELD: 4 SERVINGS.

linda hutten
HAYDEN, IDAHO

Your family will be delighted with this spin on a classic dish. You will be amazed at how easy it is to prepare!

GOLDEN CHICKEN CASSEROLE

PREP 5 minutes | **BAKE** 30 minutes

- 2 cups cubed cooked chicken
- 1 can (20 ounces) unsweetened pineapple chunks, drained
- 1 jar (12 ounces) apricot preserves *or* spreadable fruit
- 1 can (10-3/4 ounces) condensed cream of chicken soup, undiluted
- 1 can (8 ounces) water chestnuts, drained

Hot cooked rice

In a bowl, combine the first five ingredients. Transfer to a greased 2-qt. baking dish. Bake, uncovered, at 350° for 30 minutes or until heated through. Serve over rice.

YIELD: 6 SERVINGS.

NUTRITION FACTS: 1 serving (prepared with reduced-fat soup and spreadable fruit; calculated without rice) equals 259 calories, 3 g fat (0 saturated fat), 44 mg cholesterol, 413 mg sodium, 41 g carbohydrate, 3 g fiber, 16 g protein. **DIABETIC EXCHANGES:** 2 lean meat, 2 fruit, 1/2 vegetable.

melanie may
FISHERS, INDIANA

Apricot preserves give a different twist to this saucy sweet-and-sour chicken. With just five ingredients, it's a snap to stir up and serve over steaming rice.

SEAFOOD RICE CASSEROLE

PREP 10 minutes | **BAKE** 45 minutes

- 3 cups cooked long grain rice
- 1/3 cup chopped onion
- 2 tablespoons chopped green chilies
- 1 can (6-1/2 ounces) chopped clams, undrained
- 1 can (5 ounces) evaporated milk
- 1/4 cup seasoned bread crumbs
- 1/2 cup shredded cheddar cheese

In a 1-1/2-qt. baking dish coated with cooking spray, combine rice, onion and chilies. In a small bowl, combine clams and milk; pour over the rice mixture. Sprinkle with crumbs and cheese. Bake, uncovered, at 350° for 45 minutes.

YIELD: 4 MAIN-DISH OR 8 SIDE-DISH SERVINGS.

NUTRITION FACTS: 1/2-cup serving (prepared with evaporated skim milk) equals 195 calories, 3 g fat (0 saturated fat), 24 mg cholesterol, 207 mg sodium, 29 g carbohydrate, 0 fiber, 12 g protein. **DIABETIC EXCHANGES:** 2 starch, 1 lean meat.

pat wieghorst
PHILLIPSBURG, NEW JERSEY

My family loves rice and clams, so I decided to combine them in this recipe. It was a hit! This dish is very filling and satisfying. Cooking and creating new recipes are two of my favorite pastimes.

SALMON CASSEROLE

PREP 10 minutes | **BAKE** 30 minutes

agnes moon
IONIA, MICHIGAN

- 1 can (7-1/2 ounces) salmon, drained, bones and skin removed
- 4 cups soft bread crumbs
- 1/2 cup chopped celery
- 1/2 cup chopped green pepper
- 1/4 cup chopped onion
- 1 tablespoon minced fresh parsley
- 3/4 cup fat-free milk
- 1 tablespoon reduced-fat mayonnaise
- 1 teaspoon ground mustard
- 1/4 teaspoon pepper
- 1 tablespoon grated Parmesan cheese
- 1/4 teaspoon paprika

In a large bowl, combine the salmon, bread crumbs, celery, green pepper, onion and parsley. In a small bowl, combine the milk, mayonnaise, mustard and pepper. Pour over salmon mixture; toss to coat evenly.

Transfer to a 1-qt. baking dish coated with cooking spray. Sprinkle with Parmesan cheese and paprika. Bake, uncovered, at 350° for 30-35 minutes or until heated through and top is golden brown.

YIELD: 4 SERVINGS.

Canned salmon is the key ingredient in this comforting casserole. Bread crumbs give it a soft texture...and mayonnaise, mustard and cheese add flavor to this old-fashioned favorite.

SOUTHWEST CORN BREAD BAKE

PREP/TOTAL TIME 30 minutes

duane & christine geyer
CORALVILLE, IOWA

- 1 can (15-1/2 ounces) chili beans, undrained
- 1 can (8-3/4 ounces) whole kernel corn, drained
- 2 tablespoons chopped onion
- 1/2 teaspoon ground cumin
- 1/2 cup all-purpose flour
- 1/2 cup cornmeal
- 2 tablespoons sugar
- 1-1/4 teaspoons baking powder
- 1/4 teaspoon salt
- 1/2 cup plus 1 tablespoon milk
- 1-1/2 teaspoons canola oil

Warm up chilly nights with this tasty casserole. It's loaded with hearty beans and corn, then topped with a from-scratch corn bread. I usually double the ingredients and bake it in a 13-in. x 9-in. baking dish for a bit longer.

about **BAKING POWDER**

Nearly all baking powder available today is double-acting. This means it contains two types of acids that react at different times. The first acid will react by creating gases when mixed with the liquid in the recipe. The second type will react by creating gases when the batter is exposed to oven heat. Our recipes are tested with double-acting baking powder, so use exactly the amount listed in the recipe.

In a bowl, combine chili beans, corn, onion and cumin. Transfer to an 8-in. square baking dish coated with cooking spray.

In another bowl, combine dry ingredients. Combine the milk and oil; stir into the dry ingredients just until moistened.

Drop by tablespoons over the chili mixture; carefully spread over the top. Bake, uncovered, at 350° for 20-25 minutes or until golden brown.

YIELD: 4 SERVINGS.

CALIFORNIA CHICKEN CASSEROLE

PREP 10 minutes | **BAKE** 45 minutes

1 can (10-3/4 ounces) condensed cream of mushroom soup, undiluted

1/3 cup milk

1 package (16 ounces) frozen California-blend vegetables, thawed

1-1/2 cups cubed cooked chicken

1-1/2 cups (6 ounces) shredded Swiss cheese, *divided*

1 jar (2 ounces) diced pimientos, drained

Salt and pepper to taste

Hot cooked rice

In a large bowl, combine soup and milk. Stir in vegetables, chicken, 1-1/4 cups cheese, pimientos, salt and pepper. Transfer to a greased 9-in. square baking dish.

Cover and bake at 350° for 40 minutes. Uncover; top with remaining cheese. Bake 5-10 minutes longer or until bubbly. Let stand for 5 minutes. Serve over rice.

YIELD: 4 SERVINGS.

debbie kokes
TABOR, SOUTH DAKOTA

I love to try new recipes, and this chicken and vegetable combo passed my family's taste test. If there are leftovers, I package them for my husband to reheat in the microwave.

SPINACH FETA STRATA

PREP 10 minutes + chilling | **BAKE** 40 minutes

10 slices French bread (1 inch thick) *or* 6 croissants, split

6 eggs

1-1/2 cups milk

1 package (10 ounces) frozen chopped spinach, thawed and squeezed dry

1/2 teaspoon salt

1/4 teaspoon ground nutmeg

1/4 teaspoon pepper

1-1/2 cups (6 ounces) shredded Monterey Jack cheese

1 cup (4 ounces) crumbled feta cheese

In a greased 13-in. x 9-in. baking dish, arrange French bread or croissant halves with sides overlapping.

In a large bowl, combine the eggs, milk, spinach, salt, nutmeg and pepper; pour over the bread. Sprinkle with cheeses. Cover and refrigerate for 8 hours or overnight.

Remove from the refrigerator 30 minutes before baking. Bake, uncovered, at 350° for 40-45 minutes or until a knife inserted near the center comes out clean. Let stand for 5 minutes before cutting. Serve warm.

YIELD: 12 SERVINGS.

pat lane
PULLMAN, WASHINGTON

This is a fairly new recipe for me, but my family loved it the first time I made it. A friend shared it with me, and it became an instant hit!

PINEAPPLE CHICKEN CASSEROLE

PREP/TOTAL TIME 30 minutes

- 2 cups cubed cooked chicken
- 1 can (10-3/4 ounces) condensed cream of mushroom soup, undiluted
- 1 cup pineapple tidbits
- 2 celery ribs, chopped
- 1 tablespoon chopped green onion
- 1 tablespoon soy sauce
- 1 can (3 ounces) chow mein noodles, *divided*

In a large bowl, combine the first six ingredients. Fold in 1 cup chow mein noodles. Transfer to a greased shallow 2-qt. baking dish. Sprinkle with remaining noodles. Bake, uncovered, at 350° for 20-25 minutes or until heated through.

YIELD: 4-6 SERVINGS.

susan warren
NORTH MANCHESTER, INDIANA

I love to cook, but with teaching school, playing handbells at church and juggling my family's schedule, I have little time in the kitchen. I'm always looking for one-dish dinners like this one that save time and cleanup.

HAM AND RICE BAKE

PREP 10 minutes | BAKE 25 minutes

- 1 can (10-3/4 ounces) condensed cream of chicken soup, undiluted
- 1 cup (4 ounces) shredded cheddar cheese, *divided*
- 1 package (16 ounces) frozen California-blend vegetables, thawed
- 1 cup cooked rice
- 1 cup cubed fully cooked ham

In a large saucepan, combine the soup and 1/2 cup cheese; cook and stir until cheese is melted. Stir in vegetables, rice and ham.

Transfer to a greased 1-1/2-qt. baking dish. Sprinkle with the remaining cheese. Bake, uncovered, at 350° for 25-30 minutes or until heated through.

YIELD: 4 SERVINGS.

sharol binger
TULARE, SOUTH DAKOTA

I can put a satisfying supper on the table in a jiffy with this recipe. I add a can of soup, rice and a few convenience items to leftover ham for a flavorful, no-fuss casserole.

CHEDDAR CABBAGE CASSEROLE

PREP 10 minutes | BAKE 45 minutes

- 2-1/2 cups coarsely crushed cornflakes
- 1/2 cup butter, melted
- 4-1/2 cups shredded cabbage
- 1/3 cup chopped onion
- 1/4 to 1/2 teaspoon salt
- 1/4 to 1/2 teaspoon pepper
- 1 can (10-3/4 ounces) condensed cream of celery soup, undiluted
- 1 cup milk
- 1/2 cup mayonnaise
- 2 cups (8 ounces) shredded cheddar cheese

Toss the cornflakes and butter; sprinkle half into a greased 13-in. x 9-in. baking dish. Layer with cabbage, onion, salt and pepper. In a large bowl, combine the soup, milk and mayonnaise until smooth. Spoon over top; sprinkle with the cheese and remaining cornflake mixture. Bake, uncovered, at 350° for 45-50 minutes or until golden brown.

YIELD: 8-10 SERVINGS.

EDITOR'S NOTE: Reduced-fat or fat-free mayonnaise is not recommended for this recipe.

alice jones
DEMOREST, GEORGIA

The flavors really blend well in this hot dish. The crunch of the crushed cornflakes adds to the texture contrast.

TORTILLA CASSEROLE

PREP 10 minutes | **COOK** 25 minutes

1 pound ground beef
1/2 cup chopped onion
1/2 cup chopped green pepper
1 envelope taco seasoning
1 can (8 ounces) tomato sauce
1 can (6 ounces) tomato paste
1/2 cup sliced ripe olives
1/4 cup water
1/2 teaspoon chili powder
2 eggs
1 cup (8 ounces) sour cream
1/4 teaspoon pepper
4 flour tortillas (7 inches)
2 cups crushed corn chips
2 cups (8 ounces) shredded Monterey Jack cheese

Crumble meat into a 2-qt. microwave-safe dish; add onion and green pepper. Cover and microwave on high for 5-6 minutes or until meat is no longer pink; drain. Stir in taco seasoning, tomato sauce, tomato paste, olives, water and chili powder. Cover and cook at 50% power for 10 minutes or until thickened, rotating dish once.

In a bowl, whisk the eggs, sour cream and pepper. Place two tortillas in an 11-in. x 7-in. microwave-safe dish. Layer with half of the sour cream mixture and meat sauce; repeat. Top with corn chips and cheese.

Microwave, uncovered, at 50% power for 10-15 minutes or until a thermometer reads 160° and cheese is melted. Let stand for 5 minutes before cutting.

YIELD: 6-8 SERVINGS.

joy clark
EVANSVILLE, WYOMING

This dish combines most of the food groups into one satisfying meal. I like to top servings with shredded lettuce, chopped tomatoes and a dollop of sour cream.

BROCCOLI CORN CASSEROLE

PREP 10 minutes | **BAKE** 45 minutes

1-1/2 cups crushed cornflakes, *divided*
1-1/4 cups soft bread crumbs (about 2 slices), *divided*
1/3 cup butter, melted, *divided*
1 can (14-3/4 ounces) cream-style corn
3 cups frozen chopped broccoli, thawed
2 eggs
2 tablespoons chopped onion
1 teaspoon salt
1/8 teaspoon pepper

In a small bowl, combine 1/4 cup of corn-flake crumbs and 1/3 cup bread crumbs. Drizzle with 2 tablespoons butter and toss to coat; set aside. In a large bowl, combine the corn, broccoli, eggs, onion, salt, pepper and the remaining cornflakes, bread crumbs and butter.

Transfer to a greased 1-1/2-qt. baking dish. Sprinkle with the reserved crumb mixture. Bake, uncovered, at 350° for 45 minutes or until a thermometer reads 160°.

YIELD: 4-6 SERVINGS.

beverly griggs
ROSEBURG, OREGON

Here's a wonderful vegetable dish that's a little different. Try it and see if your family likes it as much as mine does.

easy ONIONS

A convenient way to have fresh chopped onion on hand is to keep a peeled onion in a glass jar in the refrigerator. When you need a small amount of chopped onion for a recipe, the onion stays fresh in the jar, eliminating waste.

SOUTHWEST CHICKEN AND RICE

PREP/TOTAL TIME 10 minutes

- 2 packages (8-1/2 ounces *each*) ready-to-serve Santa Fe whole grain rice medley
- 2 packages (6 ounces *each*) ready-to-use Southwestern chicken strips, cut into chunks
- 1 can (10 ounces) diced tomatoes and green chilies, drained
- 1/2 cup shredded Monterey Jack cheese

Heat rice according to package directions. In a 2-qt. microwave-safe dish, combine chicken and tomatoes; stir in rice. Cover and microwave on high for 2-3 minutes. Sprinkle with cheese; cook 1 minute longer or until cheese is melted.

YIELD: 4 SERVINGS.

penny hawkins
MEBANE, NORTH CAROLINA

With brown rice, whole grains, tomatoes and corn, this super-fast meal is such a tasty way to get your family to eat more fiber...they won't even realize it's good for them!

HASH BROWN EGG BAKE

PREP 5 minutes | **BAKE** 45 minutes

1 package (32 ounces) frozen cubed hash brown potatoes, thawed

1 pound sliced bacon, cooked and crumbled

1 cup (4 ounces) shredded cheddar cheese, *divided*

1/4 to 1/2 teaspoon salt

8 eggs

2 cups milk

Dash paprika

In a large bowl, combine the hash browns, bacon, 1/2 cup cheese and salt. Spoon into a greased 13-in. x 9-in. baking dish. In another large bowl, whisk eggs and milk until smooth; pour over the hash brown mixture. Sprinkle with paprika.

Bake, uncovered, at 350° for 45-50 minutes or until a knife inserted near the center comes out clean. Sprinkle with remaining cheese.
YIELD: 8 SERVINGS.

EDITOR'S NOTE: This dish may be prepared in advance, covered and refrigerated overnight. Remove from the refrigerator 30 minutes before baking.

cheryl johnson
PLYMOUTH, MINNESOTA

A package of frozen hash browns makes this recipe simple to prepare. Featuring bacon and cheddar cheese, it's a tasty breakfast or brunch fare. You can even make it the night before, keep in the fridge and bake the next morning—so convenient!

SPINACH BEEF BAKE

PREP 10 minutes | **BAKE** 45 minutes

- 1 pound ground beef
- 1 jar (4-1/2 ounces) sliced mushrooms, drained
- 1 medium onion, chopped
- 2 garlic cloves, minced
- 1-1/2 teaspoons dried oregano
- 1-1/4 teaspoons salt
- 1/4 teaspoon pepper
- 2 packages (10 ounces *each*) frozen chopped spinach, thawed and squeezed dry
- 1 can (10-3/4 ounces) condensed cream of celery soup, undiluted
- 1 cup (8 ounces) sour cream
- 1 cup uncooked long grain rice
- 1 cup (4 ounces) shredded part-skim mozzarella cheese

In a skillet, brown beef; drain. Add the mushrooms, onion, garlic, oregano, salt and pepper. Add spinach, soup, sour cream and rice; mix well.

Transfer to a greased 2-1/2-qt. baking dish. Sprinkle with mozzarella cheese. Cover and bake at 350° for 45-50 minutes or until the rice is tender.

YIELD: 6-8 SERVINGS.

laverne schultz
GREENFIELD, WISCONSIN

Everyone loves the mild flavor and cheesy topping of this crowd-pleasing casserole. I usually round out this hearty meal with a tossed salad or applesauce.

CHEESY CHILI CASSEROLE

PREP 10 minutes | **BAKE** 40 minutes

- 2 cups (8 ounces) shredded Monterey Jack cheese
- 2 cups (8 ounces) shredded cheddar cheese
- 1 can (7 ounces) whole green chilies, rinsed and seeded
- 2 eggs
- 2 tablespoons all-purpose flour
- 1 can (12 ounces) evaporated milk
- 1 can (8 ounces) tomato sauce *or* 1 cup fresh salsa, drained, *divided*

In a large bowl, combine cheeses. In a greased 11-in. x 7-in. baking dish, layer cheese and chilies. Combine the eggs, flour and milk; pour over cheese mixture.

Bake at 350° for 30 minutes. Top with half the tomato sauce or salsa; bake 10 minutes longer. Let stand for 5 minutes before serving. Serve with remaining sauce.

YIELD: 8 SERVINGS.

phyllis bidwell
LAS VEGAS, NEVADA

This dish is an interesting and appetizing change to classic chili. With limited ingredients, whipping up this casserole is a cinch!

fresh SALSA

To make your own fresh salsa, combine: 4 cups chopped peeled fresh tomatoes, 1/4 cup finely chopped onion, 2 seeded and finely chopped jalapenos, 1 tablespoon each olive oil and vinegar, 1 teaspoon each ground cumin and salt, and 1 minced garlic clove. Let stand for 1 hour and serve at room temperature. Store in the refrigerator.

PORK SAUSAGE PUFF

PREP 10 minutes | **BAKE** 50 minutes

1 cup biscuit/baking mix
6 eggs, beaten
2 cups milk
2-1/2 cups cooked bulk pork sausage
    (1 pound uncooked)
1 cup (4 ounces) shredded cheddar
    cheese
1/2 teaspoon dried oregano

In a bowl, combine the biscuit mix, eggs and milk until blended. Add the cooked sausage, cheese and oregano.

Transfer to a greased 13-in. x 9-in. baking dish. Bake, uncovered, at 350° for 50-55 minutes or until a knife inserted near the center comes out clean.

YIELD: 6 SERVINGS.

EDITOR'S NOTE: This recipe can be prepared and refrigerated overnight. Remove from the refrigerator 30 minutes before baking.

christina french
ELKHART, INDIANA

I like to serve this special brunch dish to overnight guests because I can prepare it the night before. The recipe, which I changed a bit to suit our family's tastes, came from a dear lady at our church.

TOMATO BEEF AND RICE CASSEROLE

PREP 10 minutes | **BAKE** 1-1/2 hours

1 pound lean ground beef
3 cups chopped canned tomatoes with
    liquid
1 medium green pepper, chopped
1 cup uncooked long grain rice
1 large onion, chopped
1 teaspoon chili powder
1/2 teaspoon salt
1/4 teaspoon pepper

In a large bowl, combine all ingredients. Place in a greased 2-qt. baking dish. Cover and bake at 400° for 1-1/2 hours, stirring once or twice. Uncover during the last 15 minutes to brown.

YIELD: 6 SERVINGS.

linda bangert
EDWARDSVILLE, ILLINOIS

Here's a delicious dish that is very easy to make—and fast, too. The best thing, though, is that you mix everything in one bowl!

COMPANY VEGETABLE CASSEROLE

PREP 10 minutes | **BAKE** 35 minutes

1 can (14-1/2 ounces) cut green beans,
    drained *or* 2 cups frozen cut green
    beans, thawed
1 can (15-1/4 ounces) whole kernel corn,
    drained *or* 2 cups cooked fresh *or*
    frozen whole kernel corn
1 can (10-3/4 ounces) condensed cream
    of celery soup, undiluted
1/2 cup sour cream
1/2 cup shredded cheddar cheese
1/2 cup chopped onion
1/4 cup butter, melted
3/4 cup saltine crumbs
1/4 cup sliced almonds, toasted

In a large bowl, combine the beans, corn, soup, sour cream, cheese and onion. Pour into an ungreased 2-qt. baking dish.

Combine butter, crumbs and almonds; sprinkle over vegetables. Bake, uncovered, at 350° for 35-40 minutes or until bubbly.

YIELD: 6-8 SERVINGS.

leora clark
LINCOLN, NEBRASKA

A neighbor passed this on to me. I make the casserole for family dinners, reunions and potlucks, and the response is almost always the same after people taste it: "Can I have the recipe?" I grew up as the oldest of seven children, and I've been cooking for 67 of my 78 years.

SAUSAGE POLENTA BAKE

PREP 5 minutes | **BAKE** 35 minutes + standing

1-1/4 cups yellow cornmeal

1/2 teaspoon salt

4 cups boiling water

1/4 cup grated Parmesan cheese

1/2 pound bulk sweet Italian sausage

1/2 pound bulk hot Italian sausage

1 teaspoon olive oil

1 jar (26 ounces) garden-style spaghetti sauce

1-1/2 cups (6 ounces) shredded part-skim mozzarella cheese

In a large saucepan, combine the cornmeal and salt. Gradually add the boiling water, whisking constantly. Cook and stir over medium heat for 5 minutes or until mixture comes to a boil. Remove from the heat. Stir in Parmesan cheese.

Spread the polenta into a greased 13-in. x 9-in. baking dish. Bake, uncovered, at 350° for 20 minutes. Meanwhile, in a large skillet, cook sausage in oil over medium heat for 5 minutes or until no longer pink; drain. Add the spaghetti sauce; cook for 5 minutes or until heated through.

Spread over the polenta; sprinkle with mozzarella cheese. Bake 12-15 minutes longer or until cheese is melted. Let stand for 15 minutes before cutting.

YIELD: 8 SERVINGS.

taste of home
test kitchen
GREENDALE, WISCONSIN

Rustic polenta creates a tasty foundation for Italian sausage stewed in spaghetti sauce.

CHICKEN VEGGIE CASSEROLE

PREP 10 minutes | BAKE 1 hour

3 cups cubed cooked chicken
4 medium carrots, cut into chunks
3 medium red potatoes, cut into chunks
3 celery ribs, sliced
1 can (10-3/4 ounces) condensed cream
of chicken soup, undiluted
2/3 cup water
1/2 teaspoon salt
1/4 teaspoon pepper

Place chicken in a greased shallow 2-qt. baking dish. Top with carrots, potatoes and celery. Combine the soup, water, salt and pepper; pour over vegetables.

Cover and bake at 350° for 60-75 minutes or until vegetables are tender.

YIELD: 5 SERVINGS.

bonnie smith
GOSHEN, INDIANA

This comforting one-dish meal is not only easy to assemble, but it's economically priced, too. To save time, you can substitute a package of frozen vegetables.

DO-AHEAD BRUNCH BAKE

PREP 10 minutes + chilling | BAKE 1 hour 20 minutes + standing

- 8 frozen hash brown patties
- 1 package (8 ounces) thinly sliced fully cooked ham, chopped
- 1-1/4 cups shredded reduced-fat cheddar cheese, *divided*
- 2 cups fat-free milk
- 1 can (10-3/4 ounces) reduced-fat reduced-sodium condensed cream of mushroom soup, undiluted
- 1 cup egg substitute
- 1 teaspoon ground mustard
- 1/4 teaspoon pepper

Place the potato patties in a 13-in. x 9-in. baking dish coated with cooking spray. Top with ham and 1 cup cheese. Combine milk, soup, egg substitute, mustard and pepper; pour over cheese. Cover baking dish and refrigerate overnight.

Remove from refrigerator 30 minutes before baking. Bake at 350° for 1 hour. Uncover and sprinkle with the remaining cheese. Bake 20-25 minutes longer or until a knife inserted near the center comes out clean. Let stand 10 minutes before serving. **YIELD:** 12 SERVINGS.

NUTRITION FACTS: 1 serving equals 122 calories, 5 g fat (0 saturated fat), 13 mg cholesterol, 463 mg sodium, 9 g carbohydrate, trace fiber, 11 g protein. **DIABETIC EXCHANGES:** 1 meat, 1/2 starch.

joy maynard
ST. IGNATIUS, MONTANA

I wake up my clan with this convenient breakfast casserole that I assemble the night before. Loaded with hearty ham and hash browns, it's sure to start their day in a tasty way.

PARSLIED RICE WITH LEMON

PREP 10 minutes | BAKE 40 minutes

- 3 cups cooked rice
- 1 cup minced fresh parsley
- 1/2 cup shredded cheddar cheese, *divided*
- 1/3 cup chopped onion
- 1/4 cup chopped green pepper
- 1 garlic clove, minced
- 2 eggs, lightly beaten
- 1 can (12 ounces) evaporated milk
- 1/2 cup canola oil
- 3 tablespoons lemon juice
- 1 tablespoon grated lemon peel
- 1 teaspoon salt
- 1/2 teaspoon seasoned salt
- 1/2 teaspoon pepper

In a large bowl, combine the rice, parsley, 1/3 cup cheese, onion, green pepper and garlic. In another bowl, combine eggs, milk, oil, lemon juice and peel, salt, seasoned salt and pepper. Stir into the rice mixture.

Transfer to a greased 2-qt. baking dish; sprinkle with the remaining cheese. Bake, uncovered, at 350° for 40-45 minutes or until golden brown. **YIELD:** 6-8 SERVINGS.

mrs. theo jones
ODESSA, MISSOURI

I like to serve this dish at Thanksgiving and Christmas—or for that matter, anytime we have guests. It's a "no-fail" recipe.

lemon PEEL

A quick and easy way to make grated lemon peel for recipes is to use a paring knife to slice off big pieces of peel, then grind them for a few seconds in a food processor.

serves two

BISCUIT-TOPPED BEEF CASSEROLE • PAGE 269

BEEF NOODLE CASSEROLE

PREP 15 minutes | **BAKE** 20 minutes

valerie belley
ST. LOUIS, MISSOURI

Need a little comfort food? Look no further than this creamy, meaty home-style casserole.

- 2 cups uncooked egg noodles
- 1/2 pound lean ground beef
- 1 can (8 ounces) tomato sauce
- 1/4 cup chopped green onions
- 1/4 cup canned chopped green chilies
- 1 small garlic clove, minced
- 1/8 teaspoon salt
- 1/2 cup sour cream
- 2 ounces cream cheese, softened
- 1/4 cup shredded part-skim mozzarella cheese

Cook the noodles according to the package directions. Meanwhile, in a large skillet, cook beef over medium heat until no longer pink; drain. Stir in the tomato sauce, onions, chilies, garlic and salt. In a small bowl, combine sour cream and cream cheese. Drain noodles.

Place 1/2 cup of the beef mixture in a 1-qt. baking dish coated with cooking spray. Layer with half of the noodles, cream cheese mixture and cheese. Spread 1/2 cup beef mixture over cheese; repeat layers. Spoon remaining beef mixture over top.

Cover and bake at 350° for 20-25 minutes or until bubbly.

YIELD: 3 SERVINGS.

PORK CHOP SUPPER

PREP 20 minutes | **BAKE** 25 minutes

- 1 medium tart apple, cored
- 2 bone-in pork loin chops (about 3/4 inch thick and 8 ounces *each*)
- 3/4 teaspoon salt, *divided*
- 1/4 teaspoon pepper
- 2 teaspoons canola oil
- 1/3 cup uncooked long grain rice
- 2 tablespoons chopped onion
- 3/4 cup water
- 1 teaspoon chicken bouillon granules
- 2 teaspoons butter, melted
- 2 teaspoons brown sugar
- 1/8 teaspoon ground cinnamon

Cut apple widthwise in half. Peel and chop half of apple; set aside. Cut remaining half into three rings; set aside.

Sprinkle the chops with 1/2 teaspoon salt and pepper. In a large skillet, brown chops in oil for 3-4 minutes on each side. Transfer to a greased 11-in. x 7-in. baking dish; keep warm.

In same skillet, cook and stir the rice and onion in drippings until the rice is lightly browned. Stir in the water, bouillon and remaining salt. Stir in chopped apple. Bring to a boil. Reduce heat; cover and simmer for 10 minutes.

Spoon rice mixture around pork chops. In a small bowl, combine the butter, brown sugar and cinnamon; brush over apple slices. Arrange apple slices on top of chops.

Cover and bake at 350° for 25-30 minutes or until the meat juices run clear and rice is tender.

YIELD: 2 SERVINGS.

edie despain
LOGAN, UTAH

Here's a casserole supper so delicious and satisfying, there's no need for side dishes or extras. I found this stick-to-the-ribs recipe in an old cookbook.

about **APPLES**

To remove any contaminants on the skin of an apple, wash it thoroughly with soapy water and rinse it off before using. Cut out any bad or soft areas of the apple. To prevent browning, dip peeled apple slices into one part citrus juice and three parts water.

TURKEY SPAGHETTI PIE

PREP 25 minutes | **BAKE** 15 minutes

- 2 ounces uncooked spaghetti, broken in half
- 1 egg, lightly beaten
- 2 tablespoons grated Parmesan cheese
- 3 tablespoons sour cream
- 1/2 pound ground turkey
- 1/4 cup chopped green pepper
- 2 tablespoons chopped onion
- 1 teaspoon butter
- 1/3 cup tomato sauce
- 1/4 teaspoon garlic salt
- 1/4 teaspoon dried oregano

Salt and pepper to taste
- 1/3 cup shredded part-skim mozzarella cheese

Cook the spaghetti according to package directions; drain. In a bowl, combine the egg, Parmesan cheese and spaghetti. Press the spaghetti mixture onto the bottom and up the sides of a greased shallow 2-cup baking dish or 7-in. pie plate. Spread with the sour cream.

Crumble the turkey into a skillet; add the pepper, onion and butter. Cook over medium heat until meat is no longer pink; drain. Stir in the tomato sauce, garlic salt, oregano, salt and pepper. Spoon into spaghetti crust. Sprinkle with mozzarella cheese. Cover edges loosely with foil.

Bake at 350° for 15-20 minutes or until heated through and cheese is melted. Serve immediately.

YIELD: 2 SERVINGS.

colleen sherman
BAKERSFIELD, CALIFORNIA

This pie is practically a meal in itself. I usually put a green salad and crusty French rolls on the table alongside it.

CREAMY GREEN BEAN CASSEROLE

PREP 10 minutes | **BAKE** 25 minutes

- 1/2 cup condensed cream of mushroom soup, undiluted
- 1 ounce cream cheese, softened
- 1-3/4 cups frozen French-style green beans
- 5 tablespoons shredded Italian cheese blend, *divided*
- 5 tablespoons french-fried onions, *divided*
- 1/4 cup sour cream

In a small bowl, beat the soup and cream cheese until blended. Stir in green beans, 4 tablespoons Italian cheese, 4 tablespoons onions and sour cream. Transfer to a 3-cup baking dish coated with cooking spray. Sprinkle with remaining cheese and onions.

Bake, uncovered, at 350° for 25-30 minutes or until bubbly and cheese is melted. **YIELD:** 2 SERVINGS.

rosemary beaudoin
PLAINVILLE, CONNECTICUT

My scaled-down recipe takes a spin on the classic side dish. You can replace the green beans with any other frozen veggies. I like a mixture of colorful carrots, broccoli and cauliflower.

PUFFED PIZZA CASSEROLE

PREP 25 minutes | **BAKE** 20 minutes

- 1/3 pound lean ground beef
- 1/4 cup chopped onion
- 1/2 cup tomato sauce
- 3 tablespoons water
- 3 teaspoons spaghetti sauce mix
- 1/3 cup all-purpose flour
- 1/3 cup 2% milk
- 2 tablespoons beaten egg
- 1 teaspoon canola oil
- 1/2 cup shredded part-skim mozzarella cheese
- 2 tablespoons grated Parmesan cheese

In a skillet, cook the beef and onion over medium heat until meat is no longer pink; drain. Add the tomato sauce, water and spaghetti sauce mix. Bring to a boil. Reduce heat; simmer, uncovered, for 5 minutes. Meanwhile, place flour in a small bowl. Combine the milk, egg and oil; whisk into flour just until blended.

Pour meat mixture into a 3-cup baking dish coated with cooking spray. Sprinkle with mozzarella cheese. Pour flour mixture over top. Sprinkle with Parmesan cheese.

Bake, uncovered, at 400° for 20-25 minutes or until golden brown and center is set. Serve immediately.
YIELD: 2 SERVINGS.

NUTRITION FACTS: 1 serving equals 382 calories, 16 g fat (7 g saturated fat), 125 mg cholesterol, 995 mg sodium, 27 g carbohydrate, 2 g fiber, 30 g protein. **DIABETIC EXCHANGES:** 4 lean meat, 1-1/2 starch, 1 fat.

linda wilkens
MAPLE GROVE, MINNESOTA

My sister gave me this recipe many years ago. The hefty, comforting one-dish meal has a fun popover crust...and the pizza flavor makes it a favorite with all ages!

GROUND BEEF

Ground beef is often labeled using the cut of meat that it is ground from, such as ground chuck or ground round. It can also be labeled according to fat content or the percentage of lean meat to fat, such as 85% or 90% lean. The higher the percentage, the leaner the meat. Buy ground beef that is bright red in color and is in a tightly sealed package.

SOUTHWEST TURKEY CASSEROLE

PREP 20 minutes | **BAKE** 20 minutes

- 1/2 cup uncooked elbow macaroni
- 1/4 cup chopped onion
- 1/4 cup chopped sweet red pepper
- 4-1/2 teaspoons butter
- 1 tablespoon canola oil
- 1 tablespoon all-purpose flour
- 1/2 teaspoon salt
- 1/2 teaspoon ground cumin

Dash pepper

- 1 cup 2% milk
- 1 cup (4 ounces) shredded cheddar cheese
- 1 cup cubed cooked turkey
- 2/3 cup canned diced tomatoes and green chilies
- 1/3 cup frozen corn
- 1/3 cup frozen peas

Cook the macaroni according to package directions. Meanwhile, in a large skillet, saute the onion and red pepper in butter and oil until tender. Stir in the flour, salt, cumin and pepper until blended; gradually add milk. Bring to a boil; cook and stir for 1-2 minutes or until thickened. Stir in the cheese until melted.

Drain macaroni; add to cheese mixture. Stir in the turkey, tomatoes, corn and peas. Transfer to a 1-qt. baking dish coated with cooking spray. Bake, uncovered, at 350° for 20-25 minutes or until bubbly.

YIELD: 2 SERVINGS.

maria luisa reyes
BASTROP, TEXAS

When I was small, my mother and stepfather—who was head cook for an oil company—made this colorful casserole. It's been a favorite ever since!

PORTOBELLO SPAGHETTI CASSEROLE

PREP 30 minutes | **BAKE** 40 minutes

- 4 ounces uncooked spaghetti
- 3 Portobello mushrooms, stems removed and thinly sliced
- 1/4 teaspoon salt
- 1/8 teaspoon pepper
- 1 tablespoon olive oil
- 1 egg
- 1/4 cup sour cream
- 2 tablespoons grated Parmesan cheese
- 1 tablespoon minced fresh parsley
- 1-1/2 teaspoons all-purpose flour
- 1/4 teaspoon garlic powder
- 1/8 teaspoon crushed red pepper flakes
- 1-1/4 cups marinara sauce
- 3/4 cup shredded part-skim mozzarella cheese

Cook the spaghetti according to package directions. Meanwhile, in a large skillet, saute the mushrooms, salt and pepper in oil until mushrooms are tender; drain.

In a large bowl, combine the egg, sour cream, Parmesan cheese, parsley, flour, garlic powder and pepper flakes. Drain the spaghetti; add to the sour cream mixture. Transfer to a 1-1/2-qt. baking dish coated with cooking spray. Top with mushrooms and marinara sauce.

Cover and bake at 350° for 30 minutes. Uncover; sprinkle with mozzarella cheese. Bake 10-15 minutes longer or until heated through and cheese is melted. Let stand 10 minutes before serving.
YIELD: 3 SERVINGS.

mary shivers
ADA, OKLAHOMA

In the mood for a meatless meal? You can't go wrong with this easy, Italian-style casserole. You can substitute shiitakes for the portobellos if you wish!

SUMMER SQUASH BAKE

PREP 30 minutes + cooling | **BAKE** 30 minutes

- 1 pound yellow summer squash, chopped
- 1/4 cup water
- 1/4 cup chopped onion
- 1/2 teaspoon salt
- 1 egg, beaten
- 1/4 cup dry bread crumbs
- 2 tablespoons butter, melted
- Pepper to taste
- 1/2 cup shredded cheddar cheese

In a saucepan, combine squash, water, onion and salt. Bring to a boil. Reduce the heat; cover and simmer for 15-20 minutes or until squash is tender. Remove from the heat; cool.

Stir in the egg, bread crumbs, butter and pepper. Transfer to a greased 1-qt. baking dish; sprinkle with cheese. Bake, uncovered, at 350° for 30 minutes or until heated through and the cheese is melted.

YIELD: 2 SERVINGS.

sue joyce
WINSTON-SALEM, NORTH CAROLINA

My daughter-in-law created this recipe and shared it with me. I was delighted, since my husband and I were cutting down on fried foods and that's the way I had always prepared squash. The recipe is versatile...it can easily be enlarged to serve for a family dinner.

CHEESY HAM 'N' NOODLES

PREP 10 minutes | **BAKE** 30 minutes

- 3/4 cup uncooked egg noodles
- 2 tablespoons butter, *divided*
- 1 tablespoon all-purpose flour
- 2/3 cup 2% milk
- 1/2 cup cubed process cheese (Velveeta)
- 1 cup cubed fully cooked ham
- 1/2 cup frozen peas, thawed
- 2 tablespoons dry bread crumbs
- 1/4 teaspoon dried parsley flakes

Cook the noodles according to the package directions. Meanwhile, in a saucepan, melt 1 tablespoon butter; stir in the flour until smooth. Gradually add the milk. Bring to a boil over medium heat; cook and stir for 2 minutes or until thickened. Remove from the heat; stir in cheese until melted.

Drain noodles. Add noodles, ham and peas to the cheese sauce. Pour into a 3-cup baking dish coated with cooking spray. Melt remaining butter; toss with bread crumbs and parsley. Sprinkle over the top. Bake, uncovered, at 350° for 30-35 minutes or until heated through.

YIELD: 2 SERVINGS.

renee schwebach
DUMONT, MINNESOTA

I love to prepare this comforting dish because it's always an easy-to-make and successful meal. It's also a great way to use up leftover ham. Peas add color and flavor.

REUBEN CASSEROLE

PREP 15 minutes | **BAKE** 25 minutes

agnes golian
GARFIELD HEIGHTS, OHIO

Sauerkraut fans will love this hearty, layered casserole. Round out this meal for two with dinner rolls and a light fruit dessert.

- 1 can (8 ounces) sauerkraut, rinsed and well drained
- 1/8 teaspoon caraway seeds
- 1 small tomato, cut into thin wedges
- 2 tablespoons Thousand Island salad dressing
- 1 package (2 ounces) thinly sliced deli corned beef
- 1/4 cup shredded Swiss cheese
- 1/4 cup cubed rye bread
- 2 teaspoons butter, melted

Place the sauerkraut in an ungreased 3-cup baking dish; sprinkle with caraway seeds. Layer with tomato wedges, salad dressing, corned beef and Swiss cheese. Toss bread cubes and butter; sprinkle over the top.

Bake, uncovered, at 375° for 25-30 minutes or until heated through.

YIELD: 2 SERVINGS.

CHICKEN MACARONI CASSEROLE

PREP 20 minutes | **BAKE** 20 minutes

quincie ball
SHELTON, WASHINGTON

Start the evening off right with this piping hot, hearty casserole. Topped with crispy breadcrumbs, you'll love the satisfying crunch.

MUSHROOMS

Mushrooms are a staple in many cooks' kitchens because they add an earthy, even meaty flavor to dishes. For a fancy flair, substitute the mushrooms in this casserole dish with sliced cremini mushrooms.

- 2/3 cup uncooked elbow macaroni
- 2/3 cup sliced fresh mushrooms
- 2 tablespoons finely chopped onion
- 1 tablespoon finely chopped green pepper
- 1 tablespoon butter
- 3/4 cup cubed cooked chicken
- 1/2 cup shredded cheddar cheese
- 1/2 cup sour cream
- 2 tablespoons 2% milk
- 1 tablespoon chopped pimiento-stuffed olives
- 1/2 teaspoon seasoned salt
- 1/8 teaspoon pepper
- 1/4 cup soft bread crumbs
- 1 teaspoon butter, melted

Cook the macaroni according to package directions. Meanwhile, in a small skillet, saute the mushrooms, onion and green pepper in butter until tender.

In a small bowl, combine the chicken, cheese, sour cream, milk, olives, seasoned salt, pepper and vegetable mixture. Drain macaroni; add to chicken mixture.

Transfer to a 3-cup baking dish coated with cooking spray. Combine bread crumbs and butter; sprinkle over top of casserole. Bake, uncovered, at 350° for 20-25 minutes or until bubbly.

YIELD: 2 SERVINGS.

SCALLOPED POTATOES WITH HAM

PREP 25 minutes | **BAKE** 55 minutes

mark baccus
MELBOURNE BEACH, FLORIDA

When you don't want to bake a ham for Easter, this is a nice alternative. It also makes a delicious meal any time of the year.

2 teaspoons butter
2 teaspoons all-purpose flour
1/8 teaspoon salt
1/8 teaspoon pepper
Dash Cajun seasoning
1/2 cup 2% milk
1-1/2 teaspoons sherry *or* chicken broth
1 teaspoon Worcestershire sauce
1/2 cup shredded cheddar cheese, *divided*
1 medium potato, peeled and thinly sliced
1 cup cubed fully cooked ham
1/4 cup thinly sliced onion

In a small saucepan, melt the butter. Stir in flour, salt, pepper and Cajun seasoning until smooth. Gradually add milk, sherry and Worcestershire sauce. Bring to a boil; cook and stir for 1 minute or until thickened. Reduce heat; stir in 1/4 cup cheese. Remove from the heat; set aside.

Place half of the potato slices in a 1-qt. baking dish that is coated with cooking spray. Layer with the ham, onion and half of the white sauce. Repeat layers.

Cover and bake at 350° for 50-60 minutes or until the potatoes are tender. Uncover; sprinkle with remaining cheese. Bake 5-10 minutes longer or until cheese is melted.
YIELD: 2 SERVINGS.

🍳 ITALIAN HOT DISH

PREP 30 minutes | **BAKE** 40 minutes

theresa smith
SHEBOYGAN, WISCONSIN

1-1/2 cups uncooked small pasta shells
1 pound lean ground beef
1 cup sliced fresh mushrooms, *divided*
1/2 cup chopped onion
1/2 cup chopped green pepper
1 can (15 ounces) tomato sauce
1 teaspoon dried oregano
1/2 teaspoon garlic powder
1/4 teaspoon onion powder
1/8 teaspoon pepper
1/2 cup shredded part-skim mozzarella cheese, *divided*
4 teaspoons grated Parmesan cheese, *divided*

Cook the pasta according to the package directions. Meanwhile, in a large nonstick skillet coated with cooking spray, cook the beef, 1/2 cup mushrooms, onion and green pepper until meat is no longer pink; drain. Stir in the tomato sauce, oregano, garlic powder, onion powder and pepper. Bring to a boil. Reduce heat; cover and simmer for 15 minutes.

Drain pasta; place in an 8-in. square baking dish coated with cooking spray. Top with meat sauce and remaining mushrooms. Sprinkle with 1/4 cup mozzarella and 2 teaspoons Parmesan.

Cover and bake at 350° for 35 minutes. Uncover; sprinkle with remaining cheeses. Bake 5-10 minutes longer or until heated through and cheese is melted.
YIELD: 4 SERVINGS.

My husband had a poor perception of healthy food until he tried this beefy casserole. The combination of pasta, oregano, mushrooms and green peppers makes it a favorite in our house.

NUTRITION FACTS: 1 serving equals 391 calories, 12 g fat (5 g saturated fat), 65 mg cholesterol, 663 mg sodium, 36 g carbohydrate, 3 g fiber, 33 g protein. **DIABETIC EXCHANGES:** 3 lean meat, 2 starch, 2 vegetable, 1/2 fat.

CORDON BLEU BAKE

PREP 20 minutes | **BAKE** 30 minutes

- 1/2 cup water
- 3 tablespoons butter, *divided*
- 1 cup stuffing mix
- 1 cup frozen mixed vegetables, thawed
- 2/3 cup condensed cream of mushroom *or* cream of chicken soup, undiluted, *divided*
- 3/4 cup cubed cooked chicken breast
- 2 ounces thinly sliced lean deli ham, cut into strips
- 1/2 cup shredded Swiss cheese

In a small saucepan, bring the water and 1 tablespoon butter to a boil. Stir in the stuffing mix. Remove from heat; cover and let stand for 5 minutes.

Meanwhile, in a shallow 1-qt. baking dish coated with cooking spray, combine vegetables with 1/3 cup soup. Combine the chicken with remaining soup; spoon over vegetables. Layer with ham and cheese. Fluff stuffing with a fork; spoon over cheese. Melt remaining butter; drizzle over stuffing. Bake, uncovered, at 350° for 30-35 minutes or until heated through.
YIELD: 2 SERVINGS.

helen musenbrock
O'FALLON, MISSOURI

This comforting casserole is fast and easy to assemble, plus it helps use up leftovers.

CREAMY CHICKEN ENCHILADAS

PREP/TOTAL TIME: 30 minutes

- 2/3 cup condensed cream of chicken soup, undiluted
- 2/3 cup sour cream
- 2 cups shredded cooked chicken breast
- 1/2 cup shredded Monterey Jack cheese, *divided*
- 4 flour tortillas (6 inches), warmed

Combine soup and sour cream. Spread half over the bottom of an 8-in. square baking dish coated with cooking spray.

Place 1/2 cup chicken and 1 tablespoon cheese down the center of each tortilla; roll up and place in the baking dish. Top with the remaining soup mixture; sprinkle with remaining cheese.

Bake, uncovered, at 350° for 18-22 minutes or until heated through.
YIELD: 2 SERVINGS.

rachel smith
KATY, TEXAS

I love this creamy, comforting dish because it's easy, tastes amazing, freezes well and reheats easily in the microwave. If you prefer more zip, substitute pepper Jack cheese for Monterey Jack.

MUSHROOM TURKEY CASSEROLE

PREP/TOTAL TIME: 30 minutes

1-1/2 cups cubed cooked turkey
1-1/2 cups sliced fresh mushrooms
   1 cup condensed cream of chicken soup, undiluted
   1 small celery rib, chopped
   1 small carrot, grated
   1 teaspoon minced fresh parsley
1/8 teaspoon pepper
1/4 cup soft bread crumbs
   1 teaspoon butter, melted
1/2 teaspoon paprika

In a bowl, combine turkey, mushrooms, soup, celery, carrot, parsley and pepper. Divide the mixture into two greased 2-cup baking dishes.

In a small bowl, toss the bread crumbs with butter. Sprinkle half over each dish. Sprinkle with paprika. Bake, uncovered, at 350° for 15-20 minutes or until golden brown and bubbly.
YIELD: 2 SERVINGS.

NUTRITION FACTS: 1-1/2 cups (prepared with reduced-fat reduced-sodium soup) equals 326 calories, 10 g fat (4 g saturated fat), 95 mg cholesterol, 643 mg sodium, 22 g carbohydrate, 2 g fiber, 36 g protein. **DIABETIC EXCHANGES:** 3-1/2 lean meat, 1-1/2 starch.

nella parker
HERSEY, MICHIGAN

To change up the flavor, I sometimes substitute leftover cooked chicken for the turkey and stir 1/2 cup seedless white grapes into the mixture just before adding the topping.

TACO RAMEKINS

PREP 15 minutes | **BAKE** 20 minutes

1/4 pound ground beef
1/4 teaspoon chili powder
1/8 teaspoon salt
1/8 teaspoon pepper
3/4 cup biscuit/baking mix
   3 tablespoons cold water
   1 medium tomato, sliced
1/4 cup chopped green pepper
   2 tablespoons sour cream
   2 tablespoons mayonnaise
   2 tablespoons shredded cheddar cheese
   1 tablespoon chopped onion

In a skillet, cook beef over medium heat until no longer pink; drain. Stir in the chili powder, salt and pepper. Remove from the heat and set aside.

Combine biscuit mix and water to form a soft dough. Press onto the bottom and up the sides of two 10-oz. ramekins or custard cups coated with cooking spray. Fill with meat mixture; top with tomato and green pepper. Combine sour cream, mayonnaise, cheese and onion; spread evenly over top.

Bake, uncovered, at 375° for 20-25 minutes or until heated through.
YIELD: 2 SERVINGS.

barbara willmitch
YOUNGSTOWN, OHIO

I love to cook and eat all types of food, but this tasty dish is a real hit with my daughter and her friends. It has a mildly Mexican-style flavor that both young and old can enjoy.

cool **DRINK**

A refreshing, cool drink pairs nicely with the Taco Ramekins. Combine 1 cup chilled, unsweetened pineapple juice, 1-2 tablespoons lemon juice and one chilled 12-ounce can of lemon-lime soda. Fill 2 glasses with ice cubes, and pour the juice mixture over the ice.

MASHED POTATO ARTICHOKE BAKE

PREP 30 minutes | **BAKE** 15 minutes

laura mcallister
MORGANTON, NORTH CAROLINA

These jazzed-up mashed potatoes make a welcome side dish for any entree. My husband loves this bake.

- 2 medium potatoes, peeled and quartered
- 1/4 cup sour cream
- 2 tablespoons 2% milk
- 2 tablespoons mayonnaise
- 1 tablespoon butter
- 1/2 teaspoon snipped fresh dill *or* 1/8 teaspoon dill weed

Dash salt

Dash pepper

- 3/4 cup frozen artichoke hearts, thawed and chopped
- 1 green onion, chopped
- 2 bacon strips, cooked and crumbled
- 1/3 cup shredded cheddar cheese

Place the potatoes in a small saucepan and cover with water. Bring to a boil. Reduce heat; cover and cook for 10-15 minutes or until tender. Mash potatoes with sour cream, milk, mayonnaise, butter and seasonings. Stir in artichokes and onion.

Transfer to a 1-qt. baking dish coated with cooking spray. Sprinkle with bacon and cheese. Bake, uncovered, at 400° for 15-20 minutes or until heated through and cheese is melted.

YIELD: 2 SERVINGS.

FIESTA BEAN CASSEROLE

PREP 20 minutes | **BAKE** 20 minutes

- 3/4 cup kidney beans, rinsed and drained
- 1/4 cup chopped onion
- 1/4 cup chopped green chilies, drained
- 1/4 teaspoon ground cumin
- 16 Triscuits *or* other crackers
- 3/4 cup shredded cheddar cheese
- 1/2 cup 2% milk
- 1/3 cup mayonnaise
- 2 tablespoons beaten egg

Sour cream and sliced ripe olives, optional

In a small bowl, combine beans, onion, green chilies and cumin. Place eight crackers in an 8-in. x 4-in. loaf pan coated with cooking spray. Top with half of the bean mixture; layer with the remaining crackers and bean mixture. Sprinkle with cheese.

In a small bowl, combine the milk, mayonnaise and egg; pour over cheese. Bake, uncovered, at 350° for 20-25 minutes or until heated through. Serve with sour cream and olives if desired.

YIELD: 2 SERVINGS.

karen tjelmeland
ELY, IOWA

I don't recall its origin, but I have had this recipe for many years. A Triscuit cracker crust makes it a unique meatless option.

APPLE PORK CHOP CASSEROLE

beverly baxter
KANSAS CITY, KANSAS

I've loved this recipe since the first time I tried it. The apples and raisins give a nice homey flavor to the stuffing.

PREP 30 minutes | **BAKE** 30 minutes

- 2 boneless pork loin chops (3/4 inch and 8 ounces *each*)
- 2 teaspoons canola oil
- 3/4 cup water
- 1 tablespoon butter
- 1 small tart green apple, chopped
- 2 tablespoons raisins
- 1-1/2 cups crushed chicken stuffing mix
- 2/3 cup condensed cream of mushroom soup, undiluted

In a large skillet, brown meat in oil for about 5 minutes on each side. Meanwhile, in a large saucepan, combine water, butter, apple and raisins; bring to a boil. Stir in the stuffing mix. Remove from the heat; cover and let stand for 5 minutes. Fluff with a fork.

Transfer to a greased shallow 1-qt. baking dish. Top with meat. Spoon soup over meat and stuffing.

Cover and bake at 350° for 30-35 minutes or until a meat thermometer inserted into pork chops reads 160°.

YIELD: 2 SERVINGS.

MACARONI 'N' CHEESE FOR TWO

mrs. o. lick
BOYNE FALLS, MICHIGAN

This is the simplest of entrees, and perfect for cold, frosty evenings. The combination of sour cream and cheese gives this macaroni dish a distinctive taste all its own.

PREP/TOTAL TIME: 30 minutes

- 1/3 cup sour cream
- 1/3 cup milk
- 1 cup (4 ounces) shredded sharp cheddar cheese
- 3/4 cup elbow macaroni, cooked and drained
- 2 tablespoons chopped onion, optional

Paprika

In a bowl, combine the sour cream and milk. Stir in the cheese, macaroni and onion if desired.

Transfer to a greased 2-1/2-cup baking dish; sprinkle with paprika. Cover and bake at 325° for 25 minutes or until heated through.

YIELD: 2 SERVINGS.

CANDIED SWEET POTATOES

ruby williams
BOGALUSA, LOUISIANA

This nice old-fashioned side dish is perfect for the holidays and easily down-sized for two. It's a dish that can be made often to complement any meal and the touch of pineapple juice adds a nice flavor.

PREP 40 minutes | **BAKE** 15 minutes

- 1 large sweet potato
- 1/4 cup packed brown sugar
- 2 tablespoons chopped pecans
- 1 tablespoon unsweetened pineapple *or* orange juice
- 1 teaspoon lemon juice
- 1/4 teaspoon ground cinnamon
- 1 tablespoon butter

Place the sweet potato in a small saucepan; cover with water. Bring to a boil. Reduce the heat; cover and simmer for 30-40 minutes or just until tender. Drain.

When cool enough to handle, peel and cut into 1/4-in. slices. Place in a greased shallow 2-cup baking dish.

In a small bowl, combine the brown sugar, pecans, pineapple juice, lemon juice and cinnamon; sprinkle over the sweet potato slices. Dot with butter.

Bake, uncovered, at 350° for 15 minutes or until bubbly and heated through.

YIELD: 2 SERVINGS.

HAM AND POTATOES AU GRATIN

PREP 15 minutes | **BAKE** 35 minutes

- 2 cups sliced peeled potatoes, cooked
- 1 cup diced cooked ham
- 1 tablespoon finely chopped onion
- 1/3 cup butter, cubed
- 3 tablespoons all-purpose flour
- 1-1/2 cups milk
- 1 cup (4 ounces) shredded cheddar cheese
- 3/4 teaspoon salt

Dash white pepper

Minced fresh parsley

In a greased 1-qt. baking dish, combine the potatoes, ham and onion; set aside.

In a saucepan, melt butter over medium heat; stir in flour until smooth. Gradually add milk. Bring to a boil; cook and stir for 2 minutes or until mixture is thickened and bubbly. Add cheese, salt and pepper; stir until the cheese is melted. Pour over the potato mixture and stir gently to mix.

Bake, uncovered, at 350° for 35-40 minutes or until bubbly. Garnish with parsley.

YIELD: 2 SERVINGS.

novella cook
HINTON, WEST VIRGINIA

This is one of the dishes Grandma served to our family during the holidays. Now, when the family gathers and I prepare this for my grandchildren, memories of those special times at Grandma's house fill my mind. I usually double this recipe, because the leftovers are fabulous when warmed up.

CHICKEN SPAGHETTI BAKE

PREP 15 minutes | **BAKE** 20 minutes

- 3 ounces uncooked spaghetti
- 1/3 cup chopped green pepper
- 1/3 cup chopped onion
- 1 garlic clove, minced
- 1 tablespoon butter
- 1 cup cubed cooked chicken breast
- 1 can (8 ounces) tomato sauce
- 1/3 cup condensed cream of mushroom soup, undiluted
- 1/4 cup chopped fresh mushrooms
- 2 teaspoons Worcestershire sauce
- 1/2 teaspoon hot pepper sauce
- 1/8 teaspoon pepper
- 2 tablespoons grated Parmesan cheese

Cook the spaghetti according to package directions. Meanwhile, in a small skillet, saute the green pepper, onion and garlic in butter until tender.

In a large bowl, combine the green pepper mixture, chicken, tomato sauce, soup, mushrooms, Worcestershire sauce, hot pepper sauce and pepper.

Drain spaghetti; stir into the chicken mixture. Transfer to a 1-qt. baking dish coated with cooking spray. Bake, uncovered, at 350° for 20-25 minutes or until heated through. Sprinkle with Parmesan cheese.

YIELD: 2 SERVINGS.

joyce fogleman
STAFFORD, TEXAS

Leftover chicken and my grandmother's treasured recipe add up to a delectable, down-home supper that heats up chilly nights. Serve with an easy salad of tossed greens or a loaf of crusty French bread for a complete meal.

SPAGHETTI

When placing spaghetti into a pot of boiling water, carefully hold the spaghetti in the water, then ease it down into the water as it softens. When fully immersed in the water, stir the spaghetti strands to separate them.

SHRIMP & MACARONI CASSEROLE

PREP 20 minutes | **BAKE** 20 minutes

- 1 cup uncooked elbow macaroni
- 1 egg
- 1/4 cup half-and-half cream
- 2 tablespoons butter, melted
- 1/2 cup grated Parmesan cheese
- 3/4 cup shredded part-skim mozzarella cheese, *divided*
- 1 garlic clove, minced
- 1/4 teaspoon salt
- 1/8 teaspoon pepper
- 1/4 pound uncooked medium shrimp, peeled, deveined and chopped
- 3/4 cup chopped fresh spinach

Cook the macaroni according to package directions. Meanwhile, in a small bowl, combine the egg, cream and butter; set aside. Drain macaroni. Add the Parmesan cheese, 1/2 cup mozzarella cheese, garlic, salt, pepper and reserved egg mixture; toss to coat. Stir in shrimp and spinach.

Transfer to a 1-qt. baking dish coated with cooking spray. Sprinkle with remaining mozzarella cheese. Bake, uncovered, at 350° for 20-25 minutes or until shrimp turn pink and cheese is melted.

YIELD: 3 SERVINGS.

michael cohen
LOS ANGELES, CALIFORNIA

Mac and cheese goes upscale in this deliciously cheesy variation. The shrimp gives a unique twist to this popular standard.

MOZZARELLA CHICKEN BREASTS

PREP 20 minutes | **BAKE** 30 minutes

- 2 boneless skinless chicken breast halves (5 ounces *each*)
- 1/8 teaspoon pepper
- 2 slices part-skim mozzarella cheese (3/4 ounce *each*)
- 1-1/2 cups stuffing mix
- 1/2 cup chicken broth, warmed
- 2/3 cup condensed cream of chicken soup, undiluted
- 2 tablespoons white wine *or* additional chicken broth
- 1 garlic clove, minced

Sprinkle chicken with pepper; top with cheese. Place in a 1-1/2-qt. baking dish coated with cooking spray. In a small bowl, combine stuffing mix and broth; let stand for 3 minutes. Spoon around chicken.

Combine soup, wine or additional broth and garlic; spread over chicken. Cover and bake at 350° for 25 minutes. Uncover; bake 5-10 minutes longer or until chicken juices run clear.

YIELD: 2 SERVINGS.

ladonna reed
PONCA CITY, OKLAHOMA

Whip up this special dish with boneless chicken breasts, canned soup and stuffing. This entree tastes like you fussed, but it's really so simple. It's also easy to upsize for company.

MEXICAN SPOON BREAD CASSEROLE

PREP 25 minutes | **BAKE** 25 minutes

- 1/2 pound ground beef
- 1 small onion, chopped
- 2 tablespoons chopped green pepper
- 1 garlic clove, minced
- 2/3 cup tomato sauce
- 1/2 cup frozen corn, thawed
- 2 tablespoons sliced ripe olives
- 3/4 teaspoon chili powder
- 1/2 teaspoon salt
- Dash pepper

TOPPING

- 3 tablespoons cornmeal
- 1/2 cup milk
- 1/8 teaspoon salt
- 1/4 cup shredded cheddar cheese
- 1 egg, lightly beaten

In a large skillet, cook the beef, onion, green pepper and garlic over medium heat until meat is no longer pink; drain. Add the tomato sauce, corn, olives, chili powder, salt and pepper; bring to a boil. Reduce heat; simmer, uncovered, for 10 minutes.

Meanwhile, in a large saucepan, combine the cornmeal, milk and salt; bring to a boil, stirring frequently. Remove from the heat. Stir in cheese and egg.

Spoon meat mixture into an ungreased 1-qt. baking dish. Pour topping over meat mixture. Bake, uncovered, at 375° for 22-26 minutes or until a knife inserted near the center comes out clean.

YIELD: 2 SERVINGS.

paula lock
GLENWOOD, ARKANSAS

This casserole really hits the spot when it's cold outside. It's tasty and filling. It will warm you right up.

sliced **OLIVES**

To quickly slice whole pitted ripe olives, use an egg slicer. Place the olives, end to end, across the slots on the base of the slicer, then press the top down. You'll end up with neat, uniform slices.

HEARTY TORTILLA CASSEROLE

PREP 35 minutes | **BAKE** 30 minutes

- 1/2 pound ground beef
- 2 tablespoons taco seasoning
- 1/3 cup water
- 1 small onion, finely chopped
- 1 to 2 Anaheim *or* Poblano chilies, roasted, peeled and finely chopped *or* 1 can (4 ounces) chopped green chilies
- 1 jalapeno pepper, seeded and finely chopped
- 1 garlic clove, minced
- 1 tablespoon canola oil
- 1/4 cup heavy whipping cream
- 1/8 teaspoon salt
- 4 flour tortillas (8 inches)
- 1 can (16 ounces) refried beans
- 1 cup (4 ounces) shredded Monterey Jack cheese, *divided*
- 1 cup (4 ounces) shredded cheddar cheese, *divided*
- Sour cream and salsa, optional

In a skillet over medium heat, cook the ground beef until no longer pink; drain. Add the taco seasoning and water. Simmer, uncovered, for 5 minutes; remove from the heat and set aside.

In a saucepan, saute onion, chilies, jalapeno and garlic in oil until tender, about 8 minutes. Stir in cream and salt. Cover and simmer for 5 minutes.

Spread 3 tablespoons of the sauce in an ungreased 8-in. round or square baking dish. Spread about 2 teaspoons sauce on each tortilla; layer with beans, beef mixture and 2 tablespoons of each kind of cheese. Roll up and place seam side down in baking dish. Top with remaining sauce.

Bake, uncovered, at 350° for 25 minutes. Sprinkle with the remaining cheeses; bake 5 minutes longer. Serve with sour cream and salsa if desired.

YIELD: 2-4 SERVINGS.

EDITOR'S NOTE: When cutting hot peppers, disposable gloves are recommended. Avoid touching your face.

terri nelson
WARREN, MINNESOTA

Being single, I often halve this recipe to yield a meal for one plus a lunch I can take to work. When co-workers remark on how good it looks, I invite them over to try it, then pass along the recipe. It's hot but not overpowering.

SPINACH CHEDDAR BAKE

PREP 5 minutes | **BAKE** 30 minutes

- 1 package (10 ounces) frozen chopped spinach, thawed and undrained
- 1/3 cup crushed saltines (about 6 crackers)
- 1 egg, beaten
- 1/2 teaspoon onion powder

Salt to taste

- 1 cup (4 ounces) shredded cheddar cheese, *divided*

In a bowl, combine the spinach, saltines, egg, onion powder and salt. Stir in 1/2 cup cheese.

Transfer to a greased 2-cup baking dish; sprinkle with remaining cheese. Bake, uncovered, at 350° for 30 minutes or until cheese is melted and bubbly.

YIELD: 2 SERVINGS.

RASPBERRY FRENCH TOAST CUPS

PREP 20 minutes + chilling | **BAKE** 25 minutes

- 2 slices Italian bread, cut into 1/2-inch cubes
- 1/2 cup fresh *or* frozen raspberries
- 2 ounces cream cheese, cut into 1/2-inch cubes
- 2 eggs
- 1/2 cup milk
- 1 tablespoon maple syrup

RASPBERRY SYRUP

- 2 teaspoons cornstarch
- 1/3 cup water
- 2 cups fresh *or* frozen raspberries, *divided*
- 1 tablespoon lemon juice
- 1 tablespoon maple syrup
- 1/2 teaspoon grated lemon peel

Ground cinnamon, optional

Divide half of the bread cubes between two greased 8-oz. custard cups. Sprinkle with the raspberries and cream cheese. Top with remaining bread. In a small bowl, whisk eggs, milk and syrup; pour over bread. Cover and refrigerate for at least 1 hour.

Remove from refrigerator 30 minutes before baking. Bake, uncovered, at 350° for 25-30 minutes or until golden brown.

Meanwhile, in a small saucepan, combine cornstarch and water until smooth. Add 1-1/2 cups raspberries, lemon juice, syrup and lemon peel. Bring to a boil; reduce the heat. Cook; stir for 2 minutes or until thickened. Strain and discard seeds; cool slightly.

Gently stir remaining berries into syrup. Sprinkle French toast cups with cinnamon if desired; serve with syrup.

YIELD: 2 SERVINGS.

julie dixon
HAZELWOOD, MISSOURI

Spinach is one of my favorite foods, so I make this easy recipe often. Using frozen or canned spinach keeps it simple.

sandi tuttle
HAYWARD, WISCONSIN

These individual treats are a delightful twist on French toast that make any morning special. I made this recipe for my mom last Mother's Day, and we both enjoyed it.

RASPBERRIES

Purchase raspberries that are brightly colored without the hulls attached. One-half pint equals about 1 cup. When you get home, discard any that are soft, shriveled or moldy. Quickly rinse remaining berries in water, then place in a single layer in a paper towel-lined bowl. They'll stay fresh in the refrigerator for up to 3 days.

BISCUIT-TOPPED BEEF CASSEROLE

PREP 25 minutes | **BAKE** 20 minutes

1/2 pound lean ground beef
1/4 cup chopped onion
1/2 cup water
1/2 cup tomato sauce
1/4 cup tomato paste
1/8 teaspoon pepper
1 cup frozen mixed vegetables, thawed
1/2 cup shredded part-skim mozzarella cheese, *divided*
1 tube (6 ounces) refrigerated flaky buttermilk biscuits
1 teaspoon butter, melted
1/4 teaspoon dried oregano

In a small saucepan, cook beef and onion over medium heat until meat is no longer pink; drain. Stir in the water, tomato sauce, tomato paste and pepper. Bring to a boil. Reduce the heat; simmer, uncovered, for 10 minutes.

Remove from the heat; stir in vegetables and 1/4 cup cheese. Transfer to a 1-qt. baking dish coated with cooking spray (dish will be full).

Separate each biscuit horizontally in half; arrange around the edge of the dish. Brush with butter; sprinkle with oregano. Sprinkle remaining cheese over beef filling.

Bake, uncovered, at 375° for 18-22 minutes or until heated through and the biscuits are golden brown.

YIELD: 2 SERVINGS.

debbie slater
SPOKANE, WASHINGTON

This satisfying recipe has been in our family for years. I made a few adjustments to suit my household's taste. It's so flavorful, we can't get enough of it!

COMFORTING TUNA CASSEROLE

PREP 15 minutes | **BAKE** 20 minutes

1-3/4 cups uncooked wide egg noodles

6 teaspoons butter, *divided*

4 teaspoons all-purpose flour

1/4 teaspoon salt

Dash pepper

3/4 cup 2% milk

1 package (3 ounces) cream cheese, softened

1 can (3 ounces) solid white tuna, drained

2 tablespoons diced pimientos

2 teaspoons minced chives

2 slices Muenster cheese (3/4 ounce *each*)

2 tablespoons soft bread crumbs

Cook the noodles according to the package directions. Meanwhile, in a small saucepan, melt 5 teaspoons butter. Stir in flour, salt and pepper until blended; gradually add milk. Bring to a boil; cook and stir for 1-2 minutes or until thickened. Reduce heat; add the cream cheese, tuna, pimientos and chives. Cook and stir until cheese is melted.

Drain the noodles. Spread 1/4 cup tuna mixture into a 3-cup baking dish coated with cooking spray. Layer with half of the noodles, 1/2 cup tuna mixture and one slice of cheese. Repeat layers.

In a small microwave-safe bowl, melt butter; stir in bread crumbs. Sprinkle over top of casserole. Bake, uncovered, at 350° for 20-25 minutes or until bubbly.
YIELD: 2 SERVINGS.

dorothy coleman
HOBE SOUND, FLORIDA

My mother gave me the recipe for this classic casserole over 20 years ago. Sometimes I use sliced stuffed olives instead of pimientos.

CREAMY BAKED CORN

PREP 10 minutes | BAKE 40 minutes

- 1 can (8-3/4 ounces) cream-style corn
- 8 saltines, crushed
- 1 tablespoon butter, melted
- 1/8 teaspoon salt
- 1/8 teaspoon pepper
- 1 egg
- 1/4 cup 2% milk

In a small bowl, combine the corn, saltines, butter, salt and pepper. Transfer to a shallow 2-cup baking dish coated with cooking spray.

In a small bowl, whisk egg and milk; pour over corn mixture. Bake, uncovered, at 350° for 40-45 minutes or until top is golden brown.

YIELD: 2 SERVINGS.

nancy collins
CLEARFIELD, PENNSYLVANIA

This is an old recipe handed down from my mother-in-law and is an especially good accompaniment to roast beef. The corn is moist and creamy with a souffle-like topping.

GREEK FETA CASSEROLE

PREP 20 minutes | BAKE 35 minutes

- 1/2 cup uncooked elbow macaroni
- 1 egg, lightly beaten
- 2 tablespoons milk
- 1/2 cup crumbled feta cheese *or* shredded part-skim mozzarella cheese, *divided*
- 1/2 pound ground pork
- 2 tablespoons chopped onion
- 1/2 cup tomato sauce
- 1/8 to 1/4 teaspoon ground cinnamon

Cook the macaroni according to package directions; drain.

In a bowl, combine the egg, milk and 1/4 cup cheese. Stir in macaroni. Transfer to a greased 3-cup baking dish. In a skillet, cook pork and onion over medium heat until meat is no longer pink; drain. Stir in the tomato sauce and cinnamon.

Pour over macaroni mixture. Sprinkle with remaining cheese. Cover and bake at 375° for 20 minutes. Uncover; bake 12-16 minutes longer or until bubbly and heated through.

YIELD: 2 SERVINGS.

joyce hill
QUESNEL, BRITISH COLUMBIA

A touch of cinnamon and savory feta cheese give this international hot dish a special taste.

PIZZA MACARONI BAKE

PREP 25 minutes | BAKE 25 minutes

- 1/2 pound bulk pork sausage
- 1/4 cup chopped green pepper
- 2 tablespoons chopped onion
- 1/2 cup elbow macaroni, cooked and drained
- 1 can (8 ounces) tomato sauce
- 4 tablespoons grated Parmesan cheese, *divided*
- 2 tablespoons water
- 1/4 teaspoon dried oregano
- Dash pepper

In a skillet, cook sausage, green pepper and onion over medium heat until meat is no longer pink; drain. Stir in the macaroni, tomato sauce, 2 tablespoons Parmesan cheese, water, oregano and pepper.

Transfer to a lightly greased 1-qt. baking dish; sprinkle with the remaining cheese. Cover and bake at 350° for 25-30 minutes or until liquid is absorbed and casserole is heated through.

YIELD: 2 SERVINGS.

barbara kemmer
ROHNERT PARK, CALIFORNIA

I found this recipe in a cookbook over 30 years ago, when I was newly married. It's tasty and simple to prepare—just right for a busy couple. It's also easy to double for a family of four.

ITALIAN CASSEROLE

PREP 25 minutes | **BAKE** 30 minutes

- 3 ounces uncooked spaghetti
- 1 Italian sausage link, casing removed
- 1 small onion, sliced
- 1 small zucchini, sliced

Dash pepper

- 1 bacon strip, cooked and crumbled
- 1/4 cup shredded Parmesan cheese
- 1 cup spaghetti sauce, *divided*
- 2 tablespoons chopped sweet red pepper
- 1/2 cup shredded part-skim mozzarella cheese
- 12 slices pepperoni

Dash *each* dried oregano, thyme and basil

Cook the spaghetti according to package directions. Meanwhile, crumble the sausage into a small skillet; add onion. Cook over medium heat until the meat is no longer pink; drain.

Drain the spaghetti. Arrange zucchini in a shallow 1-qt. baking dish coated with cooking spray; sprinkle with pepper. Layer with the bacon, Parmesan cheese, 1/2 cup spaghetti sauce, spaghetti, remaining sauce, red pepper, sausage mixture, mozzarella cheese and pepperoni.

Sprinkle with herbs. Bake, uncovered, at 350° for 30-35 minutes or until vegetables are tender.

YIELD: 3 SERVINGS.

lee sauers
MIFFLINBURG, PENNSYLVANIA

This hearty pizza-flavored dish is perfect with toasted garlic bread and a tossed salad.

CRUNCHY BEEF BAKE

PREP 15 minutes | **BAKE** 30 minutes

- 2 cups uncooked spiral pasta
- 1 pound ground beef
- 3/4 cup chopped green pepper
- 1 garlic clove, minced
- 1 can (14-1/2 ounces) diced tomatoes, undrained
- 1 can (10-3/4 ounces) condensed cream of mushroom soup, undiluted
- 3/4 cup shredded cheddar cheese
- 3/4 teaspoon seasoned salt
- 1 can (2.8 ounces) french-fried onions

Cook the pasta according to the package directions. Meanwhile, in a Dutch oven, cook the beef, green pepper and garlic over medium heat until meat is no longer pink and green pepper is tender; drain.

Drain pasta; add to the beef mixture with the tomatoes, soup, cheese and salt.

Transfer to a greased 2-qt. baking dish. Cover and bake at 350° for 30-40 minutes. Uncover; sprinkle with the onions and bake 5 minutes longer.

YIELD: 4-6 SERVINGS.

janie moore
MARION, OHIO

I always use corkscrew noodles when preparing this casserole because the sauce seems to cling to them better than it does to flat noodles—ensuring plenty of good taste in every bite!

PORK CHOP BAKE

PREP 20 minutes | **BAKE** 45 minutes

- 2 boneless pork loin chops (5 ounces each)
- 2 teaspoons butter
- 2 medium apples, peeled and sliced
- 3/4 cup whole-berry cranberry sauce
- 1 small sweet onion, halved and thinly sliced
- 2 tablespoons brown sugar
- 1/4 teaspoon ground cinnamon

In a small nonstick skillet, brown pork chops in butter. Meanwhile, in a small bowl, combine apples, cranberry sauce and onion. Transfer to an 8-in. square baking dish coated with cooking spray. Combine brown sugar and cinnamon; sprinkle over apple mixture. Top with pork chops.

Cover and bake at 325° for 45-50 minutes or until the pork reaches 160° and the apples are tender.

YIELD: 2 SERVINGS.

shelvy ritter
PORTAGE, WISCONSIN

I first tried pork chops and apples in this bake, then I added cranberry and onion, and it was so good! I like to eat this with mashed potatoes or buttered noodles.

BROCCOLI CHEESE STRATA

PREP 15 minutes + chilling | BAKE 25 minutes

1 cup coarsely chopped fresh broccoli
2 green onions, sliced
1 tablespoon water
2 slices white bread, cubed
1/2 cup shredded cheddar cheese
4 eggs
1/2 cup 2% milk
1/2 teaspoon Dijon mustard
1/8 teaspoon dill weed
Dash ground nutmeg
Dash pepper

In a small microwave-safe dish, microwave the broccoli and onions in water on high for 1 minute; drain and set aside. Place the bread in a shallow 3-cup baking dish coated with cooking spray. Add broccoli mixture and cheese.

Combine the eggs, milk, mustard, dill, nutmeg and pepper; pour over cheese. Cover and refrigerate overnight.

Remove from the refrigerator 30 minutes before baking. Bake, uncovered, at 350° for 25-30 minutes or until a knife inserted near the center comes out clean.
YIELD: 2 SERVINGS.

mina dyck
BOISSEVAIN, MANITOBA

This recipe is an easy-to-prepare lunch for two. I enjoy it so much, I often make it just for myself and reheat the extra portion in the microwave the next day.

CORN BREAD BREAKFAST CASSEROLE

PREP 20 minutes | BAKE 20 minutes

- 1 tube (11-1/2 ounces) refrigerated corn bread twists
- 1/4 pound bulk pork sausage
- 3 eggs
- 2 tablespoons half-and-half cream
- 1/8 teaspoon pepper

Dash salt, optional

- 1/2 cup Mexican cheese blend *or* cheddar cheese
- 2 tablespoons chopped green chilies

Unroll and separate the corn bread dough along perforations into 16 pieces. Using 10 or 11 pieces, line the bottom and sides of an ungreased shallow 3-cup baking dish. Flatten and press dough pieces together to seal the perforations. Bake at 375° for 11-14 minutes or until golden brown.

Meanwhile, crumble sausage into skillet; cook over medium heat until no longer pink. Drain well and set aside.

In a bowl, combine eggs, cream, pepper and salt if desired. In the same skillet, cook and stir eggs over medium heat until completely set.

In a bowl, combine sausage, scrambled eggs, cheese and chilies. Spoon into prebaked crust. Top with remaining dough. Flatten and press together to cover top; seal edges.

Bake 18-22 minutes longer or until top is deep golden brown. Serve immediately.
YIELD: 2 SERVINGS.

EDITOR'S NOTE: This recipe was tested with Pillsbury refrigerated corn bread twists.

taste of home
test kitchen
GREENDALE, WISCONSIN

This scrumptious breakfast bake has all the flavors that will keep your family wanting more. A great start to any morning!

MOZZARELLA VEGETABLE STRATA

PREP 20 minutes | BAKE 30 minutes

- 1/2 cup sliced zucchini
- 1/3 cup sliced fresh mushrooms
- 1/3 cup chopped onion
- 2 teaspoons canola oil
- 1 tablespoon minced fresh parsley *or* 1-1/2 teaspoons dried parsley flakes
- 3/4 teaspoon minced fresh basil *or* 1/4 teaspoon dried basil
- 2-3/4 cups cubed bread
- 1/2 cup shredded part-skim mozzarella cheese
- 2 eggs
- 1/2 cup 2% milk
- 1/4 teaspoon salt
- 1/8 teaspoon pepper
- 1 plum tomato, seeded and chopped

In a small skillet, saute the zucchini, mushrooms and onion in oil until tender; drain. Stir in parsley and basil.

In an 8-in. x 4-in. loaf pan coated with cooking spray, layer half of the bread cubes and mozzarella cheese. Top with vegetables and remaining bread and cheese. In a small bowl, whisk the eggs, milk, salt and pepper. Pour over cheese. Sprinkle with tomato.

Cover and bake at 350° for 20 minutes. Uncover; bake 10-15 minutes longer or until a knife inserted near the center comes out clean. Let stand for 5 minutes before cutting.
YIELD: 2 SERVINGS.

wendy mcgowan
FONTANA, CALIFORNIA

A generous layer of sauteed vegetables adds fresh garden flavor to this moist, meatless casserole. Try it for brunch, lunch or dinner.

MACARONI SAUSAGE SUPPER

PREP 15 minutes | **BAKE** 20 minutes

- 3/4 cup uncooked elbow macaroni
- 1/3 pound bulk Italian sausage
- 2 tablespoons chopped onion
- 1 tablespoon chopped green pepper
- 1/4 cup sliced ripe olives, drained
- 2/3 cup condensed cream of mushroom soup, undiluted
- 1/4 cup 2% milk
- 1/8 teaspoon pepper
- 2 ounces process cheese (Velveeta)

Cook the macaroni according to package directions. Meanwhile, in a small skillet, cook the sausage, onion and green pepper over medium heat until meat is no longer pink; drain.

Drain the macaroni; stir into the sausage mixture. Add the olives. Transfer to a 1-qt. baking dish coated with cooking spray.

In a small saucepan over low heat, combine the soup, milk and pepper. Gradually stir in cheese until melted. Pour over sausage mixture. Bake, uncovered, at 375° for 20-25 minutes or until heated through.
YIELD: 2 SERVINGS.

joyce clauson
WISCONSIN RAPIDS, WISCONSIN

My husband and I chase winter's chill with this hearty and delicious casserole that has been a family favorite for decades. Sometimes I add a few fresh mushrooms or substitute cream of celery soup and a stalk of diced celery for extra flavor and nutrition. I heat up leftover soup for lunch the next day.

CORN CHIP BEEF BAKE

PREP 20 minutes | **BAKE** 15 minutes

- 1/2 pound lean ground beef
- 1/3 cup finely chopped onion
- 1/3 cup thinly sliced celery
- 1/3 cup finely chopped green pepper
- 1/4 teaspoon minced garlic
- 1 cup cooked brown rice
- 1 medium tomato, chopped
- 1 teaspoon lemon juice
- 1/4 teaspoon salt
- 1/4 teaspoon hot pepper sauce
- 1/4 cup mayonnaise
- 1/2 to 1 cup corn chips, crushed

In a large skillet, cook beef, onion, celery, green pepper and garlic over medium heat until the meat is no longer pink; drain. Stir in the brown rice, tomato, lemon juice, salt and hot pepper sauce; heat through. Stir in the mayonnaise.

Spoon the rice mixture into two 15-oz. baking dishes coated with cooking spray. Sprinkle with crushed corn chips. Bake, uncovered, at 350° for 13-15 minutes or until heated through.
YIELD: 2 SERVINGS.

barbara bernard
HOLYOKE, MASSACHUSETTS

After my children left home, I found it difficult to whittle down meals for two, but I eventually succeeded, and this became one of our favorites. You can easily freeze the extra portion if you're cooking for one.

SWISS ZUCCHINI BAKE

PREP 20 minutes | **BAKE** 25 minutes

- 2 small zucchini, halved lengthwise and sliced
- 1/4 cup chopped onion
- 2 eggs
- 1/2 teaspoon chicken bouillon granules
- 1/2 teaspoon Italian seasoning
- 1/4 teaspoon ground mustard
- 1/4 teaspoon pepper
- 1 cup (4 ounces) shredded Swiss cheese, *divided*

Place the zucchini and onion in a steamer basket. Place in a saucepan over I in. of water; bring to a boil. Cover and steam for 4-6 minutes or until crisp-tender; drain.

Combine eggs, bouillon, Italian seasoning, mustard and pepper; set aside.

Layer half of zucchini mixture in a I-qt. baking dish coated with cooking spray. Sprinkle with I/2 cup Swiss cheese. Repeat layers. Pour egg mixture over top.

Bake, uncovered, at 350° for 25-30 minutes or until a knife inserted near the center comes out clean.

YIELD: 2 SERVINGS.

george hascher
PHOENICIA, NEW YORK

This is a great entree for a romantic brunch for two. This cheesy, comforting bake will make you both smile.

CREAMY CHICKEN CASSEROLE

PREP 20 minutes | **BAKE** 25 minutes

jaky broussard
GREENSBORO, ALABAMA

French onion dip lends a tangy accent to this cheesy rice bake. Short prep time means you can eat deliciously without spending hours in the kitchen.

- 2/3 cup uncooked instant rice
- 1/4 cup chopped onion
- 2 teaspoons butter
- 1/2 cup 4% cottage cheese
- 1/3 cup French onion dip
- 3 tablespoons sour cream
- 1/4 teaspoon salt
- Dash white pepper
- 1/2 cup cubed cooked chicken
- 1/2 cup shredded cheddar cheese
- 2 tablespoons chopped green chilies

Cook the rice according to the package directions. Meanwhile, in a small skillet, saute onion in butter until tender; set aside. In a small bowl, combine cottage cheese, onion dip, sour cream, salt and pepper. Stir in rice and onion.

Spread half of the rice mixture into a 3-cup baking dish coated with cooking spray. Layer with chicken, 1/4 cup cheddar cheese and green chilies. Top with remaining rice mixture; sprinkle with remaining cheese.

Bake, uncovered, at 350° for 25-30 minutes or until bubbly.

YIELD: 2 SERVINGS.

MEXICAN ZUCCHINI CASSEROLE

PREP 15 minutes | **BAKE** 20 minutes + standing

- 1 egg
- 1 tablespoon canola oil
- 1/8 teaspoon salt
- 1/8 teaspoon pepper
- 1 cup shredded zucchini
- 1 tablespoon chopped seeded jalapeno pepper
- 1 tablespoon finely chopped onion
- 1/3 cup biscuit/baking mix
- 2 tablespoons shredded cheddar cheese

In a small bowl, beat egg, oil, salt and pepper. Add the zucchini, jalapeno and onion; stir to coat. Stir in the biscuit mix and cheese.

Pour into a 15-oz. baking dish coated with cooking spray. Bake at 375° for 18-20 minutes or until a toothpick comes out clean. Let stand for 10 minutes before serving.

YIELD: 2 SERVINGS.

EDITOR'S NOTE: When cutting hot peppers, disposable gloves are recommended. Avoid touching your face.

dolores kitzinger
APPLETON, WISCONSIN

Use some of your garden bounty to whip up this zesty quiche-like casserole that teams zucchini with cheese, onion, egg and jalapeno pepper. You could serve it as a meatless main dish for breakfast, lunch or dinner.

MINI TUNA CASSEROLES

PREP/TOTAL TIME 30 minutes

- 1/2 cup chopped green onions
- 2 tablespoons butter
- 2 tablespoons all-purpose flour
- 3/4 cup milk
- 1 can (6 ounces) tuna, drained
- 1 cup crushed potato chips, *divided*
- 1/4 teaspoon pepper

In a saucepan, saute the onions in butter. Stir in the flour until blended. Gradually stir in milk. Bring to a boil over medium heat; cook and stir for 2 minutes or until thickened. Remove from the heat. Stir in the tuna, 1/2 cup of potato chips and pepper.

Pour into two greased 8-oz. baking dishes. Sprinkle with remaining potato chips. Bake, uncovered, at 350° for 20-25 minutes or until hot and bubbly.

YIELD: 2 SERVINGS.

rebecca reese
JACKSBORO, TEXAS

I can whip up this dish in a hurry, and it's perfect for a light supper or luncheon for two. I always have a can of tuna on my pantry shelf, and when I prepare it, I feel I've served us a nutritious meal.

SWEET POTATO SHEPHERD'S PIE

PREP 25 minutes | **BAKE** 30 minutes

- 1 large sweet potato
- 1/2 pound lean ground beef
- 1/4 cup chopped onion
- 1 can (8-3/4 ounces) whole kernel corn, drained
- 1/2 cup tomato sauce
- Dash *each* ground cinnamon, allspice and nutmeg
- 1 tablespoon butter
- 1 tablespoon 2% milk
- 1/8 teaspoon salt
- 1/8 teaspoon pepper

Scrub and pierce sweet potato; place on a microwave-safe plate. Microwave, uncovered, on high for 10-12 minutes or until tender, turning once.

Meanwhile, in a large skillet, cook beef and onion until meat is no longer pink; drain. Add the corn, tomato sauce and spices. Place in a 1-qt. baking dish coated with cooking spray; set aside.

When cool enough to handle, cut potato in half; scoop out the pulp and place in a small bowl. Mash with butter, milk, salt and pepper. Spread evenly over meat mixture.

Bake, uncovered, at 350° for 25-30 minutes or until heated through.

YIELD: 2 SERVINGS.

tanya marcketti
GOLDEN, COLORADO

As a child, shepherd's pie was one of my favorites. But now, having cut white potatoes out of our diet, I experimented with sweet potatoes. The result is different but just as yummy!

potluck pleasers

BOW TIE BAKE

PREP 25 minutes | **BAKE** 30 minutes

1 pound ground beef
1 large onion, chopped
1 can (8 ounces) mushroom stems and pieces, drained
1/2 cup chopped green pepper
1 package (16 ounces) bow tie pasta, cooked and drained
1 can (10-3/4 ounces) condensed tomato soup, undiluted
3 cups (12 ounces) shredded part-skim mozzarella cheese, *divided*
1 can (10-3/4 ounces) condensed cream of mushroom soup, undiluted

In a large skillet, cook the beef, onion, mushrooms and green pepper over medium heat until meat is no longer pink; drain.

In a greased 3-qt. baking dish, layer half of the pasta, half of the meat mixture, all of the tomato soup and 1 cup of cheese. Top with the remaining pasta and meat mixture. Spread with mushroom soup. Sprinkle with the remaining cheese.

Bake, uncovered, at 350° for 30-45 minutes or until heated through.
YIELD: 12 SERVINGS.

EDITOR'S NOTE: As a side dish for bow tie bake, place fresh cut green beans in a saucepan; cover with water. Bring to a boil. Cook, uncovered, for 8-10 minutes or until crisp-tender; drain. Sprinkle with Italian seasoning.

cindy kemp
FOREST, ONTARIO

My cousin takes this dish to our annual family picnic. I make it for functions on my husband's side of the family and never bring home any leftovers.

BLARNEY BREAKFAST BAKE

PREP 20 minutes | **BAKE** 50 minutes + standing

1 pound bulk pork sausage
1/2 pound sliced fresh mushrooms
1 large onion, chopped
10 eggs
3 cups milk
2 teaspoons ground mustard
1 teaspoon salt
1/2 teaspoon pepper
6 cups cubed day-old bread
1 cup chopped seeded tomatoes
1 cup (4 ounces) shredded pepper Jack cheese
1 cup (4 ounces) shredded cheddar cheese

In a large skillet, cook sausage, mushrooms and onion over medium heat until meat is no longer pink; drain. In a large bowl, whisk the eggs, milk, mustard, salt and pepper.

In a greased 13-in. x 9-in. baking dish, layer half of the bread cubes, tomatoes, cheeses and sausage mixture. Repeat layers. Pour egg mixture over the top.

Bake, uncovered, at 325° for 50-55 minutes or until a knife inserted near the center comes out clean. Let stand for 10 minutes before serving.
YIELD: 12 SERVINGS.

kerry barnett-amundson
OCEAN PARK, WASHINGTON

I got this recipe from my mom, and I used it when I served an Irish brunch to my neighbors for St. Patrick's Day.

seeded TOMATOES

To seed a tomato, cut it in half horizontally and remove the stem. Holding a tomato half over a bowl or sink, scrape out the seeds with a small spoon or squeeze the tomato to force out the seeds. Then slice, dice or chop as directed in the recipe.

HAM-POTATO PHYLLO BAKE

PREP 30 minutes | **BAKE** 20 minutes

tracy hartsuff
CHARLOTTE, MICHIGAN

I'm often asked to bring this savory dish to potlucks. The phyllo is crisp and golden brown, and the dill tastes so good with the rich filling.

- 3 pounds red potatoes, peeled and thinly sliced
- 1 medium onion, chopped
- 8 tablespoons butter, *divided*
- 20 sheets phyllo dough (14 inches x 9 inches)
- 2 cups (16 ounces) sour cream
- 2 cups cubed fully cooked ham
- 2 cups (8 ounces) shredded cheddar cheese
- 7 teaspoons dill weed, *divided*
- 2 teaspoons garlic powder
- 1 teaspoon salt
- 1/2 teaspoon pepper
- 1 egg, lightly beaten
- 2 tablespoons half-and-half cream

Place potatoes in a Dutch oven and cover with water. Bring to a boil; reduce heat. Cover and cook for 10-15 minutes or until tender; drain. In a small skillet, saute the onion in 1 tablespoon butter until tender; set aside.

Melt remaining butter. Brush a 13-in. x 9-in. baking dish with some of the butter. Unroll phyllo sheets; trim to fit into dish. (Keep dough covered with plastic wrap and a damp cloth while assembling.) Place one phyllo sheet in prepared dish; brush with butter. Repeat twice.

Top with half each of the sour cream, potatoes, onion, ham and cheese. Combine 6 teaspoons dill, garlic powder, salt and pepper; sprinkle half over cheese. Layer with three phyllo sheets, brushing each with butter. Top with the remaining sour cream, potatoes, onion, ham, cheese and the seasoning mixture.

Layer with remaining phyllo dough, brushing each sheet with butter. Combine egg and cream; brush over top. Sprinkle with remaining dill.

Bake, uncovered, at 350° for 20-25 minutes or until heated through. Let stand for 5 minutes. Cut into squares.
YIELD: 12-15 SERVINGS.

MEATY SPINACH MANICOTTI

PREP 30 minutes | **BAKE** 45 minutes

2 packages (8 ounces *each*) manicotti shells
1/4 cup butter, cubed
1/4 cup all-purpose flour
2-1/2 cups milk
3/4 cup grated Parmesan cheese
1 pound bulk Italian sausage
4 cups cubed cooked chicken *or* turkey
2 packages (10 ounces *each*) frozen chopped spinach, thawed and squeezed dry
2 eggs, beaten
1 cup (4 ounces) shredded part-skim mozzarella cheese
2 jars (26 ounces *each*) spaghetti sauce
1/4 cup minced fresh parsley

Cook manicotti according to package directions. Meanwhile, melt butter in a saucepan. Stir in the flour until smooth. Gradually add milk. Bring to a boil; cook and stir for 2 minutes or until thickened. Stir in Parmesan cheese until melted; set aside. Drain manicotti; set aside.

In a large skillet, cook sausage over medium heat until no longer pink; drain. Add chicken, spinach, eggs, mozzarella cheese and 3/4 cup white sauce. Stuff into manicotti shells.

Spread 1/2 cup spaghetti sauce in each of two ungreased 13-in. x 9-in. baking dishes. Top with manicotti. Pour remaining spaghetti sauce over the top.

Reheat remaining white sauce, stirring constantly. Pour over spaghetti sauce. Bake, uncovered, at 350° for 45-50 minutes. Sprinkle with parsley.

YIELD: 14-16 SERVINGS.

pat schroeder
ELKHORN, WISCONSIN

This hearty stuffed pasta dish will feed a crowd. Tangy tomato sauce tops manicotti that's filled with a mouthwatering blend of Italian sausage, chicken, spinach and mozzarella cheese. Be prepared to share the recipe!

ITALIAN SAUSAGE EGG BAKE

PREP 20 minutes + chilling | **BAKE** 50 minutes

- 8 slices white bread, cubed
- 1 pound Italian sausage links, casings removed and sliced
- 2 cups (8 ounces) shredded sharp cheddar cheese
- 2 cups (8 ounces) shredded part-skim mozzarella cheese
- 9 eggs
- 3 cups milk
- 1 teaspoon dried basil
- 1 teaspoon dried oregano
- 1 teaspoon fennel seed, crushed

Place bread cubes in a greased 13-in. x 9-in. baking dish; set aside. In a large skillet, cook sausage over medium heat until no longer pink; drain. Spoon sausage over bread; sprinkle with cheeses.

In a large bowl, whisk the eggs, milk and seasonings; pour over casserole. Cover and refrigerate overnight.

Remove from refrigerator 30 minutes before baking. Bake, uncovered, at 350° for 50-55 minutes or until golden brown. Let stand for 5 minutes before cutting.

YIELD: 12 SERVINGS.

darlene markham
ROCHESTER, NEW YORK

This hearty entree warms up any breakfast or brunch menu with its herb-seasoned flavor.

BRUNCH STRATA

PREP 45 minutes | **BAKE** 35 minutes + standing

- 3 cups sliced fresh mushrooms
- 3 cups chopped zucchini
- 2 cups cubed fully cooked ham
- 1-1/2 cups chopped onions
- 1-1/2 cups chopped green peppers
- 2 garlic cloves, minced
- 1/3 cup canola oil
- 2 packages (8 ounces *each*) cream cheese, softened
- 1/2 cup half-and-half cream
- 12 eggs
- 4 cups cubed day-old bread
- 3 cups (12 ounces) shredded cheddar cheese
- 1 teaspoon salt
- 1/2 teaspoon pepper

In a large skillet, saute mushrooms, zucchini, ham, onions, green peppers and garlic in oil until vegetables are tender. Drain and pat dry; set aside.

In a large bowl, beat the cream cheese and cream until smooth. Beat in the eggs. Stir in the bread, cheese, salt, pepper and vegetable mixture.

Pour into two greased 11-in. x 7-in. baking dishes. Bake, uncovered, at 350° for 35-40 minutes or until a knife inserted near the center comes out clean. Let stand for 10 minutes before serving.

YIELD: 2 CASSEROLES (8 SERVINGS EACH).

arlene kay butler
OGDEN, UTAH

Ham, zucchini, mushrooms and cheese flavor this rich, hearty egg dish. It adds appeal to a breakfast or lunch buffet and cuts easily, too. Make sure you bring the recipe—everyone will want it!

about ZUCCHINI

Handle zucchini carefully; they're thin-skinned and easily damaged. Look for firm, heavy squash with moist stem ends and shiny skin. Smaller squash are generally sweeter and more tender than larger ones. One medium (1/3 pound) zucchini yields about 2 cups sliced or 1-1/2 cups shredded. Store in a plastic bag in the refrigerator crisper for 4 to 5 days. Do not wash until ready to use.

CHEESY BROCCOLI-RICE BAKE

PREP 10 minutes | **BAKE** 40 minutes

martha myers
ASH GROVE, MISSOURI

With cheese and sour cream, this lovely casserole is perfect to serve to guests or share on a buffet. It's a hearty rich-tasting side dish along with any meat.

- 1 can (10-3/4 ounces) low-fat condensed cream of broccoli soup, undiluted
- 1 can (10-3/4 ounces) low-fat cream of chicken soup, undiluted
- 2 cups fat-free milk
- 1/2 cup reduced-fat sour cream
- 2 cups (8 ounces) shredded part-skim mozzarella cheese
- 1 cup (4 ounces) shredded reduced-fat cheddar cheese
- 2 cups uncooked instant rice
- 2 cups chopped fresh broccoli
- 1 small onion, chopped
- 1 teaspoon paprika, *divided*
- 1/2 teaspoon pepper

In a large bowl, combine soups, milk and sour cream. Stir in cheeses, rice, broccoli, onion, 3/4 teaspoon of paprika and pepper.

Transfer to a 13-in. x 9-in. baking dish coated with cooking spray. Sprinkle with remaining paprika. Cover and bake at 350° for 35 minutes. Uncover; bake 5-10 minutes longer or until rice and broccoli are tender.

YIELD: 16 SERVINGS.

NUTRITION FACTS: One 1/2-cup serving equals 149 calories, 5 g fat (3 g saturated fat), 19 mg cholesterol, 280 mg sodium, 17 g carbohydrate, 1 g fiber, 9 g protein. **DIABETIC EXCHANGES:** 1 starch, 1 medium-fat meat.

CHICKEN STUFFING CASSEROLE

PREP 15 minutes | **BAKE** 30 minutes

cathy smith
WYOMING, MICHIGAN

This tasty chicken casserole is chock-full of homey, comforting flavor! It's a great way to use up leftover cooked chicken, plus it's so quick to assemble using handy pantry items.

- 2 packages (6 ounces *each*) chicken stuffing mix
- 2 cans (10-3/4 ounces *each*) condensed cream of mushroom soup, undiluted
- 1 cup milk
- 4 cups cubed cooked chicken
- 2 cups frozen corn
- 2 cans (8 ounces *each*) mushroom stems and pieces, drained
- 4 cups (16 ounces) shredded cheddar cheese

Prepare stuffing mixes according to the package directions. Meanwhile, in a large bowl, combine soup and milk; set aside. Spread the stuffing into two greased 8-in. square baking dishes. Layer with chicken, corn, mushrooms, soup mixture and cheese.

Cover and freeze one casserole for up to 3 months. Cover and bake the second casserole at 350° for 30-35 minutes or until cheese is melted.

TO USE FROZEN CASSEROLE: Remove from the freezer 30 minutes before baking (do not thaw). Bake at 350° for 1-1/2 hours. Uncover; bake 10-15 minutes longer or until heated through.

YIELD: 2 CASSEROLES (6 SERVINGS EACH).

ROASTED VEGGIE PASTA

PREP 40 minutes | **BAKE** 25 minutes

- 4 small zucchini, halved lengthwise and cut into 1-inch slices
- 2 large onions, cut into wedges
- 2 medium yellow summer squash, halved lengthwise and cut into 1-inch slices
- 2 large sweet yellow peppers, cut into 1-inch pieces
- 1 cup fresh baby carrots, halved lengthwise
- 2 tablespoons olive oil
- 3-1/2 cups uncooked fusilli pasta
- 2 cups (8 ounces) shredded fontina cheese
- 1-1/2 cups heavy whipping cream
- 1/2 cup canned diced tomatoes in sauce
- 1/2 cup grated Parmesan cheese, *divided*
- 2 garlic cloves, minced
- 1/2 teaspoon salt
- 1/4 teaspoon pepper

In a large bowl, combine first six ingredients. Transfer to two greased 15-in. x 10-in. x 1-in. baking pans. Bake at 450° for 20-25 minutes or until crisp-tender; set aside. Reduce heat to 350°.

Cook pasta according to the package directions; drain. Add the fontina cheese, cream, tomatoes, 1/4 cup Parmesan cheese, garlic, salt and pepper. Stir in vegetable mixture.

Transfer to a greased 13-in. x 9-in. baking dish (dish will be full). Sprinkle with the remaining Parmesan. Bake, uncovered, for 25-30 minutes or until bubbly.

YIELD: 16 SERVINGS (3/4 CUP EACH).

robyn baney
LEXINGTON PARK, MARYLAND

My sister gave me this recipe years ago, and it has become a favorite make-ahead and company meal. For a heartier dish, pair it with ham and dinner rolls.

POTLUCK HAM AND PASTA

PREP 40 minutes | **BAKE** 25 minutes

- 1 package (16 ounces) elbow macaroni
- 4 cups fresh broccoli florets
- 1/2 cup finely chopped onion
- 1/2 cup butter, cubed
- 1/2 cup all-purpose flour
- 1 teaspoon ground mustard
- 1 teaspoon salt
- 1/4 teaspoon pepper
- 6 cups milk
- 1 jar (15 ounces) process cheese sauce
- 2 cups (8 ounces) shredded cheddar cheese, *divided*
- 4 cups cubed fully cooked ham

Cook macaroni according to package directions, adding broccoli during the last 3-4 minutes; drain.

In a Dutch oven, saute onion in butter for 2 minutes. Stir in the flour, mustard, salt and pepper until blended. Gradually stir in milk. Bring to a boil; cook and stir for 2 minutes or until thickened. Stir in cheese sauce and 1 cup cheddar cheese until blended.

Remove from the heat; stir in the ham, macaroni and broccoli. Divide between a greased 13-in. x 9-in. baking dish and a greased 8-in. square baking dish. Sprinkle with remaining cheese.

Bake, uncovered, at 350° for 25-35 minutes or until bubbly and heated through.
YIELD: 12 SERVINGS.

nancy foust
STONEBORO, PENNSYLVANIA

This easy meal-in-one dish is a real crowd-pleaser on chilly nights. Because it bakes in two pans, you could freeze one for later, depending on your needs. It's creamy, and filling and has a wonderful ham-and-cheese flavor.

HOLIDAY BRUNCH CASSEROLE

PREP 15 minutes + chilling | **BAKE** 30 minutes + standing

- 4 cups frozen shredded hash brown potatoes
- 1 pound bulk pork sausage, cooked and drained
- 1/2 pound sliced bacon, cooked and crumbled
- 1 medium green pepper, chopped
- 2 cups (8 ounces) shredded cheddar cheese, *divided*
- 1 green onion, chopped
- 1 cup reduced-fat biscuit/baking mix
- 1/2 teaspoon salt
- 4 eggs
- 3 cups milk

In a large bowl, combine the hash browns, sausage, bacon, green pepper, 1 cup cheese and onion. Transfer to a greased 13-in. x 9-in. baking dish.

In another bowl, whisk the biscuit mix, salt, eggs and milk; pour over the top. Sprinkle with remaining cheese. Cover and refrigerate overnight.

Remove from refrigerator 30 minutes before baking. Bake, uncovered, at 375° for 30-35 minutes or until golden brown. Let stand for 10 minutes before cutting.

YIELD: 12 SERVINGS.

nelda cronbaugh
BELLE PLAINE, IOWA

If you'll be having overnight company during the holidays, you may want to consider this hearty casserole. Guests will be impressed with its bountiful filling and scrumptious flavor.

HAM & CHEESE CASSEROLES

PREP 20 minutes | **BAKE** 25 minutes

- 1-1/2 pounds uncooked egg noodles
- 3 pounds cubed fully cooked ham
- 4 cans (10-3/4 ounces *each*) condensed cream of chicken soup, undiluted
- 4 cups frozen cut green beans, thawed
- 1 cup milk
- 1/4 cup butter, melted
- 2 cups (8 ounces) shredded Colby-Monterey Jack cheese

jan schoshke
BROOKVILLE, KANSAS

I got this recipe from my mother, and I love it because it's easy and I've usually got the ingredients on hand. It also freezes well, and I can have it handy when extra guests show up. Everyone always likes it; there are never leftovers.

Cook pasta according to the package directions. Meanwhile, in a large bowl, combine the ham, soup, beans and milk. Drain pasta; pour over ham mixture and toss to coat. Transfer to two greased 13-in. x 9-in. baking dishes.

Drizzle each with butter; sprinkle with cheese. Cover and freeze one casserole for up to 3 months. Bake remaining casserole, uncovered, at 350° for 25-30 minutes or until heated through.

TO USE FROZEN CASSEROLE: Thaw in the refrigerator overnight. Remove from the refrigerator 30 minutes before baking. Bake, uncovered, at 350° for 40-45 minutes or until heated through.

YIELD: 2 CASSEROLES (8 SERVINGS EACH).

FIVE-CHEESE LASAGNA

PREP 1 hour | **BAKE** 40 minutes + cooling

- 6 packages (16 ounces *each*) lasagna noodles
- 10 pounds bulk Italian sausage
- 10 medium onions, chopped
- 30 garlic cloves, minced
- 11 cans (29 ounces *each*) tomato sauce
- 2/3 cup dried basil
- 3 tablespoons ground nutmeg
- 2 tablespoons fennel seed, crushed
- 1 tablespoon salt
- 1 tablespoon pepper
- 6 cartons (32 ounces *each*) ricotta cheese
- 10 pounds shredded mozzarella cheese
- 4 cartons (8 ounces *each*) grated Parmesan cheese
- 5 blocks (5 ounces *each*) Romano cheese, grated
- 10 packages (6 ounces *each*) sliced provolone cheese, cut into strips
- 1 cup minced fresh parsley

Cook the noodles in boiling water for 5 minutes; rinse in cold water and drain.

Cook sausage, onions and garlic until meat is no longer pink; drain. Add the tomato sauce and seasonings; bring to a boil. Reduce heat; simmer, uncovered, for 50-60 minutes.

Grease ten 13-in. x 9-in. baking dishes. In each dish, layer about 1-1/2 cups tomato sauce, four noodles, about 1-1/4 cups ricotta, 1-1/2 cups mozzarella, about 1/3 cup Parmesan, 1/4 cup Romano and three slices provolone. Repeat layers. Top with four noodles, about 1-1/2 cups of tomato sauce, 1 cup mozzarella and about 1 tablespoon minced parsley.

Bake, uncovered, at 375° for 40-50 minutes or until browned and bubbly. Let stand 10-15 minutes before serving.

YIELD: 10 CASSEROLES (12-15 SERVINGS EACH).

todd newman
LA PORTE, TEXAS

I prepared this for a Cub Scout banquet. It was easy since there was nothing to do at the last minute but cut and serve. It was a big success.

MUSTARD HAM STRATA

PREP 15 minutes + chilling | **BAKE** 45 minutes

- 12 slices day-old bread, crusts removed and cubed
- 1-1/2 cups cubed fully cooked ham
- 1 cup chopped green pepper
- 3/4 cup shredded cheddar cheese
- 3/4 cup shredded Monterey Jack cheese
- 1/3 cup chopped onion
- 7 eggs
- 3 cups milk
- 3 teaspoons ground mustard
- 1 teaspoon salt

In a greased 13-in. x 9-in. baking dish, layer bread cubes, ham, green pepper, cheeses and onion. In a large bowl, combine the eggs, milk, mustard and salt. Pour over top. Cover and refrigerate overnight.

Remove from refrigerator 30 minutes before baking. Bake, uncovered, at 325° for 45-50 minutes or until a knife inserted near the center comes out clean. Let stand for 5 minutes before cutting.

YIELD: 12 SERVINGS.

dolores zornow
POYNETTE, WISCONSIN

I had this at a bed-and-breakfast years ago. They were kind enough to give me the recipe, and I've made it many times since.

easy **POTLUCK**

Watch rummage sales and thrift stores for pretty dishes priced inexpensively. Use the dishes to take casseroles to potlucks and parties, and let your host keep the dish. Then you don't have to lose a cherished bowl or platter.

PEARL ONION BROCCOLI BAKE

PREP 20 minutes | **BAKE** 25 minutes

4 packages (8 ounces *each*) frozen broccoli cuts

4 cups frozen pearl onions

1/2 cup butter, *divided*

1/4 cup all-purpose flour

3/4 teaspoon salt

1/8 teaspoon pepper

2 cups milk

2 packages (3 ounces *each*) cream cheese, cubed

2 cups soft bread crumbs

1 cup (4 ounces) shredded cheddar cheese

In a large saucepan, cook broccoli in 1 in. of water until almost tender; drain. Cook pearl onions in 1 in. of water until almost tender; drain.

In a large saucepan, melt 1/4 cup butter; stir in flour, salt and pepper until smooth. Gradually add milk. Bring to a boil; cook and stir for 1-2 minutes or until thickened. Reduce heat; stir in the cream cheese until smooth and blended.

Place broccoli and onions in a greased 13-in. x 9-in. baking dish. Add sauce and gently stir to coat. Melt remaining butter; toss with bread crumbs. Sprinkle crumbs and cheddar cheese over vegetables.

Bake, uncovered, at 350° for 25-30 minutes or until topping is golden brown.
YIELD: 12-15 SERVINGS.

charles keating
MANCHESTER, MARYLAND

With its creamy white cheese sauce and buttery crumb topping, this dish is great comfort food. If you're looking for a mild way to dress up broccoli, this is the recipe.

ELEGANT VEGETABLE CASSEROLE

PREP 1 hour | BAKE 50 minutes

virginia anthony
JACKSONVILLE, FLORIDA

Please everyone at the table with this innovative and space-saving dish. Three traditional sides line up to create an eye-appealing medley.

PARSNIP POTATOES

- 2 pounds potatoes, peeled and cubed (about 4 medium)
- 4 medium parsnips, peeled and cubed
- 1 carton (8 ounces) reduced-fat sour cream
- 3 tablespoons fat-free milk
- 1 teaspoon salt

SQUASH

- 1 medium butternut squash (about 3 pounds), peeled and cubed
- 1/2 teaspoon salt
- 1/4 teaspoon ground nutmeg

SPINACH

- 2 eggs
- 1 tablespoon fat-free milk
- 1/4 teaspoon salt
- 2 packages (10 ounces *each*) frozen chopped spinach, thawed and squeezed dry
- 1-1/2 cups (6 ounces) shredded reduced-fat Swiss cheese
- 3/4 cup soft bread crumbs
- 1 small onion, grated

Place potatoes and parsnips in a large saucepan; cover with water and bring to a boil. Reduce heat; cover and simmer for 15-20 minutes or until tender. Drain. Mash with sour cream, milk and salt; set aside.

Place squash in another large saucepan and cover with water. Bring to a boil. Reduce heat; cover and simmer for 15-20 minutes or until tender. Drain. Mash with salt and nutmeg; set aside.

In a small bowl, whisk the eggs, milk and salt. Stir in the spinach, cheese, bread crumbs and onion.

Place half of parsnip potatoes at one end of a 13-in. x 9-in. baking dish coated with cooking spray. Add squash to dish, forming a stripe. Repeat with the spinach. Place remaining parsnip potatoes at opposite end of dish. (Dish will be full.)

Cover and bake at 350° for 45-55 minutes or until a meat thermometer inserted in the spinach reads 160°.

YIELD: 14 SERVINGS (1 CUP EACH).

NUTRITION FACTS: 1 cup equals 183 calories, 3 g fat (2 g saturated fat), 40 mg cholesterol, 410 mg sodium, 31 g carbohydrate, 6 g fiber, 10 g protein. **DIABETIC EXCHANGES:** 2 starch, 1/2 fat.

POTLUCK MUSHROOM RICE

PREP 30 minutes | **COOK** 30 minutes

3 cups water
1-1/2 teaspoons beef bouillon granules
1-1/2 cups uncooked long grain rice
2 pounds ground beef
1 large onion, chopped
1 large green pepper, chopped
1 jar (6 ounces) whole mushrooms, drained
1 can (4 ounces) mushroom stems and pieces, drained
1 celery rib, sliced
1 can (10-3/4 ounces) condensed cream of celery soup, undiluted
1 can (10-3/4 ounces) condensed cream of mushroom soup, undiluted
2 tablespoons Worcestershire sauce
1/2 teaspoon garlic powder

In a large saucepan, bring the water and bouillon to a boil. Add the rice. Reduce heat; cover and simmer for 15-20 minutes or until tender.

Meanwhile, in a large skillet, cook the beef, onion, green pepper, mushrooms and celery until the meat is no longer pink and the vegetables are tender; drain. Stir in rice, soups, Worcestershire sauce and garlic powder; mix well.

Transfer to an ovenproof Dutch oven. Cover and bake at 350° for 30 minutes or until heated through.
YIELD: 12-14 SERVINGS.

yvonne taylor
ROBSTOWN, TEXAS

Once a week at work, we'd hold potluck dinners. A co-worker brought this dish, and I left with the recipe. It's very versatile because you can add different seasonings to suit your taste.

THREE-CHEESE KIELBASA BAKE

PREP 55 minutes | **BAKE** 30 minutes

12 ounces uncooked elbow macaroni
2 pounds kielbasa or Polish sausage, halved lengthwise and sliced
1 tablespoon olive oil
2 medium onions, chopped
2 medium zucchini, quartered and sliced
2 medium carrots, grated
1/2 teaspoon minced garlic
1 jar (26 ounces) spaghetti sauce
1 can (14-1/2 ounces) stewed tomatoes
1 egg, lightly beaten
1 carton (15 ounces) ricotta cheese
2 cups (8 ounces) shredded cheddar cheese
2 cups (8 ounces) part-skim shredded mozzarella cheese
2 green onions, chopped

Cook macaroni according to the package directions. Meanwhile, in a large skillet, brown sausage in oil over medium heat; drain. Add the onions, zucchini, carrots and garlic; cook and stir for 5-6 minutes or until crisp-tender.

Stir in spaghetti sauce and tomatoes. Bring to a boil. Reduce the heat; simmer, uncovered, for 15 minutes. Drain macaroni.

In each of two greased 13-in. x 9-in. baking dishes, layer a fourth of the macaroni and meat sauce. Combine the egg and ricotta; spoon a fourth over sauce. Sprinkle with a fourth of the cheddar and mozzarella. Repeat layers. Top with green onions.

Cool one casserole; cover and freeze for up to 2 months. Cover and bake the remaining casserole at 350° for 15 minutes. Uncover; bake 15 minutes longer or until cheese is melted.

TO USE FROZEN CASSEROLE: Thaw in the refrigerator for 24 hours. Remove from refrigerator 30 minutes before baking. Cover and bake at 350° for 35-40 minutes or until heated through.
YIELD: 2 CASSEROLES (8-10 SERVINGS EACH).

kate beckman
HEMET, CALIFORNIA

This hearty casserole takes advantage of garden-fresh vegetables and handy convenience items. My aunt originally made this for family gatherings. Now I fix it any night of the week.

EGG AND SAUSAGE STRATA

PREP 15 minutes + chilling | **BAKE** 1-1/2 hours

12 slices white bread, crusts removed, cubed
1-1/2 pounds bulk pork sausage
1/3 cup chopped onion
1/4 cup chopped green pepper
1 jar (2 ounces) chopped pimientos, drained
6 eggs
3 cups milk
2 teaspoons Worcestershire sauce
1 teaspoon ground mustard
1/2 teaspoon salt
1/4 teaspoon pepper
1/4 teaspoon dried oregano

Line a greased 13-in. x 9-in. baking dish with bread cubes; set aside.

In a skillet, cook sausage with the onion and green pepper over medium heat until meat is no longer pink; drain. Stir in pimientos; sprinkle over bread.

In a bowl, beat eggs, milk, Worcestershire sauce, mustard, salt, pepper and oregano. Pour over the sausage mixture. Cover and refrigerate overnight.

Cover and bake at 325° for 1 hour 20 minutes. Uncover; bake 10 minutes longer or until a knife inserted near the center comes out clean. Let stand for 10 minutes before serving.

YIELD: 12-15 SERVINGS.

gail carney
ARLINGTON, TEXAS

I especially like to make this breakfast dish when we have weekend guests. I fix it the night before, and the next morning I can sit, eat and enjoy their company. People often think I spent hours preparing it.

PUFFY CHILE RELLENOS CASSEROLE

PREP 20 minutes | **BAKE** 40 minutes + standing

6 cans (4 ounces *each*) whole green chilies, drained
8 flour tortillas (6 inches), cut into 1-inch strips
2 cups (8 ounces) shredded part-skim mozzarella cheese
2 cups (8 ounces) shredded reduced-fat cheddar cheese
3 cups egg substitute
3/4 cup fat-free milk
1/2 teaspoon garlic powder
1/2 teaspoon ground cumin
1/2 teaspoon pepper
1/4 teaspoon salt
1 teaspoon paprika
1 cup salsa

Cut along one side of each chili and open to lie flat. Coat a 13-in. x 9-in. baking dish with cooking spray. Layer half of the chilies, tortilla strips, mozzarella and cheddar cheeses in prepared dish. Repeat layers.

In a small bowl, beat the egg substitute, milk, garlic powder, cumin, pepper and salt. Pour over cheese. Sprinkle with paprika.

Bake, uncovered, at 350° for 40-45 minutes or until puffy and a knife inserted 2 in. from the edge of the pan comes out clean. Let stand for 10 minutes before cutting. Serve with salsa.

YIELD: 12 SERVINGS.

NUTRITION FACTS: 1 piece with 4 teaspoons salsa equals 213 calories, 9 g fat (5 g saturated fat), 25 mg cholesterol, 690 mg sodium, 14 g carbohydrate, 1 g fiber, 18 g protein. **DIABETIC EXCHANGES:** 2 lean meat, 1 starch, 1 vegetable.

EDITOR'S NOTE: When cutting hot peppers, disposable gloves are recommended. Avoid touching your face.

marilyn morey
MALLARD, IOWA

Here's a wonderfully zesty casserole that's much lower in fat and easier to assemble than traditional chile rellenos. I don't remember where I got the recipe, but I've enjoyed this layered brunch entree for years.

make your OWN

To make your own egg substitute, whisk 2 large egg whites, lightly beaten, 1 tablespoon nonfat dry milk powder and 1 teaspoon canola or vegetable oil until well blended. Add 4 drops of yellow food coloring, if desired. This recipe yields 1/4 cup of egg substitute that is equivalent to 1 large egg.

BROCCOLI-CHICKEN CUPS

PREP 15 minutes | **BAKE** 20 minutes

2 tubes (10 ounces *each*) refrigerated biscuit dough

2 cups (8 ounces) shredded cheddar cheese, *divided*

1-1/3 cups crisp rice cereal

1 cup cubed cooked chicken

1 can (10-3/4 ounces) condensed cream of mushroom soup, undiluted

3 cups frozen chopped broccoli, cooked and drained

Place the biscuits in greased muffin cups, pressing dough over the bottom and up the sides. Add 1 tablespoon cheese and cereal to each cup.

In a large bowl, combine chicken, soup and broccoli; spoon into cups. Bake at 375° for 20-25 minutes or until bubbly. Sprinkle with remaining cheese.

YIELD: 10-12 SERVINGS.

shirley gerber
ROANOKE, ILLINOIS

I first sampled these when my cousin made them for a bridal shower. All the ladies raved over the fantastic flavor of their individual "casseroles."

CASSEROLE FOR A CROWD

PREP 25 minutes | **BAKE** 30 minutes

2 pounds ground beef

1 large onion, chopped

8 ounces wide egg noodles, cooked and drained

1 can (15-1/4 ounces) whole kernel corn, drained

1 can (15-1/4 ounces) peas, drained

1 can (8 ounces) mushroom stems and pieces, drained

4 cups (16 ounces) shredded cheddar cheese, *divided*

1 can (10-3/4 ounces) condensed cream of celery soup, undiluted

1-1/4 cups milk

1 tablespoon chili powder

1 tablespoon Worcestershire sauce

2 teaspoons salt

1/4 teaspoon pepper

1/4 teaspoon garlic powder

In a large skillet, cook beef and onion over medium heat until meat is no longer pink; drain. Transfer to a greased roasting pan. Stir in noodles, corn, peas and mushrooms.

In a large saucepan, combine 2-1/2 cups cheese with remaining ingredients. Cook and stir over low heat until cheese is melted. Pour over noodle mixture and mix well. Sprinkle with remaining cheese.

Bake, uncovered, at 350° for 30 minutes or until heated through.

YIELD: 12-14 SERVINGS.

fran huettner
BEAVER DAM, WISCONSIN

All five of our children and six grandchildren expect me to serve this casserole when they visit. It makes just the right amount for our growing family.

FOUR-CHEESE RICE CASSEROLE

PREP 10 minutes | **BAKE** 40 minutes

- 1 medium sweet onion, chopped
- 1/4 cup butter, cubed
- 4 cups cooked long grain rice
- 2 packages (10 ounces *each*) frozen chopped spinach, thawed and squeezed dry
- 3 cups (12 ounces) shredded part-skim mozzarella cheese, *divided*
- 1-1/2 cups shredded Parmesan cheese, *divided*
- 2 packages (8 ounces *each*) cream cheese, softened
- 1 carton (15 ounces) ricotta cheese
- 3/4 cup milk
- 1/2 teaspoon garlic powder
- 1/2 teaspoon Beau Monde seasoning

In a small skillet, saute onion in butter until tender. In a large bowl, combine the rice, spinach, 1-1/2 cups mozzarella, 1 cup Parmesan and the onion mixture.

In a large bowl, beat the cream cheese, ricotta, milk, garlic powder and Beau Monde seasoning until smooth. Add to the rice mixture and mix well.

Spoon into a greased 13-in. x 9-in. baking dish. Sprinkle with remaining mozzarella and Parmesan. Bake, uncovered, at 325° for 40-45 minutes or until heated through and cheese is melted.

YIELD: 12 SERVINGS.

EDITOR'S NOTE: This recipe was tested with Spice Islands Beau Monde seasoning. It is a blend of salt, onion powder and celery seed.

gretchen kavanaugh
OKLAHOMA CITY, OKLAHOMA

My husband and I developed this recipe to avoid making a broccoli and rice casserole that we had relied on for years. Now his folks won't let us in the door at the holidays without this dish in hand.

ONIONS NEPTUNE

PREP 20 minutes | **BAKE** 35 minutes

- 5 to 6 medium sweet onions, sliced and separated into rings
- 1/2 cup butter, softened, *divided*
- 2 cans (6 ounces *each*) lump crabmeat, drained, *divided*
- 3 cups (12 ounces) shredded Swiss cheese
- 1 can (10-3/4 ounces) condensed cream of mushroom soup, undiluted
- 1/2 cup evaporated milk
- 1/2 teaspoon salt
- 1/4 teaspoon pepper
- 12 to 16 slices French bread (1/4 inch thick)

In a large skillet, saute onions in 1/4 cup butter until tender. Remove from the heat; gently stir in half of the crab. Spread into a greased 13-in. x 9-in. baking dish. Top with remaining crab. Combine the cheese, soup, milk, salt and pepper; spoon over crab.

Spread the remaining butter over one side of each slice of French bread; place buttered side up over the casserole. Bake, uncovered, at 350° for 35-45 minutes or until golden brown.

YIELD: 12 SERVINGS.

todd noon
GALLOWAY, NEW JERSEY

I serve this dish as an appetizer and often add whatever ingredients I have handy, such as mushrooms or sun-dried tomatoes. Whether I serve it "as is" or jazz it up, it's always delicious.

potlucks for KIDS

Young children often don't like casserole-type foods that are available at potlucks. To make sure the kids will eat, bring hot dogs to cook. Put them in buns and cut them in half to make it easier for little hands to hold.

SAUSAGE MOZZARELLA SUPPER

PREP 20 minutes | **BAKE** 1-1/4 hours

- 20 pounds link *or* bulk Italian sausage, sliced *or* crumbled
- 3 gallons spaghetti sauce
- 16 cups sliced fresh mushrooms
- 6 cups tomato juice
- 3 large onions, chopped
- 3 tablespoons Italian seasoning
- 2 tablespoons salt
- 1 tablespoon pepper
- 12 pounds spiral pasta, cooked and drained
- 5 pounds part-skim mozzarella cheese, sliced
- 8 pounds shredded part-skim mozzarella cheese

In several large skillets, brown sausage; drain. In several large kettles, combine the spaghetti sauce, mushrooms, tomato juice, onions, Italian seasoning, salt and pepper. Stir in sausage.

Grease eight 6-qt. baking dishes. Layer half of the noodles, sliced cheese and meat sauce in pans. Repeat layers. Sprinkle shredded cheese equally over each pan.

Cover and bake at 350° for 1 hour. Uncover; bake 15 minutes longer or until cheese is melted.

YIELD: 150-175 SERVINGS.

clara honeyager
MUKWONAGO, WISCONSIN

I've used this for church meals, and it's mighty tasty. Everyone seems to enjoy it!

PHILLY BEEF 'N' PEPPER STRATA

PREP 15 minutes + chilling
BAKE 1-1/4 hours + standing

- 7 cups cubed Italian bread
- 3-3/4 cups julienned sweet red, yellow *and/or* green peppers
- 1/4 cup chopped onion
- 3/4 pound cooked roast beef, cut into thin strips
- 2 cups (8 ounces) shredded Monterey Jack cheese
- 8 eggs
- 2-1/4 cups milk
- 2 tablespoons Dijon mustard
- 1/2 teaspoon salt
- 1/2 teaspoon pepper

Place a third of the bread cubes in a greased 13-in. x 9-in. baking dish. Layer with a third of the peppers, onion, roast beef and cheese. Repeat layers twice. In a large bowl, whisk eggs, milk, mustard, salt and pepper; pour over top. Cover and refrigerate for 8 hours or overnight.

Remove from the refrigerator 30 minutes before baking. Bake, covered, at 325° for 1 hour. Uncover; bake 15-20 minutes longer or until a knife inserted near the center comes out clean. Let stand for 10 minutes before serving.

YIELD: 12 SERVINGS.

betty claycomb
ALVERTON, PENNSYLVANIA

Here's a mouthwatering entree for brunch, lunch or dinner that's quick to fix. It combines several convenient ingredients for a large casserole that's pleasing to all who try it.

JULIENNE

A food that is "julienned" means that it is cut into long, thin matchstick strips that are about 2 inches long and 1/8 inch thick.

CHICKEN POTATO CASSEROLE

PREP 20 minutes | **BAKE** 45 minutes

- 6 large baking potatoes, peeled and cubed
- 1-1/2 cups water
- 2 pounds boneless skinless chicken breasts, cut into 1-inch cubes
- 2 cups (16 ounces) sour cream
- 3/4 cup shredded cheddar cheese
- 1/2 cup butter, softened
- 1/4 cup shredded Parmesan cheese
- 1 envelope onion soup mix
- 1/4 cup finely chopped fresh spinach
- 1/4 cup shredded carrot
- 1/4 teaspoon salt
- 1/4 teaspoon garlic powder
- 1/4 teaspoon pepper
- 1/4 cup dry bread crumbs

Place the potatoes and water in a 3-qt. microwave-safe dish. Cover and microwave on high for 12-15 minutes or until tender. Meanwhile, divide chicken between two greased 8-in. square baking dishes.

Drain the potatoes and place in a large bowl. Add the sour cream, cheddar cheese, butter, Parmesan cheese, soup mix, spinach, carrot, salt, garlic powder and pepper; mash until smooth. Spoon over chicken; sprinkle with bread crumbs.

Bake one casserole, uncovered, at 350° for 45-50 minutes or until chicken is no longer pink. Cover and freeze remaining casserole for up to 3 months.

TO USE FROZEN CASSEROLE: Thaw in the refrigerator overnight. Remove from the refrigerator 30 minutes before baking. Bake as directed.

YIELD: 2 CASSEROLES (6 SERVINGS EACH).

kersten campbell
PULLMAN, WASHINGTON

This savory, satisfying casserole is real comfort food that freezes so well. Thaw it in the fridge overnight, then pop it into the oven when you get home the next day for a super-easy supper.

CLASSIC TURKEY TETRAZZINI

PREP 30 minutes | **BAKE** 30 minutes

1 package (16 ounces) spaghetti
2 medium onions, chopped
9 tablespoons butter, *divided*
1 pound sliced fresh mushrooms
1 large sweet red pepper, chopped
1/2 cup all-purpose flour
1 teaspoon salt
6 cups milk
1 tablespoon chicken bouillon granules
6 cups cubed cooked turkey breast
1 cup grated Parmesan cheese
1-1/2 cups dry bread crumbs
4 teaspoons minced fresh parsley

Cook spaghetti according to package directions. Meanwhile, in a Dutch oven, saute onions in 6 tablespoons butter until tender. Add the mushrooms and red pepper; saute 4-5 minutes longer.

Stir in flour and salt until blended. Gradually whisk in milk and bouillon. Bring to a boil; cook and stir for 2 minutes or until thickened. Stir in turkey and Parmesan cheese; heat through. Remove from the heat.

Drain spaghetti; add to turkey mixture and mix well. Transfer to one greased 13-in. x 9-in. baking dish and one greased 11-in. x 7-in. baking dish.

Melt remaining butter; toss with bread crumbs. Sprinkle over casseroles. Bake, uncovered, at 350° for 30-35 minutes or until heated through. Sprinkle with parsley.
YIELD: 16 SERVINGS.

shannon weddle
BERRYVILLE, VIRGINIA

This classic casserole is so easy to make and works well with either leftover turkey or fresh turkey cutlets. You can also substitute flavored bread crumbs for the plain ones and jarred, roasted red peppers for the fresh variety.

WILD RICE BRUNCH CASSEROLE

PREP 20 minutes | **BAKE** 40 minutes

- 1 package (4 ounces) wild rice
- 1-1/2 pounds fresh asparagus, trimmed and cut into 1-inch pieces
- 2 cups cubed fully cooked ham
- 5 tablespoons butter, *divided*
- 12 eggs
- 1/2 cup milk
- 1 teaspoon salt
- 1/4 teaspoon pepper

CHEESE SAUCE

- 2 tablespoons canola oil
- 3 tablespoons all-purpose flour
- 1 cup milk
- 2 cups (8 ounces) shredded Colby *or* Gouda cheese
- 1/2 teaspoon ground ginger

Dash white pepper

Cook rice according to package directions. Spread in greased 13-in. x 9-in. baking dish; set aside.

Place asparagus and 1/2 in. of water in a large saucepan; bring to a boil. Reduce heat; cover and simmer for 3-5 minutes or until crisp-tender. Drain and set aside.

In a large skillet, saute the ham in 2 tablespoons butter until lightly browned. Spoon over wild rice.

In a large bowl, whisk the eggs, milk, salt and pepper. In the same skillet, heat remaining butter until hot. Add the egg mixture; cook and stir over medium heat until eggs are completely set. Spoon over ham; top with asparagus.

For sauce, heat oil in a saucepan. Stir in flour until smooth. Gradually stir in milk. Bring to a boil; cook and stir for 2 minutes or until thickened. Reduce heat; add the cheese, ginger and pepper. Cook and stir 2 minutes longer or until cheese is melted.

Pour over casserole. Cover and bake at 325° for 30 minutes. Uncover; bake 10-15 minutes longer or until a thermometer reads 160°.

YIELD: 10-12 SERVINGS.

meredith berg
HUDSON, WISCONSIN

Wild rice is one of our state's prized foods. Paired with our garden specialty—fresh asparagus—you won't want to miss this recipe!

about **WILD RICE**

Wild rice is a dark-hulled, aquatic grass native to North America. It has a chewy texture and nutty flavor. Grains expand 3 to 4 times their original size when cooked and some of the kernels may pop, allowing you to see their white insides. Wild rice should be rinsed before cooking.

GOLDEN HARVEST POTATO BAKE

PREP 40 minutes | **BAKE** 25 minutes

- 5 pounds Yukon Gold potatoes, peeled and cubed
- 2 medium sweet potatoes, peeled and cubed
- 5 large carrots, cut into 2-inch pieces
- 3 garlic cloves, minced
- 1 teaspoon dried tarragon
- 1 cup (4 ounces) shredded cheddar cheese, *divided*
- 1/2 cup milk
- 2 eggs
- 2 tablespoons cider vinegar
- 1 tablespoon butter
- 1 teaspoon salt
- 1 teaspoon dried parsley flakes
- 1/2 to 1 teaspoon pepper

Place potatoes, carrots, garlic and tarragon in a Dutch oven; cover with water. Bring to a boil. Reduce the heat; cover and cook for 15-20 minutes or until tender. Drain.

In a large bowl, mash the vegetables. Stir in 1/2 cup cheese, milk, eggs, vinegar, butter, salt, parsley and pepper until blended.

Transfer to a greased 13-in. x 9-in. baking dish; sprinkle with remaining cheese. Bake, uncovered, at 325° for 25-30 minutes or until a thermometer reads 160°.

YIELD: 16 SERVINGS.

pat tomkins
SOOKE, BRITISH COLUMBIA

This brightly-colored casserole features two kinds of potatoes. It fits well with any holiday entree.

CREAMY TURKEY CASSEROLE

PREP 15 minutes | **BAKE** 40 minutes

- 1 can (10-3/4 ounces) condensed cream of celery soup, undiluted
- 1 can (10-3/4 ounces) condensed cream of mushroom soup, undiluted
- 1 can (10-3/4 ounces) condensed cream of onion soup, undiluted
- 5 ounces process cheese (Velveeta), cubed
- 1/3 cup mayonnaise
- 4 cups cubed cooked turkey
- 1 package (16 ounces) frozen broccoli cuts, thawed
- 1-1/2 cups cooked white rice
- 1-1/2 cups cooked wild rice
- 1 can (8 ounces) sliced water chestnuts, drained
- 1 jar (4 ounces) sliced mushrooms, drained
- 1-1/2 to 2 cups salad croutons

In a large bowl, combine the soups, cheese and mayonnaise. Stir in the turkey, broccoli, rice, water chestnuts and mushrooms.

Transfer to a greased 13-in. x 9-in. baking dish. Bake, uncovered, at 350° for 30 minutes; stir. Sprinkle with the croutons. Bake 8-12 minutes longer or until bubbly.

YIELD: 12 SERVINGS.

EDITOR'S NOTE: Reduced-fat or fat-free mayonnaise is not recommended for this recipe.

mary jo o'brien
HASTINGS, MINNESOTA

This supper puts Thanksgiving leftovers to terrific use. I sometimes make turkey just so I have the extras for the casserole!

CHEESY NOODLE CASSEROLE

PREP 25 minutes | **BAKE** 25 minutes

- 2 packages (1 pound *each*) wide egg noodles
- 1/2 cup butter, cubed
- 1/4 cup all-purpose flour
- 1 teaspoon garlic salt
- 1 teaspoon onion salt
- 5 to 6 cups milk
- 2 pounds process cheese (Velveeta), cubed

TOPPING

- 1/2 cup dry bread crumbs
- 2 tablespoons butter, melted

Cook noodles according to the package directions; drain. Meanwhile, in a Dutch oven, melt butter. Stir in the flour, garlic salt and onion salt until smooth; gradually stir in milk. Bring to a boil; cook and stir for 2 minutes or until thickened. Add the cheese; stir until melted. Stir in the noodles.

Transfer to two greased shallow 2-qt. baking dishes. Combine bread crumbs and butter until crumbly; sprinkle over casseroles. Bake, uncovered, at 350° for 25-30 minutes or until golden brown.

YIELD: 2 CASSEROLES (12 SERVINGS EACH).

shirley mckee
VARNA, ILLINOIS

This rich, cheesy side dish is such an excellent meal extender that I always keep it in mind whenever I feel my menu needs a boost. It's a quick and easy casserole to fix…and is always devoured in a hurry!

GREEK CHICKEN NACHOS

brenda murphy
SPOKANE, WASHINGTON

PREP/TOTAL TIME 30 minutes

- 2 packages (10 ounces *each*) lemon-pepper marinated chicken breast fillets
- 2 cans (15 ounces *each*) garbanzo beans *or* chickpeas, rinsed and drained
- 1/2 cup Italian salad dressing
- 4 cups coarsely crushed tortilla chips
- 1 package (4 ounces) crumbled tomato and basil feta cheese
- 1 cup chopped tomatoes
- 1 cup Greek olives, chopped
- 2 cups (8 ounces) shredded part-skim mozzarella cheese

Cook the chicken in batches on an indoor grill for 6-8 minutes or until the juices run clear.

Meanwhile, place garbanzo beans and salad dressing in a food processor; cover and process until smooth. Dice chicken. In an ungreased 13-in. x 9-in. baking dish, layer half of the bean mixture, tortilla chips, chicken, feta cheese, tomatoes, olives and mozzarella cheese. Repeat layers.

Bake, uncovered, at 325° for 8-10 minutes or until cheese is melted.
YIELD: 12 SERVINGS.

These delicious nachos are perfect on Greek-cuisine night with family or friends, but don't treat them like an appetizer! Packed with chicken, cheese and all your favorite Greek flavors, these nachos make for a hearty, filling meal.

SUPREME PIZZA CASSEROLE

PREP 20 minutes | **BAKE** 30 minutes

nancy foust
STONEBORO, PENNSYLVANIA

This yummy pizza dish is perfect for the whole family. The tempting combination of pepperoni and spices will keep everyone wanting more!

- 8 ounces uncooked fettuccine
- 2 pounds ground beef
- 1 medium onion, chopped
- 2 cans (8 ounces *each*) mushroom stems and pieces, drained
- 1 can (15 ounces) tomato sauce
- 1 jar (14 ounces) pizza sauce
- 1 can (6 ounces) tomato paste
- 1/2 teaspoon sugar
- 1/2 teaspoon garlic powder
- 1/2 teaspoon onion powder
- 1/2 teaspoon dried oregano
- 4 cups (16 ounces) shredded part-skim mozzarella cheese, *divided*
- 1 package (3-1/2 ounces) sliced pepperoni
- 1/2 cup grated Parmesan cheese

Cook fettuccine according to the package directions. Meanwhile, in a Dutch oven, cook the beef and onion over medium heat until meat is no longer pink; drain. Stir in the mushrooms, tomato sauce, pizza sauce, tomato paste, sugar and seasonings. Drain pasta; stir into meat sauce.

Divide half of the mixture between two greased 2-qt. baking dishes; sprinkle each with 1 cup mozzarella cheese. Repeat layers. Top each with pepperoni and Parmesan cheese.

Cover and bake at 350° for 20 minutes. Uncover; bake 10-15 minutes longer or until heated through.

YIELD: 2 CASSEROLES (8 SERVINGS EACH).

CROWD CHICKEN CASSEROLE

PREP 20 minutes | **BAKE** 20 minutes

- 10 cups diced cooked chicken
- 10 cups chopped celery
- 2 cups slivered almonds
- 2 bunches green onions with tops, sliced
- 2 cans (4 ounces *each*) chopped green chilies
- 2 cans (2-1/4 ounces *each*) sliced ripe olives, drained
- 5 cups (20 ounces) shredded cheddar cheese, *divided*
- 2 cups mayonnaise
- 2 cups (16 ounces) sour cream
- 5 cups crushed potato chips

In a very large bowl, combine the first six ingredients; add 2 cups cheese. In a small bowl, combine mayonnaise and sour cream; add to chicken mixture and toss to coat.

Transfer to two greased 3-qt. baking dishes. Sprinkle with chips and remaining cheese. Bake, uncovered, at 350° for 20-25 minutes or until heated through.
YIELD: 2 CASSEROLES (12 SERVINGS EACH).

marna dunn
BULLHEAD CITY, ARIZONA

If you're looking to feed a big group, here's your recipe! It's full of ooey-gooey goodness that will hit the spot on a cool fall day. The potato chips add a kid-friendly crunch, too.

TUNA NOODLE CUPS

PREP 30 minutes | **BAKE** 30 minutes

- 8 ounces medium egg noodles
- 2 cups frozen peas and carrots
- 1 small onion, finely chopped
- 1 can (6-1/2 ounces) tuna, drained
- 2 cups (8 ounces) shredded cheddar cheese
- 3 eggs
- 1 can (12 ounces) evaporated milk
- 1/2 cup water

Cook the noodles according to the package directions; drain and place in a large bowl. Add the peas and the carrots, onion, tuna and cheese. In a small bowl, combine the eggs, milk and water; stir into the noodle mixture. Spoon into greased muffin cups.

Bake at 350° for 30-35 minutes or until a knife comes out clean. Cool for 5 minutes; loosen edges with a knife to remove from cups. Serve immediately.
YIELD: ABOUT 1-1/2 DOZEN.

marlene pugh
FORT MCMURRAY, ALBERTA

Older kids can get a jump on preparing dinner by stirring up these miniature tuna casseroles. Or serve them for brunch with fresh fruit, a tossed salad and rolls.

AU GRATIN POTATOES AND HAM

PREP 45 minutes | **BAKE** 45 minutes

- 20 pounds red potatoes
- 8 pounds fully cooked ham, cubed
- 4 cans (10-3/4 ounces *each*) condensed cream of celery soup, undiluted
- 1/2 cup all-purpose flour
- 8 cups milk
- 6 pounds process cheese (Velveeta), cubed
- 2 teaspoons pepper
- 2 teaspoons paprika

Place the potatoes in several stockpots and cover with water. Bring to a boil. Reduce the heat; cover and cook for 15-20 minutes or until tender. Drain.

Peel if desired and cut into cubes. Place about 6 cups of potatoes in each of eight greased 13-in. x 9-in. baking dishes. Add about 3-1/2 cups of cubed ham to each dish.

In the same kettles, combine soup, flour and milk until smooth. Bring to a boil; cook and stir for 2 minutes or until thickened. Add cheese, pepper and paprika. Reduce heat and cook until cheese is melted.

Pour about 2-1/4 cups of sauce into each pan. Cover and bake at 350° for 40 minutes. Uncover and bake 5-10 minutes longer or until bubbly.
YIELD: 8 CASSEROLES (10 SERVINGS EACH).

evie pond
IPSWICH, SOUTH DAKOTA

With hearty chunks of ham and red potato in a creamy cheese sauce, this dish appeals to all at any gathering.

CABBAGE ROLL CASSEROLE

PREP 20 minutes | **BAKE** 55 minutes

- 2 pounds ground beef
- 1 large onion, chopped
- 3 garlic cloves, minced
- 2 cans (15 ounces *each*) tomato sauce, *divided*
- 1 teaspoon dried thyme
- 1/2 teaspoon dill weed
- 1/2 teaspoon rubbed sage
- 1/4 teaspoon salt
- 1/4 teaspoon pepper
- 1/4 teaspoon cayenne pepper
- 2 cups cooked rice
- 4 bacon strips, cooked and crumbled
- 1 medium head cabbage (2 pounds), shredded
- 1 cup (4 ounces) shredded part-skim mozzarella cheese

In a large skillet, cook beef, onion and garlic over medium heat until meat is no longer pink; drain. Stir in one can of tomato sauce and seasonings. Bring to a boil. Reduce heat; cover and simmer for 5 minutes. Stir in rice and bacon; heat through. Remove from the heat.

Layer a third of the cabbage in a greased 13-in. x 9-in. baking dish. Top with half of the meat mixture. Repeat layers; top with remaining cabbage. Pour the remaining tomato sauce over top.

Cover and bake at 375° for 45 minutes. Uncover; sprinkle with cheese. Bake 10 minutes longer or until cheese is melted. Let stand for 5 minutes before serving.

YIELD: 12 SERVINGS.

NUTRITION FACTS: 1 piece equals 230 calories, 8 g fat (4 g saturated fat), 44 mg cholesterol, 620 mg sodium, 18 g carbohydrate, 3 g fiber, 20 g protein. **DIABETIC EXCHANGES:** 3 vegetable, 2-1/2 lean meat, 1/2 fat.

doreen martin
KITIMAT, BRITISH COLUMBIA

I layer cabbage and a ground beef filling, lasagna-style, in this hearty casserole that cabbage roll lovers will savor.

CABBAGE

Cut the head of cabbage in half or quarters. Make a V-shaped cut around the core and remove. To shred by hand, place the halves or quarters cut side down on a cutting board. With a large sharp knife, carefully cut into thin slices.

WILD RICE CHICKEN DINNER

PREP/TOTAL TIME 30 minutes

- 2 packages (8.8 ounces *each*) ready-to-serve long grain and wild rice
- 2 packages (16 ounces *each*) frozen French-style green beans, thawed
- 2 cans (10-3/4 ounces *each*) condensed cream of celery soup, undiluted
- 2 cans (8 ounces *each*) sliced water chestnuts, drained
- 2/3 cup chopped onion
- 2 jars (4 ounces *each*) sliced pimientos, drained
- 1 cup mayonnaise
- 1/2 cup milk
- 1 teaspoon pepper
- 6 cups cubed cooked chicken
- 1 cup slivered almonds, *divided*

Heat rice according to package directions. Meanwhile, in a Dutch oven, combine the green beans, soup, water chestnuts, onion, pimientos, mayonnaise, milk and pepper. Bring to a boil. Reduce the heat; cover and simmer for 5 minutes. Stir in chicken and rice; cook 3-4 minutes longer or until chicken is heated through.

Transfer half of the mixture to a serving dish; sprinkle with 1/2 cup almonds. Serve immediately. Pour the remaining mixture into a greased 13-in. x 9-in. baking dish; cool. Sprinkle with remaining almonds. Cover and freeze for up to 3 months.

TO USE FROZEN CASSEROLE: Thaw in the refrigerator overnight. Cover and bake at 350° for 40-45 minutes or until heated through.

YIELD: 2 CASSEROLES (6-8 SERVINGS EACH).

EDITOR'S NOTE: Reduced-fat or fat-free mayonnaise is not recommended for this recipe.

lorraine hanson
INDEPENDENCE, IOWA

With chicken, green beans and the nice crunch of water chestnuts and almonds, this casserole has everything you need. Using ready-to-serve wild rice makes putting it together a breeze.

SPICY NACHO BAKE

PREP 1 hour | **BAKE** 20 minutes

2 pounds ground beef

2 large onions, chopped

2 large green peppers, chopped

2 cans (28 ounces *each*) diced tomatoes, undrained

2 cans (15-1/2 ounces *each*) hot chili beans

2 cans (15 ounces *each*) black beans, rinsed and drained

2 cans (11 ounces *each*) whole kernel corn, drained

2 cans (8 ounces *each*) tomato sauce

2 envelops taco seasoning

2 packages (13 ounces *each*) spicy nacho tortilla chips

4 cups (16 ounces) shredded cheddar cheese

In a Dutch oven or large kettle, cook the beef, onions and green peppers over medium heat until meat is no longer pink; drain. Stir in the tomatoes, beans, corn, tomato sauce and taco seasoning. Bring to a boil. Reduce heat; simmer, uncovered, for 30 minutes (mixture will be thin).

In each of two greased 13-in. x 9-in. baking dishes, layer 5 cups of tortilla chips and 4-2/3 cups of meat mixture. Repeat layers. Top each with 4 cups of tortilla chips and 2 cups of cheese.

Bake, uncovered, at 350° for 20-25 minutes or until golden brown.

YIELD: 2 CASSEROLES (15 SERVINGS EACH).

anita wilson
MANSFIELD, OHIO

I made this hearty, layered Southwestern casserole for a dinner meeting once, and now I'm asked to bring it every time we have a potluck. Everybody loves the ground beef and bean filling and the cheesy topping.

COUNTRY BEAN BAKE

PREP 25 minutes | **BAKE** 65 minutes

- 2 pounds bulk pork sausage
- 1 can (16 ounces) Boston baked beans
- 1 can (16 ounces) kidney beans, rinsed and drained
- 1 can (15-1/4 ounces) lima beans, rinsed and drained
- 1 can (15 ounces) butter beans, rinsed and drained
- 1 can (8 ounces) unsweetened crushed pineapple, drained
- 1 medium tart apple, peeled and shredded
- 1 small onion, diced
- 1/2 cup ketchup
- 1/2 cup molasses
- 1 tablespoon lemon juice
- 1 cup (4 ounces) shredded cheddar cheese

In a large skillet, cook the sausage over medium heat until no longer pink; drain. In a large bowl, combine the sausage, beans, pineapple, apple, onion, ketchup, molasses and lemon juice.

Transfer to a greased 3-qt. baking dish. Cover and bake at 325° for 60-70 minutes or until thickened and bubbly.

Uncover; sprinkle with the cheese. Bake 5 minutes longer or until cheese is melted. **YIELD:** 15 SERVINGS (2/3 CUP EACH).

gloria jarrett
LOVELAND, OHIO

This recipe of my mom's makes the best baked beans I have ever eaten. I've taken them to summer and fall picnics, Super Bowl parties, family reunions, etc. and am always asked for the recipe. An added bonus? Make-ahead convenience!

MAKEOVER SLOPPY JOE MAC AND CHEESE

PREP 1 hour | **BAKE** 30 minutes

- 1 package (16 ounces) elbow macaroni
- 3/4 pound lean ground turkey
- 1/2 cup finely chopped celery
- 1/2 cup shredded carrot
- 1 can (14-1/2 ounces) diced tomatoes, undrained
- 1 can (6 ounces) tomato paste
- 1/2 cup water
- 1 envelope sloppy joe mix
- 1 small onion, finely chopped
- 1 tablespoon butter
- 1/3 cup all-purpose flour
- 1 teaspoon ground mustard
- 3/4 teaspoon salt
- 1/4 teaspoon pepper
- 4 cups 2% milk
- 1 tablespoon Worcestershire sauce
- 8 ounces reduced-fat process cheese (Velveeta), cubed
- 2 cups (8 ounces) shredded cheddar cheese, *divided*

Cook macaroni according to the package directions. Meanwhile, in a large nonstick skillet, cook the turkey, celery and carrot over medium heat until meat is no longer pink and vegetables are tender; drain. Add the tomatoes, tomato paste, water and sloppy joe mix. Bring to a boil. Reduce heat; cover skillet and simmer for 10 minutes, stirring occasionally.

Drain macaroni; set aside. In a large saucepan, saute the onion in butter until tender. Stir in the flour, mustard, salt and pepper until smooth. Gradually add the milk and Worcestershire sauce. Bring to a boil; cook and stir for 1-2 minutes or until thickened. Remove from the heat. Stir in the process cheese until melted. Add the macaroni and 1 cup cheddar cheese and mix well.

Spread two-thirds of macaroni mixture in a 13-in. x 9-in. baking dish coated with cooking spray. Spread turkey mixture to within 2 in. of edges. Spoon remaining macaroni mixture around edges of pan. Cover and bake at 375° for 30-35 minutes or until bubbly. Uncover; sprinkle with the remaining cheddar cheese. Cover and let stand until cheese is melted.

YIELD: 10 SERVINGS.

NUTRITION FACTS: 1 cup equals 353 calories, 12 g fat (7 g saturated fat), 54 mg cholesterol, 877 mg sodium, 42 g carbohydrate, 3 g fiber, 20 g protein. **DIABETIC EXCHANGES:** 2 starch, 1-1/2 fat, 1 reduced-fat milk.

taste of home
test kitchen
GREENDALE, WISCONSIN

Decreasing the butter and replacing the half-and-half with milk helped cut a whopping 658 calories and more than half the fat from the original version of this casserole. Even though the cholesterol and sodium was reduced, this healthy hot dish offers all the heart-warming comfort of the original high-calorie submission.

POTATO STUFFING CASSEROLE

PREP 50 minutes | **BAKE** 30 minutes

- 5 pounds potatoes, peeled and quartered
- 5 medium onions, finely chopped
- 4 celery ribs, chopped
- 1 cup butter
- 2 tablespoons poultry seasoning
- 1 tablespoon *each* dried savory, thyme and marjoram
- 2 teaspoons salt
- 1/2 teaspoon pepper
- 1 package (14 ounces) seasoned stuffing cubes
- 1/2 to 3/4 cup chicken *or* turkey broth

Place potatoes in a Dutch oven and cover with water. Bring to a boil. Reduce heat; cover and cook for 15-20 minutes or until tender. Meanwhile, in a large skillet, saute onions and celery in butter for 6-8 minutes or until tender. Stir in seasonings; set aside.

Drain potatoes; mash in a large bowl. Stir in seasoned stuffing cubes. Stir in the vegetable mixture and enough broth to reach desired moistness.

Transfer to two greased shallow 2-qt. baking dishes (dishes will be full). Cover and bake at 350° for 30-35 minutes or until heated through.

YIELD: 17 CUPS.

EDITOR'S NOTE: This dressing is best served as a side dish, rather than stuffed into poultry.

eleanor howell
FALMOUTH, MAINE

This treasured family recipe provides the goodness of potatoes and stuffing in every forkful. We look forward to it every year for Thanksgiving.

general recipe index

◆ Recipe includes Nutrition Facts and Diabetic Exchanges.

alphabetical recipe index

◆ Recipe includes Nutrition Facts and Diabetic Exchanges.